Lecture Notes in Computer Scier

T0238311

Commenced Publication in 1973
Founding and Former Series Editors:
Gerhard Goos, Juris Hartmanis, and Jan van Leeuwen

Bernhard M. Hämmerli   Robin Sommer (Eds.)

Detection of Intrusions and Malware, and Vulnerability Assessment

4th International Conference, DIMVA 2007
Lucerne, Switzerland, July 12-13, 2007
Proceedings

 Springer

Volume Editors

Bernhard M. Hämmerli
Acris GmbH und HTA Lucerne
Bodenhofstraße 29, 6005 Luzern, Switzerland
E-mail: bmhaemmerli@acris.ch

Robin Sommer
International Computer Science Institute
1947 Center St. Suite 600
Berkeley, CA 94704, USA
E-mail: robin@icsi.berkeley.edu

Library of Congress Control Number: 2007930209

CR Subject Classification (1998): E.3, K.6.5, K.4, C.2, D.4.6

LNCS Sublibrary: SL 4 – Security and Cryptology

ISSN   0302-9743
ISBN-10   3-540-73613-1 Springer Berlin Heidelberg New York
ISBN-13   978-3-540-73613-4 Springer Berlin Heidelberg New York

Springer is a part of Springer Science+Business Media

springer.com

© Springer-Verlag Berlin Heidelberg 2007
Printed in Germany

Typesetting: Camera-ready by author, data conversion by Scientific Publishing Services, Chennai, India
Printed on acid-free paper   SPIN: 12089918   06/3180   5 4 3 2 1 0

Preface

On behalf of the Program Committee, it is our pleasure to present to you the proceedings of the 4th GI International Conference on Detection of Intrusions and Malware, and Vulnerability Assessment (DIMVA). Each year DIMVA brings together international experts from academia, industry and government to present and discuss novel security research. DIMVA is organized by the special interest group Security—Intrusion Detection and Response of the German Informatics Society (GI).

The DIMVA 2007 Program Committee received 57 submissions from 20 different countries. All submissions were carefully reviewed by Program Committee members and external experts according to the criteria of scientific novelty, importance to the field and technical quality. The final selection took place at a Program Committee meeting held on March 31, 2007, at Università Campus Bio-Medico di Roma, Italy. Twelve full papers and two extended abstracts were selected for presentation at the conference and publication in the conference proceedings. The conference took place during July 12–13, 2007, at the University of Applied Sciences and Arts Lucerne (HTA Lucerne) in Switzerland. The program featured both theoretical and practical research results grouped into five sessions. The keynote speech was given by Vern Paxson, International Computer Science Institute and Lawrence Berkeley National Laboratory. Another invited talk was presented by Marcelo Masera, Institute for the Protection and Security of the Citizen. Peter Trachsel, Deputy Head of the Federal Strategic Unit for IT in Switzerland, gave a speech during the conference dinner. The conference program further included a rump session organized by Sven Dietrich of Carnegie Mellon University; and it was complemented by the third instance of the European capture-the-flag contest CIPHER, organized by Lexi Pimenidis of RWTH Aachen.

We sincerely thank all those who submitted papers as well as the Program Committee members and our external reviewers for their valuable contributions to a great conference program.

For further details about DIMVA 2007, please refer to the conference Web site at http://www.dimva.org/dimva2007.

July 2007

Bernhard Hämmerli
Robin Sommer

Organization

Organizing Committee

General Chair   Bernhard Hämmerli (HTA Luzern)
Program Chair   Robin Sommer (LBNL/ICSI)
Sponsor Chair   Dirk Schadt

Program Committee

Roland Büschkes   RWE, Germany
Weidong Cui   Microsoft Research, USA
Marc Dacier   Eurécom, France
Hervé Debar   France Télécom, France
Sven Dietrich   Carnegie Mellon University, USA
Toralv Dirro   McAfee, Germany
Holger Dreger   Siemens CERT, Germany
Mohamed Eltoweissy   Virginia Tech, USA
Ulrich Flegel   University of Dortmund, Germany
Felix C. Freiling   University of Mannheim, Germany
Dirk Häger   BSI, Germany
Bernhard Hämmerli   HTA Lucerne, Switzerland
Marc Heuse   n.runs, Germany
Ming-Yuh Huang   Boeing, USA
Erland Jonsson   Chalmers University, Sweden
Klaus Julisch   IBM Research, USA
Angelos Keromytis   Columbia University, USA
Hartmut König   BTU Cottbus, Germany
Christian Kreibich   ICSI, USA
Christopher Kruegel   TU Vienna, Austria
Pavel Laskov   Fraunhofer FIRST, Germany
Wenke Lee   Georgia Tech, USA
Jun Li   Tsinghua University, China
Javier Lopez   University of Malaga, Spain
John McHugh   Dalhousie University, Canada
Michael Meier   University of Dortmund, Germany
R. Sekar   Stony Brook University, USA
Roberto Setola   Univ. CAMPUS Bio-Medico Rome, Italy
Doug Tygar   UC Berkeley, USA
Giovanni Vigna   UC Santa Barbara, USA

External Reviewers

Periklis Akritidis	Thomas Biege	Matt Burnside
Michael Collins	Gabriela Cretu	Michael E. Locasto
Jason Franklin	Jan Goebel	Van Hau Pham
Thorsten Holz	Engin Kirda	Ulf Larson
Corrado Leita	Igor Nai	Peng Ning
Vern Paxson	Michalis Polychronakis	Maurizio Sajeva
Sebastian Schmerl	Yingbo Song	Olivier Thonnard
Jouni Viinikka	Nicholas Weaver	

Steering Committee

Chairs	Ulrich Flegel (University of Dortmund)
	Michael Meier (University of Dortmund)
Members	Roland Büschkes (RWE)
	Christopher Kruegel (TU Vienna)
	Marc Heuse (n.runs)
	Pavel Laskov (Fraunhofer FIRST)
	Klaus Julisch (IBM Research)

DIMVA 2007 was organized by the Special Interest Group Security – Intrusion Detection and Response (SIDAR) of the German Informatics Society (GI), in cooperation with the IEEE Task Force on Information Assurance and the Information Security Society Switzerland.

Support

The main sponsor of DIMVA 2007 was Secude Headquarter, Lucerne, Switzerland. We sincerely thank them for their support.

Table of Contents

Host Security

Extensible Web Browser Security

Mike Ter Louw, Jin Soon Lim, and V.N. Venkatakrishnan

Department of Computer Science,
University of Illinois at Chicago
{mter,jlim,venkat}@cs.uic.edu

Abstract. In this paper we examine the security issues in functionality extension mechanisms supported by web browsers. Extensions (or "plug-ins") in modern web browsers enjoy unlimited power without restraint and thus are attractive vectors for malware. To solidify the claim, we take on the role of malware writers looking to assume control of a user's browser space. We have taken advantage of the lack of security mechanisms for browser extensions and have implemented a piece of malware for the popular Firefox web browser, which we call BROWSER-SPY, that requires no special privileges to be installed. Once installed, BROWSER-SPY takes complete control of a user's browser space and can observe all the activity performed through the browser while being undetectable. We then adopt the role of defenders to discuss defense strategies against such malware. Our primary contribution is a mechanism that uses code integrity checking techniques to control the extension installation and loading process. We also discuss techniques for runtime monitoring of extension behavior that provide a foundation for defending threats due to installed extensions.

1 Introduction

The Internet web browser, arguably the most commonly used application on a network connected computer, is becoming an increasingly capable and important platform for millions of today's computer users. The web browser is often a user's window to the world, providing them an interface to perform a wide range of activity including email correspondence, shopping, social networking, personal finance management, and professional business.

This usage gives the browser a unique perspective; it can observe and apply contextual meaning to sensitive information provided by the the user during very personal activities. Furthermore, the browser has access to this information *in the clear*, even when the user encrypts all incoming and outgoing communication. This high level of access to sensitive, personal data warrants efforts to ensure its complete confidentiality and integrity.

Ensuring that the entire code base of a browser addresses the security concerns of confidentiality and integrity is a daunting task. For instance, the current distribution of the Mozilla Firefox browser has a build size of 3.7 million lines of code (as measured using the `kloc` tool) written in a variety of languages that include C, C++, Java, JavaScript and XML. These challenges of size and implementation language diversity make it difficult to develop a "one-stop shop" solution for this problem. In this paper, we focus on the equally significant subproblem of ensuring confidentiality and integrity in a

B. M. Hämmerli and R. Sommer (Eds.): DIMVA 2007, LNCS 4579, pp. 1–19, 2007.

browser in the presence of browser extensions. We discuss this problem in the context of Mozilla Firefox, the widely used free (open source) software browser, used by about 70 million web users [1].

Browser extensions (or "add-ons") are facilities provided to customize the browser. These extensions make use of interfaces exported by the browser and other plugins to alter the browser's behavior. Though the build of Firefox is platform-specific (such as one for Windows XP, Linux or Mac OS X), extensions are primarily platform-independent based on the neutral nature of JavaScript and XML, the predominant languages used to implement them.

Even though extensions plug directly into the browser, there is no provision currently in Firefox to provide protection against malicious extensions. One way to do this is to disallow extensions altogether. Firefox is able to do this when started in debugging mode, which prevents any extension code to be loaded. However, typical installation and execution in the normal mode allow extensions to be executed. Extensions offer useful functionality, as evidenced by the popularity of their download numbers [2], to several thousands of users who use them. Dismissing the security concerns about extensions by turning them off ignores the problem.

To understand the impact of running a malicious extension, we set for ourselves the goal of actually crafting one. Surprisingly, we engineered a malicious extension for the Firefox browser we call BROWSERSPY, with modest efforts and in less than three weeks. Once installed, this extension takes complete control of the browser. As further testimony, a recent attack was launched on the Firefox browser using a malware extension known as FormSpy [8], that elicited widespread media coverage and concern about naive users.

There are two main problems raised by the presence of our malware extension and the FormSpy extension:

- *Browser code base integrity* A malicious extension can compromise the integrity of the browser code base when it is installed and loaded. We demonstrate (by construction) that a malicious extension can subvert the installation process, take control of a browser, and hide its presence completely.
- *User data confidentiality and integrity* A malicious extension can read and write confidential data sent and received by the user, even over an encrypted secure connection. We demonstrate this by having our extension collect sensitive data input by a user while browsing and log it to a remote site.

In this paper we present techniques that address these problems. To address extension integrity, our solution empowers the end-user with complete control of the process by which code is selected to run as part of the browser, thereby disallowing installation integrity threats due to malware. This is done by a process of *user authorization* that detects and refuses to allow the execution of extensions that are not authorized by the end user.

To address the second challenge of data confidentiality and integrity, we augment the browser with support for policy-based monitoring of extensions by interposition mechanisms retrofitted to the Spidermonkey JavaScript engine and other means (Section 5).

A key benefit of our solution is that it is targeted to *retrofit* the browser. We consider this benefit very important, and have traded off potentially better solutions to achieve this benefit. Other benefits of our approach are that it is convenient, user-friendly and poses very acceptable overheads. Our implementation is robust, having been tested with several Firefox extensions.

This paper is organized as follows. A discussion of related work appears in Section 2. We present the main details behind our malware extension in Section 3. We present our solution to the extension integrity problem in Section 4 and address data confidentiality in Section 5. We evaluate these approaches with several Firefox add-ons and discuss their performance in the above sections individually. In Section 6 we conclude.

2 Related Work

We examined extension support in four contemporary browsers: Firefox, Internet Explorer (IE), Safari and Opera. Among the four browsers that we studied, only the Safari browser does not support the concept of extensions. The remaining three possess extensible architecture but do not have security mechanisms addressing extension-based threats. For instance, IE primary extension mechanism is through Browser Helper Objects (BHO). The PestPatrol malware detection website lists hundreds of malware that use BHOs [5]. Furthermore, the integrity and confidentiality of the end-user's private data used in the browser is also not addressed in recent mechanisms such as "protected-browser-mode" [4] in Windows Vista.

The problem of safely running extensions in a browser is in many ways similar to the problem of executing downloaded untrusted code in an operating system. This is a well known problem, and has propelled research in ideas such as signed code, static analysis, proof-carrying code, model-carrying code and several execution monitoring approaches. Below, we discuss the applicability of these solutions to the browser extension problem highlighting several technical and practical reasons.

Signed code. The Firefox browser provides support for signed extensions; however, this is hardly used in practice. A search of extensions in the Firefox extensions repository addons.mozilla.org revealed several thousand unsigned extensions and only two that were signed. In addition, we note that signed extensions merely offer a first level of security. They only guarantee that they are from the browser distribution site and are unmodified in transit; no assurance is provided regarding the security implications of running the extension.

Static analysis. A very desirable approach for enforcing policies on extension code is by use of static analysis. Static analysis has been employed in several past efforts in identifying vulnerabilities or malicious intent. The primary advantages of using static analysis are the absence of execution overhead and runtime aborts, which are typical of dynamic analysis based solutions.

It is difficult to employ static analysis for JavaScript code without making conservative assumptions, however. A first example is the *eval* statement in JavaScript that allows a string to be interpreted as executable code. Without knowing the runtime values of the arguments to the *eval* statement, it is extremely difficult—if not impossible—to determine the runtime actions of the script. Another problem is tracing the flow of object references in a prototype-based object oriented language such as JavaScript. For instance, variable assignment to or from an array element or object property (when the object is indexed as an associative array) can decisively hamper the tracking of object reference flow as references are stored or retrieved.

Consequently, recent efforts that trace JavaScript code [11] use runtime approaches to track references. An exception is [13] that employs static analysis for JavaScript for detecting *cross-site scripting* (XSS) attacks. In their approach, scenarios like the above are handled by a conservative form of tainting. This is suitable for their purpose of preventing XSS attacks as evidenced by their experimental results, and the fact that typical scripts from web pages are not expected to have complex *eval* constructs. This approach is unsuitable for statically analyzing extension code in JavaScript, however. Almost half (45%) of the extensions that we tested make heavy use of complex *eval* constructs, while all generously use objects as associative arrays, making static analysis very hard.

PCC and MCC. The difficulties for static analysis make frameworks such as proof-carrying code (PCC) [10] unsuitable for this problem. It will be difficult to produce proofs for extensions that make heavy use of constructs such as *eval* as part of their code. The typical approach to employ PCC in scenarios that require runtime data is to: (a) transform the original script with runtime checks that enforce the desired security property, and (b) produce a proof that the transformed program respects this property. The proof in this case is primarily used to demonstrate the correctness of the placement of runtime checks.

In the browser situation, transformation needs to be made before all *eval* statements. Policy enforcement would still be carried out by runtime checks, and therefore we did not adopt this route of using PCC. Another solution is model-carrying-code [12] which employs runtime techniques to learn the behavior of code that will be downloaded. The difficulty in using this approach is in obtaining test suites for exhaustive code coverage required for approaches based on runtime learning of models.

Execution monitoring. Several execution monitoring techniques [14,6,7] have previously looked at the problem of safely executing malicious code. The closest related project to our approach is by Hallaraker and Vigna [7]. This was the first work that looked at the security issues of executing malicious code in a large mainstream browser. Their focus is on protection against pages with malicious content rather than the ensuring the integrity of a browser's internal operations. For them it is not necessary to address the problem of browser code integrity, as scripts from web pages are sandboxed to prevent them from performing sensitive actions. In contrast we address the extension installation integrity problem, as extension code is unmonitored and can perform many sensitive operations.

To effectively regulate extension behavior, a runtime monitor must be able to determine the particular extension responsible for each operation. A direct adaptation of their execution monitoring approach does not provide this ability, and is therefore not suited for runtime supervision of extensions. To fill this void we describe two new *action attribution* mechanisms making use of browser facilities and JavaScript interposition in Section 5.

(a) Extension hiding from the browser UI.   (b) Data collector receiving sensitive information.

Fig. 1. Two views of the BROWSERSPY extension in operation.

3   A Malware Extension

To gain a better understanding of the threat posed by a malware extension, we set ourselves the task of actually writing one. The motivations for creating the malicious software are to: (a) help us identify the scope of threats malicious extensions pose by understanding the facilities available to an extension in a browser, (b) increase our understanding of architecture-level and implementation-level weaknesses in the browser's extension manager, (c) give us a practical estimate in understanding the ease with which malware writers may be able to craft such extensions, and (d) provide a concrete implementation of a malicious extension to serve as a benchmark for malware analysis.

Extension Capabilities. BROWSERSPY, the extension we authored, is capable of harvesting every piece of form data (e.g., passwords) submitted by the user, including those sent over encrypted connections. Furthermore, once the extension enters the system, it ensures that it remains undetectable by users (Figure 1 (a)).

Once BROWSERSPY is installed, it begins collection of personal data that will ultimately fall into the hands of an attacker. As a user navigates the Internet, BROWSERSPY harvests the URLs comprising their browsing history and stores them in a cache. Any username and password pairs that are stored in Firefox's built-in password manager are retrieved, along with the URL of the site they pertain to. Form data that the user submits finds its way into the extension as well. All of this information is stored and periodically sent over the network to a remote host.

Given enough data the spy can effectively steal the identity of the person using the browser. Intercepted form fields can give an attacker credit card numbers, street addresses, Social Security Numbers, and other highly sensitive information. The username / password pairs can readily provide access to the user's accounts on external sites. The history items can give the attacker a profile of the victim's browsing patterns, and serve as candidate sites for further break-in attempts using the retrieved set of username /

password pairs. Figure 1 (b) shows a remote window collecting sensitive information about the user.

To mimick a spyware attack more closely, BROWSERSPY employs stealth to prevent the user from knowing that anything unusual is being conducted. The extension uses two techniques to shroud itself from Firefox's installed extensions list. First, the extension simply removes itself from the list so that the user won't see it. Second, it injects itself into a (presumably benign) extension, Google Toolbar (Figure 1 (a)). The latter method serves as a technique to guard the extension from being discovered should the user inspect the files on her system. The injection process is even successful at infecting code signed browser extensions,[1] as the browser does not check the integrity of these extensions following installation.

A common technique practiced by malware is covert information flow mechanisms [9] for transmission. To mimic this behavior, our final stealth tactic deliberately delays delivery of sensitive data to the remote host. We cache the information and send it out in periodic bursts to offset the network activity from the event that triggers it, making it harder for an observant user to correlate the added traffic with security sensitive operations. Thus, the composite effect of some relatively easy measures employed by our extension is alarming.

Extension entry vectors. The typical process of extension installation requires the user to download and install the extension through a browser interface window. Though the BROWSERSPY extension can be installed this way, this is not the only route by which this malicious extension can be delivered to a browser. It can be delivered by preexisting malware on the system without involving the browser. It can also be delivered outside the browser given user account access for a short duration. These entry vectors are all too common with unpatched systems, public terminals, and naive users who do not suspect such threats.

Extension development effort. Very little effort was required to create this extension. The lack of any security in the browser's Extension Manager module assisted in its speedy creation. It only took one graduate student (who had no prior experience in developing extensions) three weeks working part time to complete this extension. We present this information merely to argue the ease with which this task can be accomplished. We note that this period of three weeks is merely an upper bound of effort for creating malicious extensions. Malware writers have more resources, experience and time to create extensions that could be more stealthy, perhaps employing increasingly sophisticated covert mechanisms for information transmission.

Our implementation techniques. We started by studying the procedure of how extensions are created, installed and executed in the system. Firefox extensions make use of the *Cross-Platform Component Object Model* (XPCOM) framework, which provides a variety of services within the browser such as file access abstraction. We carefully studied interfaces to the XPCOM framework available for use by an extension, and discerned that one could easily program event observers for various operations performed

---

[1] Case in point, the code in the Google Toolbar extension is signed by Google, Inc.

Table 1. The malware extension exploits the use of these XPCOM interfaces to perform attacks

XPCOM Interface	Usefulness to perform malicious behavior
nsIHistoryListener	By attaching an event listener of this type to each open document, the browser notifies the malware when a new document is opened.
nsIHttpChannel	By attaching an event listener to this interface, the browser grants the malware a chance to inspect query parameters before submission.
nsIPasswordManager	The malware invokes a method provided by this interface which reveals all of the user's stored passwords.
nsIRDFDataSource	This interface provides the malware with write access to one of the Extension Manager's critical internal data objects.

by the browser. We implemented the spying features based on four of these event observers as itemized in Table 1.

We make unconventional use of the XPCOM framework to achieve hiding mechanisms in our spyware implementation. To simply disappear from the browser user interface, we use a standard interface (Table 1) to manipulate an internal data object belonging to Firefox's Extension Manager. This exposes a flaw in the browser implementation, full access to an object is exported where it should remain at most read-only to the extension code base.

Injecting the BROWSERSPY extension into another extension requires copying a file into the target's directory and then appending some text to the target's chrome.manifest (a file containing declarations instructing the browser how to load an extension). The absence of file access restrictions on extension code easily allow this injection attack. It is actually a more subtle and fundamental flaw in the implementation of Firefox that allows such attacks to be carried out with ease. Instead of storing user preferences in a data file and reading them for later use, the browser generates JavaScript code every time the user changes her preferences, and executes this file on startup. This is poor design from a security perspective. If the integrity of this file is compromised the browser can easily be attacked. Our BROWSERSPY extension precisely exploits such implementation weaknesses.

Through mostly normal use of the services Firefox provides to extensions, we have been able to concretely demonstrate much cause for concern.

4   Our Approach to Enhance Security

Firefox's vulnerabilities can be strengthened to make all of the BROWSERSPY attacks unsuccessful. As mentioned in the introduction section, this requires us to enforce the following requirements:

Requirement 1   Ensure the integrity of the browser's code base.
Requirement 2   Protect sensitive user data from being accessed or modified by the extension code base.

A browser that adheres to Requirement 1 prevents the BROWSERSPY extension from injecting itself into the browser's code base. Implicitly, this first requirement also

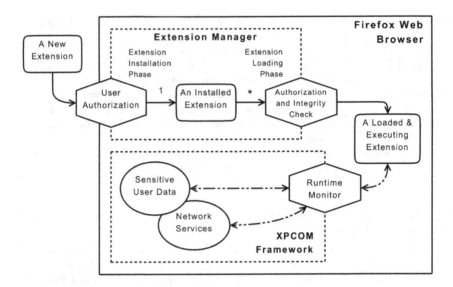

Fig. 2. Overview of Firefox's extensible architecture (hexagons represent functionality added to improve security). Extensions must be user authorized and uncorrupted to get loaded into the browser. Extension access to XPCOM is controlled by policies defined in the runtime monitor.

disallows unauthorized extensions to access sensitive data, contributing to the fulfillment of Requirement 2.

A high level architecture of our solution is presented in Figure 2. Browser code base integrity is addressed in our approach by a mechanism of user authorization which we describe in the remainder of this section. Protection of sensitive information is addressed in Section 5 through monitoring mechanisms that control extensions' access to the XPCOM framework.

4.1 Extension Installation and Loading

It is important to understand a browser's code base to clarify the issues surrounding its integrity. Firefox and other extensible browsers, when installed in a fairly secure fashion, have at least two components to their code base:

1. *Browser core*, the code directly loaded by invoking the browser executable.
2. *User code base*, additional program code loaded from among the user's files as the browser starts up.

We analyze the browser core and user code base to determine how the concepts of code authorization apply to each.

By default the code in the browser core must be granted full privileges within the browser, and we say that the user has authorized this by the basic act of installing the browser. This authorization is typically enforced by making the browser core not modifiable by an ordinary (unprivileged) user account. The files that constitute the core have their owner set to the superuser, and do not allow write privileges for any other users and groups. In addition to the code directly loaded by invoking the browser executable, there can be extensions installed as part of the browser core. For the purposes of this paper we include them in the browser core, as they share authorization properties with it.

The code that makes up the user code base is also authorized by the act of installation. This typically takes the form of the user confirming the install of an extension via the browser's graphical user interface. As the browser runs with the privileges of the user who invoked it, the browser is capable of installing extensions into the user code base on behalf of the user.

A critical aspect to browser security is the integrity of user code base, given that the browser core is well protected. If the user code base of the web browser is compromised, the end user is vulnerable to attack by malware such as the BROWSERSPY extension. The following two principles are fundamental to the user code base integrity:

Principle 1 Code should not be introduced into the user code base of the browser without the user's authorization.

Principle 2 Code that is part of the user code base of the browser should not be modified without the user's authorization.

It is necessary that browsers with an extensible architecture enforce these principles.[2] Integrity of the user code base can not be guaranteed unless both are upheld.

As indicated in Section 3, the Firefox web browser is vulnerable to attack against both principles. Installing an extension outside of a browser session by emulating the Firefox's installation routine is one way of introducing code into the user code base. This can be done without the user's knowledge or consent, thus betraying Principle 1. Furthermore, modification of the user code base of the browser can be realized by conducting an injection attack on a trusted extension, as the BROWSERSPY extension does. The injection is performed without the authorization of the user, which violates Principle 2.

Code signing. One potential solution to this problem is to require all extensions to be delivered to the user's browser with their code signed by a trusted entity. In this scenario, the user code base can be validated at any time to determine if its integrity has been undermined. However, Firefox has a design flaw in its current implementation of signed extensions that precludes the effectiveness of this solution. It only validates code at the time an extension is installed; when the browser loads an extension for execution, no integrity check is performed, making it easy for the BROWSERSPY extension to inject code into signed extensions. Firefox can not uphold Principle 2 without a fix to maintain code integrity, and a solution to this requires re-architecting the browser.

A way to detect the addition of code to the user code base is required to enforce Principle 1, even for code that has been signed by a trusted provider. The detection mechanism must implement an indicator of what extensions are currently part of the

---

[2] We note that even though this threat exists for other programs that are present in the user's account, the threat on the browser is especially critical due to nature of sensitive information available to it.

user code base, enabling newly introduced extensions to be differentiated from the set of previously authorized ones. This indicator needs to be secure against tampering by an agent other than the user, as the user is the *sole* authorizing agent with respect to what extensions are part of the user code base. A system based simply on remotely signed extensions does not provide these facilities, and thus can not ensure that all additions to the user code base are user authorized.

User signed extensions. A solution aimed at providing a better protection layer for the browser code base must certainly allow for unsigned extensions in order for it to offer any practical benefit. As previously mentioned, an extension distributor such as Mozilla may not be willing to provide any assurances with regard to third-party code by signing extensions on their behalf. Yet, users still want to allow such extensions into their user code base, as evidenced by the popularity of unsigned extension downloads. This poses a dilemma.

Our solution to this dilemma is to empower the user with the ability to sign extensions that are included in her user code base. Once the user has indicated approval for the unsigned code to become integrated into the user code base, we provide tools for the user to sign and suitably transform the code so that at any point its integrity can be verified. After the conversion to a user-signed extension is accomplished, we augment the browser with support for maintaining assurance of its user code base integrity. This thwarts injection attacks by malicious code (e.g., BROWSERSPY). These user signed extensions thus enhance resiliency of the browser code base to unauthorized modification.

User signed extensions also enable a convenient mechanism for the user to tightly control what is allowed into the user code base. Extensions can be allowed execution based on whether or not they have been signed by the user.[3]

Implementation approach. To prevent a malicious extension from tainting the trusted code base of Firefox, we have developed a prototype implementation of user signed extensions. The remainder of this section describes this implementation in detail.

The default behavior of the browser core has been augmented in two places:

1. *Extension installation*, performed once each time an extension is installed or updated to a more recent version.
2. *Extension loading*, occurring each time a new browser session is begun.

During installation, our solution assists the user in signing extension code so that it can be safely incorporated into the user code base. During loading, each extension loaded from the user code base is tested for code integrity before allowing it to be introduced into the browser session. If an extension has not been signed by the user, Firefox will not load it. Loading will also be denied to any extension for which integrity verification has failed. Figure 2 displays these steps as an extension makes its way into a browser session for execution.

Extension certificates. User extension signing is performed by generating a certificate (Figure 3) for each installed extension which can be used for the purposes of authorization and integrity checking. These certificates are composed of two sections:

---

[3] They may be further monitored for confidentiality and integrity policies as described in Section 5.

Absolute file paths   File hashes (SHA-256)

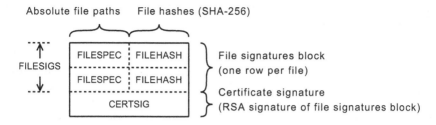

Fig. 3. A user signed extension certificate, employed to verify authorization and integrity of untrusted code

1. FILESIGS, used to verify the integrity of the extension's files.
2. CERTSIG, used to verify the integrity of FILESIGS.

Every file that comprises the extension is represented by a signature in the FILESIGS section of the certificate. Each file's signature is composed of its absolute path (FILESPEC) and a SHA-256 content hash (FILEHASH). By comparing the list of files present in the extension at load time with FILESIGS, the browser detects if a file has been added to or removed from the user code base without authorization. Through comparison of each file's hash value at load time with their respective FILEHASH, the browser notices if one of the trusted files has been illicitly modified. Firefox will refuse to load any extension that is revealed by these detection mechanisms to have violated user code base integrity.

The certificate signature CERTSIG is the RSA signed MD5 hash value of FILESIGS. As an extension is loaded, the browser generates another FILESIGS corresponding to the load-time state of the extension's root directory. The browser is then able to determine whether the file signatures represented in the certificate are valid by computing a hash of the extension's load-time FILESIGS and comparing it to the hash stored in CERTSIG. This check will fail if any of the following events have occurred subsequent to installation:

1. a file is added to or removed from the extension
2. a file is added to or removed from FILESIGS
3. one of an extension's files is modified
4. one of the certificate's FILEHASH is modified

Upon detection of these forms of corruption, the browser will rule not to load the extension.

The integrity of a certificate signature is protected by having the user sign it via RSA public-key cryptography. This signing by the user is what explicitly authorizes the extension to become part of the user code base. If the signature is tampered with, the browser will not be able to derive the hash value of FILESIGS, which must be decoded from CERTSIG to validate the certificate. In such a case, the browser will refuse to load the extension.

Key safeguarding. It is necessary to protect the user's public and private keys that are used in this solution, as they are the root of the security provided by user signed extension certificates.

An attacker can circumvent authorization if he gains access to the private key. He can modify user signed extensions and sign them himself by emulating the browser's certificate generation process. Since we expect extension based browser attacks to be launched by a malicious agent with user level access, and the user's private key is likely to be stored in local file space under user control, additional security is needed to protect the private key.

The enhanced protection is provided by encoding the private key using AES encryption. This encoded private key is made available to the browser, which prompts the user for her AES passphrase whenever the RSA private key is needed for extension installation. As only the user knows the passphrase, the private key is not accessible to attackers.

A different exploit is possible if an attacker is able to overwrite the user's public key with one of his own. In this scenario the browser is fooled into accepting extensions that are signed by the attacker and refusing those that are signed by the user. This privilege swap attack is possible because only the public key is used in the certificate validation process (private key safeguards do not come into play).

To protect the public key from this attack, our solution stores the key file as part of the browser core; writing to the key file requires administrative (root) privileges, though reading can still be performed by the user. This makes the key invulnerable to attack by an agent with only user level access.

Usability. It is well understood that a security solution that is invasive or difficult to use will face resistance in user uptake. If users decide they would rather not use the security solution then the benefits it provides can not be realized. With this concept in mind, the solution presented here is implemented in the least intrusive way possible.

Recall that the user must provide an AES passphrase in order to decrypt the private key needed for code signing. The browser prompts the user for this passphrase during installation. This is the minimal burden that our integrity mechanism imposes on the user.

The browser could require the user to authorize each extension when it is loaded, which would require the user to authenticate every time the browser starts up. Instead, authorization is performed only during extension installation. This way the user has to authenticate only on rare occasion: when installing or upgrading an extension. The system is just as secure as one which performs load-time authentication, and exhibits greater usability.

Another usability concern is apparent during the certificate generation phase of extension installation. As the user is performing the infrequent activity of adding a new extension, she may decide to add more than one. A multiple installation situation is especially likely when a periodic software update is triggered by the browser. Considering that each certificate generated requires the user to authenticate, installing several extensions could frustrate the user by repeatedly prompting for her password.

The obvious solution is to authenticate the user once, and then perform the certificate generation in bulk. This is the approach taken by our implementation. Once the user

Table 2. Top 20 most popular extensions from `addons.mozilla.org` tested with our implementation. Drawn from the top 23 as we elected to skip platform dependent and non-English language extensions.

1. Download Statusbar	6. Forecastfox	11. Web Developer	16. Map+
2. FlashGot	7. Tab Mix Plus	12. Cooliris Previews	17. StumbleUpon
3. NoScript	8. VideoDownloader	13. DownThemAll!	18. Foxmarks
4. Adblock Plus	9. Foxytunes	14. FireBug	19. Clipmarks
5. FireFTP	10. Fasterfox	15. Torrent Search	20. Answers

has decrypted the private key needed for signing, it is used to sign all the necessary certificates before being zeroed and deallocated.

Care must be taken when performing multiple installation based on a single authentication. It is highly important that the user always know what is signed as a result of authentication. If this issue is not regarded, a malicious extension could be injected among the other extensions to be installed without the user's knowledge. To defend against this attack, our implementation displays a list of all extensions that will be signed on the user's behalf before authentication is required. The user can decide to generate certificates for all extensions that are pending installation, or for none of them. Additionally, authorization decisions can be made per-extension. Screen shots of our changes to the installation mechanism can be found on the project website [3].

4.2   Install Protection Experimental Analysis

The solution was tested to determine its compatibility with popular browser extensions and its impact on Firefox's speed. The 20 most popular extensions for Firefox were used as a basis for our performance evaluation (listed in Table 2).

Compatibility testing. Determining compatibility was done by running the extensions in the test environment and exercising their core functionality. As some extensions provide a large feature set, it would have been difficult to exercise their total functionality. In our tests, 18 out of 20 extensions performed flawlessly. The extension Forecastfox elected to force registration of its XPCOM components using an `.autoreg` file, which the browser deletes following registration. The Foxytunes extension renamed its platform-specific component DLL to remove the platform identifier. These two user code base integrity violations are the result of actions taken that other extensions were able to avoid through different approaches to the same task. We also note that in general it is not possible for automated mechanisms to reason about the safety of these file manipulation operations, and hence the only option is to disallow them.

Performance overheads. To evaluate performance in terms of speed, we benchmarked the extension loading and installation phases under five conditions. For each test, we installed from one to five extensions and measured:

1. the time needed to generate the user signed certificates during installation,

Table 3. Extension installation integrity system benchmarks. The system used was a modified version of Firefox 2.0, running on Ubuntu 6.06 LTS, on an AMD Athlon 64 X2 3800+ (2GHz), 2GB RAM. The extensions tested were the top five from Table 2.

Installation / Loading performance benchmark	Number of extensions installed				
	1	2	3	4	5
Total time spent generating certificates (s)	18.6	38.1	53.5	75.6	94.7
Average time spent per certificate generated (s)	18.6	19.1	17.8	18.9	18.9
Percent of generation time spent signing certificates	99.5	99.5	99.9	99.9	99.8
Total time spent validating certificates (s)	0.75	1.50	2.30	3.00	3.70
Average time spent per certificate validated (ms)	748	750	767	750	740
Percent of validation time spent verifying signatures	90.5	92.3	95.8	95.3	96.4

2. the time needed to validate the certificates during loading, and
3. the time spent performing RSA cryptography during items 1 and 2.

The cryptography implemented uses 128-bit passphrases for AES, 512-bit keys for RSA, and SHA-256 for file hashing. MD5 is used to hash FILESIGS for use in generating CERTSIG.

The results of our speed tests are shown in Table 3. It takes the implementation about 18.7 seconds on average to generate a certificate. The benchmarks indicate over 99.5% of that time is spent signing the certificate using RSA.

Extension loading takes a little longer than a stock installation of Firefox. It takes about 751 ms for each certificate to be validated, of which there is one per extension. For validation of the certificate signature, we again observe that over 90% of the time is spent applying RSA cryptography.

We estimate that by using the browser's native RSA implementation, a significant benefit to performance would be gained. The RSA implementation we use is written in JavaScript. Due to its nature as an interpreted language, JavaScript is slow running for computationally intensive algorithms as present in RSA. We chose RSA in Java-Script as it is the easiest drop-in solution for our purpose of generating a stand-alone patch for the browser. If Firefox were modified such that its internal C++ public key cryptography routines be made available for use by the Extension Manager, we believe the performance of certificate generation could be greatly enhanced. Improved RSA performance would also allow us to use greater length keys, increasing the browser's resilience to attack.

It is apparent that the AES and SHA-256 cryptography routines do not noticeably impact performance. If a faster RSA implementation were employed, the significance of the other two cryptographic functions would likely increase.

We acknowledge the importance that the solution be optimized for greater extension load-time performance, as it is the common case when contrasted against extension installation. When comparing the speed of loading to installation in our prototype, it is conspicuous that the system is optimized for loading.

5   Extension Execution

User signed extensions disallow the user code base from unauthorized changes. However, this doesn't address the threat of a malicious extension installed with user consent. Once installed, it can corrupt the integrity of the user code base or even the browser core by making changes to the runtime state of the browser. Our BROWSERSPY extension hides itself using this mechanism; it alters the runtime state of the Extension Manager affecting display of the list of installed extensions.

The second phase of our solution therefore involves controlling an extension's access to critical browser services (XPCOM) via runtime monitoring. (The XPCOM services are discussed in length [7] along with many useful references.) Ordinarily, extensions enjoy unrestricted access to every interface of this framework. Our focus in this section is mainly on the mechanisms and infrastructure needed for a runtime monitoring solution governing access to the XPCOM interface.

The default security manager for JavaScript uses policies such as the *same origin* policy and the *signed script* policy. Firefox enforces these policies for web content pages, however does not so restrain internal JavaScript operations. Moreover, these policies are oblivious to browser overlays (explained below), another regular feature present in extensions. A straightforward adaptation of the use of these policies on extensions is not suitable for these reasons.

The action attribution problem. To enforce policies on a per-extension basis, it is necessary to identify the extension requesting each XPCOM operation. Unfortunately, Firefox does not have sufficient mechanism in place to establish identity due to the presence of *file overlays*. Extensions can provide these overlays to core portions of the web browser, which may extend and selectively mask the browser core. This integration is handled by Firefox in a way that does not retain means to identify the extension that applied the overlay. Through a malicious execution of this procedure, an extension can anonymously inject program code into the base functionality of the browser. Therefore, our solution to the action attribution problem has two parts: for overlay and non-overlay files.

Handling non-overlaid files. Policy enforcement mechanisms are comparatively simpler for non-overlaid files. In this case, the executable statements they contain are traced back to the extension that issued them. This data is compiled into the set of extensions contributing to any specific operation, used for the basis of policy decisions. The procedure of tracing the origin of a single operation involves getting the URL of the currently executing script (maintained by the browser's JavaScript interpreter *Spidermonkey*) and deriving an extension identifier from it. We have implemented this action attribution mechanism and discuss the performance later in this section.

Handling overlaid files. JavaScript statements present in overlay files require special handling. When a command is executed from one of these files, the script filename available to the runtime monitor points to the target of the overlay. This target is usually part of the browser core—not part of the extension that the code originated from—resulting in the action attribution problem explained earlier.

We have devised a way to provide the means of associating actions of overlay files with their extension of origin. Our approach is based on automatic interposition of "delimiting statements" around blocks of code that qualify as entry and exit points. These statements enable us to identify the executing extension for all code evaluated within the enclosed block.

The opening statements that we interpose manipulate a stack (maintained in the browser core) by pushing an extension identifier onto it. The interposed closing statements subsequently access the stack to pop the identifier off. An indicator of which extension is issuing the intermediate code is then found at the top of the stack. A *try-finally* construct wraps the function body to ensure that we pop the stack in the event of a return statement or thrown exception.

Spidermonkey is adapted to perform the interposition. Out of the box it provides us with an API capable of compiling JavaScript statements into bytecode (in preparation for execution), and another interface to decompile bytecode back into its original JavaScript. Specifically, support was added to the decompiler so that it can do the needed interposition.

The technique employed is to compile JavaScript into bytecode, then feed the bytecode into the interposing decompiler. This procedure is conducted once per extension, at the time the extension is installed. The performance of this operation is comparable to the rewriting technique in [11] with the advantage that it does not have to run every time the browser application is launched.

The above infrastructure is sufficient to handle overlaid code. However, a total solution to the overlay problem requires stripping the JavaScript code from overlay files, transforming it using interposition, and stitching the file back together. We are currently adding support to our infrastructure to handle this straightforward operation, and therefore report the performance of this interposition mechanism on non-overlaid files later in this section.

Analysis of interposition mechanisms. Under the interposition technique, a malicious extension may attempt manipulation of the active extension stack to spoof its extension ID, allowing access to XPCOM with elevated privileges and circumvention of stateful policies. Although this attack is theoretically possible, significant effort is required to mount it in our environment where user code base integrity is assured. Assuring a segment of code will not exploit this deficiency is difficult, stemming from the challenges in static analysis of JavaScript code.

Protection against this attack can be provided by an additional security layer that uses randomization. A signed, extension-specific magic number is given as an argument to the interposed stack manipulation code. This makes it harder for a generic attack to be constructed that is successful for more than a single targeted user. To achieve generality, the extension must self-modify by discovering and incorporating the magic number into its attack code. This is hard to do in our environment where extension integrity is continually enforced, as the malware must morph prior to installation.

Policies. With infrastructure in place, we have implemented six policies on non-overlaid extension code. They are representative of the types of policies enforceable using this solution, and are described in Table 4.

Table 4. The example policies that were created and tested with the runtime monitoring solution

Policy name	What it does	Granularity
XPCOM-ALLOW	Allow all access to a XPCOM interface	per extension
XPCOM-DENY	Deny all access to a XPCOM interface	per extension
SAME-ORIGIN	Allow access to same-origin domains	per extension
XPCOM-SAFE	Deny all access to XPCOM while SSL is in use.	per extension
PASS-RESTRICT	Deny access to the password manager	all extensions
HISTORY-FLOW	Prevent URL history leaks via output streams	all extensions

Table 5. Performance micro-benchmarks for the default browser behavior and two different action attribution methods. The execution time of selected functions within the top five most popular extensions is measured over 1000 runs. The same test platform described at Table 3 was used.

Extension	Function	Stock (ms)	File Lookup (ms)	Overhead (%)	Interposition (ms)	Overhead (%)
Adblock Plus	abp_init()	14.1	14.5	2.8	15.4	9.2
Download Statusbar	init()	4.5	4.7	4.4	5.0	11.1
FireFTP	changeDir()	26.4	29.4	11.4	32.6	23.5
FlashGot	getLinks()	4.2	4.4	4.8	4.6	9.5
NoScript	nso_save()	14.2	16.7	17.6	18.7	31.7
Average				8.2		17.0

The first four policies are extension specific. Complex policies can be composed of these rules to allow only the level of access an extension needs to function. The policies XPCOM-SAFE and PASS-RESTRICT are conservative policies that disallow access to sensitive data. PASS-RESTRICT and HISTORY-FLOW are enforced globally. HISTORY-FLOW is unique in that it is stateful. If any extension is detected accessing Firefox's URL history interface, that extension will be disallowed further access to interfaces of type nsIOutputStream. This protects writes to files and network sockets over a single session.

Performance. To evaluate the performance of our approach to action attribution, we wrapped functions within the five most popular Firefox extensions with benchmarking code. One thousand iterations of each function were performed in: (a) an unmodified browser, and (b) a browser using the filename lookup mechanism, and (c) a browser using the interposition technique on overlay files.

We observed a modest overhead of 8.2% on average to apply our policies using filename lookup. The interposition mechanism was slightly slower, imposing an overhead of 17.0% on average. The additional impact is not detrimental considering that overlay code is typically short, thus causing minimal difference in the overall user experience. Our experience in operating the browser with active runtime monitoring and policy enforcement did not indicate perceivable overhead.

6   Conclusion

We authored a malicious extension as proof-of-concept that security concerns exist in modern extensible web browsers. We selected the open source browser Firefox as our target platform, because it suffers many of these flaws.

The threat of malicious extensions was addressed using two mechanisms: (1) a mechanism by which the installation integrity of extensions is validated at load-time, and (2) infrastructure for runtime monitoring and policy enforcement of extensions to further prevent attacks on browser core integrity and sensitive data confidentiality.

Our changes to Firefox insure that the browser allows only extensions installed by the user to be loaded, and detects unauthorized changes made to installed extensions. This modification seals the outside installation vector for malicious extensions by disallowing standard and injection type installations external to a browser session. We enabled the browser to monitor a significant portion of extension code at runtime and effect policy on a per-extension basis. The monitoring infrastructure and the set of policies that we have created represent only a starting point. More research is needed for designing a comprehensive suite of policies that can be enforced on extensions with acceptable overheads on usability.

We are currently pursuing efforts to integrate our extension integrity checking prototype into the Firefox browser main source tree. Our malicious extension is available through private circulation for malware researchers.

References

1. Information from http://en.wikipedia.org/wiki/Mozilla_Firefox
2. Information from http://addons.mozilla.org
3. Project website. http://research.mike.tl/view/Research/ ExtensibleWebBrowserSecurity
4. Protected mode in vista ie7. http://blogs.msdn.com/ie/archive/2006/02/09/528963.aspx
5. eTrust Pest Patrol. Pests detected by pestpatrol and classified as browser helper object http://www.pestpatrol.com/pestinfo2005
6. Goldberg, I., Wagner, D., Thomas, R., Brewer, E.A.: A secure environment for untrusted helper applications: confining the wily hacker. In: USENIX Security Symposium (1996)
7. Hallaraker, O., Vigna, G.: Detecting Malicious JavaScript Code in Mozilla. In: Proceedings of the IEEE International Conference on Engineering of Complex Computer Systems (ICECCS), pp. 85–94, Shanghai, China (June 2005)
8. Kirk, J.: Trojan cloaks itself as firefox extension. Infoworld magazine (July 2006)
9. Lampson, B.W.: A note on the confinement problem. Communications of the ACM 16(10) (1973)
10. Necula, G.C.: Proof-carrying code (ACM SIGACT and SIGPLAN). In: ACM Symposium on Principles of Programming Languages (POPL), pp. 106–119. ACM Press, New York (1997)
11. Reis, C., Dunagan, J., Wang, H., Dubrovsky, O., Esmeir, S.: Browsershield: Vulnerability-driven filtering of dynamic html. In: USENIX Symposium on Operating Systems Design and Implementation (OSDI) (2006)
12. Sekar, R., Venkatakrishnan, V.N., Basu, S., Bhatkar, S., DuVarney, D.C.: Model carrying code: A practical approach for safe execution of untrusted applications. In: ACM Symposium on Operating Systems Principles (SOSP) (2003)

13. Vogt, P., Nentwich, F., Jovanovic, N., Kirda, E., Kruegel, C., Vigna, G.: Cross site scripting prevention with dynamic data tainting and static analysis. In: Network and Distributed System Security Symposium (NDSS), San Diego (2007)
14. Wahbe, R., Lucco, S., Anderson, T., Graham, S.: Efficient software-based fault isolation. In: Proceedings of the Symposium of Operating System Principles (1993)

On the Effectiveness of Techniques to Detect Phishing Sites

Christian Ludl, Sean McAllister, Engin Kirda, and Christopher Kruegel

Secure Systems Lab, Technical University Vienna
{chris2,sean,ek,chris}@seclab.tuwien.ac.at

Abstract. Phishing is an electronic online identity theft in which the attackers use a combination of social engineering and web site spoofing techniques to trick a user into revealing confidential information. This information is typically used to make an illegal economic profit (e.g., by online banking transactions, purchase of goods using stolen credentials, etc.). Although simple, phishing attacks are remarkably effective. As a result, the numbers of successful phishing attacks have been continuously increasing and many anti-phishing solutions have been proposed. One popular and widely-deployed solution is the integration of blacklist-based anti-phishing techniques into browsers. However, it is currently unclear how effective such blacklisting approaches are in mitigating phishing attacks in real-life. In this paper, we report our findings on analyzing the effectiveness of two popular anti-phishing solutions. Over a period of three weeks, we automatically tested the effectiveness of the blacklists maintained by Google and Microsoft with 10,000 phishing URLs. Furthermore, by analyzing a large number of phishing pages, we explored the existence of page properties that can be used to identify phishing pages.

1 Introduction

Online services simplify our lives. They allow us to access information ubiquitously and are also useful for service providers because they reduce the operational costs involved in offering a service. For example, online banking over the web has become indispensable for customers as well as for banks. Unfortunately, interacting with an online service such as a banking web application often requires a certain degree of technical sophistication that not all Internet users possess. For the last couple of years, such naive users have been increasingly targeted by phishing attacks that are launched by miscreants who are aiming to make an easy profit by means of illegal financial transactions. Phishing is a form of electronic identity theft in which a combination of social engineering and web site spoofing techniques are used to trick a user into revealing confidential information with economic value. In a typical attack, the attacker sends a large number of spoofed (i.e., fake) e-mails to random Internet users that appear to be coming from a legitimate business organization such as a bank. The e-mail urges the recipient (i.e., the potential victim) to update his personal information. Often, the e-mail also warns the recipient that the failure to comply with

B. M. Hämmerli and R. Sommer (Eds.): DIMVA 2007, LNCS 4579, pp. 20–39, 2007.

the request will result in the suspending of his online banking account. Such ungrounded threats are common in social engineering attacks and are an effective technique in persuading users.

When the unsuspecting victim follows the phishing link that is provided in the e-mail, he is directed to a web site that is under the control of the attacker. The site is prepared in a way such that it looks familiar to the victim. That is, the phishers typically imitate the visual corporate identity of the target organization by using similar colors, icons, logos and textual descriptions. In order to "update" his personal information, the victim is asked to enter his online banking login credentials (i.e., user name and password) to access the web site. If a victim enters his valid login credentials into the fraudulent web site, the phisher can then impersonate the victim. This may allow the attacker to transfer funds from the victim's account or cause other damage. Because victims are directly interacting with a web site that they believe they know and trust, the success rate of such attacks is very high. Note that although phishing has been receiving wide media coverage (hence, causing the number of Internet users who have heard of phishing to increase), such attacks still remain effective as phishers have been adapting their social engineering attempts accordingly. For example, many phishing e-mails now ask the victims to validate their personal information for "security purposes", supposedly because the targeted organization would like to protect them against the phishing threat.

According to the Anti-Phishing Working Group [2], the phishing problem has grown significantly over the last years. For example, the number of unique phishing web sites has exploded from 7,197 in December 2005 to 28,531 in December 2006. Also, financial losses stemming from phishing attacks have risen considerably, to more than $2.8 billion in the last year according to Gartner Inc. [8].

The phishing problem has become so serious that large IT companies such as Microsoft, Google, AOL and Opera have recently started announcing browser-integrated, blacklist-based anti-phishing solutions. However, one important question that still remains is how effective such blacklist-based solutions are in dealing with the phishing problem.

In this paper, we report our findings on analyzing the effectiveness of two popular blacklist-based anti-phishing solutions. We automatically tested the effectiveness of the blacklists maintained by Google and Microsoft over a three week period. During this time, we tested the blacklists with 10,000 phishing URLs. Furthermore, by analyzing a large number of phishing pages, we experimentally explored the existence of page properties that can be used to identify phishing pages.

The contributions of this paper are as follows:

– We show that blacklist-based solutions are actually quite effective in protecting users against phishing attempts. In our experiments, Google recognized almost 90% of the malicious URLs at the time of the initial check.
– By analyzing a large number of phishing pages, we built a classification model that attempts to use the properties of a page (e.g., number of password fields, number of external links, etc.) to distinguish between malicious and

legitimate pages. We believe our model can be used to improve existing anti-phishing approaches (e.g., such as the built-in phishing detection heuristics used by IE 7).

2 Related Work

A number of anti-phishing solutions have been proposed to date. Some approaches attempt to solve the phishing problem at the e-mail level. That is, they try to prevent phishing e-mails from reaching the potential victims by means of filters and content analysis. Obviously, such techniques are closely related to anti-spam research. In fact, anti-spam techniques (e.g., such as Bayesian filters) have proven to be quite effective in also intercepting phishing e-mails. Unfortunately, the effectiveness of anti-spam techniques often depends on many critical factors such as regular filter training and the availability of anti-spam tools. Furthermore, filtering, no matter how efficient, is not perfect and some phishing e-mails may manage to get through the filters and reach potential victims (i.e., strengthening the belief that the e-mail is legitimate).

Microsoft and Yahoo have also defined e-mail authentication protocols (i.e., Sender ID [16] and DomainKeys [32]) that can be use to verify if a received e-mail is authentic. The main disadvantage of these solutions, however, is that they are currently not used by the majority of Internet users.

Several academic, browser-integrated solutions (i.e., client-side techniques) have been proposed to date to mitigate phishing attacks. Well-known solutions in literature are SpoofGuard [3, 26] and PwdHash [24, 23]. SpoofGuard looks for phishing symptoms (e.g., obfuscated URLS) in web pages and raises alerts. Pwd-Hash, in contrast, creates domain-specific passwords that are rendered useless if they are submitted to another domain (e.g., a password for www.gmail.com will be different if submitted to www.attacker.com). Our anti-phishing tool, AntiPhish [11] takes a different approach and keeps track of where sensitive information is being submitted. That is, if it detects that confidential information such as a password is being entered into a form on an untrusted web site, a warning is generated and the pending operation is canceled.

An interesting solution that has been proposed by Dhamija et al. [5] involves the use of a so-called dynamic security skin on the user's browser. The technique allows a remote server to prove its identity in a way that is easy for humans to verify, but difficult for phishers to spoof. The disadvantage of this approach is that it requires effort by the user. That is, the user needs to be aware of the phishing threat and check for signs that the site he is visiting is spoofed. In fact, in a later study [6], Dhamija et al. report that more than 20% of the users do not take visual cues into consideration when surfing and that visual deception attacks can fool even the most sophisticated users.

Lui et al. [30] analyze and compare legitimate and phishing web pages to define metrics that can be used to detect a phishing page. A web page is classified as a phishing page if its visual similarity value is above a pre-defined threshold.

The most popular and widely-deployed techniques, however, are based on the use of blacklists of phishing domains that the browser refuses to visit. For example, Microsoft has recently integrated a blacklist-based anti-phishing solution into its Internet Explorer (IE) 7 browser. The browser queries lists of blacklisted and whitelisted domains from Microsoft servers and makes sure that the user is not accessing any phishing sites. Microsoft's solution is also known to use some heuristics to detect phishing symptoms in web pages [27, 15]. Obviously, to date, the company has not released any detailed public information on how its anti-phishing techniques function.

Other browser-integrated anti-phishing tools include Google Safe Browsing [25], NetCraft tool bar [18], eBay tool bar [7] and McAfee SiteAdvisor [12]. Similar to the Microsoft IE 7 anti-phishing protection, Google Safe Browsing uses blacklists of phishing URLs to identify phishing sites. The disadvantage of the approach is that non blacklisted phishing sites are not recognized. In contrast, NetCraft assesses the phishing probability of a visited site by trying to determine how old the registered domain is. The approach partially uses a database of sites that are maintained by the company. The downside of the approach, hence, is that new phishing sites that are not in the database might not be recognized. Similarly, SiteAdvisor is a database-backed solution that is, however, mainly designed for protection against malware-based attacks (e.g., spyware, Trojan horses, etc.). It includes automated crawlers that browse web sites, perform tests and create threat ratings for each visited site. Unfortunately, just like other blacklist or database-based solutions, SiteAdvisor cannot recognize new threats that are unknown and not in the database. The eBay solution is specifically designed for eBay and PayPal and involves the use of a so-called "Account Guard" that changes color if the user is on a spoofed site.

Verisign has also been providing a commercial anti-phishing service [28]. The company is crawling millions of web pages to identify "clones" in order to detect phishing web sites. Furthermore, just like other large companies such as Microsoft, McAfee and Google, blacklists of phishing web sites are maintained.

Note that one problem with crawling and blacklists proposals could be that the anti-phishing organizations will find themselves in a race against the attackers. This problem is analogous to the problems faced by anti-virus and anti-spam companies. Obviously, there is always a window of vulnerability during which users are susceptible to attacks. Furthermore, listing approaches are only as effective as the quality of the lists that are maintained. Hence, one interesting research question is how effective such blacklists are in mitigating attacks.

In late 2006, two studies appeared that compared the effectiveness of the Google and Microsoft blacklists. One study, which was paid for by Microsoft, unsurprisingly concluded that the Microsoft blacklist is superior [19]. The other study, initiated by Mozilla, drew the opposite conclusion [17]. Thus, we felt that a third, independent evaluation would be valuable. In addition, the two studies mentioned above only consider whether a phishing URL was blacklisted at one point in time. However, no attempt was made to assess whether phishing URLs were added at a later time, or whether they were never added at all. Hence, a key difference of our study is that we take these questions into account.

Also, independently and concurrently from our work, Zhang et al. [33] have also performed a similar study that investigates the efficiency of anti-phishing solutions. The authors have created an automated test-bed with which they have tested the detection rates of mostly blacklist-based anti-phishing solutions. An important difference of our work is that our tests and experimental data include 10,000 phishing URLs collected over a three week period lasting from December 2006 to January 2007. In comparison, Zhang et al.'s dataset includes 100 phishing URLs collected over a period of three days in November 2006. Furthermore, in our work, besides investigating the efficiency of popular blacklists, we also experimentally explored the existence of page properties that can be used to identify phishing pages.

3   Scope of Study

The goal of this paper is to analyze the effectiveness of anti-phishing solutions. More precisely, we are interested in assessing techniques that are capable of classifying individual web pages. To qualify for our study, a technique must be capable of determining whether a page is legitimate or a phishing page, given only the URL and the page's source code. We did not consider mechanisms that aim to prevent users from visiting a phishing site (e.g., by recognizing phishing mails). Also, we did not evaluate solutions that attempt to protect sensitive user information from being leaked to the phishers (e.g., by replacing passwords with site-specific tokens, or by using novel authentication mechanisms). Currently, there are two main approaches to classify visited web pages without any additional information. The first one is based on URL blacklists. The second approach analyzes properties of the page and (sometimes) the URL to identify indications for phishing pages.

Blacklists: Blacklists hold URLs (or parts thereof) that refer to sites that are considered malicious. Whenever a browser loads a page, it queries the blacklist to determine whether the currently visited URL is on this list. If so, appropriate countermeasures can be taken. Otherwise, the page is considered legitimate. The blacklist can be stored locally at the client or hosted at a central server.

Obviously, an important factor for the effectiveness of a blacklist is its coverage. The coverage indicates how many phishing pages on the Internet are included in the list. Another factor is the quality of the list. The quality indicates how many non-phishing sites are incorrectly included into the list. For each incorrect entry, the user experiences a false warning when she visits a legitimate site, undermining her trust in the usefulness and correctness of the solution. Finally, the last factor that determines the effectiveness of a blacklist-based solution is the time it takes until a phishing site is included. This is because many phishing pages are short-lived and most of the damage is done in the time span between going online and vanishing. Even when a blacklist contains many entries, it is not effective when it takes too long until new information is included or reaches the clients.

For our study, we attempted to measure the effectiveness of popular blacklists. In particular, we studied the blacklists maintained by Microsoft and Google. We believe that these blacklists are the ones that are most wide-spread, as they are used by Internet Explorer and Mozilla Firefox, respectively.

Page analysis: Page analysis techniques examine properties of the web page and the URL to distinguish between phishing and legitimate sites. Page properties are typically derived from the page's HTML source. Examples of properties are the number of password fields, the number of links, or the number of unencrypted password fields (these are properties used by SpoofGuard [3]).

The effectiveness of page analysis approaches to identify phishing pages fundamentally depends on whether page properties exist that allow to distinguish between phishing and legitimate sites. Thus, for our study, we aimed to determine whether these properties exist, and if so, why they might be reasonable candidates to detect phishing pages.

In a first step, we defined a large number of page properties that can be extracted from the page's HTML code and the URL of the site. Then, we analyzed a set of phishing and legitimate pages, assigning concrete values to the properties for each page. Finally, using the collected data as training input, we applied machine-learning techniques to create a web page classifier. The resulting classifier is able to distinguish well between phishing and legitimate classifiers, with a very low false positive rate. This indicates that the aforementioned page properties that allow one to identify malicious pages do in deed exist, at least for current phishing pages.

It seems that Microsoft has drawn a similar conclusion, as the new Internet Explorer browser also features a phishing page detection component based on page properties. This component is invoked as a second line of defense when a blacklist query returns no positive result for a visited URL. As part of our study, we attempted to determine the features that are most relevant to the IE for identifying phishing sites. We observed that the IE model looks different than the one we have built, and also detects less phishing pages.

4 Experimental Setup

In this section, we first discuss the anti-phishing solutions that we chose to examine. Then, we describe the test data that was collected to conduct our experiments.

4.1 Anti-phishing Solutions

In the previous section, we outlined the scope of our study. In particular, we explained our focus on solutions that analyze web pages for indications of phishing, namely blacklist-based and page analysis techniques. To evaluate the effectiveness of these approaches, it is desirable to select solutions that are in wide-spread use. This is important so that the results of the study are relevant. Also, a wide-spread solution has a higher likelihood of being well-supported and maintained, thus making the result of the study meaningful. Consider a study that evaluates the effectiveness of a blacklist that is not updated. While this study will probably conclude that blacklists are very ineffective, these results are not very insightful.

For this study, we decided to analyze the effectiveness of the anti-phishing solutions used by the Microsoft Internet Explorer 7 and Mozilla Firefox 2. The reasons for this choice are the following: First, these two applications are the most-used web browsers on the Internet. Second, both browsers recently introduced anti-phishing mechanisms, and one can assume that these mechanisms will be the most widely deployed anti-phishing solutions in the near future. Note that we did not include the Opera browser in our study because the company announced a phishing filter only shortly after we started our experiments.

Internet Explorer 7: Microsoft recently introduced the version 7 of its popular Internet Explorer (IE) browser, which was automatically deployed to millions of computers around the world via Microsoft's Windows update web site. One of the most important, new features of this browser is its anti-phishing support. To this end, the IE 7 uses both an online database of reported phishing sites as well as heuristics that analyze web pages to determine the potential risk of a web site [27, 15]. This makes the Internet Explorer an optimal selection for our study, as it uses both a blacklist and page analysis approaches to identify phishing attempts.

For the user, the anti-phishing support has the following visible effects: If a site is a reported phishing site, the address bar of the browser turns red and the web site turns into a full page warning about the potential dangers of the site. The user can then choose to either proceed to the site or close the page. If the site is not found in the blacklist of reported scam pages, but the page heuristics detect a possible phishing attempt, the address bar turns yellow and a warning symbol appears at the bottom of the screen.

Mozilla Firefox: Mozilla Firefox is considered the only serious competitor to the Microsoft IE, which currently dominates the browser market. Since version 2.0, Firefox includes anti-phishing support. The browser can connect to any available blacklist provider, using a documented, open protocol. Currently, however, only the Google blacklist servers[1] are pre-configured. The anti-phishing approach of Firefox is solely based on blacklists and does not use any form of page analysis to warn the user of potential scams. By default, Firefox uses regularly downloaded lists and does not perform blacklist lookups with each web connection. The user, however, can also choose to use live blacklists. When a visited URL is on the blacklist, Firefox turns the web page into a black-and-white version and displays a warning message.

---

[1] Google's blacklist is also used by the Google safe browsing toolbar [9].

4.2   Test Data

For our study, a large number of phishing pages were necessary. We chose `phishtank.com` as a source of phishing URLs. The information from this site is freely available and the amount of reported phishing sites is very large (approximately five hundred new phishing reports every day). There are other providers of blacklist data, but their feeds are typically only available for a fee, and their reports tend to focus on particular phishing incidents [4] (for example, a large scale phishing attack towards a particular institution, with multiple site mirrors and copies of spoofed emails), whereas the phishtank datasets focus on the URL itself, thereby making it more appropriate to our goals. The free availability of this information is also a very important aspect to our research, as phishtank is neither affiliated with Microsoft nor with Mozilla, making the results more objective. The URLs were extracted from a XML feed [20] of verified and (then) online phishing sites. In addition to saving the URLs we made local copies of each site. This was important, as most phishing sites are only online for a short period of time and the page source was needed later for evaluating the effectiveness of page analysis techniques. Note that even when attempting to download phishing sites immediately, a significant fraction of these sites was already down (and thus, no longer available for further analysis).

Table 1. (a) Domains that host phishing sites. (b) Popular phishing targets.

(a)

No domain (numerical)	3,864
.com	1,286
.biz	1,164
.net	469
.info	432
.ws	309
.jp	307
.bz	256
.nz	228
.org	156
.de	111
.ru	106
.us	105

(b)

paypal	1,301
53.com	940
ebay	807
bankofamerica	581
barclays	514
volksbank	471
sparkasse	273
openplan	182
Total	5,069

Note that phishtank is a community-driven site that lives from submissions made by its users. Hence, this approach has the disadvantage that some reported sites may not be phishing sites. Phishtank uses a system based on verification by other users, who can vote whether a page is a phishing page or not. These votes are weighted by the experience and the rank the user has within the community. Nevertheless, it is possible that even a page that is verified by phishtank users to be malicious is in fact legitimate. Therefore, we cannot completely rule out the possibility that some samples are false positives. Also, note that we were not able to investigate how often phishes reported by Google and Microsoft appeared on phishtank. This is because we do not have access to the full blacklist used at Microsoft (which is queried via SOAP requests) and because we believe that the Google blacklist that is available online is not complete (i.e., we suspect that the Google blacklist does not include IPs that have been taken down or that are not relevant anymore).

We started the collection of phishing pages on 15. December 2006, with the goal of gathering 10,000 URLs. This goal was reached after about three weeks, on 4. January 2007. During this time a webcrawler periodically checked the collected URLs and when possible downloaded the sites to our local repository. If the download failed the crawler checked the site again on its next run and continued doing so for 48 hours after the site was first added to our database. For the 10,000 URLs that we collected, we were only able to download the page sources of 4,633 sites. This clearly underlines the short time span that many phishing pages are online. In Table 1(a), the leading top level domain names of the phishing sites are listed. Note that the largest fraction of pages is not hosted under any domain, but uses only numerical IP addresses. Among the remaining sites, a large variety of domains can be observed.

We also analyzed the sites that were spoofed most often by checking for hostnames of legitimate sites in the phishing sites URL. This is also a property we checked for in the page analysis (see section 6.1). The results are shown in Table 1(b). Not surprisingly, both paypal and ebay were among the top three. Most other frequently targeted victims are online portals of banks. The eight most targeted victims alone account for more than 50% of the phishing URLs that we observed. Further analysis of current phishing targets based on Google's blacklist can be found at [13].

5   Study of Blacklist Effectiveness

To study the effectiveness of the blacklists provided by Microsoft (used by the Internet Explorer) and Google (used by Firefox), we periodically checked whether our most recently collected URLs from phishtank.com were already blacklisted. Depending on the initial response, we either saved the positive answer (i.e., the site is blacklisted) and stopped to check the URL, or we continued to send requests with not-yet blacklisted URLs. In the latter case, we stopped after the first positive response and saved the received data together with a timestamp.

Automated analysis: Because of the large amount of data that needed to be processed, an automated solution to check URLs was necessary. Hence, we had to exchange data with the two blacklist servers directly, without going through the browser. This task was quite easy for the Google blacklist server because the blacklist protocol and the specifications of the request and response formats are public [25, 21].

Of course, the situation is different for Microsoft's blacklist server, for which no public protocol information is available. The first problem that we faced was that the information between the IE and Microsoft is exchanged over an encrypted SSL connection. To discover more details about the protocol, we first set up an Apache SSL server. Then, we created a self-signed certificate and stored this certificate in our Internet Explorer. In addition, we added an entry for Microsoft's blacklist server `urs.microsoft.com` to the `hosts` file of the machine that the Internet Explorer was running on. The idea was to let the Microsoft blacklist server URL point to our SSL server. As a result, the browser contacted our server for each blacklist request. At this point, we were able to decrypt the messages that were arriving at our server, and we discovered that the communication was implemented via SOAP messages. We could then forward these messages to the real Microsoft server, and received responses that we could further analyze.

Analyzing the blacklist protocol, we observed that the URL of each visited page is stripped from any GET data at the end of the URL and then sent to the server for checking. This is different from the Google protocol, which always includes the complete URL. On sites that include iframes, a single request was sent for each iframe. This can lead to performance problems and was subsequently changed by Microsoft [29]. That is, before the change was introduced, an HTML page with an embedded iframe that linked to a known phishing site was reported as being a phishing site itself. After the change, we observed that the browser ignored iframe links. Hence, if we created a "phishing" page that used iframes and linked to a known phishing site, our phishing page would not be detected. During our experiments, we also noticed that the request and response pairs to the blacklist server often included lookup strings and responses for domains such as `microsoft.com`. Unfortunately, we were not able to determine the reason for these lookups. However, we could confirm that the browser version and the IP address of the computer that the browser is running on is sent to the Microsoft servers with each request (which is indicated in the privacy statement in [14]).

Analysis results: When checking the results of our test run, we recognized that for the 10,000 different URLs that we sent to both servers, only Google returned appropriate answers for all of them. However, we received only 6,131 responses from the Microsoft server. After further analysis of the data, we had to draw the conclusion that the Microsoft server was using some sort of rate limiting and locked us out because of too many requests. As a result, we unfortunately have less comprehensive data from the Microsoft blacklist. Nevertheless, we believe that we still have sufficient data to provide meaningful statistics for the Microsoft blacklist.

The results of the experiment are shown in Table 2. Initially, when we first requested the status for a URL, Google had 6,414 URLs on its blacklist. During the remaining time, 108 additional URLs were added to the blacklist. Thus, Google had blacklisted a total of 6,522 URLs (out of the 10,000 analyzed) at the end of our experiment. Microsoft sent a positive result for 3,095 URLs initially, and 331 later, which yields a total of 3,426 blacklisted pages. Because of the different absolute numbers of checked URLs, the table also shows the relative values. Given our results, we observe that Google's blacklist appears to have

Table 2. Blacklist responses for phishing URLs

	Google	Microsoft
Sites	10,000 (100.00%)	6,131 (100.00%)
BL initially	6,414 (64.14%)	3,095 (50.48%)
BL delayed	128 (1.28%)	331 (5.40%)
BL total	6,522 (65.22%)	3,426 (55.88%)

more coverage, although the fraction of malicious pages that are detected are not too encouraging in both cases.

One problem with the results above is that they do not differentiate between phishing sites that are online (and thus, present a danger for users) and those that are offline. Many phishing sites have a very short lifetime, and as described in Section 4.2, we were only able to download the source for 4,633 of the 10,000 URLs we collected. Of course, maintainers of blacklists cannot include a URL when they cannot check the page that the URL is referring to. Thus, it is fairer to check the blacklist responses only for those pages that could be accessed. To this end, for the next experiment, we only considered those URLs for which both the Microsoft server and the Google server returned a response, and which could be successfully downloaded. For this, the data set contained a total of 3,592 URLs. The results are shown in Table 3. Interestingly, the hit rate is significantly higher in this case, suggesting that there are probably many URLs reported that are never considered for blacklisting because they are offline. Also, one can be seen that the gap between Google's blacklist and the one by Microsoft has increased, showing that Google delivers significantly better results.

Table 3. Blacklist responses for live phishing sites

	Google	Microsoft
Sites	3,595 (100.00%)	3,592 (100.00%)
BL initially	3,157 (87.89%)	2,139 (59.55%)
BL delayed	84 (2.34%)	274 (7.63%)
BL total	3,241 (90.23%)	2,413 (67.18%)

For the next experiment, we analyzed the response times for URLs that were not initially blacklisted, but were entered into the list after some delay. More precisely, we considered all URLs that have not initially been blacklisted by a server, and measured the time until we first received a positive blacklist response. The fasted addition to the Microsoft blacklist occurred after 9:07 minutes, while it took 9 days and almost 6 hours for the slowest. Google's fastest addition took 19:56 minutes, the slowest 11 days and 20 hours. On average, it took Microsoft 6.4 hours to add an initially not blacklisted entry (with a standard deviation of 6.2 hours). For Google, it took somewhat longer (on average 9.3 hours, with a standard deviation of 7.2 hours). Note that due to our test setup, we are not able to precisely measure the shortest listing times. This is because we do not continuously check URLs, but perform lookups periodically every 20 minutes. The shortest amount of time that passed between receiving the URL from phishtank and checking it for the first time was 7:33 minutes (for both servers). The longest period until checking Google's blacklist were 1:43 hours, and 2:10 for Microsoft's (due to unexpected problems with our scripts). In general, the results show that adding new entries to the blacklist often takes a considerable amount of time. However, only few entries were added overall, and the responses received from a server for a URL rarely changed over time.

Discussion: Looking at our results for two widely-used blacklists, we can conclude that this approach is quite successful in protecting users, especially when considering only URLs that refer to sites that are online. Especially Google, which has correctly recognized almost 90% of the malicious URLs at the time of the initial check, appears to be an important and powerful component in the fight against phishing.

Finally, it is worth pointing out that blacklist approaches may sometimes be defeated by simple obfuscation tricks, as reported in [1]. The basic idea of this attack is to replace single slashes with double slashes in phishing URLs, thereby defeating a simple blacklist string comparison. Both Firefox and Internet Explorer 7 were vulnerable to this kind of evasion.

6 Study of Page Analysis Effectiveness

To study the effectiveness of page analysis techniques, we first wish to answer the more basic question of whether page properties actually exist that allow one to distinguish between malicious (phishing) pages and legitimate (benign) ones. To answer this basic question, we define a number of properties that can be extracted from the source and the URL of web pages (described in Section 6.1). Once we define the page properties that we are interested in, we extract them from a set of phishing and normal (legitimate) pages. Based on the extracted properties, we use machine learning techniques to attempt to build a model to distinguish between malicious and legitimate pages. When such a model can be built, this implies that the properties must reflect some difference between phishing pages and normal ones. However, when such a classification model cannot be built, we have to conclude that the properties that we have defined do not allow to distinguish between phishing and legitimate pages. Our efforts of classifying web pages are discussed in Section 6.2. Finally, in Section 6.3, we use our properties to analyze the effectiveness of the page analysis heuristics implemented by Microsoft Internet Explorer 7.

6.1 Page Properties

As mentioned previously, we need to define appropriate properties to characterize a web page before it can be analyzed for indications that might reveal it as a phishing site. Not all of these properties have the same significance towards the probability of being a phishing site, but those that do not matter are then considered irrelevant by the data mining tool and therefore not included in the final decision tree. The following is the list of 18 properties that we consider. Our features are mostly extracted from the HTML source of a page. Two features are derived from the page's URL.

- **Forms:** Phishing pages aim to trick users into providing sensitive information. This information is typically entered into web forms. Thus, the *number of forms* (which is counted by this property) might provide an indicator to distinguish between phishing and legitimate pages, because some phishing sites ask the user to enter more than just his username and password (TAN numbers in banking applications and similar).
- **Input fields:** Because of the importance and prevalence of web forms on phishing pages, we aimed to define additional properties that characterize their structure in more detail. We specified properties that count the number of *input fields, text fields, password fields, hidden fields,* and *other fields.* The category *other fields* summarizes all input elements that are not member of any of the four more specific classes. Examples for *other fields* are radio buttons or check boxes.
- **Links:** Another important, general characteristic of every web page is its link structure. This not only takes into account links to other web pages, but also includes links to embedded images. Interestingly, many phishing pages contain links to the site they spoof, often to include original page elements from the victim page. To recognize such pages, we include properties that count the number of *internal links* to resources located in the page's domain as well as *external links* to resources stored on other sites. These links are extracted from a page by looking for <a> tags in the HTML source. By scanning for <img> tags, we extract links to *internal images* and *external images.* In addition, there is a category called *other links,* which counts the number of links included by other HTML tags (such as links to style sheets or JavaScript code, using the <link> tag). Furthermore, we explicitly count the number of (internal and external) links over a secure connection (i.e., by specifying an https target), using the *secure links* property. The same is done for images (*secure images*). Finally, to underline the importance of external links for finding phishing pages, we also define the category *external references,* which holds the sum of the number of *external links* and *external images.*
- **Whitelist references:** As mentioned previously, phishing pages often contain references to resources on their victims' sites. This fact is partly captured by the properties that count the number of external references. However, we can go one step further and analyze all external references for the presence of links that are particularly suspicious. An external reference is suspicious when it points to a resource on a site that is a frequent target of phishing. To find such links, we check whether any of the links on a page refer to a resource on a trusted site. Trusted sites are those that appear on a

whitelist. More precisely, we used a whitelist compiled by Google [10] that at the time of writing (February 2007) contained 2,431 entries that were considered trusted. This whitelist is freely available, in contrast to a similar whitelist maintained by Microsoft, which is stored in encrypted form in the Windows registry.

- **Script tags:** To distinguish between sites that make ample use of JavaScript and plain text pages, we count the number of JavaScript tags on a page and store it in the *script tags* property.

- **Suspicious URL:** This and the following property are derived from the URL of the page that is analyzed, and not from the page's source.

  An important goal of phishers is to make the phishing page appear as similar as possible to the spoofed one. Phishers often include parts of the URL they spoof into the URL of their phishing pages (for example, as part of the hostname, or in the path field). To capture such behavior, we search the URL for appearances of fragments of trusted pages. More precisely, we make use of the domains stored in Google's whitelist, and we check whether any of the trusted domains appear in the URL of the page that is currently analyzed. Hence, we perform a simple string search and determine whether any of the domains on the whitelist appear as a substring in the current URL. For example, www.ebay.com is on Google's whitelist. To check whether the current URL is suspicious, we check it for the presence of the substring ebay. Unfortunately, this approach can raise false positives, especially when trusted domains are very short. To mitigate this problem, we decided to only check for the appearance of domain names that have five or more characters. In addition, we manually added a few shorter domain names (such as ebay or dell) that are known to be frequently targeted by phishers. The remaining whitelist then contained 1,830 domains.

- **Uses SSL:** Another characteristic that was analyzed for each page is whether it is accessed over SSL (https) or not. In our preliminary studies, we observed that not many phishing sites make use of a secure server. One explanation could be that it is not straightforward to obtain a trustworthy certificate. Hence, not having such a certificate causes the browser to display a warning message, thereby alerting the user.

Of course, we are aware of the fact that our properties might not be complete. Furthermore, determined attackers could evade defense systems based on these properties (for example, by making use of Flash). However, the aim of our study is to understand whether current phishing pages can be identified based on page properties. Thus, we believe that our selection is reasonable and reflects the structure and methods that phishers use today. Also, our property list covers most page attributes that are checked by SpoofGuard [3], a tool that analyzes pages for phishing indicators. One property that is used by SpoofGuard, but that we have not included are checks for techniques that attempt to obfuscate links. These techniques are already handled (checked) by browsers, which raise appropriate warning (Firefox 2) or error messages (Internet Explorer 7). As a result, they are no longer effective and, as a consequence, no longer used by phishers.

6.2 Classification Model

Based on the properties defined in the previous section, we built a classification model that attempts to use these properties to distinguish between malicious and legitimate pages.

As the set of phishing sites, we used the 4,633 pages that were successfully downloaded during our experiments (as discussed in Section 4.2) plus about 1100 pages that we collected before starting the blacklist analysis, resulting in 5751 analyzed sites. To obtain a set of legitimate pages, we had to collect a reasonable amount of comparable benign sites. Since the targets of phishers are mostly login pages, we used Google's `inurl:` operator to search for login pages. More precisely, we used Google to search for pages where one of the following strings `login`, `logon`, `signin`, `signon`, `login.asp`, `login.php` and `login.htm` appears in the URL. After downloading 5,124 pages, we manually removed from our data set all pages that were the result of a 404 error (indicating the the page was not found) as well as pages that were obviously no login pages (e.g., blog entries that just happened to contain the string `login` in the URL. This left us with 4,335 different benign web sites for further analysis.

To prepare the data for the following classification process, we extracted one feature vector for each page in the sets of phishing and legitimate pages. Every feature vector has one entry for each of the 18 properties that we have defined. When analyzing the feature vectors, we observed that there were many vectors that had identical values, especially in case of the phishing pages. This was the result of certain, identical phishing pages that appeared under several URLs (sometimes, an identical phishing page appeared under a few hundred different URLs). To prevent a bias in the classification model, focusing on the properties of certain phishing pages that appear frequently, we decided to include into the classification process only unique feature vectors. That is, when a number of different pages are characterized by the same feature vector, this vector is only considered once by the classification process. As a result, we ended up with 680 feature vectors for the set of phishing pages, and 4,149 for the set of legitimate pages.

Using the input data described above, we applied the J48 algorithm to extract a decision tree that can classify pages as legitimate or phishing. J48 is an implementation of the classic C4.5 decision tree algorithm [22] in Weka [31], a well-known data mining tool. We selected the C4.5 classifier for two reasons. First, we believe that a decision tree provides intuitive insight into which features are important in classifying a data set. Second, the C4.5 algorithm is known to work well for a wide range of classification problems.

Without stripping down our data to unique feature vectors, Weka created decision trees with a bias towards the properties of the most frequently appearing sites, thus delivering different results. The root node (i.e., whitelist references) stays the same. However, the count of external links gains far more importance, as it is the first node of the right subtree.

The runtimes for generating a decision tree with Weka heavily depend on the size of the input set. With our above mentioned data sets, the building of the models took 0.54 seconds for the IE data, respectively 1.29 seconds for the

Table 4. Confusion matrix for page classifier

	Classified as legitimate	Classified as phishing
Legitimate page	4,131	18
Phishing page	115	565

number of whitelist references, the number of external and internal links, and the property that captures suspicious URLs. The fact that these page properties are close to the root indicates that they are most effective in discriminating between phishing and legitimate sites. Indeed, when analyzing the paths that lead to the leaves with the largest fraction of phishing pages, one can observe that the presence of many external and few internal references is evidence of a malicious site. This is even more so when these external references point to sites that are common phishing victims (that is, URLs on the whitelist). Also, a suspicious URL is a good indication of a phishing page. When looking for strong evidence of legitimate pages, one will typically find many internal links and internal images (and the absence of a suspicious URL).

6.3   Analysis of Internet Explorer Heuristics

In the next step, we attempted to determine those features that the Internet Explorer page analysis heuristics considers most important to identify phishing pages. Of course, since we were only able to do black-box testing, we can only make assumptions about the inner workings of the phishing filter and how it determines the "phishiness" of a webpage.

We first used the Internet Explorer to classify our sets of legitimate and phishing pages. The process of analyzing web pages was automated, due to the large amount of data. We developed a Browser Helper Object (BHO) (i.e., IE plug-in) that was visiting pages and reporting on the results of the page analysis heuristics. After each page was visited, the BHO was used to delete all temporary files (such as browser history and cookies). This was to ensure that the next site visited would not be treated differently because of any cached information from previous pages. In addition, we had to work around the problem that the Internet Explorer offers no possibility to turn off the communication with the blacklist server. Fortunately, we could reuse the server that we previously set up to analyze the protocol between the browser and the Microsoft blacklist server. More precisely, we intercepted all blacklist requests by the browser during this analysis run and provided a response that indicated that the visited site was not blacklisted, thereby forcing IE to resort to its page analysis heuristics.

Examining the results, we observed that the Internet Explorer raised no false warnings (that is, all legitimate sites were recognized as such). This is better than the model that we introduced in the previous section. However, the browser was also less successful in identifying phishing pages (only 1,867 of the 4,633 original phishing pages, or slightly more than 40% were correctly classified). This is likely the result of a design decision to suppress false alarms as the most important goal. In any case, even a 40% classification accuracy is valuable when considering that no false positives are raised. This is particularly true when page analysis techniques are employed as a second line of defense with a blacklisting approach. When only using page heuristics to detect phishing sites, good coverage is probably only achievable when a few false positives are tolerated (as shown in the previous sections).

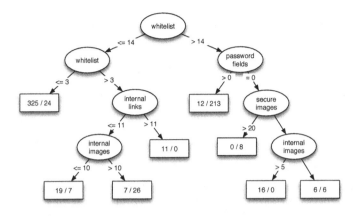

Fig. 2. Decision tree for Internet Explorer

Once the classification effectiveness of the Internet Explorer was analyzed quantitatively, we attempted to understand which properties were most important for the decision process. To this end, we used the Weka J48 algorithm to build a decision tree based on the set of phishing pages only. More precisely, as input data set, we used the 680 unique feature vectors and the labels that IE assigns to the corresponding pages. That is, the set contained on one hand 284 feature vectors of pages that were correctly identified as malicious, and 396 feature vectors of phishing pages that were incorrectly classified as benign. The idea was to extract a model that would indicate which properties (together with the properties' values) are most important for the Internet Explorer to label a phishing site as malicious. Figure 2 shows a reduced version of the decision tree for this experiment. Note that the number of references that are in the whitelist plays a central role for classification. When the number of such references is less than four, the page is almost always classified as benign. The fact that there are nine pages with less than three whitelist references might very well be attributed to the fact that our whitelist (which is from Google) is slightly different that the one used by Microsoft. Other indicators are less significant, but one can see that the number of links to pages and images also seem to be taken into account.

7   Conclusion

In this paper, we reported our findings on analyzing the effectiveness of two popular anti-phishing solutions. We tested the anti-phishing solutions integrated into the Firefox 2 (i.e., Google blacklists) and Microsoft's Internet Explorer 7 over a period of three weeks. We fed these blacklists 10,000 phishing URLs to measure their effectiveness in mitigating phishing attacks. Furthermore, by analyzing a large number of phishing pages, we report page properties that can be used to identify phishing pages and improve existing solutions. Our findings show that blacklist-based solutions are actually quite effective in protecting users against phishing attempts and that such solutions are an important and useful component in the fight against phishing.

Acknowledgments

This work has been supported by the Austrian Science Foundation (FWF) under grants P-18764, P-18157, and P-18368.

References

[1] Firefox 2.0.0.1 Phishing Protection Bypass (2007)
https://bugzilla.mozilla.org/show_bug.cgi?id=367538
[2] Anti-Phishing Working Group (APWG). APWG Homepage (2007)
http://www.antiphishing.org/
[3] Chou, N., Ledesma, R., Teraguchi, Y., Boneh, D., Mitchell, J.: Client-side defense against web-based identity theft. In: 11th Annual Network and Distributed System Security Symposium (NDSS '04), San Diego (2005)
[4] Utter, D.: Sites Want To Hook And Gut Phishers (2006)
http://www.securitypronews.com/insiderreports/insider/
spn-49-20061114SitesWantTo HookAndGutPhishers.html
[5] Dhamija, R., Tygar, J.D.: The battle against phishing: Dynamic security skins. In: Proceedings of the 2005 symposium on Usable privacy and security, pp. 77–88. ACM Press, New York (2005)
[6] Dhamija, R., Tygar, J.D., Hearst, M.: Why Phishing Works. In: Proceedings of the Conference on Human Factors In Computing Systems (CHI) 2006, Montreal, Canada, ACM Press, New York (2006)
[7] eBay. eBay tool bar (2007) http://pages.ebay.com/ebaytoolbar/
[8] Gartner Press Release. Gartner Says Number of Phishing E-Mails Sent to U.S. Adults Nearly Doubles in Just Two Years (2006)
http://www.gartner.com/it/page.jsp?id=498245
[9] Google. Google Toolbar for Firefox (2006)
http://www.google.com/tools/firefox/toolbar/FT3/intl/en/
[10] Google. Google Whitelist (2007) http://sb.google.com/safebrowsing/update?
version=goog-white-domain:1:-1
[11] Kirda, E., Kruegel, C.: Protecting Users against Phishing Attacks. The Computer Journal (2006)
[12] McAfee. McAfee SiteAdvisor (2007) http://www.siteadvisor.com
[13] Sutton, M.: A Tour of the Google Blacklist (2007)
http://portal.spidynamics.com/blogs/msutton/archive/2007/01/04/
A-Tour-of-the-Google-Blacklist.aspx
[14] Microsoft. Microsoft Internet Explorer Privacy Statement (2006),
http://www.microsoft.com/windows/ie/ie7/privacy/ieprivacy_7.mspx
[15] Microsoft. Phishing Filter FAQ (2007) https://phishingfilter.microsoft.com
/faq.aspx
[16] Microsoft. Sender ID Home Page (2007) http://www.microsoft.com/mscorp/
safety/technologies/senderid/default.mspx
[17] Mozilla. Firefox 2 Phishing Protection Effectiveness Testing (2006)
http://www.mozilla.org/security/phishing-test.html

[18] NetCraft. Netcraft anti-phishing tool bar (2007) `http://toolbar.netcraft.com`
[19] Robichaux, P., Phishing, G.: Evaluating Anti-Phishing Tools for Windows (2006), `http://www.3sharp.com/projects/antiphishing/gone-phishing.pdf`
[20] Phishtank. Phishtank feed: validated and online (2007) `http://data.phishtank.com/data/online-valid/index.xml`
[21] Provos, N.: Phishing Protection: Server Spec: Lookup Requests (2007) `http://wiki.mozilla.org/Phishing_Protection:_Server_Spec#Lookup_Requests`
[22] Quinlan, R.: C4.5: Programs for Machine Learning. Morgan Kaufmann, San Francisco (1993)
[23] Ross, B., Jackson, C., Miyake, N., Boneh, D., Mitchell, J.C.: A Browser Plug-In Solution to the Unique Password Problem (2005) `http://crypto.stanford.edu/PwdHash/`
[24] Ross, B., Jackson, C., Miyake, N., Boneh, D., Mitchell, J.C.: Stronger Password Authentication Using Browser Extensions. In: 14th Usenix Security Symposium (2005)
[25] Schneider, F., Provos, N., Moll, R., Chew, M., Rakowski, B.: Phishing Protection Design Documentation (2007) `http://wiki.mozilla.org/Phishing_Protection:_Design_Documentation`
[26] SpoofGuard. Client-side defense against web-based identity theft (2005) `http://crypto.stanford.edu/SpoofGuard/`
[27] Sharif, T.: IE Blog: Phishing Filter (2005), `http://blogs.msdn.com/ie/archive/2005/09/09/463204.aspx`
[28] Verisign. Anti-Phishing Solution (2005) `http://www.verisign.com/verisign-business-solutions/anti-phishing-solut%ions/`
[29] W3C. IEBlog:IE7 Phishing Filter Performance Update is Now Available (2007) `http://blogs.msdn.com/ie/archive/2007/01/31/ie7-phishing-filter-perform%ance-update-is-now-available.aspx`
[30] Wenyin, L., Huang, G., Xiaoyue, L., Min, Z., Deng, X.: Detection of phishing webpages based on visual similarity. In: 14th International Conference on World Wide Web (WWW): Special Interest Tracks and Posters (2005)
[31] Witten, I.H., Frank, E.: Data Mining: Practical machine learning tools and techniques, 2nd edn. Morgan Kaufmann, San Francisco (2005)
[32] Yahoo. Yahoo! AntiSpam Resource Center (2007) `http://antispam.yahoo.com/domainkeys`
[33] Zhang, Y., Egelman, S., Cranor, L., Hong, J.: Phinding Phish: Evaluating Anti-Phishing Tools. In: Network and IT Security Conference: NDSS 2007, San Diego, California (2007)

Protecting the Intranet Against "JavaScript Malware" and Related Attacks*

Martin Johns and Justus Winter

Security in Distributed Systems (SVS)
University of Hamburg, Dept of Informatics
Vogt-Koelln-Str. 30, D-22527 Hamburg
{johns,4winter}@informatik.uni-hamburg.de

Abstract. The networking functionality of JavaScript is restricted by the Same Origin Policy (SOP). However, as the SOP applies on a document level, JavaScript still possesses certain functionality for cross domain communication. These capabilities can be employed by malicious JavaScript to gain access to intranet resources from the outside. In this paper we exemplify capabilities of such scripts. To protect intranet hosts against JavaScript based threats, we then propose three countermeasures: *Element Level SOP*, *rerouting of cross-site requests*, and *restricting the local network*. These approaches are discussed concerning their respective protection potential and disadvantages. Based on this analysis, the most promising approach, *restricting the local network*, is evaluated practically.

> *We're entering a time when XSS has become the new Buffer Overflow and JavaScript Malware is the new shellcode.*
>
> Jeremiah Grossman [6]

1 Introduction

Web browsers are installed on virtually every contemporary desktop computer and the evolution of active technologies like JavaScript, Java or Flash has slowly but steadily transformed the web browser into a rich application platform. Furthermore, due to the commonness of Cross Site Scripting (XSS) vulnerabilities [3] the number of XSS worms [25] is increasing steadily. Therefore, large scale execution of malicious JavaScripts is a reality nowadays. Additionally, if no XSS flaw is at hand, a simple well written email usually suffices to lure a potential victim into visiting an innocent looking web page that contains a malicious payload. For all these reasons, the browser was recently (re)discovered as a convenient tool to smuggle malicious code behind the boundaries of the company's firewall. While earlier related attacks required the existence of a security vulnerability in the browser's source code or libraries, the attacks which are covered in

---

* This work was supported by the German Ministry of Economics (BMWi) as part of the project "secologic", www.secologic.org.

B. M. Hämmerli and R. Sommer (Eds.): DIMVA 2007, LNCS 4579, pp. 40–59, 2007.
© Springer-Verlag Berlin Heidelberg 2007

this paper simply employ the legal means that are provided by today's browser technology.

Within this context, the term "JavaScript Malware" was coined by J. Grossman [6] in 2006 to describe this class of script code that stealthy uses the web browser as vehicle for attacks on the victim's intranet. In this paper we exemplify capabilities of such scripts and propose first defensive approaches.

1.1   Definitions

This paper focuses on web browser based attacks that target intranet resources. Therefore, we frequently have to differentiate between locations that are either within or outside the intranet. For this reason, in the remainder of this paper we will use the following naming conventions:

Local IP-addresses: The specifier *local* is used in respect to the boundaries of the intranet that a given web browser is part of. A local IP-address is therefore an address that is located inside the intranet. Such addresses are rarely accessible from the outside.

Local URL: If a URL references a resource that is hosted on a local IP-address, we refer to is as *local URL*.

The respective counterparts *external IP-address* and *external URL* are defined accordingly.

1.2   Transparent Implicit Authentication

With the term *implicit authentication* we denote authentication mechanisms, that do not require further interaction after the initial authentication step. For example the way HTTP authentication is implemented in modern browsers requires the user to enter his credential for a certain web application only once per session. Every further request to the application's restricted resources is outfitted with the user's credentials automatically.

Furthermore, with the term *transparent implicit authentication* we denote authentication mechanisms that also execute the initial authentication step in a way that is transparent to the entity that is being authenticated. For example NTLM authentication [4] is such an authentication mechanism for web applications. Web browsers that support the NTLM scheme obtain authentication credentials from their underlying operating system. These credentials are derived from the user's operating system login information. In most cases the user does not notice such an automatic authentication process at all. Often such mechanism are summarized under the term "Single Sign On" (SSO).

Especially in the intranet context transparent implicit authentication is used frequently. This way the company makes sure that only authorized users access restricted resources without requiring the employees to remember additional passwords or execute numerous, time-consuming authentication processes on a daily basis.

The firewall as a means of authentication. A company's firewall is often used as a means of transparent implicit authentication: The intranet server are positioned behind the company's firewall and only the company's staff has access to computers inside the intranet. As the firewall blocks all outside traffic to the server, it is believed that only members of the staff can access these servers. For this reason intranet server and especially intranet web server are often not protected by specific access control mechanisms. For the same reason intranet applications often remain unpatched even though well known security problems may exist and home-grown applications are often not audited for security problems thoroughly.

1.3   Cross Site Request Forgery

Cross Site Request Forgery (XSRF / CSRF) a.k.a. *Session Riding* is a client side attack on web applications that exploits implicit authentication mechanisms. The actual attack is executed by causing the victim's web browser to create HTTP requests to restricted resources. This can be achieved e.g., by including hidden images in harmless appearing webpages. The image itself references a state changing URL of a remote web application, thus creating an HTTP request (see Figure 1). As the browser provides this requests automatically with authentication information, the target of the request is accessed with the privileges of the person that is currently using the attacked browser. See [26] or [2] for further details.

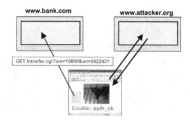

Fig. 1. A CSRF attack on an online banking site

2   Attacking the Intranet with JavaScript

2.1   Using a Webpage to Get Access to Restricted Web Resources

As described in Section 1 many companies allow their employees to access the WWW from within the company's network. Therefore, by constructing a malicious webpage and succeeding to lure an unsuspecting employee of the target company into visiting this page, an attacker can create malicious script code that is executed in the employee's browser. As current browser scripting technologies possess certain network capabilities and as the employee's browser is executed on a computer within the company's intranet and the employee is in general outfitted with valid credentials for possibly existing authentication mechanisms (see

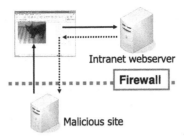

Fig. 2. Using a webpage to access restricted web servers

Section 1.2), any script that runs inside his browser is able to access restricted intranet resources with the same permissions as the employee would.

In the next Sections we examine the actual network capabilities and restrictions of existing active browser technologies and exemplify how these capabilities can be used to circumvent authentication schemes.

2.2 A Closer Look at JavaScript

For security reasons, the networking functions of client-side browser technologies are subject to major restrictions. We describe these restrictions only in respect to JavaScript, but similar concepts apply to e.g., Flash or Java applets.

Network capabilities: Foremost JavaScript is limited to HTTP communication only. Furthermore, a script is not allowed to communicate with arbitrary HTTP hosts. This is enforced by the *Same Origin Policy (SOP)*: The Same Origin Policy was introduced by Netscape Navigator 2.0 [24]. It defines and limits various rights of JavaScript. The origin of an element is defined by the protocol, the domain and the port that were used to access this element. The SOP is satisfied when the origins of two elements match. All explicit network functionality of JavaScript is restricted to communication with targets that satisfy the SOP. This effectively limits a script to direct communication with its origin host.

There is only one possibility for JavaScript to create HTTP requests to targets that do not satisfy the SOP: The script can dynamically include elements like images from foreign hosts into the document's DOM tree [9].

Access rights: Additionally, the SOP defines the access rights of a given script. A JavaScript is only allowed access to elements that are part of a document which has been obtained from the same origin as the JavaScript itself. In this respect, the SOP applies on a *document level*. Thus, if a JavaScript and a document share a common origin, the SOP allows the script to access all elements that are embedded in the document. Such elements could be e.g., images, stylesheets, or other scripts. These granted access rights hold even if the elements themselves where obtained from a different origin.

Example: The script `http://exa.org/s.js` is included in the document `http://exa.org/i.html`. Furthermore `i.html` contains various images from `http://picspicspics.com`. As the script's and the document's origin match, the script has access to the properties of the images, even though their origin differs from the script's.

A loophole in the SOP: As explained above, the cross-domain networking capabilities of JavaScript are restricted by the SOP. However, this policy allows dynamically including elements from cross domain HTTP hosts into the DOM tree by a JavaScript in its container document. This exception in the networking policy and the fact that the SOP applies on a document level creates a loophole in SOP, as this policy allows partial cross domain access. Depending on the type of the element that was included in the document, the JavaScript's capabilities to gain information by the inclusion differs. In the next sections we explain how this loophole can be exploited for malicious purposes.

2.3 Portscanning the Intranet

It was shown by various parties [19,21,7] how malicious web pages can use its capability to port-scan the local intranet. While the specific techniques vary, the general approach is always the same:

1. The script constructs a local URL that contains the IP-address and the port that shall be scanned.
2. Then the script includes an element in the webpage that is addressed by this URL. Such elements can be e.g., images, iframes or remote scripts.
3. Using JavaScript's time-out functions and eventhandlers like `onload` and `onerror` the script can decide whether the host exists and the given port is open: If a time-out occurs, the port is probably closed. If an `onload`- or `onerror`-event happens, the host answered with some data, indicating that the host is up and is listening on the targeted port.

To launch such an discovery attack, the malicious script needs to know the IP-range of the local intranet. In case this IP-range is unknown to the attacker, he can use a Java-Applet [17] to obtain the IP-address of the computer that currently executes the web browser which is vehicle of the attack. Using this address the attacker's script can approximate the intranet's IP-range.

Limitation: Some browsers like Firefox enforce a blacklist of forbidden ports [23] that are not allowed in URLs. In this case JavaScript's port scanning abilities are limited to ports that are not on this list. Other browsers like Internet Explorer allow access to all ports.

2.4 Fingerprinting of Intranet Hosts

After determining available hosts and their open ports, a malicious script can try to use fingerprinting techniques to get more information about the offered services. Again the script has to work around the limitations that are posed by the SOP. For this reason the fingerprinting method resembles closely the port-scanning method that was described above [19,7].

The basic idea of this technique is to request URLs that are characteristic for a specific device, server, or application. If such a URL exists, i.e., the request for this URL succeeds, the script has a strong indication about the technology that is hosted on the fingerprinted host. For example, the default installation of the Apache web server creates a directory called "icons" in the document root of the web server. This directory contains image files that are used by the server's directory listing functionality. If a script is able to successfully access such an image for a given IP-address, it can conclude that the scanned host runs an Apache web server. The same method can be used to identify web applications, web interfaces of network devices or installed scripting languages (e.g., by accessing PHP eastereggs).

2.5   Attacking Intranet Servers

After discovering and fingerprinting potential victims in the intranet, the actual attack can take place. A malicious JavaScript has for example the following options:

Exploiting unpatched vulnerabilities: Intranet hosts are frequently not as rigorously patched as their publicly accessible counterparts as they are believed to be protected by the firewall. Thus, there is a certain probability that comparatively old exploits may still succeed if used against an intranet host. A prerequisite for this attack is that these exploits can be executed by the means of a web browser [7].

Opening home networks: The following attack scenario mostly applies to home users. Numerous end-user devices like wifi routers, firewall appliances or DSL modems employ web interfaces for configuration purposes. Not all of these web interfaces require authentication per default and even if they do, the standard passwords frequently remain unchanged as the device is only accessible from within the "trusted" home network.

If a malicious script was able to successfully fingerprint such a device, there is a certain probability that it also might be able to send state changing requests to the device. In this case the script could e.g., turn off the firewall that is provided by the device or configure the forwarding of certain ports to a host in the network, e.g., with the result that the old unmaintained Windows 98 box in the cellar is suddenly reachable from the internet. Thus, using this method the attacker can create conditions for further attacks that are not limited to the web browser any longer.

Cross protocol communication: Wade Alcorn showed in [1] how multi-part HTML forms can be employed to send (semi-)valid messages to ASCII-based protocols. Prerequisite for such an attempt is that the targeted protocol implementation is sufficient error tolerant, as every message that is produced this way still contains HTTP-meta information like request-headers. Alcorn exemplified the usage of an HTML-form to send IMAP3-messages to a mail-server which are interpreted by the server in turn. Depending on the targeted server, this method might open further fingerprinting and exploitation capabilities.

2.6   Leaking Intranet Content by Breaking DNS-Pinning

The SOP should prevent cross domain access to content hosted on intranet web servers. In 1996 [27] showed how short lived DNS entries can be used to weaken this policy.

Example: Attacking an intranet host located at 10.10.10.10 would roughly work like this:

1. The victim downloads a malicious script from www.attacker.org
2. After the script has been downloaded, the attacker modifies the DNS answer for www.attacker.org to 10.10.10.10
3. The malicious script requests a web page from www.attacker.org (e.g via loading it into an iframe)
4. The web browser again does a DNS lookup request for www.attacker.org, now resolving to the intranet host at 10.10.10.10
5. The web browser assumes that the domain values of the malicious script and the intranet server match, and therefore grants the script unlimited access to the intranet server.

To counter this attack modern browsers employ "DNS pinning": The mapping between a URL and an IP-address is kept by the web browser for the entire lifetime of the browser process even if the DNS answer has already expired. While in general this is an effective countermeasure against such an attack, unfortunately there are scenarios that still allow the attack to work: Josh Soref has shown in [28] how in a multi session attack a script that was retrieved from the browser's cache still can execute this attack. Furthermore, we have recently shown [13] that current browsers are vulnerable to breaking DNS pinning by selectively refusing connections.

Using this attack, the script can access the server's content. With this ability the script can execute refined fingerprinting, leak the content to the outside or locally analyze the content in order to find further security problems.

Based on our findings, Kanatoko Anvil [16] demonstrated recently, that a successful anti DNS-pinning attack also effects some browser plugins, like the Flash player. As the Flash player's scripting language ActionScript supports low level socket communication, such an attack extends the adversary's capabilities towards binary protocols.

2.7   Attacks That Do Not Rely on JavaScript

Intranet exploration attacks like portscanning do not necessary have to rely on JavaScript. It has been shown recently [5] that attacks similar to the vectors show in Sections 2.3 can be staged without requiring active client-side technologies. Instead timing analysis is employed.

Currently these attacks rely on a certain, not-standardized behaviour of the Firefox web browser: In general whenever a browser's rendering engine encounters an HTML element that includes remote content into the page, like image, `script` or `style`-tags, the browser sends an asynchronous HTTP request to retrieve the remote resource and resumes rendering the web page. However, the `link`-tag does not adhere to this behaviour. Instead the rendering engine stops the rendering process until the HTTP request-response pair, that was initiated because of the tag, has terminated. Thus, by creating a webpage that contains a `link`-element, that references a local URL, and an `image`-element, that is requested from the attacker's host, the attacker can use timing analysis to conclude if in fact an actual host can be reached under a given local URL. Employing this technique, an attacker can reliably create a mapping of the local lan. However, the timing differences between the response time of a RST-package, that was generated because of a closed port, and an actual HTTP-response are hard to measure from the attacker's position. For this reason fingerprinting attacks are not yet feasible. As research in the area of these attack techniques is comparatively young and web browsers are still evolving, it is probable that there exist more attack vectors which do not rely on active technologies.

2.8 Analysis

In the most cases CSRF attacks (see Section 1.3) target authentication mechanisms that are executed by the web browser, e.g., by creating hidden HTTP requests that contain valid session cookies. The attacks covered in this paper are in fact CSRF attacks that target an authentication mechanism which is based on physical location: As discussed in Section 1.2, the firewall is used as a means of transparent implicit authentication which is subverted by the described attacks.

The main problem in the context of the specified issues is that the attacked intranet servers have very limited means to protect themselves against such attacks. All they receive are HTTP requests from legitimate users, sometimes even in a valid authentication context. Therefore, at the server side it is not always possible to distinguish between requests that were intended by the user and requests that were generated by a malicious JavaScript. In some cases evidence like external referrers or mismatching host headers are available but this is not always the case. Furthermore, some of the described attacks will still work even when the server would be able to identify fraudulent requests.

Thus, a reliable protection mechanism has to be introduced at the client side. Only at the client-side all required context information concerning the single requests is available. Furthermore, to stop certain attacks, like the exploitation of unpatched vulnerabilities, it has to be prevented that the malicious request even reaches the targeted host.

3   Defense Strategies

In this section we discuss four possible strategies to mitigate the threats described in Section 2. At first we assess to which degree already existing technology can be employed. Secondly we examine whether a refined version of the Same Origin

Policy could be applied to protect against malicious JavaScript. The third technique shows how general client-side CSRF protection mechanisms can be extended to guard intranet resources (a prior version of this approach was originally proposed by us in [14]). The final approach classifies network locations and deducts access rights on the network layer based on this classification. For every presented mechanism, we assess the anticipated protection and potential problems.

3.1 Turning Off Active Client-Side Technologies

An immediate solution to counter the described attacks is to turn of active client-side technologies in the web browser. To achieve the intended protection at least JavaScript, Flash and Java Applets should be disabled. As turning off JavaScript completely breaks the functionality of many modern websites, the usage of browser-tools that allow per-site control of JavaScript like the NoScript extension [10] is advisable.

Protection: This solution protects effectively against active content that is hosted on untrusted web sites. However, this approach does not protect against attacks, that do not rely on active technologies (see Section 3.1).

Furthermore, if an XSS weakness exists on a web page that is trusted by the user, he is still at risk. Compared to e.g. Buffer Overflows, XSS is a vulnerability class that is often regarded to be marginal. This is the case especially in respect to websites that do not provide serious services, as an XSS hole in such a site has only a limited attack surface in respect to causing "real world" damage. For this reason such web sites are frequently not audited thoroughly for XSS problems.

Any XSS hole can be employed to execute the attacks that are subject of this paper. This is the analogy between XSS and Buffer Overflows, that was mentioned in the introducing quote by J. Grossman: As a Buffer Overflow enables the attacker to run the shellcode in a trusted binary, an XSS vulnerability enables the attacker to run script code in the context of a trusted web application and therefore inside the victims browser.

Drawbacks: In addition to the limited protection, an adoption of this protection strategy will result in significant obstacles in the user's web browsing. The majority of modern websites require active client-side technologies to function properly. With the birth of the so-called "Web 2.0" phenomenon this trend even increases. The outlined solution would require a site-specific user-generated decision which client-side technologies should be permitted whenever a user visits a website for the first time. For this reason the user will be confronted with numerous and regularly occurring configuration dialogues. Furthermore, a website's requirements may change in the future. A site that does not employ JavaScript today, might include mandatory scripts in the future. In the described protection scenario such a change would only be noticeable due to the fact that the web application silently stopped working correctly. The task to determine the reason for this loss of functionality lies with the user.

3.2   Extending the SOP to Single Elements

As discussed in Section 2 a crucial part of the described attacks is the fact that the SOP applies on a document level. This allows a malicious JavaScript to explore the intranet by including elements with local URLs into documents that have an external origin. Therefore, a straight forward solution would be to close the identified loophole by extending the SOP to the granularity of single objects:

Definition 1 (Element Level SOP). *In respect to a given JavaScript an element satisfies the* Element Level SOP *if the following conditions are met:*
- *The element has been obtained from the same location as the JavaScript.*
- *The document containing the element has the same origin as the JavaScript.*

Only if these conditions are satisfied the JavaScript
- *is allowed to access the element directly and*
- *is permitted to receive events, that have been triggered by the element.*

Jackson et. al describe in [12] a similar approach. In their work they extend the SOP towards the browser's history and cache. By doing so, they are able to counter attacks that threaten the web user's privacy.

Protection: Applying the SOP on an element level would successfully counter attacks that aim to portscan the intranet or fingerprint internal HTTP-services (see Sections 2.3 and 2.4). These attacks rely on the fact that events like onerror that are triggered by the inclusion of local URLs can be received by attacker provided JavaScript. As the origin of this JavaScript and the included elements differs, the refined SOP would not be satisfied and therefore the malicious JavaScript would not be able to obtain any information from the inclusion attempt.

However, refined and targeted fingerprinting attacks may still be feasible. Even if elements of a different origin are not directly accessible any longer, side effects that may have been caused by these elements are. E.g., the inclusion of an image causes a certain shift in the absolute positions of adjacent elements, which in turn could be used to determine that the image was indeed loaded successfully. Furthermore, the attacks described in Section 2.5 would still be possible. Such an attack consists of creating a state-changing request to a well known URL, which would still be allowed by the refined policy. Also the content leaking attack described in Section 2.6 would not be prevented. The basis of the attack is tricking the browser to believe that the malicious script and the attacked intranet server share the same origin. Nonetheless, the feasibility of these still working attacks depends on detailed knowledge of the intranet's internal layout. As obtaining such knowledge is prevented successfully by the outlined countermeasure the protection can still be regarded as sufficient, provided the attacker has no other information leak at hand.

Drawbacks: The main disadvantage of this approach is its incompatibility to current practices of many websites. Modern websites provide so called *web APIs* that allow the inclusion of their services into other web applications. Such services are for example offered to enable the inclusion of external cartography material into webpages. Web APIs are frequently implemented using remote JavaScripts that are included in the targeted webpage by a `script`-tag. If a given browser starts to apply the SOP on an element level, such services will stop working.

A further obstacle in a potential adoption of this protection approach is the anticipated development costs, as an implementation would require profound changes in the internals of the web browser.

3.3 Rerouting Cross-Site Requests

As discussed in Section 2.8, the attacks shown in Section 2 are CSRF attacks which exploit the fact that the firewall is used as a means of transparent implicit authentication. In [14] we proposed *RequestRodeo* a client side countermeasure against CSRF attacks in general. This section presents a refined version of our original concept that is geared towards protecting companies' intranets against JavaScript Malware.

RequestRodeo's protection mechanism is based on a classification of outgoing http requests:

Definition 2 (entitled). *A given HTTP request is classified to be* entitled *if and only if:*
- *It was initiated because of the interaction with a web page and*
- *the URLs of the originating page and the requested page satisfy the SOP.*
Only requests that were identified to be entitled *are permitted to carry implicit authentication information.*

According to this definition, all *unentitled* requests are "cross site requests" and therefore suspicious to be part of a CSRF attack and should be treated with caution. Cross-site request are fairly common and an integral part of the hyperlink-nature of the WWW. Therefore, a protection measure that requires the cancellation of such requests is not an option.

Instead we proposed to remove all authentication information from these requests to counter potential attacks. However, in the given case the requests do not carry any authentication information. They are implicitly authenticated as their origin is inside the boundaries that are defined by the firewall. For this reason other measures have to be taken to protect local servers. Our proposed solution introduces a *reflection service* that is positioned on the outer side of the firewall. All *unentitled* requests are routed through this server. If such a request succeeds, we can be sure that the target of the request is reachable from the outside. Such a target is therefore not specifically protected by the firewall and the request is therefore permissible.

The method that is used to do the actual classification is out of scope of this paper. In [14] we introduced a client side proxy mechanism for this purpose, though ultimately we believe such a classification should be done within the web browser.

Example: As depict in figure 3a a web browser requests a webpage from a server that is positioned outside the local intranet. In our scenario the request is

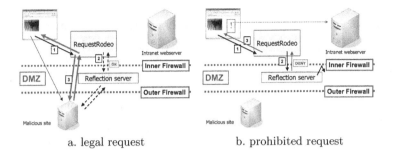

a. legal request b. prohibited request

Fig. 3. Usage of a reflection service

unentitled. It is therefore routed through the reflection service. As the reflection service can access the server unhindered, the browser is allowed to pose the request and receives the webpage's data. The delivered webpage contains a malicious script that tries to request a resource from an intranet web server (see figure 3b). As this is a cross domain request, it also is *unentitled* and therefore routed through the reflection service as well. The reflection service is not able to successfully request the resource, as the target of the request lies inside the intranet. The reflection service therefore returns a warning message which is displayed by the web browser.

Position of the service: It is generally undesirable to route internal web traffic unprotected through an outside entity. Therefore the reflection service should be positioned between the outer and an inner firewall. This way the reflection service is treated as it is not part of the intranet while still being protected by the outer firewall. Such configurations are usually used for DMZ (demilitarized zone) hosts.

Protection: The attack methods described in Section 2.3 to Section 2.5 rely on executing a JavaScript that was obtained from a domain which is under (at least partial) control of the attacker. In the course of the attack, the JavaScript creates HTTP requests that are targeted to local resources. As the domain-value for local resources differs from the domain-value of the website that contains the malicious script, all these requests are detected to be cross-site request. For this reason they are classified as *unentiteld.* Consequently, these request are routed through the reflection service and thus blocked by the firewall (see Figure 3).

Therefore, the usage of a reflection service protects effectively against malicious JavaScript that tries to either port-scan the intranet (see Section 2.3), fingerprint local servers (Section 2.4) or exploit unpatched vulnerabilities by sending state changing requests (Section 2.5).

The main problem with this approach is its incapability to protect against attacks that exploit the breaking of the web browser's DNS pinning feature (see Section 2.6). Such attacks are based on tricking the browser to access local resources using an attacker provided domain-name (e.g., `attacker.org`). Because of this attack method, all malicious requests exist within that domain and are therefore not recognised to be suspicious. Thus, these requests are not routed through the reflection service and can still execute the intended attack. As long as modern web browsers allow the breaking of DNS pinning, the protection provided by this approach is not complete. However, executing such an attack successfully requires detailed knowledge on the particular properties of the attacked intranet. As obtaining knowledge about the intranet is successfully prevented by the countermeasure, the feasibility of anti-DNS-pinning based attacks is questionable.

Drawbacks: Setting up such a protection mechanism is comparatively complex. Two dedicated components have to be introduced: The reflection service and an add-on to the web browser that is responsible for classification and routing of the HTTP requests. Furthermore, a suitable network location for the reflection service has to exist. As small-scale and home networks rarely contain a DMZ, the user either has the choice of creating one, which requires certain amounts of networking knowledge, or to position the reflection service outside the local network, which is objectionable.

The most appropriate deployment scenario for the proposed protection approach is as follows: Many companies already require their employees to use an outbound proxy for WWW-access. In such cases the classification engine, that is responsible for routing non-trusted request through the reflection service, could be included in the existing central proxy. This way all employees are transparently using the protection measure without additional configuration effort.

3.4   Restricting the Local Network

As introduced in Section 1 we refer to addresses that are located within the intranet as *local*. This notation implies a basic classification that divides network addresses into either *local* or *external* locations. If the web browser could determine to which group the origin and the target of a given request belong, it would be able to enforce a simple yet effective protection policy:

Definition 3 (restricted local network). *Hosts that are located inside a restricted local network are only accessible by requests that have a local origin. Therefore, inside such a network all HTTP requests with an external origin that target at a local resource are forbidden.*

With *requests with an external origin* we denote requests that were generated in the execution context of a webpage that was received from an external host. Unlike the proposed solution in Section 3.3 this classification does not take the domain-value of the request's origin or target into account. Only the actual IP-addresses are crucial for a policy-based decision.

Protection: All the attack methods specified in Section 2 depend on the capability of the malicious script to access local elements in the context of a webpage that is under the control of the attacker: The portscanning attack (Sec. 2.3) uses elements with local URLs to determine if a given host listens on the URL's port, the fingerprinting (Sec. 2.4) and local CSRF (Sec. 2.5) methods create local URLs based on prior application knowledge, breaking DNS-pinning (Sec. 2.6) tries to let the browser believe that an attacker owned domain is mapped to a local IP-address, and even the methods that do not rely on JavaScript (Sec. 3.1) require the usage local URLs to function. Therefore, the attacker's ability to successfully launch one of the specified attacks depends on his capability to create local HTTP requests from within a webpage under his control. By definition the attacker's host is located outside the intranet. Thus, the starting point of the attack is external. As the proposed countermeasure cancels all requests from an external origin to local resources, the attacker is unable to even bootstrap his attack.

Drawbacks: The configuration effort of the proposed solution grows linearly with the complexity of the intranet. Simple networks that span over a single subnet or exclusively use private IP-addresses can be entered fairly easy. However, fragmented networks, VPN setups, or mixes of public and private address ranges may require extensive configuration work.

Furthermore, another potential obstacle emerges when deploying this protection approach to mobile devices like laptops or PDAs. Depending on the current location of the device, the applicable configuration may differ. While a potential solution to this problem might be auto-configuration based on the device's current IP-address, overlapping IP-ranges of different intranets can lead to ambiguities, which then consequently may lead to holes in the protection.

3.5   Comparison of the Proposed Protection Approaches

As the individual protection features and disadvantages of the proposed approaches have already been discussed in the preceding sections, we concentrate in this section on aspects that concern either potential protection, mobility or anticipated configuration effort (see Table 1). The technique to *selectively turn of active technologies* (see Section 3.1) is left out of this discussion, due to the approach's inability to provide any protection in the case of an exploited XSS vulnerability.

Protection: The only approach that protects against all presented attack vectors is introducing a *restricted local network*, as this is the sole technique that counters effectively anti DNS-pinning attacks. However, unlike the other attack methods that rely on inherent specifics of HTTP/HTML, successfully attacking DNS-pinning has to be regarded as a flaw in the browser implementation. Therefore, we anticipate this problem to be fixed by the browser vendors eventually. If this problem is solved, the anticipated protection of the other approaches may also be regarded to be sufficient.

Configuration effort & mobility: The *element level SOP* approach has the clear advantage not to require any location-depended configuration. Therefore, the mobility of a device protected by this measure is uninhibited. But as some sites' functionality depends on external scripts, adopters of this approach instead would have to maintain a whitelist of sites, for which document level access to cross-domain content is permitted. As the technique to *reroute cross-site requests* requires a dedicated reflection service, the provided protection exists only in networks that are outfitted accordingly, thus hindering the mobility of this approach significantly. Also a *restricted local network* depends on location specific configuration, resulting in comparable restrictions. Furthermore, as discussed above, a *restricted local network* might lead to extensive configuration overhead.

Conclusion: As long as breaking DNS-pinning is still possible with current browsers, an evaluation ends in favor of the *restricted local network* approach. As soon as this browser flaw has been removed, *rerouting cross-site request* appears to be a viable alternative, especially in the context of large-sized companies with non-trivial network set-ups. Before an *element level SOP* based solution is deployed on a large scale, the approach has to be examined further for the potential existence of covert channel (see Section 3.2).

Table 1. Comparison of the proposed protection approaches

	No JavaScr.	Element SOP	Rerout. CSR	Restr. network
Prohibiting Exploring the Intranet	(+)*	(+)*	+	+
Prohibiting Fingerprinting Servers	+	+	+	+
Prohibiting IP-based CSRF	-	-	+	+
Resisting Anti-DNS Pinning	+	-	-	+
Mobile Clients	+	+	-	-
No Manual Configuration	-**	+	-	-

+: supported, -: not supported, *: Protection limited to JS based attacks, **: Per site configuration.

4   Evaluation

4.1   Implementation

Based on the discussion above, we chose to implement a software to enforce a *restricted local network*, in order to evaluate feasibility and potential practical problems of this approach [30].

We implemented the approach in form of an extension to the Firefox web browser. While being mostly used for GUI enhancements and additional functions, the Firefox extension mechanism in fact provides a powerful framework to alter almost every aspect of the web browser. In our case, the extension's functionality is based mainly on an XPCOM component which instantiates a nsIContentPolicy [22]. The nsIContentPolicy interface defines a mechanism that was originally introduced to allow the development of surf-restriction plug-ins, like parental control systems. It is therefore well suited for our purpose.

By default our extension considers the localhost (127.0.0.1), the private address-ranges (10.0.0.0/8, 192.168.0.0/16 and 172.16.0.0/12) and the link-local subnet (169.254.0.0/16) to be *local*. Additionally the extension can be configured manually to include or exclude further subnets in the local-class.

Every outgoing HTTP request is intercepted by the extension. Before passing the request to the network stack, the extension matches the IP-addresses of the request's origin and target against the specifications of the address-ranges that are included in the local-class. If a given request has an external origin and a local target it is dropped by the extension.

By creating a browser extension, we hope to encourage a wider usage of the protection approach. This way every already installed Firefox browser can be outfitted with the extension retroactively. Furthermore, in general a browser extension consists of only a small number of small or medium sized files. Thus, an external audit of the software, as it is often required by companies' security policies, is feasible.

An alternative to implementing a browser extension would have been to realize the outlined protection mechanism in the form of a client-side web proxy. A proxy has the advantage of not being restricted to one single browser brand. Furthermore, such a proxy could be installed company wide at a central location, thus minimizing configuration and maintenance effort. Unfortunately establishing the origin for a given HTTP request is a non-trivial task outside the web browser. Achieving this within a proxy requires substantial alteration of incoming HTML content (see [14]), which is an error prone exercise, due to dynamic content creation by JavaScript.

4.2   Practical Evaluation

Our testing environment consisted of a PC running Ubuntu Linux version 6.04 which was located inside a firewalled subnet employing the 192.168.1.0/24 private IP-address range. Our testing machine ran an internal Apache webserver listening on port 80 of the internal interface 127.0.0.1. Furthermore, in the same subnet an additional host existed running a default installation of the Apache webserver also listening on port 80. The web browser that was used to execute the tests was a Mozilla Firefox version 2.0.0.1. with our extension installed. The extension itself was configured using the default options.

Besides internal testing scripts, we employed public available tools for the practical evaluation of our implementation. To test the protection abilities against portscanning and fingerprinting attacks, we used the JavaScript portscanner from SPI Dynamics that is referenced in [19]. To evaluate the effectiveness against anti DNS-pinning attacks we executed the online demonstration provided by [15] which tries to execute an attack targeted at the address 127.0.0.1.

The results turned out as expected. The portscanning and fingerprinting attempts were prevented successfully, as the firewall rejected the probing requests of the reflection service. Also as expected, the anti DNS-pinning attack on the local web server was prevented successfully. Furthermore the extension was able to detect the attack, as it correctly observed the change of the adversary's domain (in this case 1170168987760.jumperz.net) from being remote to local.

4.3   Limitations

During our tests we encountered a possible network setup that may yield problems with our approach. A company's web-services are usually served from within a DMZ using public IP-addresses. Unfortunately, the "local"/"external"-classification of hosts located in a DMZ is not a straight-forward task. As the hosts' services are world-reachable the respective IPs should be classified as "external" to allow cross-domain interaction between these services and third party web applications. However, in many networks the firewall setup allows connections that origin from within the company's network additional access rights to the servers positioned in the DMZ. For example internal IPs could be permitted to access the restricted FTP-port of the webserver to update the server's content. Thus, in such setups a malicious JavaScript executed within the intranet also possesses these extended network capabilities.

5   Related Work

In this section we sum up related publications. As, to the best of our knowledge, no work has been published yet that directly deals with the threats to the intranet specified in this paper, we describe approaches that deal with related web application threats in general. We thereby focus on protection mechanisms that are positioned at the client side. If applicable we discuss if the described approaches can be extended to protect the intranet against JavaScript based attacks.

Lam et al. [20] discus the reconnaissance probing attack (see Section 2.3) as a tool to identify further victims in the context of web-server worm propagation. They propose several options for client-side defense mechanisms, like limiting the number of cross-domain requests. However, as they address the issues only in the context of large scale worm propagation and DDoS attacks, these measures do not promise to be effective against targeted intranet-attacks. The paper contains an excellent analysis of existing restrictions posed by different web browsers, like number of allowed simultaneous connections.

Vogt et al. [29] propose a combination of static analysis and dynamic data tainting to stop the effects of XSS attacks. The outlined approach does not identify or stop the actual injected script but instead aims to prohibit resulting leakage of sensitive information. To achieve this, their technique employs an enhanced JavaScript engine. The added features of this modified engine are twofold: For one, the flow of sensitive data, like cookie-values, through the script can be tracked dynamically. This way the mechanism detects and prevents the transmission of such data to the adversary. Furthermore, via static analysis, all control flow dependencies in scripts that handle sensitive information are established. This is done to identify indirect and hidden channels that could be abused for data leakage. If such channels are identified, their communication with external hosts is prevented.

In a related approach, Kirda et al. [18] describe Noxes, an application-level firewall that examines incoming HTML data in respect to potential sources for information leaks. Based on this analysis the firewall dynamically creates connection rules, to stop HTTP requests that are suspicious to transport confidential data, like cookie values. Noxes is concerned with the data content of outgoing requests and not with the target. For this reason the described algorithm is not applicable in the context of this paper. However, the protection approach, canceling suspicious HTTP requests, is closely related to our solution proposed in Section 3.4. A combination of both approaches to extend the respective range of protection is therefore possible.

Ismail et al. [11] describe a local proxy based solution towards protection against reflected XSS attacks. The proxy examines the GET and POST parameters of outgoing HTTP request for the existence of potential problematic characters like "<". If such characters are found in one of the parameters, the proxy also checks the respective HTTP response if the parameter is included verbatim and unencoded in the resulting webpage. If this is the case, the proxy concludes a potential XSS attack and encodes the offending characters itself.

A more general protection approach is described by Hallaraker and Vigna [8]. Their paper shows how to modify the JavaScript-engine of a web browser to allow behaviour based analysis of JavaScript execution. Using this newly introduced capability, they apply intrusion detection mechanisms to e.g., prevent denial of service or XSS attacks. While the paper does not address the threats that are subject of our work, it may be possible to extend their work towards detecting and preventing JavaScript Malware. To verify this assumption further research work is necessary.

Finally, as already mentioned in Section 3.2, Jackson et al. [12] describe a solution to a related issue: Current browser technologies grant JavaScript certain capabilities to access information about the user's browsing history and cache content. These capabilities enable the adversary to create scripts that compromise the privacy of the user. In order to prevent such attacks, [12] extends the Same Origin Policy to also apply to cache and history information. This has the effect, that a JavaScript can only obtain cache and history information about elements that have the same origin as the script itself. As browsing history and cache content information can provide hints about the existence and particularities of intranet servers without requiring the attacker to generate any network traffic, an adoption of the described countermeasures is advisable in addition to applying the here proposed mechanisms.

6   Conclusion and Future Work

We showed that carefully crafted script code embedded in webpages is capable to bypass the Same Origin Policy and thus can access intranet resources. For this reason simply relying on the firewall to protect intranet HTTP server against unauthorized access is not sufficient. As it is not always possible to counter such attacks at the server side, we introduced and discussed four distinct client-side countermeasures. Based on this discussion, we implemented a Firefox extension to enforce a *restricted local network*.

While our implementation reliably provides protection against the specified threats, this protection comes with a price, as additional configuration overhead and potential problems concerning mobile clients exist. Furthermore, our solution fixes a problem that occurs because of fundamental flaws in the underlying concepts - HTTP and the current JavaScript security model. Therefore future research in this area should specifically target these shortcomings to provide the basis for a future web browser generation that is not susceptible any longer to the attacks that have been discussed in this paper.

References

1. Alcorn, W.: Inter-protocol communication. Whitepaper (11/13/06) (August 2006)
   http://www.ngssoftware.com/research/papers/
   InterProtocolCommunication.pdf
2. Burns, J.: Cross site reference forgery - an introduction to a common web application weakness. Whitepaper (2005)
   https://www.isecpartners.com/documents/XSRF_Paper.pdf
3. Endler, D.: The evolution of cross-site scripting attacks. Whitepaper, iDefense Inc. (May 2002) http://www.cgisecurity.com/lib/XSS.pdf
4. Glass, E.: The ntlm authentication protocol. (03/13/06) (2003) [online]
   http://davenport.sourceforge.net/ntlm.html
5. Grossman, J.: Browser port scanning without javascript. (08/01/07) (November 2006) Website http://jeremiahgrossman.blogspot.com/2006/11/browser-port-scanning-with out.html
6. Grossman, J.: Javascript malware, port scanning, and beyond. Posting to the websecurity mailing list (July 2006) http://www.webappsec.org/lists/websecurity/
   archive/2006-07/msg00097.html
7. Grossman, J., Niedzialkowski, T.C: Hacking intranet websites from the outside. Talk at Black Hat USA 2006 (August 2006) http://www.blackhat.com/presentations/
   bh-usa-06/BH-US-06-Grossman.pdf
8. Hallaraker, O., Vigna, G.: Detecting malicious javascript code in mozilla. In: Proceedings of the IEEE International Conference on Engineering of Complex Computer Systems (ICECCS), pp. 85–94 (June 2005)
9. Le Hegaret, P., Whitmer, R., Wood, L.: Document object model (dom). W3C recommendation (January 2005) http://www.w3.org/DOM/
10. InformAction. Noscript firefox extension. Software (2006)
    http://www.noscript.net/whats
11. Ismail, O., Eto, M., Kadobayashi, Y., Yamaguchi, S.: A proposal and implementation of automatic detection/collection system for cross-site scripting vulnerability. In: 8th International Conference on Advanced Information Networking and Applications (AINA04), (March 2004)
12. Jackson, C., Bortz, A., Boneh, D., Mitchell, J.C.: Protecting browser state from web privacy attacks. In: Proceedings of the 15th ACM World Wide Web Conference (WWW 2006) (2006)
13. Johns, M. (somewhat) breaking the same-origin policy by undermining dns-pinning. Posting to the Bug Traq Mailinglist (August 2006)
    http://www.securityfocus.com/archive/107/443429/30/180/threaded
14. Johns, M., Winter, J.: Requestrodeo: Client side protection against session riding. In: Piessens,F. (ed.) Proceedings of the OWASP Europe 2006 Conference, refereed papers track, Report CW448, pp. 5 – 17. Departement Computerwetenschappen, Katholieke Universiteit Leuven (May 2006)
15. Kanatoko. Stealing information using anti-dns pinning (30/01/07) (2006) Online demonstration. webpage, http://www.jumperz.net/index.php?i=2&a=1&b=7

16. Kanatoko. Anti-dns pinning + socket in flash (19/01/07) (January 2007) Website
    http://www.jumperz.net/index.php?i=2&a=3&b=3
17. Kindermann, L.: My address java applet (11/08/06) (2003) Webpage
    http://reglos.de/myaddress/MyAddress.html
18. Kirda, E., Kruegel, C., Vigna, G., Jovanovic, N.: Noxes: A client-side solution for
    mitigating cross site scripting attacks, security. In: Security Track of the 21st ACM
    Symposium on Applied Computing (SAC 2006) (April 2006)
19. SPI Labs. Detecting, analyzing, and exploiting intranet applications using
    javascript. Whitepaper (July 2006)
    http://www.spidynamics.com/assets/documents/JSportscan.pdf
20. Lam, V.T., Antonatos, S., Akritidis, P., Anagnostakis, K.G.: Puppetnets: Misus-
    ing web browsers as a distributed attack infrastructure. In: ACM Conference on
    Computer and Communications Security (CCS'06), pp. 221–234 (2006)
21. Petkov, P.: Javascript port scanner (11/08/06), August (2006) Website
    http://www.gnucitizen.org/projects/javascript-port-scanner/
22. XUL Planet. nsicontentpolicy. API Reference (11/02/07) (2006) webpage
    http://www.xpcomref/ifaces/nsIContentPolicy.html
23. Mozilla Project. Mozilla port blocking (11/13/06) (2001) Webpage
    http://www.mozilla.org/projects/netlib/PortBanning.html
24. Ruderman, J.: The same origin policy (01/10/06) (August 2001) Webpage
    http://www.mozilla.org/projects/security/components/same-origin.html
25. Samy: Technical explanation of the myspace worm (01/10/06) (October 2005) web-
    site http://namb.la/popular/tech.html
26. Schreiber, T.: Session riding - a widespread vulnerability in today's web applica-
    tions. Whitepaper, SecureNet GmbH (December 2004)
    http://www.securenet.de/papers/Session_Riding.pdf
27. Princeton University Secure Internet Programming Group. Dns attack scenario
    (February 1996) Webpage
    http://www.cs.princeton.edu/sip/news/dns-scenario.html
28. Soref, J.: Dns: Spoofing and pinning (14/11/06) (September 2003) Webpage
    http://viper.haque.net/~timeless/blog/11/
29. Vogt, P., Nentwich, F., Jovanovic, N., Kruegel, C., Kirda, E., Vig, G.: Cross site
    scripting prevention with dynamic data tainting and static analysis. In: 14th An-
    nual Network and Distributed System Security Symposium (NDSS 2007) (2007)
30. Winter, J., Johns, M.: Localrodeo: Client side protection against javascript malware
    (01/02/07) (January 2007) webpage http://databasement.net/labs/localrodeo

On the Effects of Learning Set Corruption in Anomaly-Based Detection of Web Defacements

Eric Medvet and Alberto Bartoli

DEEI, University of Trieste, Via Valerio, Trieste
emedvet@units.it, bartolia@units.it

Abstract. Anomaly detection is a commonly used approach for constructing intrusion detection systems. A key requirement is that the data used for building the resource profile are indeed attack-free, but this issue is often skipped or taken for granted. In this work we consider the problem of corruption in the learning data, with respect to a specific detection system, i.e., a web site integrity checker. We used corrupted learning sets and observed their impact on performance (in terms of false positives and false negatives). This analysis enabled us to gain important insights into this rather unexplored issue. Based on this analysis we also present a procedure for detecting whether a learning set is corrupted. We evaluated the performance of our proposal and obtained very good results up to a corruption rate close to 50%. Our experiments are based on collections of real data and consider three different flavors of anomaly detection.

1 Introduction

Anomaly detection is a powerful and commonly used approach for constructing intrusion detection systems. With this approach the system constructs automatically a profile of the resource to be monitored, starting from a collection of data representing normal usage (the learning set). Once this profile has been established the system signals an anomaly whenever the actual observation of the resource deviates from the profile, on the assumption that any anomalies represent evidence of an attack.

A key requirement is that the learning set is indeed attack-free, otherwise the presence of attacks would be incorporated in the profile and, thus, considered as a normal status. Although this requirement is crucial for the effectiveness of anomaly detection, in practice the absence of attacks in the learning set is either taken for granted or verified "manually". While such a pragmatic approach may be feasible in a carefully controlled environment, it clearly becomes problematic in many scenarios of practical interest. Building a large number of profiles for resources immersed in their production environment, for example, cannot be done by inspecting each learning set "manually" to make sure there were no attacks. A cross-the-fingers approach, on the other hand, can only lead to the construction of potentially unreliable profiles.

B. M. Hämmerli and R. Sommer (Eds.): DIMVA 2007, LNCS 4579, pp. 60–78, 2007.

In this work we focus on the problem of corruption in the learning set, i.e., a learning set containing records which do not represent a "normal" condition for the observed resource. We think that focussing on this fundamental issue could broaden the scope of anomaly-based detection frameworks. For example, in order to apply anomaly-based monitoring on a large scale—to hundreds or even thousands of resources—it is necessary to build a large number of learning sets, one for each resource to be monitored (e.g., [1] monitored many web applications at the same time). It is clearly not feasible to "manually" check each learning set to make sure there are no attacks hidden in it. The fact that profiles could have to be updated periodically in order to reflect changes in legitimate usage of resources (e.g., [2]) may only exacerbate this problem.

We restrict our analysis to a specific detection system that we developed earlier, i.e., an anomaly-based web site integrity checker [3,4]. This tool is able to monitor many remote web pages automatically using an anomaly detection approach, which may help in triggering prompt reactions in the presence of unauthorized modifications. The tool builds an individual profile for each monitored page, by simply observing that page for a while. The process is fully automatic, i.e., no prior knowledge about content and appearance of the monitored page is required. The scope of our analysis is clearly narrowed by the specific detection system that we consider, but we believe that our approach may be of interest also for other forms of detection systems.

A roadmap to deal with the problem of potentially corrupted learning sets involves: (1) *understanding*, i.e., evaluating quantitatively the effects of a corrupted learning set on the effectiveness of anomaly detection; (2) *detecting*, i.e., being able to discriminate between a corrupted learning set and a clean one; and, possibly, (3) *mitigating*, i.e., preserving an acceptable performance level of the detection system in spite of a corrupted learning set. In this paper we focus on the first two steps. Our experiments are based on collections of real data and consider three different flavors of anomaly detection. We first assess the effects of a corrupted learning set on performance, in terms of false positives and false negatives. This analysis enabled us to gain important insights into this rather unexplored issue. Based on this analysis we also present a procedure for detecting automatically whether a learning set contains corrupted records. This procedure may be used for handling large collections of datasets automatically, raising an alert to a human operator only for those which look suspicious (much like the alerts raised after the learning phase has completed). We evaluated the performance of this procedure and obtained very good results up to a corruption rate close to 50%.

2   Related Work

Broadly speaking, anomaly detection is an instance of *inductive learning classification* in which the goal is to build a profile able of discriminating between only two classes—i.e., normal and anomalous—using learning data corresponding to a single class—i.e., normal [5,6,7,8]. In the inductive machine learning field the corruption of learning set is indicated as *noise*, which is generally subdivided in two categories: attribute noise and class noise. The former consists in records for which one or more attributes are not really representative of the corresponding class, whereas the latter concerns records of the dataset which are wrongly labeled. A comparison between the effects of the two different types of noise on classifier accuracy is presented in [9]; our work refers to a very specific instance of the inductive machine learning problem and considers only class noise.

Concerning class noise, there is a substantial amount of work proposing solutions for identifying and then removing the corrupting (mislabled) records. More in general, this issue can be addressed with *outlier detection* techniques [10]. We have not investigated whether such techniques can be applied to our framework, that is characterized by a small learning set—usually a few tens of records. In this work we are merely concerned with the problem of detecting whether the learning set is indeed clean or contains some amount of class noise.

An important method for finding mislabeled records in the learning set is given in [11]. The idea consists in building a set of filtering classifiers from only part of the learning set and then testing whether data in the remaining part also belong to the profile. The learning set is partitioned in a number of subsets and, for each subset, a filtering classifier is trained using the remaining part of the learning set. Each record of the learning set is then input to each of the filtering classifiers. The cited paper proposes and evaluates several criteria for merging the labels generated by the filtering classifiers. The method should be able to identify outliers regardless of the specific classifier being used, hence, regardless of the chosen model for the data. A very similar approach, specifically tailored to large datasets, is proposed in [9]. Our work differs from these proposals in that we do not partition the learning set in smaller sets. This can be an advantage in the cases—our test scenario is indeed one of them—where learning sets may be very small and thus a further division will lead to a ineffective classifier: such cases are considered by Forman and Cohen [12] in their comparative study about machine learning applied to small learning set.

Concerning specifically anomaly detection, we are not aware of works covering both the understanding and detecting phases of the problem of corrupted learning sets. We are only aware of a few published experiments about the effects of a corrupted learning set—i.e., only the understanding phase. Hu et al. [13] consider an anomaly-based host intrusion detection system and compare the performance of Robust Support Vector Machines (RSVMs), conventional Support Vector Machines and nearest neighbor classifiers using 1998 DARPA BSM data set. Besides experimenting with clean learning sets, they consider also artificially corrupted learning datasets and find that RSVM are more robust to noise.

A similar analysis is proposed by Mahoney and Chan [14]. The authors present an IDS which detects anomalies in packet header fields. In addition to the normal effectiveness evaluation (with 1999 DARPA dataset), they experiment also with smaller and corrupted learning sets. They motivate this choice based on the practical difficulty in obtaining attack-free learning sets. The authors test their tool in a real environment and retune the tool every day based on the data collected on the previous day. A significant loss in detection rate is highlighted, but the relation between loss and corruption is not analyzed because the corruption level is not measured accurately.

A radically different approach to the problem of corrupted learning sets is that of *unsupervised anomaly detection*. With these techniques learning set records do not need to be labelled as clean or attack-related and the detection method itself is intrinsically robust to a certain amount of noise. Along this line, Laskov et al. [15] present a network IDS based on a formulation of a one-class Support Vector Machine (SVM) [16], whereas Wang and Stolfo [17] present a network IDS where anomalies with respect to the profile are based on the the Mahalanobis distance. These techniques usually work on learning datasets much larger than ours, which often consists of only a few tens of records.

3   The Test Scenario: Web Site Defacement Detection

3.1   Motivation and Framework

Our analysis is based on a specific detection system that we developed earlier, i.e., an anomaly-based web site integrity checker [3]. This tool is aimed at monitoring the integrity of remote web pages automatically while remaining fully decoupled from them, in particular, without requiring any prior knowledge about content or appearance of the monitored resources. The tool builds an individual profile for each monitored page, by simply observing that page for a while, and signals an anomaly whenever a page deviates from its profile. Full details can be found in [4], in particular concerning performance, limitations and open issues.

The issue of learning set corruption is particularly significant in this scenario for two key reasons. First, the learning set for each page is usually small. We decided that the monitoring of a new page should require the gathering of learning data for a few days at most. Since readings taken every few minutes usually exhibit very little difference, the result is that a learning set typically consists of a few tens of readings. It follows that the learning set is so small that even a little amount of corruption (e.g., a single corrupting reading) could have significant impact. Second, it is necessary to update the profile periodically [4]. Assuming a visual inspection of each new learning set is clearly not an option: the tool must be able to retune itself automatically.

Although we focus on a web site integrity checker, however, we considered a more general anomaly-based framework. We consider a source of information producing a sequence of *readings* $\{i_1, i_2, \dots\}$ which is input to a *detector* (Fig. 1). The detector will classify each reading as being either *normal* or *anomalous*. The detector consists internally of a *refiner* followed by an *aggregator*, both described in the next sections. In our scenario the source of information is a web page, univocally identified by an URL, and each reading consists of the document downloaded from that URL.

Detector Architecture. The refiner implements a function that takes a reading i and produces a fixed size numeric vector $v = R(i)$. The details of the

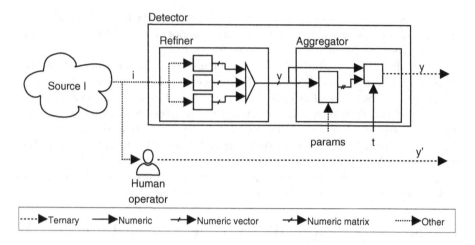

Fig. 1. Detector architecture. Different arrow types correspond to different types of data.

transformation are problem specific. In our case the transformation involves evaluating and quantifying many features of a web page related to both its content and appearance. The refiner is internally composed by one or more *sensors*. A sensor S is a component which receives as input the reading i and outputs a fixed size vector of real numbers v_S. The output of the refiner is composed by concatenating the output of all sensors. Sensors are functional blocks and have no internal state: $v = R(i)$ depends only on the current input i and does not depend on any prior reading. In our case we consider a refiner producing a vector $v = R(i)$ of 1466 elements, obtained by concatening the outputs from 43 different sensors (Sect. 3.2).

The aggregator is the core component of the detector and it is the one that actually implements the anomaly detection. In a first phase, that we call the *learning phase*, the aggregator collects a number of readings in order to build the profile of the resource; during this phase, the aggregator is not able to classify readings. In a second phase, the *monitoring phase*, the aggregator compares the current reading against the profile and considers it as anomalous whenever it is too much different from the profile. The output in the monitoring phase depends on an external parameter called *normalized discrimination threshold* (threshold for short), which affects the sensitivity-specificity tradeoff of the detector. We denote the threshold by t and the output of the refiner for reading i_k by v_k.

The aggregator performs the *learning phase* on a learning sequence obtained with the first l readings $\{v_1, \ldots, v_l\}$, that we denote S_{learning}. With this procedure the aggregator sets the values for some internal numeric parameters $\{p_1, \ldots, p_m\}$, that constitute the profile P of the resource. During the learning phase, the output y_k for each reading i_k is always y_k = unable, meaning that the aggregator is currently unable to classify the reading.

After the learning phase, the aggregator enters the *monitoring phase*, in which it considers the monitoring sequence obtained with the remaining readings $\{v_{l+1}, v_{l+2}, \dots\}$, that we denote $S_{\text{monitoring}}$. In this phase the aggregator compares each reading against the profile P established in the learning phase. The output y_k for each reading i_k is given by a function $F^A_{\text{compare}}(v_k, P, t)$ that may return either y_k = negative (meaning the reading is normal) or y_k = positive (meaning the reading is anomalous).

We built 3 different aggregators, which differ in the way they exploit application-specific knowledge in order to elaborate the outputs produced by the refiner. The details are presented in the next sections.

3.2 Prototype Details

Sensors. The 43 sensors contained in our refiner can be grouped in 5 categories, based on the way they extract information from readings. A brief description of each category follows. Table 1 summarizes salient information about sensor categories and indicates the number of sensors and the corresponding size for the vector v portion in each category.

Table 1. Sensor categories and corresponding vector portion sizes

Category	Number of sensors	Vector size
Cardinality	25	25
RelativeFrequencies	2	117
HashedItemCounter	10	920
HashedTree	2	200
Signature	4	4
Total	43	1466

Cardinality sensors. Each sensor in this category outputs a vector composed by only 1 element v^1. The value of v^1 corresponds to the measure of some simple feature of the reading (e.g., the number of lines).

The features taken into account by the sensors of this category are:

- Tags: block type (e.g., the output v^1 of the sensor is a count of the number of block type tags in the reading), content type, text decoration type, title type, form type, structural type, table type, distinct types, all tags, with `class` attribute;
- Size attributes: byte size, mean size of text blocks, number of lines, text length;
- Text style attributes: number of text case shifts, number of letter-to-digit and digit-to-letter shifts, uppercase-to-lowercase ratio;
- Other items: images (all, those whose names contain a digit), forms, tables, links (all, containing a digit, external, absolute).

RelativeFrequencies sensors. Each sensor S in this category outputs a vector composed by n_S elements $v = |v^1, \dots, v^{n_S}|$. Given a reading i, S computes the relative frequency of each item in the item class analyzed by S (e.g., lowercase letters), whose size is known and equal to n_S. The value of the element v^k is equal to the relative frequency of the k -th item of the given class.

This category includes two sensors. One analyzes lowercase letters contained in the visible textual part of the resource ($n_S = 26$); the other analyzes HTML elements of the resource—e.g., HTML, BODY, HEAD, and so on—with $n_S = 91$.

HashedItemsCounter sensors. Each sensor S in this category outputs a vector composed by n_S elements $v = |v^1, \dots, v^{n_S}|$ and works as follows. Given a reading i, S: (1) sets to 0 each element v^k of v; (2) builds a set $L = \{l_1, l_2, \dots\}$ of items belonging to the considered class (e.g., absolute linked URLs) and found in i; note that L contains no duplicate items; (3) for each item l_j, applies a hash function to l_j obtaining a value $1 \leq k_j \leq n_S$; (4) increments v^{k_j} by 1.

This category includes 10 sensors, each associated with one of the following item classes: image URLs (all images, only those whose name contains on or more digits), embedded scripts, tags, words contained in the visible textual part of the resource and linked URLs. The link feature is considered as 5 different sub-features, i.e., by 5 different sensors of this group: all external, all absolute, all without digits, external without digits, absolute without digits. All of the above sensors use a hash function such that $n_S = 100$, except from the sensor considering embedded scripts for which $n_S = 20$. Note that different items could be hashed on the same vector element. We use a large vector size to minimize this possibility, which cannot be avoided completely however.

HashedTree sensors. Each sensor S in this category outputs a vector composed by n_S elements $v = |v^1, \dots, v^{n_S}|$ and works as follows. Given a reading i, S: (1) sets to 0 each element v^k of v; (2) builds a tree H by applying a sensor-specific transformation on the HTML/XML tree of i (see below); (3) for each node $h_{l,j}$ of the level l of H, applies a hash function to $h_{l,j}$ obtaining a value $k_{l,j}$; (4) increments $v^{k_{l,j}}$ by 1. The hash function is such that different levels of the tree are mapped to different adjacent partitions of the output vector v, i.e., each partition is "reserved" for storing information about a single tree level.

This category includes two sensors, one for each of the following transformations:

- Each start tag node of the HTML/XML tree of reading i corresponds to a node in the transformed tree H. Nodes of H contain only the type of the tag (for example, TABLE could be a node of H, whereas <TABLE CLASS="NAME"> could not).
- Only nodes of the HTML/XML tree of reading i that are tags in a predefined set (HTML, BODY, HEAD, DIV, TABLE, TR, TD, FORM, FRAME, INPUT, TEXTAREA, STYLE, SCRIPT) correspond to a node in the transformed tree H. Nodes of H contain the full start tag (for example, <TD CLASS="NAME"> could be a node of H, whereas <P ID="NEWS"> could not).

Both sensor have $n_S = 200$ and use $2, 4, 50, 90$ and 54 vector elements for storing information about respectively tree levels $1, 2, 3, 4$ and 5; thereby, nodes of level 6 and higher are not considered.

Signature sensors. Each sensor of this category outputs a vector composed by only 1 element v^1, whose value depends on the presence of a given attribute. For a given reading i, $v^1 = 1$ when the attribute is found and $v^1 = 0$ otherwise.

This category includes 4 sensors, one for each of the following attributes (rather common in defaced web pages):

- has a black background;
- contains only one image or no images at all;
- does not contain any tags;
- does not contain any visible text.

Aggregators. As observed in Sect. 3.1, we built 3 different aggregators. They exploit different levels of application-specific knowledge and are described in the next sections. Recall that the learning sequence consists of a sequence $S_{\text{learning}} = \{v_1, \dots, v_l\}$ obtained from the first l readings, where each v_k is a vector with 1466 elements.

TooManyFiringElements. This aggregator does not exploit any application-specific knowledge. A reading is labelled as anomalous whenever too many elements of v_k are too much different from what expected.

During the learning procedure the aggregator computes the mean η_i and standard deviation σ_i for each element v_k^i, across all vectors in $S_{\text{learning}} = \{v_1, \dots, v_l\}$. During the monitoring phase the aggregator counts the number of *firing elements*, i.e., those elements whose value is too much different from what expected. An element fires when its value v^i is such that $|v^i - \eta_i| \geq 3\sigma_i$. If the number of firing elements is at least Nt, the reading is classified as anomalous ($N = 1466$ is the size of each vector, t is the threshold).

Note that this aggregator handles all vector elements in the same way, irrespective of how they have been generated by the refiner. Thus, for example, elements generated by a signature sensor are handled in the same way as those generated by hashed. Moreover, the aggregator does not consider any information possibly associated with pairs or sets of elements, i.e., elements generated by either the same sensor or by sensors in the same category.

TooManyFiringSensors. This aggregator exploits some degree of domain-specific knowledge: it "knows" that the vector elements are partitioned in slices and each slice corresponds to a specific sensor. The profile constructed in the learning phase is also partitioned, with one partition associated with each sensor.

In the monitoring phase this aggregator transforms each slice in a boolean, by applying a sensor-specific transformation that depends on the profile (i.e., on the partition of the profile associated with that sensor). When the boolean obtained from a slice is true, we say that the corresponding sensor *fires*. If the number of sensors that fire is at least Mt, the reading is classified as anomalous ($M = 43$ is the number of sensors, t is the threshold).

We describe the details of the learning phase and monitoring phase below. All sensors in the same category are handled in the same way.

Cardinality. In the learning procedure the aggregator determines mean η and standard deviation σ of the values $\{v_1^1, \ldots, v_l^1\}$—recall that Cardinality sensors output a vector composed by a single value. In the monitoring phase a sensor fires if its output value v^1 is such that $|v^1 - \eta| \geq 3\sigma$.

RelativeFrequencies. A sensor in this category fires when the relative frequencies (of the class items associated with the sensor) observed in the current reading are too much different from what expected. In detail, let n_S be the size of the slice output by a sensor S. In the learning phase, the aggregator performs the following steps: (i) evaluates the mean values $\{\eta_1, \ldots, \eta_{n_S}\}$ of the vector elements associated with S; (ii) computes the following for each reading v_k of the learning sequence ($k \in [1, l]$):

$$d_k = \sum_{i=1}^{n_S} |v_k^i - \eta_i| \tag{1}$$

(iii) computes mean η and standard deviation σ of $\{d_1, \ldots, d_l\}$.
In the monitoring phase, for a given reading v, the aggregator computes:

$$d = \sum_{i=1}^{n_S} |v^i - \eta_i| \tag{2}$$

The corresponding sensor fires if and only if $|d - \eta| \geq 3\sigma$.

HashedItemsCounter. Let n_S be the size of the slice output by a sensor S. In the learning procedure, the aggregator computes for each slice element the minimum value across all readings in the learning sequence, i.e. $\{m_1, \ldots, m_{n_S}\}$. In the monitoring phase S fires if and only if at least one element v^i in the current reading is such that $v^i < m_i$.
The interpretation of this category is as follows. Recall that each slice element is a count of the number of times an item appears in the reading (different items are hashed to different slice elements). Any non-zero element in $\{m_1, \ldots, m_{n_S}\}$, thus, corresponds to items which appear in every reading of the learning sequence. In the monitoring phase the sensor fires when there is at least one of these "recurrent items" missing from the current reading.

HashedTree. Sensors in this category are handled in the same way as those of the previous category, but the interpretation of a firing is slightly different. Any non-zero element in $\{m_1, \ldots, m_{n_S}\}$ corresponds to a node which appear in every reading of the learning sequence, at the same level of the tree. In the monitoring phase the sensor fires when a portion of this "recurrent tree" is missing from the current reading (i.e., the sensor fires when the tree corresponding to the current reading is not a supertree of the recurrent tree). We omit further details for simplicity, as they can be figured out easily.

Signature. A sensor in this category fires when its output is 1. Recall that these sensors output a single element vector, whose value is 1 whenever they find a specific attribute in the current reading.

As an aside, note that not only the aggregator exploits domain-specific knowledge, it also exploits knowledge about the refiner (e.g., regarding the number of sensors and size of each slice).

TooManyFiringGroups. This aggregator works similarly to the previous one. It transforms slices into boolean values in the same way as above. However, rather then considering all sensors as being equivalent, this aggregator "knows" that sensors are grouped in categories. If the number of categories with at least one sensor that fires is at least Kt, the reading is classified as anomalous ($K = 5$ is the number of categories, t is the threshold).

As we noticed in our previous works, sensors belonging to the same category tend to exhibit a similar behaviour in terms of false positives [3,4]. This aggregator thus exploits domain-specific knowledge more deeply than the previous one.

4   Experiments

4.1   Dataset

In order to perform our experiments, we built a dataset as follows. We observed 15 web pages for about one year, collecting a reading for each page every 6 hours, thus totalling about 1350 readings for almost each web page. These readings compose the *negatives sequences*—one negative sequence S_N for each page: we visually inspected them in order to confirm the assumption that they are all genuine, that is, none of them was a defacement. Table 2 presents a list of the observed pages, which includes pages of e-commerce web sites, newspapers web sites, and alike. Pages differ in size, content and dynamicity and are the same that we observed for a shorter period in [4].

Then we built a single *positive sequence* S_P composed by 100 readings extracted from a publicly available defacement archive.[1] Defacements composing S_P were not related with any of the 15 resources that we observed—as pointed out above none of these resources was defaced during our monitoring period. The next section explains how we used S_P readings in order to simulate attacks to the monitored resources.

4.2   Methodology

We wanted to gain insight about how a given aggregator A copes with a corrupted learning sequence S_{learning}, i.e., when S_{learning} contains readings that must be classified as anomalous. We considered different *corruption rates* r, i.e.,

---

[1] Our selection is available online at http://www.units.it/bartolia/download/ BartoliMedvetAttackSet.zip

Table 2. List of web resources composing our dataset. Change frequency is a rough approximation of how often non minor changes were applied to the resource, according to our observations. Concerning Amazon – Home page and Wikipedia – Random page, we noted that most of the content section of the resource changed at every reading, independently from the time.

	Change frequency	Monitoring period	# of readings
Amazon – Home page	Almost every reading	9/19/05–9/1/06	1340
Ansa – Home page	Every 4–6 hours	9/19/05–9/1/06	1340
Ansa – Rss sport	Every 4–6 hours	9/19/05–9/1/06	1340
ASF France – Home page	Weekly	9/19/05–9/1/06	1340
ASF France – Traffic page	Less than weekly	9/19/05–9/1/06	1340
Cnn – Businnes	Every 4–6 hours	9/19/05–9/1/06	1340
Cnn – Home page	Every 4–6 hours	9/19/05–9/1/06	1340
Cnn – Weather	Daily	9/19/05–9/1/06	1340
Java – Top 25 bugs	Less than weekly	12/1/05–9/1/06	1096
Repubblica – Home page	Every 4–6 hours	9/19/05–9/1/06	1340
Repubblica – Tech. and science	Every 2–3 days	9/19/05–9/1/06	1340
The Server Side – Home page	Every 2–3 days	12/1/05–9/1/06	1095
The Server Side – Tech talks	Weekly	12/1/05–9/1/06	1096
Univ. of Trieste – Home page	Weekly	9/19/05–9/1/06	1342
Wikipedia – Random page	Every reading	9/19/05–9/1/06	1337

different fractions of positive reading in S_{learning}. We measured A effectiveness, in terms of false positive rate (FPR), false negative rate (FNR) and area under the ROC curve (A_{ROC}).

For each aggregator A, corruption rate r and page p:

– We constructed a learning sequence S_{learning} as follows. (1) We extracted a sequence $S = \{i_0^n, \ldots, i_{125}^n\}$ of 125 consecutive readings from the negative sequence S_N of the page p. (2) We split S in two subsequences: S'_{learning} composed by the first $l = 50$ readings and S'_{test} composed by the last 75 readings. (3) We constructed S_{learning} by replacing the $50 \cdot r$ final readings of S'_{learning} with a positive reading extracted from the positive sequence S_P and repeated $50 \cdot r$ times (for simulating a defacement occurred while collecting the learning data). Note that r represents the percentage of S_{learning} that is corrupted.
– We constructed a test sequence S_{test} for evaluating the profile built with the corrupted learning sequence S_{learning} as follows. (4) We inserted at the beginning the sequence S'_{test} obtained at the previous step. (5) We appended 75 different positives extracted at random from the positive sequence S_P (and including the one that corrupted S_{learning}). In other words S_{test} is composed of 150 readings, the expected output should be negative in the first half and positive in the second half.

We repeated the above experiment several times, with $N_S = 10$ different negative sequences S at step 1 and with $N_p = 10$ different positive readings at step 3.

For each tuple $\langle$page p, aggregator A, corruption rate $r\rangle$, thus, we performed $N_S N_p = 100$ experiments evaluating FPR, FNR and A_{ROC} in each experiment. The values in the next sections are the average values obtained across all 15 pages in our dataset.

5 Results

5.1 Uncorrupted Learning Sequence

In this section, we present the results obtained for the 3 aggregators presented in Sect. 3.1 evaluated on an uncorrupted learning sequence, i.e., with $r = 0$. The values obtained for FPR, FNR and A_{ROC} in these conditions will serve as a comparison baseline.

Table 3 shows FPR and FNR for the 3 aggregators as a function of the threshold t. The same results are plotted in Fig. 2 in the form of ROC curves. It is clear that TooManyFiringGroups outperforms the other aggregators. In particular, Tab. 3 confirms that, with $t = 0.9$, TooManyFiringGroups never misclassifies a negative reading as positive, while it wrongly undetects only 1.9% of positive readings (i.e., defacements). Such values can not be obtained with any t value for the two other aggregators. This results confirms the intuition that domain-specific knowledge may be very beneficial in the design of an aggregator (this is similar to, e.g., choosing values for conditional probabilities in a Bayesian network [18]).

Table 3. FPR and FNR for the 3 aggregators and several t values obtained with $r = 0$, i.e., with uncorrupted learning sequences, expressed in percentage. Values corresponding to $t = t_{\mathrm{opt}}$ for each aggregator are bolded (see below).

Aggregator (A)	t	0.01	0.05	0.10	0.20	0.30	0.40	0.50	0.60	0.70	0.90	0.95
TooManyFiringGroups	FPR	-	-	76.8	-	52.9	-	29.4	-	4.2	**0.0**	-
	FNR	-	-	0.0	-	0.0	-	0.0	-	0.0	**1.9**	-
TooManyFiringSensors	FPR	76.8	55.2	39.0	18.1	10.1	**5.4**	2.8	1.6	0.7	0.0	0.0
	FNR	0.0	0.0	0.0	0.0	4.5	**5.7**	9.2	12.9	13.3	49.8	91.6
TooManyFiringInputs	FPR	65.7	**11.4**	5.0	1.3	0.0	0.0	0.0	-	-	-	-
	FNR	0.0	**5.2**	13.3	27.8	74.1	94.1	100.0	-	-	-	-

The choice of the threshold t depends on the desired trade-off between FPR and FNR. We have emphasized in bold in Tab. 3 the values corresponding to the lowest value of FPR + FNR—just one of the possible performance indexes. We observe that the 3 aggregators have different values for the respective optimal threshold t_{opt}. Assigning the same weight to false positive and false negatives may or may not be appropriate in all scenarios. For example, in the web site defacement detection scenario, one could tolerate some false positive in order to be sure of not missing any defacement. On the contrary, in the spam detection problem, one could accept some undetected spam message while not tolerating a genuine e-mail being thrown away.

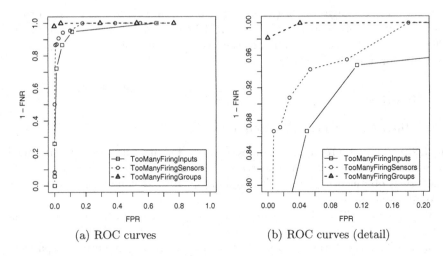

(a) ROC curves   (b) ROC curves (detail)

Fig. 2. ROC curvers for the 3 aggregators obtained with $r = 0$, i.e., with uncorrupted learning sequences. The plot on the right shows the area with FPR and FNR lower than 20%.

5.2   Corrupted Learning Sequence

In this section, we present the results concerning the effectiveness of the aggregators when corrupted learning sequences are used. We experimented with the following values for the corruption rate r, including 0 (the uncorrupted sequence): $0, 0.02, 0.05, 0.1, 0.2, 0.35, 0.5, 0.75$. Being $l = 50$ the size of the learning sequence, these rates mean that respectively $0, 1, 3, 5, 10, 18, 25, 38$ positive readings have been inserted in the learning sequence.

Table 4 shows FPR and FNR for the 3 aggregators with varying values of the corruption rate r. These results refer to the optimal threshold t_{opt} determined as explained above for $r = 0$.

Not surprisingly, increasing the corruption rate results in an increment of FNR for each aggregator. In other words, the more corrupted the learning sequence, the less sensitive to attacks the aggregator. Increasing the corruption rate also results in a decrease of FPR, due to the fact that the learning sequence, and hence the profile, becomes less and less page-specific. Although performance appears to quickly become unacceptable, varying the threshold may greatly help, as clarified in the following. The reason is because the above data corresponds to a threshold t that is optimal for an *uncorrupted* learning sequence, but this value is not necessarily optimal for a *corrupted* one.

A more general characterization of the performance of each aggregator is given in Fig. 3, which plots A_{ROC} as a function of the corruption rate r. As such, each point in this graph provides a performance index capturing *all* possible values for the threshold t. We found that A_{ROC} does *not* decrease monotonically when the corruption rate increases. On the contrary there is an A_{ROC} increase

Table 4. FPR and FNR, obtained with $t = t_{opt}$ (see Tab. 3) and presented in percentage, for the aggregator with different values for r

	TooManyFiringGroups		TooManyFiringSensors		TooManyFiringInputs	
	FPR	FNR	FPR	FNR	FPR	FNR
r	$t = t_{opt} = 0.9$		$t = t_{opt} = 0.4$		$t = t_{opt} = 0.05$	
0.00	0.0	1.9	5.4	5.7	11.4	5.2
0.02	0.0	73.4	0.1	12.4	6.5	5.6
0.05	0.0	77.6	0.1	12.9	5.5	6.3
0.10	0.0	83.9	0.0	69.5	2.5	75.8
0.20	0.0	87.5	0.1	99.9	2.5	99.4
0.35	0.0	86.7	0.1	99.9	2.6	99.6
0.50	0.0	77.6	0.1	99.7	2.8	99.6
0.75	0.0	87.7	0.3	99.8	11.3	99.4

when $r < 0.05$, the entity of the improvement being dependent on the specific aggregator. In other words, a very small corruption in the learning sequence is beneficial for all aggregators from the A_{ROC} point of view. This suggests that under a modest corruption there is some point of the ROC curve of each aggregator—i.e., some value of t—for which FPR and FNR are acceptable and, maybe, even slightly better than with an uncorrupted learning sequence. Of course, finding that point would require the knowledge of the corruption rate. The slight increase in A_{ROC} is probably due to the fact that a small amount of noise (i.e., corruption) may balance the overfitting effect, which affects negatively FPR and may be an issue in pages that are less dynamic and whose corresponding learning sets are hence less representative.

The relation between FPR + FNR and t is shown in Fig. 4, which plots one curve for each corruption rate. The lowest point of each curve corresponds to $t = t_{opt}$. We remark again that one could choose to minimize a different function of FPR and FNR. The essential issues of our arguments would not change, however. Figure 4 illustrates two important facts. First, the optimal threshold depends on the corruption rate. That is, a threshold optimized for an uncorrupted learning sequence is not necessarily the best threshold for a corrupted learning sequence. Second, performance with a corrupted learning sequence are not necessarily worse than with an uncorrupted learning sequence. For example, decreasing t improves the FPR + FNR index significantly, especially for the TooManyFiringSensors aggregator. Table 5 summarizes the improvements exhibited by the aggregators using the optimal value t_{opt} for two salient r values.

A key lesson from these experiments is that the aggregators may remain practically useful (i.e., they exhibit acceptable FPR and FNR) even in the presence of a moderate degree of corruption in the learning sequence. The problem is, turning this observation into a practically usable procedure is far from being immediate: one should know the corruption rate in order to select a suitable working point, but this is precisely the unknown entity.

Table 5. Aggregators optimal working point for two different corruption rates and corresponding FPR and FNR, presented in percentage

Aggregator (A)	r	t_{opt}	FPR	FNR	FPR + FNR
TooManyFiringGroups	0.0	0.9	0.0	1.9	1.9
	0.05	0.5	0.2	0.8	1.0
TooManyFiringSensors	0.0	0.4	5.4	5.7	11.1
	0.05	0.1	1.5	0.0	1.5
TooManyFiringInputs	0.0	0.05	11.4	5.2	16.6
	0.05	0.05	5.5	6.3	11.8

6   A Corruption Detection Procedure

We have seen in the previous section that the impact of the corruption rate r on FPR and FNR is not linear. In particular, it can be observed that the change in FPR and FNR is much sharper when r increases from 0 to 0.02 than when r increases from 0.02 to 0.05 (see Tab. 4). The effects on performance, thus, are much stronger when switching from a clean learning sequence to a corrupted learning sequence than with a moderate increase of a (non-zero) corruption rate. We performed a number of experiments, not shown here for space reasons, to verify that this phenomenon does occur in a broad range of operating conditions. We exploited the above observation for building a simple yet effective corruption detection procedure, which is presented below.

6.1   Description

The objective is to determine whether a given learning sequence S^0_{learning} is corrupted. The key idea is quite simple. We build three profiles, one with S^0_{learning} and the other with two learning sequences obtained by artificially corrupting S^0_{learning} with 1 or 3 positive readings. Then we measure performance of the three profiles on a *same* sequence S_{check}. If we observe a strong change in FPR and/or FNR when switching from the first profile to the other two profiles, then S^0_{learning} was probably clean, otherwise it was probably already corrupted.

In detail, let $S'_P = \{i^p_0, \ldots, i^p_n\}$ be a set of n positive readings. We construct S_{check} with a mixture of genuine readings and positive readings. Then we proceed as follows. (1) We tune the aggregator on S^0_{learning}; we measure FPR^0 and FNR^0 on the check sequence S_{check}; (2) For a given i^p_i in S'_P, we construct two learning sequence $S^{1,i}_{\text{learning}}$ and $S^{3,i}_{\text{learning}}$ by replacing respectively 1 and 3 random readings of S^0_{learning} with i^p_i; we tune the aggregator on these learning sequences; we measure the corresponding performance on S_{check} ($\text{FPR}^{1,i}$, $\text{FNR}^{1,i}$, $\text{FPR}^{3,i}$ and $\text{FNR}^{3,i}$). (3) We repeat the previous step for each i^p_i of S'_P and evaluate mean and standard deviation of the performance indexes.

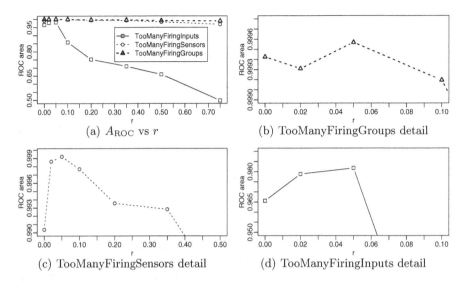

Fig. 3. The area under the ROC curve (A_{ROC}) vs the corruption rate r. Figures 3(b), 3(c) and 3(d) show salient A_{ROC} values for the 3 aggregators separately.

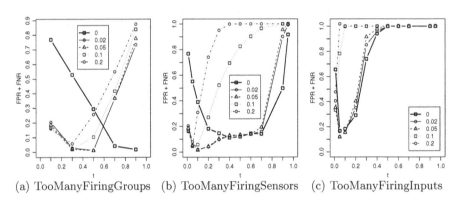

Fig. 4. Effectiveness of aggregators, as sum of FPR and FNR, plotted vs the aggregator normalized discrimination threshold t, for different modest corruption rates including $r = 0$. The lowest point of each curve corresponds to the optimal working point $t = t_{\text{opt}}$ in the given conditions.

The original learning sequence S^0_{learning} is deemed corrupted if and only if at least one of the following holds:

$$\text{FPR}^0 - \text{FPR}^\eta \geq m\text{FPR}^\sigma \tag{3}$$

$$\text{FNR}^0 - \text{FNR}^\eta \geq m\text{FNR}^\sigma \tag{4}$$

where m corresponds to a sensitivity parameter of the procedure.

6.2　Evaluation and Results

We measured the effectiveness of our procedure as follows. (1) We generated an uncorrupted learning sequence; (2) we artificially corrupted this sequence with a positive reading repeated until the end of the sequence (much like Sect. 4.2) and then (3) we applied the procedure. We experimented with $n = 5$ and several corruption rates r: 0, 0.01, 0.05, 0.1, 0.2, 0.35, 0.5. For each learning sequence, S_{check} contained 50 positive readings and 50 negative readings of the page described by the learning sequence. For each pair $\langle r, page \rangle$, we repeated the test 25 times, with $N_S = 5$ different learning sequences at step 1 and $N_p = 5$ different positive readings at step 2.

Whenever the procedure stated that the learning sequence was corrupted, the test counted as a true positive if $r \neq 0$ and as a false positive otherwise. Whenever the procedure stated that the learning sequence was *not* corrupted, the test counted as a false negative if $r \neq 0$ and as a true negative otherwise.

Figure 5(a) shows the ROC curves, obtained experimenting with different values for m. It can be seen that with TooManyFiringSensors and TooManyFiringInputs the procedure exhibits unsatisfactory performance, in that FPR is never smaller than 0.6 irrespective of m (see also what follows). With TooManyFiringGroups, on the other hand, it appears to exhibit an ideal behavior.

Figure 5(b) plots the positive rate with $m = 1$ as a function of the corruption rate r (the optimum would correspond to a positive rate 0 for $r = 0$ and 1 otherwise). This figure clearly shows that the procedure achieves the optimum (at least in our benchmark) with the TooManyFiringGroups aggregator: it detects each corrupted learning sequence while not misclassifiying any clean sequence. With the two other aggregators, on the other hand, it exhibits far too many false positives. We interpret this result as a consequence of the previous results in Tab. 4: when switching from a clean learning sequence to a corrupted one, the

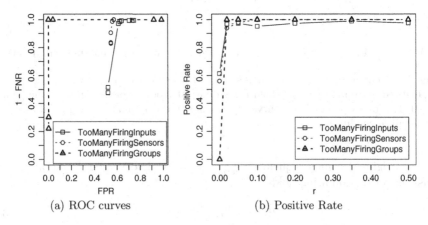

(a) ROC curves　　　　　　　　　(b) Positive Rate

Fig. 5. Effectiveness of our corruption detection procedure applied to the 3 aggregators. Figure on the left shows ROC curves. Figure on the right plots positive rates for the procedure applied with $m = 1$.

performance change is not sufficiently strong, with TooManyFiringSensors and TooManyFiringInputs.

Another important result from Fig. 5(b) is that the detection accuracy of corrupted sequences is very high over the whole range of r.

7   Concluding Remarks

We attempted to understand the rather unexplored effects of a corrupted learning set in an anomaly-based detection system, with reference to a very specific form of detection. We quantified the impact of the corruption rate on performance indexes (FPR, FNR and A_{ROC}) over many different working points for our detectors. Our experiments confirmed the obvious intuition on the positive correlation between corruption rate and aggregator sensitivity: i.e., as the corruption rate increases the false negative rate (FNR) increases and the false positive rate (FPR) decreases.

We found also the interesting result that a corrupted learning set does not necessarily lead to worse performance, at least for moderate corruption rates. We observed that the threshold leading to best performance depends on the corruption rate (which is unknown, however).

Finally, the previous analysis enabled us to develop a novel *automatic* procedure capable of detecting whether the learning set is corrupted. The procedure differs from other noise detection algorithms in the fact that it does not divide the learning set in smaller sets: this can be an advantage in the cases where learning sets are very small and a further division is not possible. We tested the procedure with our detectors and found that for one of them, the most effective, the procedure exhibits optimal behavior: it is able to detect all the corrupted sets (for each corruption rate value ranging from the minimum to 0.5) while not misclassifying any clean sequence as corrupted.

Acknowledgments

The authors are grateful to the anonymous reviewers and the shepherd for their detailed and constructive comments.

References

1. Kruegel, C., Vigna, G.: Anomaly detection of web-based attacks. In: CCS '03: Proceedings of the 10th ACM conference on Computer and communications security, pp. 251–261. ACM Press, New York (2003)
2. Shavlik, J., Shavlik, M.: Selection, combination, and evaluation of effective software sensors for detecting abnormal computer usage. In: KDD '04: Proceedings of the tenth ACM SIGKDD international conference on Knowledge discovery and data mining, pp. 276–285. ACM Press, New York (2004)
3. Bartoli, A., Medvet, E.: Automatic Integrity Checks for Remote Web Resources. IEEE Internet Computing 10(6), 56–62 (2006)

4. Bartoli, A., Medvet, E.: Anomaly-based Detection of Web Site Defacements. In submission (2006) Available at http://www.units.it/~bartolia/abstract/AnomalyBasedDetectionOfWebSiteDefacements.pdf

5. Lane, T., Brodley, C.E.: An application of machine learning to anomaly detection. In: Proceedings of the Twentieth National Information Systems Security Conference, Gaithersburg, MD, The National Institute of Standards and Technology and the National Computer Security Center, National Institute of Standards and Technology. vol. 1, pp. 366–380 (1997)

6. Lane, T.D.: Machine learning techniques for the computer security domain of anomaly detection. PhD thesis, Purdue University, Major Professor-Carla E. Brodley (2000)

7. Li, K., Teng, G.: Unsupervised svm based on p-kernels for anomaly detection. In: First International Conference on Innovative Computing, Information and Control - vol II (ICICIC'06) 2, pp. 59–62 (2006)

8. Baah, G.K., Gray, A., Harrold, M.J.: On-line anomaly detection of deployed software: a statistical machine learning approach. In: SOQUA '06: Proceedings of the 3rd International Workshop on Software Quality Assurance, pp. 70–77. ACM Press, New York (2006)

9. Zhu, X., Wu, X.: Class noise vs. attribute noise: a quantitative study of their impacts. Artif. Intell. Rev. 22(3), 177–210 (2004)

10. Hodge, V., Austin, J.: A Survey of Outlier Detection Methodologies. Artif. Intell. Rev. 22(2), 85–126 (2004)

11. Brodley, C.E., Friedl, M.A.: Identifying Mislabeled Training Data. J. Artif. Intell. Res (JAIR) 11, 131–167 (1999)

12. Forman, G., Cohen, I.: Learning from little: comparison of classifiers given little training. In: Boulicaut, J.-F., Esposito, F., Giannotti, F., Pedreschi, D. (eds.) PKDD 2004. LNCS (LNAI), vol. 3202, pp. 161–172. Springer, New York (2004)

13. Hu, W., Liao, Y., Vemuri, V.R.: Robust Support Vector Machines for Anomaly Detection in Computer Security. In: ICMLA, pp. 168–174 (2003)

14. Mahoney, M., Chan, P.: Phad: Packet header anomaly detection for identifying hostile network traffic. Technical report, Florida Tech. CS-2001-4 (2001)

15. Laskov, P., Schäfer, C., Kotenko, I.V.: Intrusion detection in unlabeled data with quarter-sphere Support Vector Machines. In: DIMVA, pp. 71–82 (2004)

16. Tax, D.M., Duin, R.P.: Data Domain Description using Support Vectors. In: ESANN, pp. 251–256 (1999)

17. Wang, K., Stolfo, S.J.: Anomalous payload-based network intrusion detection. In: RAID, pp. 203–222 (2004)

18. Mutz, D., Valeur, F., Vigna, G., Kruegel, C.: Anomalous system call detection. ACM Trans. Inf. Syst. Secur. 9(1), 61–93 (2006)

Intrusion Detection as Passive Testing: Linguistic Support with TTCN-3
(Extended Abstract)

Krzysztof M. Brzezinski

Institute of Telecommunications, Warsaw University of Technology,
Nowowiejska 15/19, 00-665 Warszawa, Poland
kb@tele.pw.edu.pl

Abstract. We explore the idea of using the internationally standardized test language TTCN-3 (*Testing and Test Control Notation*) as a platform for Intrusion Detection (ID) systems. Intrusion detection is treated as an application of *verification by passive testing*. It is argued that TTCN contains many features embodied in various „detection languages", and is relevant for ID. As a case study, we discuss a TTCN-based IDS for detecting the *Smurf* attack.

1 Introduction

Telecommunications is a broad area, in which many distinct research communities are active. The community associated with traditional telecommunications has strongly contributed to the development of formal methods and tools, e.g., for rigorous *testing* [1]. The „new telecommunications" community, with its IETF approach, is guided by „rough consensus and working code", and is more inclined to adopt *ad-hoc* solutions. Each community tackles common problems without paying much attention to the results of the other. This leads to waste of resources. In this paper we show how the concepts developed within traditional telecommunications can be applied to an important problem of „new" telecommunications: *intrusion detection* (ID).

We treat intrusions as particular behavioral properties of a system, and intrusion detection as a verification / validation problem. Monitoring and assessing of live traffic is the natural setting for *testing*-based verification methods. We propose to use the test language TTCN-3 (*Testing and Test Control Notation*) as a possible linguistic and execution platform for ID systems. TTCN-3 is virtually unknown within the ID community. The main aim of this paper is thus to establish the relevance of this language to intrusion detection, and ultimately - to add it to the ID toolbox. For a case study, the familiar *Smurf* attack was deliberately chosen. Its simplicity should help concentrate on the features and patterns of use of the TTCN-3 language.

The rest of the paper is organized as follows. Chapter 2 provides a more formal setting for treating ID as a testing-based verification problem. Chapter 3 contains an overview of TTCN-3. In chapter 4 we give the motivation for this work and relate it to other results. Chapter 5 contains the case study. In chapter 6 the possible modifications to a TTCN-based IDS are discussed. Chapter 7 concludes the paper.

B. M. Hämmerli and R. Sommer (Eds.): DIMVA 2007, LNCS 4579, pp. 79–88, 2007.

2 Background - Reasoning About Behaviors

In the early phases of the system life-cycle, it is in principle possible to formally prove whether a set of properties holds in a system under design. In the late (cut-in, operation) phases, an *implementation* is no longer a formal mathematical object. It is treated as a *black box*. Its qualitative (functional) and quantitative (performance-related) properties can only be *measured*. *Testing* and *monitoring* are two distinct [2], generic techniques of such measurements. The aim is to evaluate the behavior of an implementation w.r.t. its design specification (*verification*) or a set of properties reflecting user expectations, irrespective of the design specification (*validation*). We now provide a more formal basis for treating ID as a testing problem.

A distributed system S is composed of a set of active, non-distributed (at a given abstraction level) entities, communicating over passive channels. This corresponds to a generic *protocol* model attributed to Merlin (1982). A *manifestation*, or *instance* of behavior results from an *execution* (a *run*) of a system. It is a *trace* of observable events. The nature of these events depends on the chosen level of abstraction. *System behavior* B_S is a (possibly infinite) set of behavior instances that a system can manifest. A *specification P* is a reference, or a model, of system behavior - it expresses a set of „interesting" traces. A generic verification problem is to check whether the system behavior corresponds to its model, or whether ($B_S \sim P$) holds. The existence (but not necessarily *a priori* knowledge or non-mutability) of this model is a fundamental assumption inherent in the idea of verification. This is also the case for intrusion detection in general [3], and, what may not be obvious, for *any* particular ID paradigm, be it *misuse detection, anomaly detection*, or a *specification-based approach* [4,5,6].

In testing-based verification, a system is a black-box implementation I, whose behavior B_I is *a priori* unknown. The validity of ($B_I \sim P$) now has to be established solely by inspecting the *observed manifestations* of behavior B_I^{obs}. I is called *Implementation Under Test* (IUT), and a system of which IUT is a part (in which I is *embedded*) is called *System Under Test* (SUT). Testing consists in evaluating (the behavior of) a IUT in particular circumstances (conditions). The *active* testing paradigm considers this activity as consisting of three elements: (a) stimulating a SUT in order to place an IUT in one of the pre-defined conditions (states); (b) observing the behavior of SUT in *this* situation; and (c) comparing the observation to a model, in order to issue a *verdict*. In testing parlance, the „pre-defined conditions" are related to *test purposes* [7]. In *passive* testing, a test system does not apply stimuli; instead, it waits for an IUT to „place itself" in one of the conditions, in which its behavior would be *symptomatic*.

One of the reasons for considering a particular set of traces as a specification is to establish a *design specification* P_D for a prospective implementation I. A typical P_D can be found, e.g., in standards for protocols, developed by ETSI, ITU-T, IETF, etc. ($B_I \sim P_D$) means: *I implements*, or *conforms to*, a P_D. If *not* ($B_I \sim P_D$), then I is said to be *faulty*. For a reference specification P that is *not* a design specification, the semantics of the ~ relation may be better characterized by the notion of *correspondence* or *satisfaction* (rather than implementation or conformance). Verification thus consists in establishing the validity of ($B_I \sim P_D$), while validation consists in establishing the validity of ($B_I \sim P$).

3 The TTCN Language

To reason about the behavioral properties, including those related to intrusions, a suitable *language* with its underlying semantic base is required. To bring some order to numerous linguistic approaches used for intrusion detection, [8] classifies the languages used in this field into: *event languages* for describing and constructing elementary events from the observed data; *response languages* to specify actions to be taken in reaction to a detected attack, *reporting languages* to specify a convenient format for attack reports; *correlation languages* to reason about attacks at a „meta" level (i.e., when the elementary events are the attack detection reports); *exploit languages* for specifying the procedure for performing an attack (a problem dual to ID); and *detection languages*, a.k.a. *attack languages*, which provide mechanisms and abstractions for identifying the manifestation of an attack. In the sequel we deal only with detection and event languages, and consider TTCN-3 in this context.

The TTCN-3 language was presented and discussed, e.g., in [9]. However, in line with the aims of this work, a more detailed overview is indicated. The standardized specification of the language and its environment is contained in the ETSI standard [10]. It currently consists of seven published volumes, 1: Core Language, 2: Tabular Presentation Format (TFT), 3: Graphical Presentation Format (GFT), 4: Operational Semantics, 5: Runtime Interface (TRI), 6: Control Interface (TCI), 8: the IDL to TTCN-3 mapping. Further standardization is pending (vol. 7 on the use of ASN.1, vol.9 on XML, vol.10 on documentation tags, vol.11 on the C mapping). TTCN-3 is a re-designed version of TTCN-2 (*Tree and Tabular Combined Notation* [11]).

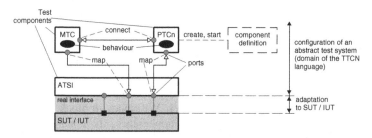

Fig. 1. Abstract view of a TTCN-3 test configuration. Master test component (MTC) may start and communicate with many parallel test components (PTC) through connected ports. A system under test (SUT) is reached through an ATSI interface, by mapped ports.

A TTCN-3 program is referred to as an *Abstract Test Suite* (ATS). It expresses the configuration (fig.1) and behavior of an *abstract test system*, which is composed of a set of concurrently executing *test components* TC: a unique *Master Test Component* (MTC) and possibly many *Parallel Test Components* (PTC). A component is characterized by a set of its *ports*, through which it may communicate with other components. Two kinds of communication acts (and thus two port types) are distinguished: *message passing* and *remote procedure call*. Procedure port types were introduced in TTCN-3, as a step towards extending the application scope of the language to cover *software testing*.

A test configuration is set up dynamically, by *creating* the instances of statically defined components, *connecting* the given ports of MTC/PTC components, and *mapping* the component ports to the ports of an Abstract Test System Interface ATSI (a special kind of component). These mapped ports, referred to as PCOs (*Points of Control and Observation*) are the means of communication with a SUT/IUT.

The main notational unit of TTCN-3 is a *module*, which is composed of a definition part and a control part. The definition part contains the definitions of types, constants, templates, ports, components, and component behaviors: functions and test cases. Syntactically, a test case (a name for a *single* test) defines the behavior of a MTC. Dynamically, a MTC may create and start multiple PTCs, with their behaviors defined as functions. The control part governs the execution of individual test cases, by means of language constructs that, in general, use the verdicts of previous test cases as conditions for the execution of further tests.

The *look-and-feel* of the core (textual) notation of TTCN-3 has been purposely redesigned to be similar to general programming languages. This makes TTCN-3 different from the previous versions of the language, which were considered too „peculiar" to be acceptable to the programming community [9]. The remaining, semantically equivalent notations of TTCN-3 (TFT and GFT) are rarely used.

Despite the shallow similarity to programming languages, TTCN-3 is specialized in its ability to express a particular kind of programs: *tests*. To this end it includes:

- the *send* and *receive* operations for asynchronous message passing on a given port;
- *templates* (called *constraints* in previous versions of the language): a particular kind of data structure that combines the features of a constant, a variable, and a data type. A template is used to explicitly define a concrete data value for *send* operations, and to implicitly define (or generate) a set of values, any of which will be accepted (or *matched*) by a *receive* operation;
- *timers*; an expiration of a timer is recognized by means of an operation similar to a *receive*. The pragmatics of the use of timers covers, e.g., assuring a limited execution time, and inferring a „no response" event;
- *alternative behavior* (*alt*): a list of alternatives, composed of a (possibly guarded) operation and a following instruction block. Within an *alt* block, each alternative is „tried" in the order of its syntactic appearance. If none can be executed successfully (e.g., for a receive operation, if there is no matching message awaiting reception), then the *alt* block is entered again, with a new „snapshot" of the state of environment. According to the pragmatics of *active* testing, within an *alt* block there is usually either a single *send* alternative (i.e., a tester sends a stimulus), or a list of many branches in which the awaited response is received and dealt with (i.e., the *receive* operations for alternative SUT responses and the *timeout* operations indicating the lack of response);
- *verdicts*: values {*pass, fail, inconc, none, error*} of a special *verdicttype*; by assigning a verdict, the outcome of a test case is made known to the control part.

One of the most important aspects of TTCN-3 standardization is that it also covers the abstract architecture of a test system and its implementation-oriented mappings. In the implementation domain, the ATSI ports must be „properly connected" to a SUT. The implementation of such connection is hidden from a TTCN program and delegated to a SUT Adapter (SA) module. The SA technology is the subject of part 5 of the Standard. Similarly, the functionality and the interface of a Coder-Decoder (CD) module has been standardized in part 6. This, in principle (although not always in practice) makes the adaptation of a test system to a particular SUT a routine task. The joint functionality of a SA and a CD is to deliver and handle the events expressed as values of a TTCN-3 type system. This is the general scope of an *event language*. The TTCN-3 technology allows a leeway in distributing this functionality among a SA, a CD, and a test program expressed in TTCN. In particular, it is possible to deliver a raw bitstring to a test program, if the templates for *receive* operations are thus defined. However, in practice the message definitions in TTCN-3 are structural, and a decoder will have to deliver data in chunks that reflect this structure.

4 Motivation and Aims

The following attack and event languages are characteristic of the Internet and CS community: EFSM automata [12], Regular Expressions for Events (REE) [13], Behavioral Monitoring Specification Language (BMSL) [6], Parallel Environment (PE) grammars to specify trace policies [5], Attack Language for State-based Intrusion Detection (STATL) [8], Auditing Specification Language (ASL) [14], Trace Description Language (TDL) / Filter Description Language (FDL) [15], the Bro language [16], Network Event Recognition Language (NERL) [17]. This variety is discouraging, and gives impression of „re-inventing the wheel". On the other hand, we have discovered many similarities between the features of these languages and the *test* language TTCN. These similarities, displayed by languages developed separately and for different purposes, suggest the existence of their common, underlying core. This corroborates our perception of ID as a *verification / testing* problem. One way to assess the practical virtue of this methodological proposition is to see what „mileage" the ID community can get from taking over, and adapting, the testing concepts. This idea was hinted in several sources [17], but has not been developed further. Some elements of passive testing using TTCN are discussed in [18]. The general need for the Internet community to acquire the TTCN technology is voiced in [19]. The only identified direct precursor of our work is [20], in which a TTCN-based system is proposed for on-line validation of the service deployment process, and the idea of „abusing the (TTCN) notation for online testing purposes" is submitted. The authors also suggest, as an item for further work, the possible use of their system for ID.

Initially, TTCN was developed strictly within the framework of *conformance testing* of black-box implementations of communication protocols in a layered (e.g., OSI) system [11]. This framework only covers the *logical* behavior and explicitly excludes other, mostly non-functional properties, such as performance, robustness, and scalability. It was natural for a TTCN community to try and extend the applicability of the language, e.g., by proposing its experimental modifications for performance testing (PerfTTCN [18], TimedTTCN-3 [21]), real-time properties (Real-Time TTCN [22]), and interoperability testing. All these modifications respected the main paradigm of *active* testing. Our work is different in that it keeps the language intact, but modifies the *pragmatics* of its use.

5   Case Study - Detecting *Smurf* with TTCN-3

We have developed and programmed in TTCN-3 passive tests for a number of attacks, including *Ping of Death*, *Smurf* and *Neptune* [3,23]. Here, to show how the common problems (patterns) of ID may be expressed in TTCN, we report on the experiment with *Smurf* (fig.2a).

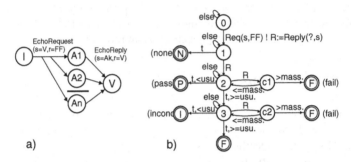

a)   b)

Fig. 2. The *Smurf* attack. (*a*) the idea: an intruder (I) broadcasts spoofed *EchoRequest* ICMP packets with a victim (V) address as a source; the recipients (A) send unsolicited replies to V; (*b*) the detection algorithm: after an initial attacking request is received in phase 0, a first response is expected (1), then responses are counted (2), and, if in doubt, counted again (3).

In the initial phase (0) of the detection algorithm (fig.2b), the test awaits the attacking *EchoRequest* packet. Then, until a verdict is issued, the test considers only *EchoReply* packets (R) that may have been sent in response to this initial packet. A timeout *t* is used to limit the duration of consecutive detection phases. In phase 1, the test awaits the first possible response. If it does not appear, the test ends with the idle verdict NONE. In phase 2, the consecutive R packets are counted: if their number is MASSIVE, then the test ends immediately with a FAIL. If, after timeout, this number is less that USUAL, then it is inferred that an attack has not developed - the verdict is PASS. If the number of responses is moderate, in phase 3 the responses are counted again. Exceeding the MASSIVE count ends the test with a FAIL verdict. If the number of accumulated responses is less than USUAL, a „prudent" verdict INCONC is issued. If this number exceeds the threshold again, the verdict is FAIL.

The semantics of the verdicts provided by TTCN-3 was originally defined for *active* testing, and had to be re-considered in a passive setting. In the example above, PASS means: „a symptomatic behavior was detected, but *according to this test* it was qualified as benign", INCONC means: „a symptomatic behavior was detected that could not be assessed *by this test*", and FAIL means: „an intrusion was detected".

The TTCN-3 implementation of the algorithm is presented in fig.3. The whole test suite (consisting of only one test case) is defined in the module *TestSmurfAttack* (line 1). The test case *SmurfSearch* (line 49) defines the behavior of a Master Test Component (MTC) named *Sniffer* (10). This component uses (is equipped with) port *p* (10), defined as a unidirectional input port (9) for messages of the type *Icmp* (5). At the start of the test case execution, the *Sniffer* component is implicitly created and starts to execute its behavior defined in (56..61). Port *p* is mapped (56) to the port of the test system interface (component defined in line 11, and referenced as a TSI in 49). This, at run-time, implicitly creates and initiates the connection, through the SUT adapter, with a network link which is being „tapped". This operation is invisible at the level of a test program. The required SA functionality and packet decoding functions (that deliver the received IP packets as values of TTCN-defined types) must be implemented (programmed) separately. Indeed, in the experiments they were fully implemented, which turned out to be relatively easy. These modules can be re-used.

```
 1 module TestSmurfAttack {
 2     const integer USUAL := 11;
 3     const integer MASSIVE := 100;
 4     const float DET_TIME := 10.0;
 5     type record Icmp {
 6         charstring src,
 7         charstring dst,
 8         integer msgtype };
 9     type port ICMPport message { in Icmp };
10     type component Sniffer { port ICMPport p; }
11     type component MyTSI { port ICMPport p; }
12 function TrackPings (in charstring src_addr)
13     runs on Sniffer {
14     var integer counter := 0;
15     timer t := DET_TIME;
16     var template Icmp answer := {
17         src := ?,
18         dst := src_addr,
19         msgtype := 0 }; // echo reply
20     //--- Phase 1
21     t.start;
22     alt {
23     [] t.timeout { return; } // setverdict (none)
24     [] p.receive(answer) { t.stop; }
25     [] p.receive { repeat; } }
26     //--- Phase 2
27     t.start;
28     alt {
29     [] t.timeout { if (counter < USUAL) {
30         setverdict (pass); return; } }
31     [] p.receive(answer) {
32         counter := counter + 1;
33         if (counter > MASSIVE) { setverdict (fail); return; };
34         else { repeat; } }
35     [] p.receive { repeat; } }

36     //--- Phase 3
37     t.start;
38     counter := 0;
39     alt {
40     [] t.timeout {
41         if (counter < USUAL) { setverdict(inconc); }
42         else { setverdict(fail); } }
43     [] p.receive(answer) {
44         counter := counter + 1;
45         if (counter > MASSIVE) { setverdict (fail); }
46         else { repeat; } }
47     [] p.receive { repeat; } }
48 } // end function
49 testcase SmurfSearch () runs on Sniffer system MyTSI {
50     var Icmp bcast_found;
51     var charstring victim;
52     var template Icmp broadcast_request := {
53         src := ?,
54         dst := pattern "*255",
55         msgtype := 8 }; // echo request
56     map (self:p, system:p);
57     p.trigger(broadcast_request) -> value bcast_found;
58     victim := bcast_found.src;
59     TrackPings(victim);
60     if (getverdict == fail) {
61         log("Smurf alert - the victim is " & victim); }
62 } // end testcase
63 control { do {} while (execute(SmurfSearch()) != fail); }
64 } // end module
```

Fig. 3. The source text of the TTCN-3 module defining an IDS for the *Smurf* attack

The test program uses two templates: *broadcast_request* (52), which matches attacking requests coming from any source towards any victim, and *answer* (16), which matches the responses destined towards a particular victim, which are the essence of the attack. To be precise, in the example *template variables* are used; this construct, introduced in a recent release of TTCN-3, allows for greater flexibility.

To wait at port *p* for an attacking message, i.e., the one matching the template *broadcast_request*, the *trigger* operation is used. It is a variant of the *receive* operation that „silently" removes a message from a receiving queue if this message does not match a template. Here, the *trigger* operation is used in a stand-alone, blocking way; its semantics is equivalent to an *alt* block with only one alternative, which is „tried" in a loop until a successful match is found. When a candidate attacking message is received, the value of its sender address field *src* is taken as the victim address (58). With this value a function *TrackPings*, which implements the rest of the algorithm, is called (59). When this function returns, a test verdict is read (60) and, for a *fail* verdict, information on the victim address is produced. The test is executed in a loop specified in the control part (63), until a *fail* verdict is issued.

Within the function *TrackPings* (12), each phase of the algorithm is specified in a separate *alt* block. The alternatives of each block serve to control time (DET_TIME, 4) assigned to each phase (23,29,40), to receive „expected" response packets (24,31,43), and to receive and ignore any other responses (25,35,47). For illustration, this time *receive* operations are used instead of a *trigger*. The function also makes use of the *repeat* (to immediately re-enter an *alt* block) and *return* instructions.

6 Issues and Improvements

After a potential attacking message is received, the test considers only the responses to *this* message, and remains „deaf" to attacks initiated by messages that occur outside the initial waiting period (phase 0). To overcome this problem, the current centralized arrangement (fig.4a) may be replaced by a distributed architecture (fig.4b).

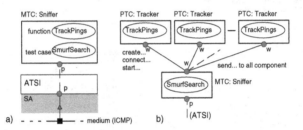

Fig. 4. Two configurations of a TTCN-based IDS for a *Smurf* attack: *(a)* centralized - with a single test component; *(b)* distributed - with separate PTCs for individual instances of an attack

The MTC now awaits the potential attacking messages, and for each such message immediately creates an instance of a *Tracker* PTC (*...Tracker.create*), connects its own port *w* with a corresponding port of the new instance (*connect...:w,mtc:w*), and starts the function *TrackPings* on this component, with the address of a potential victim. Additionally, the MTC receives each *EchoReply* packet and broadcasts it (*...send() to all component*) to all the started Trackers for further processing. All the operations concerned with comparing addresses and counting responses are now realized in independent test modules, which opens up the possibility of implementing these in separate hardware nodes. If physical broadcast is used for internal communication, then a high-performance, scalable system becomes feasible. Our experiments were conducted using the OpenTTCN tool (www.openttcn.com), in which distribution is treated in a peculiar way: SUT adapters may indeed be distributed, but the test components may not. We have found that in this environment, using readily available hardware platforms, it is possible to run at least 200 test components in parallel. In general, the number of required test components is related to the number of contexts that must have their local state tracked during the testing process. It is currently accepted that, for ID, up to 1 million contexts may have to be handled [24]. This is a „large" number, apparently beyond the reach of current TTCN-3 execution environments. However, the application of TTCN-3 to load and benchmarking tests has shown that at least tens of thousands of contexts can be handled successfully, and that a suitable structure of a test program and optimization of the execution environment can bring vast quantitative improvements [25].

7 Conclusions and Further Work

We advocated the use of TTCN-3 as a potential platform for Intrusion Detection Systems. It is internationally standardized, unlike multiple solutions currently used by the ID community. We have found it relevant and suitable for this particular application domain. Due to space restrictions, a systematic comparison of TTCN-3 with typical attack detection languages (such as STATL [8] and NERL [17]) had to be skipped, but the provided example should allow the reader to spot their similarity.

As pointed out in [19], the availability of TTCN-3 tools is still far from the expectations of the Internet community. There are relatively few, fairly expensive, commercially available TTCN-3 tools (www.ttcn-3.org), including: OpenTTCN Tester (Finland; a tool chosen for experiments), TT Workbench (TestingTechnology, Germany), TTCN-3 toolbox (Danet, Germany), Tau Tester (Telelogic, Sweden), MessageMagic (ELVIOR, Estonia), and a recent addition: TTCN-3 Express (Metarga + Fraunhofer, Germany). The interest of ID community could lead to developing open-source TTCN-3 tools, and availability of such tools seems to be the key enabler.

Intrusion detection and testing have often been presented as fundamentally different, or alternative activities [5]. This work is an attempt at harmonizing the concepts and results of these research areas from the practical, tool-oriented perspective. We have only touched (in ch.2) the theory behind the use of TTCN. The application of this theory (esp. its *passive* testing branch [2,26]) to ID deserves a thorough treatment. As an element of such research, we have developed a taxonomy that tries to capture the dimensions of ID from the perspective of testing. This taxonomy (which is being prepared for publication) explains the place of our experiment and its relation to the general paradigms of ID. In particular, it shows that TTCN-based intrusion detection is not limited to network-oriented and specification-based ID paradigms, and that missed observations (an important ID problem) are a manifestation of *observation infidelity* inherent in passive / distributed testing. It also seems to generate new research challenges, such as *truly active* ID: a test system might actively stimulate a SUT so that its intrusion-related behavior, *if present*, becomes „more symptomatic".

Acknowledgments. Early versions of TTCN-3 tests for attacks were developed by T.Kaminski [23], under this author's supervision. G.Danielewicz contributed to the verification of tests. Vesa-Matti Puro of OpenTTCN kindly provided the tools. This work was supported by the Polish Government Research Grant N517 008 31/1429.

References

1. ITU-T Z.500, Framework on Formal Methods in Conformance Testing. Geneva (1997)
2. Brzezinski, K.M.: Towards Practical Passive Testing. In: Proc. PDCN'05, Innsbruck (2005)
3. Labib, K., Vemuri, V.R.: Detecting And Visualizing Denial-of-Service and Network Probe Attacks Using Principal Component Analysis. In: Proc. SAR'04, La Londe (2004)

4. Debar, H., Dacier, M., Wespi, A.: Towards a Taxonomy of Intrusion Detection Systems. Computer Networks. Int. J. Comp. and Telecomm. Networking 31(9) (1999)
5. Ko, C., Ruschitzka, M., Levitt, K.: Execution Monitoring of Security-critical Programs in Distributed Systems: A Specification-based Approach. In: Proc. IEEE SSP (1997)
6. Uppuluri, P., Sekar, R.: Experiences with Specification-based Intrusion Detection. In: Lee, W., Mé, L., Wespi, A. (eds.) RAID 2001. LNCS, vol. 2212, Springer, Heidelberg (2001)
7. Ledru, Y., et al.: Test Purposes: Adapting the Notion of Specification to Testing. In: Proc. ASE'2001, San Diego (2001)
8. Eckmann, S.T., Vigna, G., Kemmerer, R.A.: STATL: An Attack Language for State-based Intrusion Detection. In: JCS'02 (2002)
9. Grabowski, J., Wiles, A., Willcock, C., Hogrefe, D.: On The Design of the New Testing Language TTCN-3. In: Proc. Testcom'2000 (2000)
10. ETSI ES 201 873. Methods of Testing and Specification; The Testing and Test Control Notation version 3 (release: 3.2.1, 2007-02)
11. ISO/IEC 9646. Information Technology; Open Systems Interconnection; Conformance Testing Methodology and Framework; Parts 1-7
12. Orset, J.-M., Alcalde, B., Cavalli, A.: An EFSM-Based Intrusion Detection System for Ad Hoc Networks. In: Peled, D.A., Tsay, Y.-K. (eds.) ATVA 2005. LNCS, vol. 3707, Springer, Heidelberg (2005)
13. Sekar, R., Uppuluri, P.: Synthesizing Fast Intrusion Prevention / Detection Systems from High-Level Specifications. In: Proc. USENIX'99 (1999)
14. Sekar, R., Cai, Y., Segal, M.: A Specification-Based Approach for Building Survivable Systems. In: Proc. NISSC'98 (1998)
15. Hofmann, R., et al.: Distributed Performance Monitoring: Methods, Tools, and Applications. IEEE Trans. on Parallel and Distributed Systems 5(6) (1994)
16. Paxson, V.: Bro: a System for Detecting Network Intruders in Real-Time. Computer Networks 31, 23–24 (1999)
17. Bhargavan, K., Gunter, C.: Requirements for a Practical Network Event Recognition Language. Electronic Notes in Theoretical Computer Science 70(4) (2002)
18. Schieferdecker, I., Stepien, B., Rennoch, A.: PerfTTCN, a TTCN Language Extension for Performance Testing. In: Proc. 10th IWTCS, Cheju Island (1997)
19. Sabiguero, A., Baire, A., Floch, A., Viho, C.: Using TTCN-3 in the Internet Community: an Experiment with the RIPng Protocol. In: Proc. 2nd TTCN-3 User Conference (2005)
20. Deussen, P.H., Din, G., Schieferdecker, I.: A TTCN-3 Based Online Test and Validation Platform for Internet Services. In: Proc. ISADS'03 (2003)
21. Dai, Z.: TimedTTCN-3, a Real-time Extension for TTCN-3. In: Proc. TestCom'02, Berlin (2002)
22. Walter, T., Grabowski, J.: Test Case Specification with Real-Time TTCN. In: Proc. 7 GI/ITG Technical Meeting on 'Formal Description Techniques for Distributed Systems', Berlin (1997)
23. Kaminski, T.: New Applications of the TTCN-3 Language. MSc. Thesis, Institute of Telecommunications, Warsaw University of Technology (in Polish) (2006)
24. Bononi, F., Mitzenmacher, M., Panigrahy, R., Singh, S., Varghese, G.: Beyond Bloom Filters: From Approximate Membership Checks to Approximate State Machines. In: Proc. SIGCOMM'06 (2006)
25. Din, G., Rentea, G.: Using TTCN-3 to Design Performance Tests. In: Proc. TTCN-3 UC, Berlin (2006)
26. Netravali, A.N., Sabnani, K.K., Viswanathan, R.: Correct Passive Testing Algorithms and Complete Fault Coverage. In: König, H., Heiner, M., Wolisz, A. (eds.) FORTE 2003. LNCS, vol. 2767, Springer, Heidelberg (2003)

Characterizing Bots' Remote Control Behavior

Elizabeth Stinson and John C. Mitchell

Department of Computer Science, Stanford University, Stanford, CA 94305
{stinson,mitchell}@cs.stanford.edu

Abstract. A botnet is a collection of bots, each generally running on a compromised system and responding to commands over a "command-and-control" overlay network. We investigate observable differences in the behavior of bots and benign programs, focusing on the way that bots respond to data received over the network. Our experimental platform monitors execution of an arbitrary Win32 binary, considering data received over the network to be tainted, applying library-call-level taint propagation, and checking for tainted arguments to selected system calls. As a way of further distinguishing locally-initiated from remotely-initiated actions, we capture and propagate "cleanliness" of local user input (as received via the keyboard or mouse). Testing indicates behavioral separation of major bot families (agobot, DSNXbot, evilbot, G-SySbot, sdbot, Spybot) from benign programs with low error rate.

1 Introduction

Botnets have been instrumental in distributed denial of service attacks, click fraud, phishing, malware distribution, manipulation of online polls and games, and identity theft [2,18,19,25,33,30]. As much as 70% of all spam may be transmitted through botnets [4] and as many as $\frac{1}{4}$ of all computers may be participants in a botnet [37]. A bot master (or "botherder") directs the activities of a botnet by issuing commands that are transmitted over a command-and-control (C&C) overlay network. Some previous network-based botnet detection efforts have attempted to exploit this ongoing C&C behavior or its side effects [3,6,25]. Our work investigates the potential for host-based behavioral bot detection. In particular, we test the hypothesis that the behavior of installed bots can be characterized in a way that distinguishes malicious bots from innocuous processes. We are not aware of any prior studies of this topic.

Each participating bot independently executes each command received over the C&C network. A bot command takes some number of parameters (possibly zero) – each of a particular type – in some fixed order. For example, many bots provide a web-download command, which commonly takes two parameters; the first is a URL that identifies a remote resource (typically a file) that should be downloaded, and the second is the file path on the host system at which to store the downloaded data. A botnet, therefore, constitutes a *remotely programmable platform* with the set of commands it supports forming its API.

Many parameterized bot commands are implemented by invoking operating system services on the host system. For example, the web-download command

B. M. Hämmerli and R. Sommer (Eds.): DIMVA 2007, LNCS 4579, pp. 89–108, 2007.
© Springer-Verlag Berlin Heidelberg 2007

connects to a target over the network, requests some data from that target, and creates a file on the host system; all of these actions (connect, network send and receive, and file creation) are performed via execution of system calls. Typically, a command's parameters provide information used in the system call invocation. For example, the `connect` system call takes an IP address argument, which identifies the target host with which a connection should be established. Implementations of the web-download command obtain that target host IP from the given URL parameter. Thus, execution of many parameterized commands causes system call invocations on arguments obtained from those parameters.

In this paper, we test the experimental hypothesis that the remote control of bots through parameterized commands separates bot behavior from normal execution of innocuous programs. We postulate that a process exhibits external or remote control when it uses data received from the network (an untrusted source) in a system call argument (a trusted sink). We test our hypothesis via a prototype implementation, BotSwat, designed for the environment in which the vast majority of bots operate: home users' PCs running Windows XP or 2000 [25]. BotSwat can monitor execution of an arbitrary Win32 binary and interposes on the run-time library calls (including system calls) made by a process. We consider data received over the network to be tainted and track tainted data as it propagates via dynamic library calls to other memory regions. We identify execution of parameterized bot commands when tainted arguments are supplied to select *gate functions*, which are system calls used in malicious bot activity.

Our experimental results suggest that the presence of network packet contents in selected system call arguments is an effective indicator for malicious Win32 bots, including tested variants of agobot, DSNXbot, evilbot, G-SySbot, sdbot, and Spybot. Bots from these families constitute 98.2% of malicious bots seen in the wild [18]. While these bots may implement commands in significantly different ways, similarities in the way they respond to external control allow a single approach to identify them. Additionally, the thousands of variants of each such family generally differ in ways that will not affect our ability to detect them; this is in contrast to traditional anti-malware signature scanners which may require a distinct signature for each variant [38]. Moreover, our generic approach does not rely on a particular command-and-control communication protocol (e.g., IRC) or botnet structure (e.g., centralized or peer-to-peer).

Since our prototype implementation only has visibility into memory-copying calls made via a Dynamically Linked Library (DLL), we introduce strategies to counteract the effects of *out-of-band* memory copies – those which occur outside of the interposition mechanism. In particular, we perform *content-based tainting*, which considers a memory region tainted if its contents are identical to a known tainted string. We also introduce *substring-based tainting*, whereby a region will be considered tainted if its contents are a substring of any data received by the monitored process over the network. These strategies are applied upon calls by a monitored process into *taint propagation functions*, which are DLL functions used to copy or convert the contents of memory. Applying these strategies allows us to effectively identify bot behavior even when all of the bot's calls to memory-copying functions occur out-of-band, which may be the case if the bot statically links in C library functions.

A consequence of BotSwat's use of library-call-level taint propagation is that bots could apply out-of-band encryption functions (e.g., XOR) to network data and consequently defeat detection by the prototype implementation. This is a limitation of our current testing platform rather than a deficiency in the characterization of bot remote-control behavior. Our testing of versions of agobot, which encrypt C&C communications via dynamic calls to the OpenSSL library, indicates that remote control behavior can still be identified (even when communications are encrypted), given visibility into the cryptographic function calls. Current botnet C&C communications tend to be unencrypted [19].

While both bots and benign programs may create files, interact with the network, and execute programs, we are able to separate bot behavior from that of benign programs by distinguishing between remotely-initiated and locally-initiated actions. We tested applications typical to the target environment (home-user PCs) which exhibit extensive network interaction. Early testing revealed that a benign program may use some tainted value in a system call argument as a result of local user input. For example, when a user downloads a webpage via a browser then clicks on a hypertext link therein, the browser will consequently request the content stored at the linked URL. In so doing, the browser will invoke system calls (e.g., connect, send) on tainted arguments (the URL). If user input were not tracked, this sequence of events would look similar to bot execution of the web download command. To account for this phenomenon in our experimental assessment, we designed and implemented a user-input module that identifies data values resulting from local user input as received via the keyboard or mouse. These clean strings are used to identify instances of local control. Our testing of eight benign programs over a variety of activities common to those applications resulted in eight total flagged behaviors (five different) whereas testing six bots resulted in a total of 202 flagged behaviors (18 different).

In Sect. 2, we provide background information on bots. Section 3 describes our experimental method, and Sect. 4 details our prototype implementation. Our experimental results are given in Sect. 5. We discuss the potential for and challenges to applying our findings for real-time host-based bot detection in Sect. 6. Section 7 describes related work and Sect. 8 provides concluding remarks.

2   Bots and Botnets

A botnet is a network of compromised machines that can be remotely controlled by a bot master over a command-and-control (C&C) network. Individual bots connect to a rendezvous point – commonly an IRC server and channel, access to which may require password authentication – and await commands.

2.1   Bot Families and Variants

The Honeynet Project identifies four main Win32 bot families: (1) the agobot family – the most well known; (2) the sdbot family – the most common; (3)

DSNXbot; and (4) mIRC-based bots [25]. A family is "a new, distinct sample of malicious code," whereas a variant is "a new iteration of the same family, one that has minor differences but that is still based on the original" [36]. Variants may be created by augmenting the functionality of a bot (e.g., adding a new exploit for use in spreading) or by applying "packing transformations" (such as compression and encryption) to a bot binary [36,38]. We tested at least one variant from each of the first three major Win32 bot families (agobot, sdbot, and DSNXbot) as well as evilbot and Spybot. Data from McAfee suggests that bots from these tested families collectively constitute 98.2% of known variants (as of June 2005) [18]. Since bots in the wild may link in C library functions statically or dynamically, we tested bots under both conditions.

capability	ago	DSNX	evil	G-SyS	sd	Spy
change C&C server	√	√		√	√	√
create/manage clone		√		√	√	
clone attacks		√				
create spy				√	√	
kill process	√			√		√
open/execute file	√	√		√	√	√
keylogging		√				√
create directory						√
delete file/directory		√				√
list directory		√				√
move file/directory						√
DCC send file		√				√
act as http server						√
create port redirect	√	√		√	√	√
other proxy	√					
download file	√	√		√	√	√
DNS resolution	√			√	√	
UDP/ping floods	√		√	√	√	
other DDoS floods	√			√		√
scan/spread	√	√		√	√	√
spam	√					
visit URL	√			√	√	

Fig. 1. Bot capabilities

2.2   Bot Capabilities and Commands

Figure 1 provides a summary of some of the functionality exported by the tested bots. The shaded cells represent activities that are detected by BotSwat as described in Sect. 5. Note that, of the 22 different bot activities listed, 21 are implemented as parameterized commands by each of the bots that provides that capability. The exception is keylogging, which – for both of the bots that perform it – logs the captured keystrokes to a file whose name is statically configured. This chart reflects the bot versions we tested; different variants from each of these families may export more or less functionality.

Candidate Commands. Since our characterization of bot behavior exploits the fact that command parameters are often used in system call arguments, we identify a bot's *candidate commands* as those which take at least one parameter that is subsequently used (in whole or in part) in an argument to a critical system function. Our method considers *non-candidate commands*, those which take no parameters or parameters with only "local meaning" to the bot, out-of-scope.

Any bot execution of a received command is an instance in which that bot is being remotely controlled. The remote control behavior associated with a particular command consists of all the actions taken by the bot as a direct consequence of receipt of that command. Not all commands result in an equal amount of remote control behavior; e.g., a command that asks a bot to return its ID (some statically-configured value) to the bot controller entails fewer actions than the described web-download command. We approximate a command's remote control behavior by identifying the number of distinct system calls invoked during a successful execution of that command; these values were obtained through bot source code inspection. A bot's *total potential remote control behavior*, then, is the sum of the remote-control behavior of each of that bot's commands (Table 1, Row 1). Our coverage of that potential can be measured by summing the remote-control behavior of each of a bot's candidate commands (Table 1, Row 2). The complete list of system calls used in the tallies can be found in [52]. The number of system calls invoked by a bot's candidate commands accounts for around 64 to 79% of the system calls invoked over all of the bot's commands. Interestingly enough, the non-candidate commands that cause the highest number of system call invocations generally perform beneficial tasks (from the perspective of the compromised host); specific examples of this can be found in [52].

Table 1. The number of system calls invoked during successful execution of commands

	ago	DSNX	evil	GSyS	sd	Spy
# syscalls invoked over all cmds	591	145	5	187	173	202
# syscalls invoked over candidate cmds	417	114	5	122	110	145

3 Experimental Method

We developed a host-based method that identifies instances of external control, whereby a process uses data it received from an untrusted source in a system call argument without having received intervening (local) user input implicitly or explicitly agreeing to this use.

Tainting Component. This component identifies when untrusted data is received by the system (taint instantiation) and tracks that data as it propagates to other memory regions (taint propagation). For our method, taint instantiation occurs upon network receive, and taint propagation keeps track of memory regions to which tainted data is written. This component exports an interface that enables querying whether a particular memory region is considered tainted.

User Input Component. This purpose of this component is to identify actions that are initiated by the local application user. A primary challenge in designing this component is to identify the data values corresponding to mouse input events where this mapping (from event to value) is heavily application-dependent and not typically exposed (i.e., available via a library call). This component exports an interface that enables learning whether a data value or memory region is considered clean or whether a syscall invocation is likely the result of user input.

Behavior-Check Procedure. Triggered by invocation of selected system calls, this procedure queries the tainting and user-input components to determine whether to flag the invocation as exhibiting external control. Invocations on arguments that contain more bytes of tainted than clean data are flagged.

4   Implementation

This section describes the interposition approach and the tainting, user-input, and behavior-check instrumentation used to evaluate our hypothesis.

4.1   Library and System Call Interposition

We use the `detours` library provided by Microsoft Research for library- and system-call interposition [9]. Our platform consists of a set of functions that we want to interpose upon, a replacement function for each, and a mechanism for performing interposition. The replacement functions contain the tainting, user-input, and behavior-check instrumentation. This platform is packaged as a DLL that can be injected into a target process upon its creation. Our implementation consists of approximately 70,000 lines of C++ code and, for the purpose of conducting thorough experiments, may intercept up to 2,200 API functions.

4.2   Tainting Module

Our tainting module operates dynamically at the library-call level and considers data received over the network to be tainted; consequently, network receive functions (e.g., `recv`, `WSARecv`) are instrumented as taint instantiators. Taint propagation functions include those which copy memory from a source to a destination buffer (e.g., `memcpy`), convert a buffer's contents to a numeric value (e.g., `atoi`), or convert one numeric value to another (e.g., `htons`). Taintedness can be a property of memory addresses, strings, or numeric values. A total of 172 different functions (enumerated in [52]) were instrumented as taint propagators.

As a result of out-of-band memory copies, our mechanism may possess one of two flawed views regarding a particular memory region. If a destination region D is written to with tainted data via an out-of-band operation, we will not know that D should be considered tainted. Our belief that D does not contain tainted data is a *false negative*. Similarly, a tainted region T may be written to via an out-of-band operation with untainted data; in this case, our belief that T is tainted is a *false positive*. We perform content-matching to reduce false positives and content-based and substring-based tainting to reduce false negatives.

To reduce false positives, we perform *content-matching*: for a believed-to-be-tainted memory region M, before taking any action on the basis of M's supposed taintedness (where actions include propagating taint or flagging a system call invocation), we confirm that M's contents match the relevant portion of the network receive buffer N from which M allegedly descended. The information needed to perform such a comparison (an identifier of N, the offset into N from which this tainted data descended, the number of bytes of tainted data, etc.) is stored in the data structure describing a tainted memory region.

There are three conditions under which a region may be considered tainted: address-based, content-based, and substring-based. Under *address-based tainting*, a memory region is considered tainted if its address range overlaps with that of a known tainted region. With *content-based tainting*, a memory region will be considered tainted if its contents are identical to a known tainted string. Under *substring-based tainting*, a memory region will be considered tainted if its contents are a substring of any data received over the network by this process.

The tainting module may run in one of two modes, which differ in the conditions used to determine taintedness. Under *cause-and-effect propagation*, a memory region is considered tainted if the address-based or content-based conditions hold. Under *correlative propagation*, a memory region will be considered if any of the three conditions holds. Consequently, these modes differ in the amount of resilience provided against out-of-band copies. Cause-and-effect propagation was designed for the case where the majority of memory-copies made by a monitored process are visible to the interposition mechanism. We refer to this as cause-and-effect propagation since, in applying it, there is a tight causal relationship between receipt of some data over the network and use of that data in a system call argument. That is, we can point to a sequence of memory copies from a network receive buffer to a system call argument buffer. Correlative propagation, on the other hand, was designed for the case where most or all memory copies occur out of band – such as can occur when a bot statically links in C library functions. This mode is referred to as correlative propagation since, in applying it, we are ultimately identifying when data received over the network correlates to that used in system call arguments.

Upon a call to a taint propagation function f, that function's relevant arguments are checked for taintedness via applying the appropriate conditions, given the mode, and performing content-matching. Given a tainted source argument, taint propagation proceeds in the following way. For source buffers, we ensure that the tainted portion of that buffer is a known tainted string and its address range is a known tainted region. If f copies some portion of this source buffer to a destination buffer, the corresponding portion of the destination region is transitively marked tainted. If, on the other hand, f converts the source buffer to a numeric value, we add the numeric result to our collection of tainted numbers. Finally, if the tainted source argument is a number which f converts to another number, we add the destination value to our set of tainted numbers.

4.3   User Input Module

Our implementation tracks local user input as received via the keyboard or mouse and considers subsequent use of such clean data, such as in a system call argument, innocuous. Obtaining the data value corresponding to a keystroke is generally straightforward as the system generates a message in response to keyboard input for the target application identifying the key or character. Our implementation monitors such messages and creates, for each line of keyboard input, a clean string consisting of the previously input characters.

Obtaining the data value corresponding to a mouse input event is more challenging as the system generates, upon receipt of such an event, a message which merely identifies the target window, type of event (e.g. left button down), and coordinate pair within that window at which the event occurred. The actual data value corresponding to such an event is application-defined and not available via a library call. Our implementation addresses this opacity via exploiting locality of reference; in particular, our goal was to identify when an application was executing code to handle a user-input event. We posited that any data values referenced during execution of such code could be considered clean and that in this way we could infer a set of data values corresponding to a user input event.

For a Windows user input event E, an application calls `DispatchMessage` in order to invoke that application's predefined handler for E. The handler must process E prior to returning from `DispatchMessage` [35] and may invoke system calls in its processing. Thus, upon entry to `DispatchMessage` and until return from it, we add any string referenced by any interposed-upon function to our collection of clean strings.

4.4   Behavior-Check Procedure

Our ability to identify bot behavior relies in part on our selection of appropriate system calls and their arguments to check for taintedness and cleanliness. The collection of bot capabilities (Fig. 1) informed our selection of system calls (gates) and their particular arguments (sinks); these are described below. The algorithm is as follows. If the sink type is numeric, if the argument value is tainted, we flag the invocation; otherwise, we pass control to the system call. While a numeric value will either be considered tainted or not, buffer arguments may contain some number of bytes of tainted and/or clean data. If the sink type is a data buffer which contains no tainted data, control is passed to the system call. Otherwise, we query the user-input module to determine whether that buffer also contains clean data. If not, the invocation is flagged; if so, this procedure will flag the invocation only if the argument contains more bytes of tainted than clean data.

A *behavior* is a general description of an action that may be detected via checking particular arguments for one or more system calls. The same gate function may be instrumented to detect multiple different behaviors. Conversely, multiple library functions may be instrumented to check for a single behavior. Table 2 contains the complete list of behaviors and the gate functions for each behavior. In general, we favored instrumenting lower-level API functions as gates; e.g., instrumenting `NtOpenFile` as a gate enables us to detect all behaviors that entail listing a directory, deleting a file, or replacing a file since the higher-level API functions for these tasks ultimately call into `NtOpenFile`.

Table 2. Detected behaviors and the gate functions for each behavior

	Behavior	gate function
B1	tainted open file	NtOpenFile
B2	tainted create file	NtCreateFile
B3	tainted program execution	CreateProcess{A,W}
B4	tainted process termination	NtTerminateProcess
B5	bind tainted IP	NtDeviceIoControlFile
B6	bind tainted port	NtDeviceIoControlFile
B7	connect to tainted IP	connect; WSAConnect
B8	connect to tainted port	connect; WSAConnect
B9	tainted send	NtDeviceIoControlFile; SSL_write
B10	derived send	NtDeviceIoControlFile; SSL_write
B11	sendto tainted IP	sendto; WSASendTo
B12	sendto tainted port	sendto; WSASendTo
B13	tainted set registry key	NtSetValueKey
B14	tainted delete registry key	NtDeleteValueKey
B15	tainted create service	CreateService{A,W}
B16	tainted delete service	OpenService{A,W}
B17	tainted HttpSendRequest	HttpSendRequest{A,W}
B18	tainted IcmpSendEcho	IcmpSendEcho{A,W}

Two behaviors (tainted send and derived send) require a bit more explanation. *Tainted send* occurs when data received over one connection (or socket) is sent out on another; e.g., when a bot is acting as a proxy, it echoes out on a second socket the data heard on the first. Since an application may commonly receive and send certain fixed strings over a variety of connections, we do not perform content-based or substring-based tainting for such strings. The set of such strings is small, application-specific, and generally consists of protocol header fields; e.g., a browser's set includes HTTP/1.1 and Accept-Range. Consequently, the tainted send behavior is not flagged for transmission of routine messages that do not otherwise contain tainted data. *Derived send* occurs when a system call is invoked on some tainted input to obtain a result that is then sent on the network. Various data leaking commands match derived send, such as those which take a parameter identifying a registry key and return its value.

5   Experimental Evaluation

This section provides the results of testing our experimental hypothesis that the remote control behavior of bots can be detected via checking selected system calls for tainted arguments. To determine the utility of this characterization of remote control, we compare the effects of detected commands to those of all commands. Finally, we measure whether benign programs exhibit remote control.

5.1   Bot Experiment Setup

We edited the source code of each bot by altering its C&C parameters such that, when executed, that bot would connect to a C&C server under our control. We then built two versions of each bot: one which dynamically linked in C library functions (DYN) and a second which statically linked these in (STAT). We then executed each bot binary, injecting our DLL into the newly-spawned bot process so as to intercept its API calls (as described in 4.1). We were then able to exercise each bot over its set of commands and monitor the effects of each such command.

5.2   Terminology

When BotSwat *flags* a system call invocation, we say that a behavior is *detected*. If flagging this invocation is incorrect, we refer to this as a *false positive*. Any behavior flagged for a benign program is considered a false positive. If BotSwat fails to flag a system call invocation on an argument that contains data received over the network (most likely because BotSwat does not know that this argument should be considered tainted), we say a behavior is *exhibited* but not detected and refer to this as a *false negative*. We say that a command is detected when BotSwat correctly flags at least one behavior exhibited by that command. Note that many commands exhibit more than one behavior; therefore, a particular command may exhibit a false negative but still be detected.

5.3   Bot Results

In summary, we found that the external or remote control behavior of bots can be measured by identifying system call invocations which use tainted parameters. Moreover, the effects of a bot's detected commands account for the majority of the effects of all of a bot's commands (where effects are measured via number of system call invocations). Bots in general exhibit a great volume and diversity of behaviors. Table 3 provides a summary of our test results. Row 1 identifies the total number of commands provided by each of the tested bots. The number of those commands that take at least one parameter that is subsequently used (in whole or in part) in a critical system function is provided in row 2. The 3rd row gives the number of candidate commands that were detected using cause-and-effect propagation (C&E) for bots built with C library functions dynamically linked in (DYN). The last row shows the number of candidate commands detected using correlative propagation (CORR) on bots built with statically linked in C library functions (STAT). We did not have a version of evilbot which dynamically linked in C library functions.

Detection of Commands on Dynamically-Linked Bots. The best detection occurs under cause-and-effect propagation on dynamically-linked bots, since these conditions provide the best visibility into the bot's use of data received over the network. Only three total candidate commands were not detected in this mode: agobot's `harvest.registry` and scanning commands. Agobot's

Table 3. Summary of bot command detection

	ago	DSNX	evil	GSyS	sd	Spy
# cmds	88	28	5	56	50	36
# candidate cmds	36	14	5	26	20	15
# detected cmds (DYN, C&E)	33	14	N/A	26	20	15
# detected cmds (STAT, CORR)	31	10	5	12	12	15

scanning commands use a transformation of a received parameter in a system call argument. Taintedness was not propagated across this transformation operation; thus, `scan.start` and `scan.startall` were not detected. Also, the same set of commands was detected (and the same behaviors flagged for each command) for agobot whether that bot encrypted C&C messages via dynamic calls to the OpenSSL library or not. Thus, detection of remote control is resilient to command encryption, given visibility into the cryptographic function calls.

Detection of Commands on Statically-Linked Bots. Since all tested bots either primarily or exclusively use C library functions for memory copying, static linking severely hinders visibility into a bot's use of received data. We were still, however, able to detect execution of many of the bots' candidate commands by correlating received network data to system call arguments. We explore below the effects of detected vs. undetected commands and provide some evidence that these undetected commands are significantly less harmful than are the detected commands. Many of the undetected commands rely on the previous execution of a command this *is* detected under these conditions. In particular, three of DSNX's four undetected commands (75%), seven of sdbot's eight (87.5%), and seven of G-SySbot's fourteen (50%) perform clone management; this functionality only makes sense when a clone exists to be managed. The command that creates a clone – for each of these three bots – was detected under STAT, CORR. There were three false positives under this mode; in all cases, the incorrectly flagged behavior was in fact malicious but not an example of external control.

The candidate commands that were not detected under STAT, CORR share a common property that could be used to produce even better detection results. Specifically, 24 of the 28 undetected commands use `sprintf` to format the argument buffers passed to system calls. The call to this buffer-formatting function was not visible to BotSwat (under STAT) and thus it was not able to infer that the resulting argument buffers contained (among other data) strings received over the network. Statistical tests that measure how similar an argument buffer is to data received over the network may provide significant gains here.

The Effects of Detected Commands Relative to All Commands As discussed in Sect. 2.2, not all commands result in an equal amount of remote control behavior. [1] We find that the commands we are able to detect for each bot – even under STAT, CORR – account for the majority of that bot's total potential remote control behavior. For Spybot, e.g., under STAT, CORR, the number of system calls invoked during execution of detected commands is 145 (Table 4) and during execution of all commands is 202 (Table 1). The same pattern held for all tested bots and is a consequence of the relative severity of commands we are able to detect even under these conditions.

Table 4. The number of system calls invoked during successful execution of candidate and detected commands

	ago	DSNX	evil	GSyS	sd	Spy
# syscalls invoked by candidate cmds	417	114	5	122	110	145
# syscalls ... detected cmds (DYN, C&E)	393	114	N/A	122	110	145
# syscalls ... detected cmds (STAT, CORR)	386	110	5	99	99	145

Bots Exhibit Volume and Diversity of Behaviors. For each bot command, we counted the number of distinct behaviors correctly detected in a successful execution of that command. Then we tallied these values across commands, giving us the number of times each behavior was detected for each bot (Fig. 2). It is not uncommon for execution of a single command to result in detection of multiple behaviors. Executing a port redirect command, e.g., generally results in four detected behaviors: binding a tainted port (B6), connecting to a tainted IP (B7), connecting to a tainted port (B8), and tainted send (B9). Note that in practice the raw number of detected bot behaviors might be much larger since execution of certain commands may cause the same behavior to be repeatedly flagged. Such is the case with denial-of-service (DoS) commands, which often cause a particular behavior to be flagged with transmission of each DoS packet. We note that the distribution of detected behaviors across bot families is not uniform; e.g., behavior B11 (sendto tainted IP) is frequently flagged in agobot but never in DSNXbot and only rarely in G-Sys, sd, and Spybots. Such differences may be leveraged to perform classification of an encountered bot as more likely to be a variant of a particular family.

5.4   Benign Program Results

We tested eight benign applications that exhibit extensive network interaction across a variety of activities typical to these programs. False positives in this context are any instances in which a system call invocation is flagged. This could arise from imperfections in our user-input module implementation, which

---

[1] We approximate the remote control behavior associated with a particular command via tabulating the number of distinct system calls invoked in a successful execution of that command. Then the bot's total potential remote control behavior is the sum of these values across all of that bot's commands.

	B1	B2	B3	B4	B5	B6	B7	B8	B9	B10	B11	B12	B13	B14	B15	B16	B17	B18
ago	5	6	7	2	1	5	14	2	14	1	7	3	1	1	1	1	0	0
DSNX	4	4	2	0	0	1	6	4	8	0	0	0	0	0	0	0	0	0
evil	0	0	5	0	0	0	0	0	0	0	0	0	0	0	0	0	0	0
G-SyS	1	1	8	0	0	1	8	4	10	1	1	1	0	0	0	0	3	1
sd	1	1	2	0	0	1	8	4	10	1	1	1	0	0	0	0	3	1
Spy	4	5	1	1	0	2	4	3	1	0	1	1	0	0	0	0	0	0
Total	15	17	25	3	1	10	40	17	43	3	10	6	1	1	1	1	6	2

Fig. 2. The number of times each behavior was detected, over all of a bot's commands

may not be able to infer that a system call invocation is the result of local user input. Alternatively, a benign program may genuinely exhibit external or remote control. There were eight false positives: two for the browser, three for the email client, two for the IRC client, and one for the IRC server. The programs, activities across which their behavior was traced, and results are described below.

Benign Program Testing. We tested a browser (firefox), email client (Eudora), IRC client (mIRC), ssh client (putty), FTP clients (WS_FP and SecureFX), anti-virus (AV) signature updater (Symantec's LuComServer_3_0.exe), and IRC server (Unreal IRCd). Since the majority of systems infected with bots are those of home users (who do not typically run server programs) [32], we tested against only one server program. We note, however, that server programs may, at an abstract level, be designed to respond to certain types of external control (that exerted by the client).

We used the browser to visit a variety of sites, some containing linked-in images. Once at a site, we clicked on hypertext links, downloaded files specified by links, saved the web page's contents to a file, executed downloaded programs from within the browser, etc. With the email client, we received, composed, replied to, forwarded, and sent email, including and excluding attachments, and including and excluding HTML. We also saved and executed received attachments from within the email client. We exercised the IRC client over a range of its capabilities: connecting to a server and channel, messaging, DCC file transfer, etc. We used the ssh client to connect to and execute commands on a remote host. Using FTP clients, we connected to and browsed various FTP sites, navigated across directories (alternatively using the mouse and keyboard), and downloaded files. We tested the AV signature updater via establishing a base state with stale virus definitions files then instructing the updater to get the latest AV signatures. Finally, the IRC server was networked to other servers and serviced clients.

Benign Program Results. We present the results of running under correlative propagation (which has the most relaxed requirements for taintedness) with the user-input module enabled. Four of the eight false positives occur as a result of the automatic downloading of linked-in images performed in rendering an HTML document. Two of these were exhibited by the browser and two by the email client, both upon receipt of an HTML document containing an <IMG SRC="..."> element. Receipt of such an element causes the application to request the content specified in the SRC URL. Also, when the user receives an email with an attachment, Eudora automatically creates a file of the same name (as the received file), which causes the tainted open file behavior (B1).

The mIRC client generated two false positives as a result of performing Direct Client Protocol (DCC) file receipt. These false positives reveal limitations in our user-input module implementation. In preparation for DCC file transfer, the file sender provides an IP and port to the recipient via a network message. The recipient then creates a TCP connection to the sender using the specified IP and port. Therefore, behaviors B7 (connecting to a tainted IP) and B8 (connecting to a tainted port) were flagged. Prior to the chat client creating such a connection, however, the client asks the user whether he wishes to perform this operation and will only proceed if the user responds affirmatively. Our user-input module was not able to infer the connection between the user input agreeing to this behavior (via a dialog box) and the values used to create the network connection.

The IRC server repeatedly exhibited the tainted send behavior (B9) – which identifies when data heard over one socket is sent out on another. Clearly this behavior is expected, since the overriding purpose of an IRC server is to participate in a chat network, which entails receiving messages and sharing those with its clients and/or other servers.

Benign Results Discussion. We find it interesting that most of the detected behaviors of benign programs may be known to carry a risk and thus our flagging of these behaviors may not be totally inappropriate. In particular, [53] recommends disabling DCC file receipt so as to avoid malware infection (2 behaviors); the automatic downloading of linked-in images performed by the email client and browser may be exploited to perform DoS attacks [50] (4 behaviors); and email attachments are a known malware propagation vector (1 behavior).

Table 5 summarizes the detection of behaviors across all tested programs. Note that a single run of any such program may exhibit fewer behaviors depending upon the inputs to that particular run-time instance. In general, bots exhibit high volume (202 across all bots and all commands, as in Fig. 2) and great diversity (18 different) of behaviors. By contrast, only eight behaviors total (five different) were flagged over execution of all benign programs even when testing under the most liberal taint propagation mode, correlative. We discuss how one might handle these false positives in Sect. 6. Finally, we acknowledge the limitations of black-box dynamic testing; that is, there may be other inputs to these benign programs that would result in flagging additional behaviors. Similarly, it may be the case that higher fidelity taint propagation (e.g., assembly-code-level tainting) reveals additional behaviors. That said, all programs (malicious and benign) were tested using the same system, and the demonstrated behavioral gap between bots and benign applications under these conditions is dramatic.

Table 5. For each tested program, the number of distinct behaviors detected

	# distinct behaviors	which behaviors
agobot	16	B1 - B16
GSySbot	12	B1 - B3, B6 - B12, B17, B18
sdbot	12	B1 - B3, B6 - B12, B17, B18
Spybot	10	B1 - B4, B6 - B9, B11, B12
DSNXbot	7	B1 - B3, B6 - B9
evilbot	1	B3
Eudora	3	B1, B7, B17
Firefox	2	B7, B9
mIRC	2	B7, B8
Unreal IRCd	1	B9
putty	0	N/A
SecureFX	0	N/A
Symantec AV updater	0	N/A
WS_FTP	0	N/A

5.5   Performance Results

Function interception via the `detours` library imposes an overhead of fewer than 400 nanoseconds per invocation [9]. We measured the overall performance impact of BotSwat's instrumentation via scripting a bot to receive then execute various commands; the bot's performance was measured natively and under each of the two propagation modes. The overall measured performance overhead is 2.81% when using cause-and-effect propagation and 3.87% under correlative.

6   Potential for Host-Based, Behavioral Bot Detection

Signature-based anti-malware mechanisms suffer from several critical limitations, including the inability to detect novel malware instances or obfuscated variants and the need to continuously update their signature sets [34,38]. A recent study found that even the most effective anti-virus vendor failed to detect a significant percentage of malware samples found in the wild [42]. Behavior-based approaches to malware detection provide a powerful alternative: the ability to detect entire classes of malware including previously unseen instances. The primary challenge is to identify a useful behavioral characterization: one which identifies behavior fundamental to a class of malware but which is not generally exhibited by innocuous programs. The data presents a compelling argument that our characterization meets these criteria; the very behavior that makes bots most useful to their installers (their programmability) provides the basis for detection.

Our prototype implementation was designed to test the effectiveness of our behavioral characterization; a secure implementation of our method must be able to detect and differentiate such remote control behavior in a way that is difficult for malware to adaptively evade and subvert. Designing such a system is a research problem unto itself. We highlight some of the fundamental challenges and tradeoffs in building a bot detection mechanism based on our findings.

Process Monitoring Mechanism. The mechanism that enables visibility into a process's actions may also be referred to as a *sandbox*. There are two primary design considerations: *visibility*, which refers to the type and granularity of events visible to the sandbox, and *isolation*, which refers to the difficulty of a monitored process to evade or subvert the sandbox. The (user-space) in-line function hooks [9] used in the prototype implementation provide high visibility (as the interposition code runs in the same address space as the monitored application) but very weak isolation [8,10]. Kernel-space system call interposition and Virtual Machine Introspection [24] are additional possibilities.

Tainting Challenges and Tradeoffs. Since a malicious bot may evade detection via performing data movement (or data transformation) operations out-of-band, coverage is a critical aspect of the system's security. There appears at present to be a fundamental tradeoff in dynamic tainting modules between coverage and performance; i.e., tainting implementations that provide thorough coverage (as in [12]) exact significant performance penalties. Also, if there are operations across which taintedness is not propagated (e.g., writes to persistent storage or pipes), surely such avenues will be used to launder tainted data. Propagating taint more thoroughly may result in more flagged behaviors and false positives.

User Input Module Challenges. There are two types of attacks specific to this component: spoofing user input events and genuinely obtaining user input. Exposure to user-input-spoofing attacks may be minimized by incorporating a kernel-level component that identifies receipt of user input events. The latter attack, however, highlights the fundamental challenge in this module's design. In particular, since the meaning of user input events is inherently application-defined, a user-input module must rely on the application that received a user-input event to implicitly or explicitly identify the semantics of that input. Consequently, if a malicious process is able to legitimately obtain *any* local user input, that process may be able to arbitrarily assign meaning to that input.

System Inputs and Outputs. An interesting question is which processes to monitor using the detection mechanism. A reasonable decision may be to not monitor known benign programs. Such a decision would inevitably cause attackers to explore ways in which such known benign programs could be coopted to do the attackers' bidding (as in [50]). In either case, a general decision must be made about when to label something a bot. A reasonable tradeoff may be to require some volume and diversity of behaviors; then a lower threshold more narrowly constrains the attacker's arena but may also result in more false positives. Additionally, one could whitelist certain behaviors known to be generated by particular applications during their legitimate operation (as in Sect. 5.4). A final option may be to identify and flag execution of commands – sequences of correlated behaviors – rather than individual behaviors.

7   Related Work

Applications of Tainting Analysis Tainting has been applied statically, dynamically, at a language level, via an interpreter, an emulator, compiler extensions, etc. [1,11,12,14,15,20,27]. Most commonly, security-motivated tainting has been used to identify vulnerabilities in or exploitations of non-malicious programs.

Host-Based Intrusion Detection. The problem of distinguishing execution of an installed malicious bot from that of innocuous processes differs from that explored by much previous run-time, host-based, anti-malware research, which has focused on identifying when a host program (generally assumed to be non-malicious) has been exploited [5,12,13,21,28]. While a bot may be spread via leveraging such exploits, monitoring execution of an installed bot using one of these mechanisms will generally not result in the bot being identified as malicious since no exploit of a local host program is entailed in normal bot execution. Other behavior-based research has been done to identify rootkits and spyware [23,49,7,31]. [31] identifies *extrusions*: stealthy outgoing network connection made by malicious processes. User-intended (legitimate) outgoing network connections include those preceded in time by receipt of user input. A difference between our work and theirs is that, for us, outgoing network connections are only one of 18 behaviors of interest; also, we are interested in the semantics of user-input events, not merely their occurrence at some point in time.

Botnet Detection. Host-based approaches include scanning the contents of files and memory for certain byte sequences as well as content-based filtering, which identifies receipt of packets containing known bot-command keywords, as in Norton Intrusion Prevention. Network-based approaches to botnet detection include those which: (a) detect secondary effects of botnets [6,3]; (b) set up honeypots to obtain bot binaries then infiltrate those botnets [25,41,40]; (c) mitigate the effects of a botnet at a DDoS victim [22]; (d) apply content-based Network Intrusion Detection System (NIDS) signatures [16]; (e) apply heuristics to IRC channel traffic to identify likely C&C rendezvous points; (f) identify IRC NICK messages likely to have been generated by bots [44]; (g) track and correlate various types of NIDS alarms to identify *bot-infection sequences* [43]; (h) perform analysis of flow data to identify suspected bots then likely conversations between such suspected bots and their C&C servers [45]. Challenges for these approaches include: changing the C&C protocol or botnet topology; encrypting or otherwise obfuscating C&C communications; altering the timing of bot-related events and port scanning activity so as to stay below detection thresholds; bots which employ non-worm-like spreading behavior; coverage of C&C rendezvous points; running a botnet entirely within a single administrative domain; etc.

8   Conclusions

Botnets present a serious and increasing threat, as launching points for attacks including spam, distributed denial of service, sniffing, keylogging, and malware distribution. Our work explores whether the execution of malicious bots can be distinguished from that of innocuous programs. We provided a characterization of the remote control behavior of bots, identified the fraction of current bot remote-control behavior covered by this characterization, built a prototype implementation, and evaluated our hypothesis against six bots from five different families and a variety of benign applications typical to the target environment. We introduce techniques, such as content-based and substring-based tainting, that enable us to effectively identify a bot's remote control behavior even when visibility into the memory-copying calls made by a bot is severely limited.

Experimental evaluation suggests that the external or remote control behavior of bots can be detected by identifying system call invocations which use tainted parameters. We see that the effects of a bot's candidate commands (as measured via number of system call invocations) constitute the vast majority of the effects of all of a bot's commands. We also see that bots in general exhibit a great volume and diversity of behaviors. Finally, we note that, when we track local user input and sanitize subsequent uses of it, benign programs relatively rarely exhibit the external control behavior that we're measuring. Significant challenges remain in the problem of building a secure and robust bot detection system based on these observed behavioral differences.

Acknowledgements. Thanks to the detours team at MSR and Galen Hunt in particular for helpful insights into detours. We are also grateful to David Dagon at Georgia Tech, who provided versions of agobot, and to Andrew Sakai, for testing assistance. Thanks to Tal Garfinkel and Adam Barth for helpful feedback. We thank Wenke Lee for extensive and valuable feedback on our work and on its presentation. We are very grateful to our reviewers and to our shepherd for their insightful questions and comments.

References

1. Turoff, A.: Defensive CGI Programming with Taint Mode and CGI:: UNTAINT
2. Schneier, B.: How Bot Those Nets? In Wired Magazine (July 27, 2006)
3. Dagon, D.: Botnet Detection and Response: The Network Is the Infection. In: Operations, Analysis, and Research Center Workshop (July 2005)
4. Ilett, D.: Most spam generated by botnets, says expert. ZDNet UK(September 22, 2004)
5. Wagner, D., Dean, D.: Intrusion Detection via Static Analysis. In: IEEE Symposium on Security and Privacy (May 2001)
6. Cooke, E., Jahanian, F., McPherson, D.: The Zombie Roundup: Understanding, Detecting, and Disrupting Botnets. In Steps to Reducing Unwanted Traffic on the Internet (July 2005)
7. Kirda, E., Kruegel, C., Banks, G., Vigna, G., Kemmerer, R.: Behavior-based Spyware Detection. In: Proc. 15th USENIX Security Symposium (August 2006)
8. Hoglund, G., Butler, J.: Rootkits: Subverting the Windows Kernel. Addison-Wesley, Upper Saddle River, NJ (2006)
9. Hunt, G., Brubacher, B.: Detours: Binary Interception of Win32 Functions. In: 3rd USENIX Windows NT Symposium (July 1999)

10. Butler, J.: Bypassing 3rd Party Windows Buffer Overflow Protection. In: phrack Volume 0x0b, Issue 0x3e, Phile #0x0, 7/13/2004

11. Chow, J., Pfaff, B., Garfinkel, T., Christopher, K., Rosenblum, M.: Understanding Data Lifetime via Whole System Simulation. In: Proc. of the USENIX 13th Security Symposium (August 2004)

12. Newsome, J., Song, D.: Dynamic Taint Analysis for Automatic Detection, Analysis, and Signature Generation of Exploits on Commodity Software. In: Network and Distributed Systems Symposium (February 2005)

13. Rabek, J., Khazan, R., Lewandowski, S., Cunningham, R.: Detection of Injected, Dynamically Generated, and Obfuscated Malicious Code. In: Proc. of the ACM Workshop on Rapid Malcode (October 2003)

14. Ashcraft, K., Engler, D.: Using programmer-written compiler extensions to catch security holes. In: IEEE Symposium on Security and Privacy (May 2002)

15. Locking Ruby in the Safe http://www.rubycentral.com/book/taint.html

16. LURHQ. Phatbot Trojan Analysis. http://www.lurhq.com/phatbot.html

17. Christodorescu, M., Jha, S., Seshia, S., Song, D., Bryant, R.: Semantics-Aware Malware Detection. In: IEEE Symposium on Security and Privacy (May 2005)

18. Overton, M.: Bots and Botnets: Risks, Issues, and Prevention. In: Virus Bulletin Conference, Dublin, Ireland (October 2005)

19. Ianelli, N., Hackworth, A.: Botnets as a Vehicle for Online Crime. CERT Coordination Center (December 2005)

20. perlsec http://perldoc.perl.org/perlsec.html

21. Forrest, S., Hofmeyr, S., Somayaji, A., Longstaff, T.: A Sense of Self for Unix Processes. In: IEEE Symposium on Security and Privacy (May 1996)

22. Kandula, S., Katabi, D., Jacob, M., Berger, A.: Botz-4-Sale: Surviving Organized DDoS Attacks That Mimic Flash Crowds. In: Network and Distributed System Security Symposium (May 2005)

23. Strider GhostBuster Rootkit Detection
http://research.microsoft.com/rootkit/

24. Garfinkel, T., Rosenblum, M.: A Virtual Machine Introspection Based Architecture for Intrusion Detection. In: Network & Distributed Systems Security (February 2003)

25. Honeynet Project & Research Alliance. Know your Enemy: Tracking Botnets

26. The majority of bot code was obtained from: http://tinyurl.com/3y4cfd

27. Shankar, U., Talwar, K., Foster, J., Wagner, D.: Detecting format string vulnerabilities with type qualifiers. In: Proc. 10th USENIX Security Symp. (August 2001)

28. Kiriansky, V., Bruening, D., Amarasinghe, S.: Secure execution via program shepherding. In: Proc. 11th USENIX Security Symposium (August 2002)

29. Parizo, E.: s New bots, worm threaten AIM network. SearchSecurity (December 2005)

30. Naraine, R.: Money Bots: Hackers Cas. In: on Hijacked PCs. eWeek (September 2006)

31. Cui, W., Katz, R., Tan, W.: BINDER: An Extrusion-based Break-in Detector for Personal Computers. In: Proc. of the 21st Annual Computer Security Applications Conference (December 2005)

32. Martin, K.: Stop the bots. In: The Register (April 2006)

33. Keizer, G.: Bot Networks Behind Big Boos. In: Phishing Attacks. TechWeb (November 2004)

34. Christodorescu, M., Jha, S.: Testing Malware Detectors. In: Proc. of the International Symposium on Software Testing and Analysis (July 2004)

35. MSDN Library. Using Messages and Message Queues http://tinyurl.com/27hc37
36. Symantec Internet Security Threat Report, Trends for July 05, December 05. vol. IX, Published (March 2006)
37. Sturgeon, W.: Net pioneer predicts overwhelming botnet surge. ZDNet News (January 29, 2007)
38. Symantec Internet Security Threat Report, Trends for January 06-June 06, vol. X. Published (September 2006)
39. Barford, P., Yegneswaran, V.: An Inside Look at Botnets. In: Advances in Information Security. Special Workshop on Malware Detection, Springer, Heidelberg (2006)
40. Freiling, F., Holz, T., Wicherski, G.: Botnet Tracking: Exploring a Root-Cause Methodology to Prevent Distributed Denial-of-Service Attacks. In: European Symposium On Research In Computer Security (September 2006)
41. Rajab, M., Zarfoss, J., Monrose, F., Terzis, A.: A Multifaceted Approach to Understanding the Botnet Phenomenon. In: Proc. of ACM SIGCOMM/USENIX Internet Measurement Conference (October 2006)
42. Jevans, D.: The Latest Trends in Phishing, Crimeware and Cash-Out Schemes. Private correspondence
43. Gu, G., Porras, P., Yegneswaran, V., Fong, M., Lee, W.: BotHunter: Detecting Malware Infection Through IDS-Driven Dialog Correlation. Manuscript
44. Goebel, J., Holz, T.: Rishi: Identify Bot-Contaminated Hosts by IRC Nickname Evaluation. In: 1st Workshop on Hot Topics in Understanding Botnets (April 2007)
45. Karasaridis, A., Rexroad, B., Hoeflin, D.: Wide-Scale Botnet Detection and Characterization. In: 1st Workshop on Hot Topics in Understanding Botnets (April 2007)
46. Kristoff, J.: Botnets. NANOG32 (October 2004)
47. Ramachandran, A., Feamster, N., Dagon, D.: Revealing botnet membership using DNSBL counter-intelligence. In: 2nd Workshop on Steps to Reducing Unwanted Traffic on the Internet (July 2006)
48. Grizzard, J., Sharma, V., Nunnery, C., Kang, B., Dagon, D.: Peer-to-Peer Botnets: Overview and Case Study. In: 1st Workshop on Hot Topics in Understanding Botnets (April 2007)
49. Wang, Y., Beck, D., Vo, B., Roussev, R., Verbowski, C.: Detecting Stealth Software with Strider GhostBuster. Microsoft Technical Report MSR-TR-2005-25
50. Lam, V., Antonatos, S., Akritidis, P., Anagnostakis, K.: Puppetnets: Misusing Web Browsers as a Distributed Attack Infrastructure. In: the 13th ACM Conference on Computer and Communications Security (October 2006)
51. Schneier, B.: Semantic Attacks: The Third Wave of Network Attacks. In: the Cryptogram newsletter (October 15, 2000)
52. Stinson, E., Mitchell, J.: Characterizing the Remote Control Behavior of Bots. Manuscript. http://www.stanford.edu/~stinson/pub/botswat_long.pdf
53. mIRC Help, Viruses, Trojans, and Worms. http://www.mirc.co.uk/help/virus.html

Measurement and Analysis of Autonomous Spreading Malware in a University Environment

Jan Goebel[1], Thorsten Holz[2], and Carsten Willems[2]

[1] RWTH Aachen University
Center for Computing and Communication
[2] University of Mannheim
Laboratory for Dependable Distributed Systems

Abstract. Autonomous spreading malware in the form of bots or worms is a constant threat in today's Internet. In the form of *botnets*, networks of compromised machines that can be remotely controlled by an attacker, malware can cause lots of harm. In this paper, we present a measurement setup to study the spreading and prevalence of malware that propagates autonomously. We present the results when observing about 16,000 IPs within a university environment for a period of eight weeks. We collected information about 13,4 million successful exploits and study the system- and network-level behavior of the collected 2,034 valid, unique malware binaries.

Keywords: Honeypots, Malware, Invasive Software.

1 Introduction

In the recent years, we see a shift in how attackers behave and how they try to compromise systems: large-scale worms which compromise tens or even hundreds of thousands of machines are rare now, mass-outbreaks like Code Red or Slammer did not appear in the last few years. This could have two main reasons. On the one hand, a worm does not offer the attacker any type of remote control. Once the worm is released and spreading in the wild, the attacker can not send any additional commands to the compromised machines or otherwise influence its behavior. On the other hand, the attacker does not have any *financial* advantages by releasing a worm. We observe more and more a change in the motivation behind attacks in cyberspace. While ten years ago most attacks were motivated by technical challenges or to prove certain vulnerabilities, today most attacks have a financial background, a real "underground economy" has developed [3].

One of the main problems in today's Internet are *botnets*. A botnet can be defined as a network of compromised machines which can be remotely controlled by an attacker. On every compromised machine a so called *bot* is installed which establishes a connection to a remote control network by which the attacker can issue arbitrary commands. Typical examples for these remote control networks are IRC networks or HTTP servers, but there have also been the first Peer-to-Peer based botnets in the last few years [4]. Botnets can be used by an attacker for many malicious activities: carrying out Distributed Denial-of-Service (DDoS) attacks, sending out millions of spam or phishing e-mails,

B. M. Hämmerli and R. Sommer (Eds.): DIMVA 2007, LNCS 4579, pp. 109–128, 2007.

stealing sensitive information from the compromised machines, or seeding new malware are just a few examples. With most of these activities, an attacker can also have financial advantages. A detailed introduction to the topic of botnets is given in a paper by the Honeynet Project [16].

It is hard to measure the extent of this problem and a scientific based measurement of the number of compromised machines on the Internet is missing. There are some guesses by different people which greatly vary in size. For example, Vint Cerf estimates that up to a quarter of the 600 million machines connected to the Internet may be used by cyber criminals in botnets [10]. Other popular estimates range between 12 million [19] and 70 million [17] machines infected by bots. Moreover, it remains unclear with which metrics the size of a botnet should be measured [13].

One of the side effects of botnets is the constant "background noise" in the Internet caused by propagation attempts of bots: one of the most common commands issued by the controller of a botnet is the command to scan for other vulnerable machines in order to exploit a vulnerability found and then infect that machine. Since currently hundreds or even thousands of different bot variants are propagating in the wild, they cause a measurable amount of malicious network traffic which we can study with different techniques and tools. Another source of the constant malicious network traffic we see in the Internet is caused by different kinds of *worms* which spread even years after their first release. Worms are similar compared to bots: they also try to exploit vulnerabilities on other machines and propagate further autonomously, but lack the remote control facility. We can study both kinds of malware utilizing the same methods. Other kinds of malware like for example *spyware*, *rootkits*, or *Trojan Horses* typically do not have the ability to propagate autonomously, thus their prevalence is out of scope of our study.

In this paper, we present the results from studying autonomous spreading malware during an eight week period which lasted from December 2006 to January 2007. We studied the malware prevalence within a typical university environment, in this case the network of RWTH Aachen university, which consists of three class B networks. The study consists of several steps. In the first step, we capture a binary copy of the malware that tries to exploit a vulnerability on our sensor: we use the tool *nepenthes* to simulate 21 different vulnerabilities which are commonly exploited in the wild. Additional information collected by nepenthes allow us to study the extend of malware within our analysis environment. In the second step, we perform a system-level analysis of all collected malware binaries. We study typical system-level changes applied to infected systems and common network-level behavior of compromised machines. Furthermore, we study the reaction times of common antivirus engines, which are supposed to protect end-users against this threat. Moreover, we study the remote control networks used by bots we captured.

This paper is outlined as follows: Section 2 provides an overview of related work which studies different kinds of autonomous spreading malware. In Section 3 we describe our measurement setup and give a brief background on the tools and methods used during our study. We present the analysis results in Section 4, where we focus on four different aspects of autonomous spreading malware. Finally, we give an overview of future work and conclude the paper in Section 5.

2   Related Work

A study similar to our own was conducted by Yegneswaran et al. [21]. They analyze firewall logs collected over a four month period from over 1,600 different networks world wide by contributors of the *Internet Storm Center*. The authors study the distribution, categorization, and prevalence of exploitation attempts. The collected data shows both a large quantity and wide variety of exploitation attempts on a daily basis: the authors estimate that up to 25 billion scan attempts are performed on the whole Internet every day. Furthermore, they observe that worms like Code Red or Nimda still propagate long after their original release. Compared to our study, their study is based on a condensed summary of portscan activity obtained from various firewall and IDS solutions. They do not collect high-level information like for example the malware binary that causes the attack. In our study, we also incorporate this information and thus can study the underlying methods used by the attackers as well.

A study by Moore et al. measures the victims of one particular instance of an autonomous spreading malware [8]. They study the behavior of Code Red and conclude that 359,000 computers became infected with the Code Red worm in less than 14 hours. In a similar study, Moore et al. also analyze the effects of the Slammer worm and concludes that about 75,000 hosts were infected by this malware specimen [7]. These studies only focus on one single instance of autonomous spreading malware, whereas our analysis focuses on an overview of the overall network activity caused by this kind of malware. In total, we study the effects caused by more than 2,000 unique malware binaries collected during the analysis period of eight weeks. A binary is considered unique in this context if it has a different MD5 sum.

Saroiu et al. study the amount and distribution of spyware in a university environment [14]. They analyze four common types of spyware and derive network signatures to detect the presence of this kind of malware. By analyzing a week-long passive trace of network activity, they show that at least 5.1% of active hosts within the campus network were infected with spyware, and that many computers tend to have more than one spyware program running at the same time. A broader study is performed by Moshchuk et al. in a crawler-based study of spyware on the World Wide Web [9]. Similar to Honey-Monkey [18], they crawl large parts of the Web and analyze executables and Web pages for malicious content. During a crawl in May 2005, in which they examined about 18 million URLs, they found executable files in approximately 19% of the crawled Web sites and spyware-infected executables in about 4% of the sites. Moreover, they could identify spyware in 13.4% of the 21,200 executables downloaded. Besides spyware, they are also interested in so called *drive-by* download content, i.e., Web pages that exploit a vulnerability in the visiting browser to install a piece of malware on the victim's machine. By crawling 45,000 URLs from 1,353 domains in October 2005 with an instrumented Web browser instance, they found drive-by download attempts in 0.4% of all URLs examined and drive-by attacks that exploit browser vulnerabilities in 0.2% of the examined URLs. Both studies focus on spyware, a specific kind of malware. By default, spyware does not have the capability to autonomously propagate further. In our study, we focus on malware that has the capability to *autonomously* propagate further. We also examine the additional steps performed by an attacker after he compromised the victim's system by observing the remote control network used by common bots.

There are two studies that measure the prevalence of malware in Peer-to-Peer (P2) networks. Kalafut et al. study malware in the P2P networks Limewire and OpenFT [5], whereas Shin et al. perform a similar study for the KaZaA file-sharing network [15]. In the study by Kalafut et al., they collected data for more than one month and could show that 68% of all downloadable responses in Limewire, which are either executables or archives, contain malware. However, this is caused by only a small amount of distinct malware: the top three most prevalent malware account for 99% of all the malicious responses. In contrast to this, only about 3% of the executables or archives found in OpenFT contained some kind of malware. Again, this is caused by a small number of distinct malware samples: the top three most prevalent malware account for 75% of all the malicious responses. The study by Shin et al. results in some similar conclusions: using a light-weight crawler built for KaZaA, they gathered information about more than 500,000 files returned in response to 24 common query strings. These files were examined with 364 signatures of known malicious programs, and they found that over 15% of the crawled files were infected by 52 different viruses. In contrast to these studies, we study *active* propagation by autonomous spreading malware: the malware binaries we are interested in actively search for vulnerable machines and exploit these vulnerabilities to infect the victim. Propagation via P2P networks is just *passive*: the malware binary copies itself to the shared folder of popular P2P programs and uses promising file names in order to trick a victim to open the malicious binary. No actual vulnerabilities are exploited on the victim's system, but *social engineering* is used by these malware binaries to propagate further.

Rajab et al. use a similar measurement setup to study botnets [12]. They also use nepenthes to collect malware binaries, but their malware analysis approach is significantly different from ours: they use graybox testing to extract only the network fingerprint of the binary and in a second phase they extract IRC-specific information. In contrast to this, we study the *system-level behavior* of the binary by closely monitoring its system activity. This allows us to analyze the collected binaries in more detail. Similar to our study, they also track the remote control facility used by botnets. Rajab et al. just track IRC-based botnets, whereas we also observe botnets that use other protocols for remote control. In addition, we also study other aspects of autonomous spreading malware, e.g., the reaction time of antivirus software or the behavior of malware other than bots.

3   Measurement Setup

In this section, we describe the setup of our study and describe the individual building blocks for the measurement. We use a network-based approach based on *nepenthes* [1] to collect malware binaries. Nepenthes is a *low-interaction honeypot* which aims at capturing malicious software artifacts that spread in an automated manner, like for example worms or bots. The main focus of this application is to get hold of the malware itself, i.e., to download and store a copy of the malware binary itself for further in-depth analysis. Unlike other low-interaction honeypots, nepenthes does not emulate full services for an attacker to interact with: it offers only as much interaction as is needed to exploit a vulnerability. For this reason, nepenthes is not designed for any human interaction, as the trap would be easily detected. On the contrary, for an automated attack, just a few general conditions have to be fulfilled, consequently, maximizing the effectiveness of this approach. These conditions usually include to display the correct banner information of an emulated service, as well as, some simulated commands. Therefore, the resulting service is only partly implemented.

In total, we use 21 different vulnerability modules, corresponding to commonly exploited network services. This is the default setup of nepenthes [1]. These modules provide a baseline for an estimation of the actual amount of autonomous spreading malware in the university network: they are common exploits being used by malware. However, this setup is not complete. There are other methods used by malware to propagate further, e.g., other exploits not emulated by nepenthes or other propagation strategies like e-mail. Therefore, we can only give a lower bound for the amount of autonomous spreading malware in our environment.

The usage of honeypots allows us to carry out a study like this without privacy issues: since the honeypot is just a network decoy which should not receive any network connections at all, any interaction with the honeypot is malicious by definition. We emulate vulnerable network services and only automated threats will successfully compromise our honeypot: a human attacker can easily spot the emulation.

In order to collect as many malware binaries as possible, we assign many IP addresses to the machine running nepenthes. This way, we can on the one hand collect autonomous spreading malware that sequentially exploits other systems. On the other hand, we also have a better chance to collect malware that tries to propagate further by randomly targeting other systems. The network of RWTH Aachen university, our analysis testbed, consists of three class B networks. We assigned more than 16.000 IP addresses from the whole network range to the sensor used in our study.

The sensor itself is running in a virtual machine based on Xen [2] on a Quad-CPU Pentium Xeon system with two virtual CPUs at 2,6 Ghz speed and 1 GB RAM assigned. The operating system used is Debian Linux with MySQL 5 as database software to store the collected information. During the measurement period, we used nepenthes in version 0.2.0 and did not perform any updates, in order to have a constant setup during the whole period. The average load is slightly above 1, depending on whether the antivirus engines are currently scanning or not. This means that the system is using most of its resources to emulate vulnerabilities and download malware binaries. Nepenthes itself uses about 80% of one CPU and an additional 2% to 4% are consumed by the database. A detailed study on the scalability of nepenthes is given in the paper on nepenthes [1].

In addition to the default nepenthes installation, we are running a few customized modifications to gather more detailed and statistical information on the autonomous spreading malware collected. To provide a common platform for the different analysis tools in use, we have developed a custom logging module for nepenthes, which stores all gathered information in a local MySQL database. Among these information are the IP addresses of the hostile hosts, the vulnerability modules which were triggered, the download location of the malware, as well as, the binary itself. The database is used as the basis for all other analysis utilities involved.

One of these analysis utilities is *CWSandbox* [20]. CWSandbox is a tool for *automatic behavior analysis* of malware. In contrast to the traditional approach of code analysis, the malware is viewed as a black box and only its behavior during execution is examined. This eliminates all difficulties and disadvantages of code analysis, as aspects like encryption, packing, and code obfuscation are no more relevant: the binary will decrypt and/or unpack itself and we can observe its behavior during runtime. The main disadvantage of this approach is that only one possible execution path is monitored for each execution and, therefore, analysis reports may be incomplete as not all operations of the monitored process are performed. However, our experience with CWSandbox shows that the generated analysis reports contain commonly enough details to get an overview of what a given malware binary intended to do.

In order to understand the proceeding of CWSandbox, we give a brief overview of the tool. For monitoring the behavior of a suspect file, it is executed in an instrumented Windows environment. All of its security-relevant activities are monitored, and a summarized and high-level report of the collected data is created afterwards. The monitoring, and to some degree also the controlling of the binary, is done by installing *hook functions* on several Windows API functions. Hook functions for instrumenting the following Windows objects, amongst others, exist:

- Filesystem
- Registry
- Processes and threads
- Windows service applications and kernel drivers
- Virtual memory of running processes
- Mutexes
- Windows shares
- COM objects
- Windows of running processes
- Accessing the protected storage

Besides operations on these Windows objects, the following operations are hooked as well, in order to get a more complete overview of the behavior of a given binary:

- implicit and explicit loading of DLLs
- attempt to reboot the system
- sending of ICMP packets
- using the Winsock library to establish TCP/IP connections and send/receive data via them
- retrieving system information like computer name, name of currently logged in user, ...

Each time the malware calls one of these hooked API functions, the call parameters are examined and stored into a log file. In most cases, the hook function then calls the original Windows API function, as it would be called directly by the malware. When returning from this API, the result code is examined as well and then control is delegated back to the supervised process. This whole re-routed control flow is transparent to the malware, i.e., it should *behave* normally, as if it would be running in an uncontrolled environment. There are some exceptions to the handling of the control flow, where either the call parameters of the original API function or its return result are modified by the hook function, or where the API is not called at all. Examples for this are API function that can be used to detect the presence of CWSandbox, or particular network functions, which can be restricted in several ways. For example, we only allow a certain number of outgoing TCP connections and block certain TCP ports completely in order to mitigate the risk involved during analysis.

One focus of the information extracted from an analysis run lies on the detection and recognition of network connections and the extraction of the relevant transmitted data. Therefore, CWSandbox maintains virtual connection objects for each separate network connection, analyzes the corresponding traffic data, and tries to determine the underlying protocol. In the current version, which was extended for this study, the protocols HTTP, FTP, IRC, SMTP, and IDENT can be detected independent of the network port used. If one of these protocols is detected, all relevant protocol-dependent data, like for example the username, password, or channel name used during an IRC session, is extracted and displayed in the analysis report.

As an additional analysis utility, we use four different antivirus scanners to check each of the downloaded binaries every hour for known malware. The resulting reports are also stored in the database. Prior to each scan, the scanners update their virus signatures, thus the results always reflect the latest available signature version. To keep track of changes in malware detection, each binary is always scanned with every antivirus engine. In case the output of a scanner varies from previous results, an additional entry for the affected binary is stored in the database. Thus, for each binary it is possible to determine whether it was detected by a scanner in the first place, how long it took until a new signature version detects the malware, and if a signature update modifies the name of the given malware sample. Therefore, we have some kind of timeline, indicating when a new virus was first recognized by which scanner or if a file, previously identified as virus **A**, is classified as virus **B** after a signature update occurred. The four antivirus scanners which are currently in use are *Avira AntiVir*, *BitDefender AntiVirus*, *Sophos Anti-Virus*, and *Clam AntiVirus*.

As the third analysis utility, we used the tool *botspy* [11]: if the binary collected by nepenthes is a bot or another program which offers a remote control facility, we also want to study this. Botspy is designed to be able to analyze the reports generated by CWSandbox and, if applicable, to track the remote control facility. This is for example accomplished by checking the network traffic section of the analysis report for outgoing IRC connections. Other information extracted from the report include the botnet server address (the so called *Command & Control* (C&C) server), the nickname, the user string, the channel name, and any passwords involved. With this information, botspy is able to connect to the IRC-based C&C server of the botnet and keep track of all instructions issued by the botnet herder. If the remote control facility is not based on IRC, but uses for example HTTP as the control mechanism, botspy periodically downloads the HTTP URL extracted by CWSandbox. Certain kinds of autonomous spreading malware like for example worms do not offer a remote control. In this case, botspy does not do anything. Botspy is designed to be able to track several hundred remote control facilities in parallel and also stores all collected information in a central database.

The whole measurement setup is depicted in Figure 1: with the help of nepenthes, we collect samples of autonomous spreading malware. These samples are then analyzed with the help of CWSandbox which results in a behavior based analysis report.

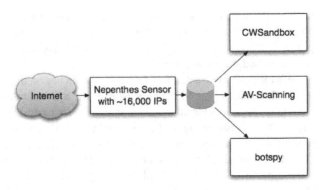

Fig. 1. Schematic Overview of Measurement Setup

In addition, several antivirus engines periodically check all collected samples and collect information about the detection and analysis rates of common antivirus software. Finally, we track the remote control facility of malware (if applicable) with the help of botspy. Thus we collect information about the infrastructure behind all this autonomous spreading malware as well.

Limitation. With the measurement setup outlined in this section, we are able to collect autonomous spreading malware with certain characteristics. First, the malware propagates further by exploiting common vulnerabilities on other systems. We only collect the malware binaries that actually exploit the vulnerabilities we emulate, thus we may miss certain samples. Secondly, we can only study malware that propagates autonomously, thus we miss malware that uses other techniques for propagation. While our measurement setup does not cover the whole range of malware out there, we nevertheless can study typical malware propagation from bots and worms.

4   Analysis of Autonomous Spreading Malware

In this section, we present measurements and analysis results of autonomous spreading malware activity within the network of RWTH Aachen University, Germany. With more than 40,000 computer-using people to support, this network offers us a testbed to study the effects of bots and worms. Our analysis is based on eight weeks of measurement, which took place during December 2006 and January 2007.

The network of RWTH Aachen university consists of three Class B network blocks (three /16 networks in CIDR notation). As noted in the previous section, the nepenthes sensor listens on about 16,000 IP addresses spread all across the network. Most of the IP addresses are grouped in a large block in one Class B network, but we have also taken care of evenly distributing smaller blocks of the sensor IPs all across the network to have a more distributed setup. This is achieved by routing smaller network blocks to the machine on which nepenthes emulates the vulnerabilities. We do not need to install additional software on end-hosts, but use a purely network-based approach.

4.1 Network-Based Analysis Results

With the help of the MySQL logging module for nepenthes, we can keep track of all connections which were established to the sensor. That includes the attacker's IP address, the target IP address and port, as well as, the vulnerability module which was triggered. More than 50 million TCP connections were established during the measurement period. Since the nepenthes sensor is a *honeypot* and has no real value in the network, it should not receive any network connections at all. Thus, the vast majority of these 50 million network connections have a malicious source. On average, more than 900,000 TCP connections were established to the nepenthes sensor per day and about 240,000 known exploits were performed every single day. Thus nepenthes recognized about 27% of all incoming connection attempts and could respond with a correct reply.

The remaining 73% of network connections are mainly caused by scanning attempts: about 75% of these connections target TCP port 80 and search for common vulnerable web applications. An additional 22% contain probe requests used by attackers during the reconnaissance phase in order to identify the network service running on a given target. About 3% of network connections contain a payload that nepenthes could not understand. By manually adding support for these missed exploitation attempts, nepenthes could be enhanced. With approaches like ScriptGen [6], the detection rates could be automatically improved in the future.

A total of more than 13,400,000 times the sensor system was *hit*. This means that so many times a TCP connection was established, the vulnerability emulation was successful, and a malware binary could be downloaded by the sensor. If one host scans linearly the whole measurement range, then we count each of these connections as a separate one. Since this skews the data, we take only the unique hostile IP addresses into account. Roughly 18,340 unique IP addresses caused those hits. Table 1 depicts the sanitized IP addresses of the ten most active attackers together with the according country. As you can see, a small number of IP addresses are responsible for a signification amount of malicious network traffic.

An analysis revealed that the distribution of attacking hosts follows a classical long-tail distribution as depicted in Figure 2. About 9,150 IPs, corresponding to about 50% of the total number of IPs observed, contacted the sensor system less then five times.

Table 1. Top Attacking Hosts with Country of Origin

IP Address:	Country:	Hits:
XXX.178.35.36	Serbia and Montenegro	216.790
XXX.211.83.142	Turkey	156.029
XXX.7.116.4	France	108.013
XXX.147.192.47	United States	107.381
XXX.92.35.23	Norway	94.974
XXX.206.128.27	United States	91.148
XXX.12.234.94	Japan	91.051
XXX.255.1.194	United States	78.455
XXX.92.35.24	Norway	78.439
XXX.29.103.225	United States	77.580

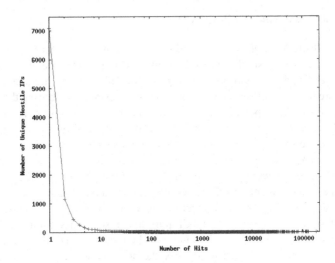

Fig. 2. Distribution of Attacking Hosts

These IPs are presumably infected with some kind of autonomous spreading malware which propagates further by scanning randomly for other victims.

The 18,340 unique IP addresses we monitored during the analysis period connected to different TCP ports on the sensor. The distribution of target ports is very biased, with more than 97% targeting TCP port 445. This port is commonly used by autonomous spreading malware that exploits vulnerabilities on Windows-based systems. Table 2 gives an overview of the distribution.

Table 2. Top Ten TCP Ports Used by Autonomous Spreading Malware

TCP Port Number	Number
445	57,015,106
135	184,695
3127	23,076
80	20,746
42	18,653
139	15,112
1023	14,709
5554	13,880
6129	27
1025	1

Closely related to the distribution of target TCP ports is the type of vulnerabilities exploited. This distribution is also dominated by the most common vulnerability on TCP port 445: the `Lsasrv.dll` vulnerability, commonly referred to as *LSASS*. Table 3 gives an overview of the vulnerability modules triggered and we see a heavy bias towards the Windows vulnerabilities related to network shares.

Table 3. Top Ten Vulnerabilities Detected by Nepenthes

Dialogue	Number
LSASSDialogue	56,652,250
PNPDialogue	361,172
DCOMDialogue	184,696
SasserFTPDDialogue	28,589
MydoomDialogue	23,076
IISDialogue	20,746
WINSDialogue	18,655
NETDDEDialogue	15,112
SMBDialogue	2,341
DWDialogue	27

The 13,4 million downloaded binaries turned out to be 2,558 unique samples. The uniqueness is determined by the MD5 hash of each binary: two binaries that have the same MD5 hash are considered to be the same binary. This is not foolproof due to the recent attacks on MD5, but so far we have no evidence that the attacking community has released different binaries with the same MD5 hash. On the other hand, this is also no strong indicator for uniqueness: if the malware binary is polymorphic, i.e., it changes with each iteration, we collect many samples which in fact are very similar. In the middle of December 2006, such a polymorphic bot was released in the form of *All.aple* worm. Unfortunately, we missed this particular worm since nepenthes could not analyze the payload send by this worm. In Section 4.2 we show preliminary results on how we can identify similar malware binaries based on behavior.

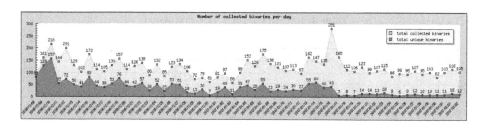

Fig. 3. Chronological Analysis of Collected Malware Binaries

The number of collected samples result in an average of one unique malware binary every 5,240 hits. Considering the number of successful exploits per day, this results in almost 46 new binaries every 24 hours. Figure 3 gives an overview of the chronological sequence for the number of collected binaries and number of unique binaries. The number of collected binary varies from day to day, ranging between 58 and 281. There are several spikes in this measurement, but no reason for these anomalies could be identified. The situation is slightly different for the number of unique binaries: in the first few days, the number of unique binaries collected per day is high, whereas this number drops after about six weeks. It seems like there is some kind of *saturation*: in the beginning, the number of unique binaries is significantly higher then in the end of the measurement period. After a certain period of time we have collected the commonly propagating malware in the measurement network and only a few new binaries are collected per day. This number varies between 6 and 16, presumably corresponding to new malware binaries released by attackers.

4.2   CWSandbox Analysis Results

In this section, we present some quantitative statistics about the analysis results of our malware collection. It should be mentioned that our collection cannot give a representative overview of current malware on the whole Internet, as on the one hand, the sample set size is not large enough and, on the other hand, it contains *only* autonomous spreading applications like bots and worms. However, for this particular subset of malicious activity, our measurement setup can give us an overview of the current threat level for a typical university environment.

From the overall collected 2,454 sample files, 2,034 could be analyzed correctly by CWSandbox, 1 failed due to a crash and 419 were no valid Win32 applications. This means that in roughly 17% of the collected samples, the resulting file was not valid. This can be explained by aborted transfers or disrupted network connectivity. One additional file of the remaining 2034 had a valid PE header, but could not be correctly initialized by the Windows Loader due to an ACCESS_VIOLATION_EXCEPTION. Each successful analysis resulted in an XML analysis report, which reflects all the security-relevant operations performed by the particular file. As we are not interested in a detailed malware analysis for single file instances in this paper, we present quantitative results extracted from the 2034 valid reports. The main focus of our statistics lies on network activities, but a few other important results are presented as well.

Table 4. Top Ten Outgoing TCP Ports Used

Remote TCP port	# samples
445	1312
80	821
139	582
3127	527
6667	403
6659	346
65520	143
7000	30
8888	28
443	16

1,993 of the 2,034 valid malware samples tried to establish some form of TCP/IP connection, either outgoing, incoming (i.e., listening connections) or both. Besides DNS requests, we have not found any single malware in our set that uses only UDP directly. 1,216 binaries were successful in the attempt to setup an outgoing TCP connection. For all the others, the remote host was not reachable or refused the connection for some other reason. Altogether, 873 different TCP remote ports have been used for outbound connection attempts, and Table 4 shows the top ten of them. Although CWSandbox is able to recognize the content of a TCP connection and infer the application protocol used, these results are not shown in this document for complexity reasons. However, it is highly probable that most connections on port 445 and 139 are aiming on further malware propagation, port 80 and 443 are used for HTTP(s) connections, 6667, 66520, 7000, 6659, and 8888 are used for IRC communication, and finally, 3127 is a backdoor of *MyDoom*.

Table 5. Top Five Listening TCP Ports Used

Local TCP port	# samples
113	497
3067	122
80	9
5554	7
1023	6

Furthermore, we have found 1,297 samples that install a TCP server for incoming connections, most of them setting up an IDENT server on port 113 for supporting IRC connections. In Table 5, the top five listening local TCP ports are presented.

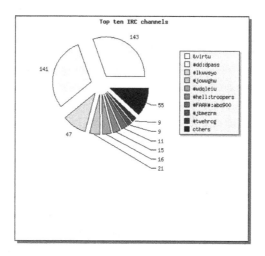

Fig. 4. Distribution of IRC Channel:Password Combinations

Since most bots rely on IRC communication, a deeper investigation of these connections is necessary. 505 samples could successfully establish a connection to an IRC server. Moreover, 352 files tried to send IRC commands over an *unestablished* connection. The reason for that is most probably bad software design. 349 of these files are variants of *GhostBot*, the other 3 are *Korgo* worms. Furthermore, we have

96 samples that try to connect to a remote host on TCP port 6667 or 7000 and fail. Adding these numbers, we have at least 953 files which try or are successful in setting up an IRC connection. The corresponding samples are most probably IRC bots. We cannot know, how many of these different binaries belong to the same bot variant or even to the same botnet. However, by taking the remote IP address, remote TCP port, IRC channel name and IRC channel password into account, we can give some estimations. This is a good indication for uniqueness: if a given binary uses the same tuple of network parameters, we can be sure that it is the same variant, although the MD5 sum of these binaries is different. Of all established IRC connections, 64 different *host:port:channel:channelpassword*-combinations have been used. As the host IP for a botnet may change, we generalize the results to the different *channel:channelpassword*-combinations and assume that each of those represent a different botnet or at least a different bot family. By generalizing the number of different combinations decreases down to 41. The most common channels are *&virtu (no password)* and *dd (password "dpass")* with 143 and 141 samples, respectively. These samples have a different MD5 sum, but based on their network behavior we argue that they are very similar. An overview of these results is given in Figure 4. Please note that all the combinations with only one corresponding malware sample are aggregated into *others*.

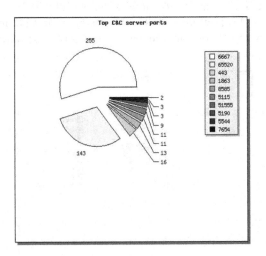

Fig. 5. TCP Ports Used for IRC Connections

When looking at the different remote TCP ports which are used for establishing an IRC connection, we see that not only the default IRC port 6667 is used, but many more. It is interesting to see that, beside some probably random ports, a lot of well known ports of other well-known protocols are used, e.g., port 80 (HTTP), port 443 (HTTPS) or port 1863 (MSN). This allows the bot to communicate through a firewall that is open for these standard protocols. Thus it is necessary to also closely observe these port when thinking about vulnerability assessment. Figure 5 shows a distribution diagram of the TCP ports observed during the study.

Table 6. Services and Kernel Drivers Installed by Collected Malware Samples

Servicename	Filename (base directory is C:\Windows\)	Kernel driver	# samples
SVKP	system32\SVKP.sys	x	15
DLLHOST32	system\dllhost.exe		8
WINHOST32	system\services.exe		2
Print Spooler	system32\spooler.exe		1
hwclock	system32\hwclock.exe		1
oreans32	system32\drivers\oreans32.sys	x	1
Windows System 32	services.exe	x	1
Windows Terminal Services	system32\vcmon.exe		1
Advanced Windows Tray	system32\vcmon.exe		1
Windows MSN	wmsnlivexp.exe		1
Windows Process Manager	system32\spoolsc.exe		1
mside	system\mside.exe		1
TCP Monitor Manager	system32\symon.exe		1
Client Disk Manager	system32\symon.exe		1
Monitor Disk Manager	system32\spoolcs.exe		1
System Restore Manager	system32\symon.exe		1

As already mentioned above, a few other interesting, system-level related results can be drawn from our analysis reports as well. After infecting a new host, nearly all malware tries to install some auto-start mechanism, such that it is activated each time the infected system reboots. This is commonly done by adding some auto-start registry keys, but some malware install a *Windows Service Application* or even a *kernel driver*. By doing that, it is much harder to detect the presence of malware. Especially in the case of kernel drivers, the malware binaries can get higher security privileges on the local system. Table 6 provides an overview of the services and kernel drivers installed by the samples we collected. In total, 21 of our collected files install a service application and 17 install a kernel driver. Since some of these binaries use the same servicename and filename for the given processes, we can learn that these were most probably installed by variants of the same malware family.

Table 7. Injection Target Processes Observed for Collected Malware Samples

Injection target process (base directory is C:\Windows\)	# samples
explorer.exe	787
system32\winlogon.exe **and** explorer.exe	101
system32\winlogon.exe	74

The observed system-level behavior can also be used to classify malware samples: if two binaries with a different MD5 sum behave similarly, we can argue that these samples belong to the same family of malware. There are several features we can use for classification. One is the registry keys created during the analysis: 1,842 samples created a registry key of the form *HKLM\Software\Microsoft\CurrentVersion\Run* in order to have an auto-start mechanism. A closer analysis revealed that only 283 unique registry keys were created, taking into account randomly created names.

As a final statistic result, Table 7 shows a summary of the windows processes, into which the malware samples injected malicious code. It is a common approach to create a new thread (or modify an existing one) in an unsuspicious windows process, e.g., `explorer.exe` or `winlogon.exe`, and perform all malicious operations from that thread. Via this proceeding, the malware becomes more stealthy and, furthermore, circumvents local firewalls or other security software that allows network connections only for trusted applications.

4.3   Antivirus Engines Detection Rates

In order to evaluate the performance of current antivirus (AV) engines, we scanned all 2,034 binaries, which we had captured with nepenthes and successfully analyzed with CWSandbox, with four common antivirus engines. This helps us to estimate the detection rate for common autonomous spreading malware and also for vulnerability assessment. These binaries are currently spreading in the wild, exploited a vulnerability in our measurement system, and could be successfully captured. In contrast to common antivirus engine evaluation tests, which rely on artificial test sets, our test set represents malware successfully spreading in the wild.

Table 8. Detection Rates for 2,034 Malware Binaries for Different AV Scanners

AV software	Absolute detection number	Relative detection rate
AntiVir	2015	99.07%
ClamAV	1963	96.51%
BitDefender	1864	91.64%
Sophos	1790	88.00%

Table 8 displays the current detection rates of each scanner with the latest signature version installed. This scan was performed one week after the measurement period, in order to give AV vendors some additional time to develop signatures and incorporate them into their products. Nevertheless, none of the tools was able to detect all malicious files and classify them accordingly. The malware reports vary significantly from one tool to another. Figure 6 gives an overview of the detected malware binaries by the four different antivirus engines.

We focus on the ClamAV results in the following and analyze the different malware families more closely. ClamAV detected 137 different *malware variants* in the test set of 2,034 samples. In total, 27 different *families* of malware could be identified. Table 9 gives an overview of the top ten different malware variants. Two families of malware clearly dominate the result: *Padobot* and *Gobot* are the two main autonomous spreading malware families we could observe within our measurement environment.

Besides these two families, also many other forms of autonomous spreading malware are currently spreading in the wild. Although Padobot and Gobot dominate the list of malware variants, the largest number of different variants was captured for *SdBot*: 35 different variants of the same family could be captured, whereas Padobot (14) and Gobot (8) had significantly less different variants.

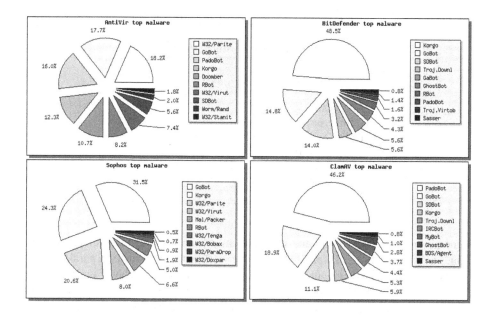

Fig. 6. Malware Variants Detected by Different Antivirus Engines

Some of the malware binaries are already known for a long time. For example, the first variants of *Blaster* were observed in the wild in August 2003. More than three years later, we captured four different variants of Blaster which are still propagating in the Internet. Similarly, three different variants of *Sasser* were captured during the measurement period. We conclude that there are still systems on the Internet which are infected for a long time, helping "old" malware binaries to propagate further.

4.4 Botspy Analysis Results

With the help of botspy, we can study the remote control networks used by the autonomous spreading malware: in case we have captured a bot, it connects to this remote control network so that the attacker can send him commands. We just want to briefly present our results when tracking these botnets for a short amount of time.

In total, we could observe 41 different botnet Command & Control (C&C) servers. Again, this behavior can be used to classify malware samples: if two binaries connect to the same C&C server, we can argue that they are similar despite the fact that they have a different MD5 sum. For example, 149 binaries connected to the IP address XXX.174.8.243 (home.najd.us). The system-level behavior of these samples is also very similar, so presumably these are just minor variants of the same malware family.

When connecting to the botnets, we could observe 33 different topics in the channel used to command the bots. The most common command used by the bot herder was related to propagation: most bots are instructed to scan for other vulnerable machines and exploit vulnerabilities on these systems. An example of such an instruction is !asc dcom135 150 3 0 -r -b -s, where the bots try to exploit the DCOM

Table 9. Top Ten Different Malware Variants

Malware Variant	Number of Samples
Worm.Padobot.M	426
Worm.Padobot.P	274
Trojan.Gobot-3	118
Trojan.Gobot-4	106
Worm.Padobot.N	101
Trojan.Downloader.Delf-35	100
Trojan.IRCBot-16	76
Trojan.Gobot.A	61
Trojan.Ghostbot.A	53
Trojan.Gobot.T	37

vulnerability on TCP port 135 and scan randomly (parameter -r) for vulnerable machines in their local class B (parameter -b) network with 150 threads in parallel. This is done for an unlimited amount of time (parameter 0) and with a delay of three seconds (parameter 3). More and more common are botnets that use non-standard IRC or encrypted communication mechanisms. For example, the command sent by the bot-herder to the bots could be an encrypted string. In total, we found 10 different botnets that use encrypted, IRC-based communication. Without a proper decryption routine, it is hard to study this kind of botnets. Currently it is unclear how we can efficiently study this kind of botnets.

Estimating the size of a given botnet is hard [13]. One possibility to estimate the size is to rely on the statistics reported by the C&C server upon connect: if the IRC server is not configured properly, it reports the number of connected clients. Moreover, we can query the server for the number of connected clients and various other status messages. Based on these numbers, the typical botnet size in our sample set varied between only a few hundred up to almost 10,000 bots.

Besides the IRC-based bots, we also found several samples of HTTP-based bots. These bots periodically query a given HTTP server and the response contains commands which are executed by the bot. Due to the rather stealthy communication channel of such bots, detection becomes harder. In addition, measuring the size of such a botnet is hard since we can only passively monitor the HTTP server. In total, we could identify three different botnets that use HTTP-based communication.

5   Conclusion and Future Work

In this paper, we have introduced a measurement method to study autonomous spreading malware in a university environment. We use several tools and techniques to capture a malware binary and then analyze the sample in detail. Based on this information, we can derive an overview of the current situation of network attacks. Moreover, we can study the typical system-level behavior of malware binaries and their activity after a successful infection. Based on more than 13,4 million downloads and 2,000 malware binaries, we presented several statistics and patterns to point out the current prevalence of malware on the Internet.

Some of the tools used in this paper can also be used in other areas. As a future research, we examine how a behavior-based analysis can be used for automated malware classification: the main problem in the area of automatic malware comparison and classification is that nowadays nearly all malware files are encrypted, compressed, or even use polymorphism to complicate their analysis and to fool signature based anti-virus software. Two versions of the very same malware may result in completely different binaries, when encrypted with different algorithms or encryption parameters. Therefore, one needs to decrypt and/or unpack the binaries before classification, which is not a trivial task. For that reason, the analysis reports created by CWSandbox are very helpful in comparing and classifying malware based on their *behavior* instead of their *code*. It is obvious that the behavior analysis of two different binary representations of the same application will result in the same, or at least very similar, reports. At the moment, we have no automated mechanisms to reduce CWSandbox analysis reports to such a high level of summarization, such that they can be compared directly. There are still a lot of side effects contained in the reports, that differ between several Windows operating systems or system environments. In the next months, we plan to build a system for *behavior-based malware classification*, in order to extend the results presented here.

With our current method, we can not study malware that uses other propagation vectors like e-mails or P2P-based propagation. With different other honeypot solution like for example *client-side honeypots* or *crawler-based honeypots* it should be possible to fill this gap and also study other kinds of malware.

Acknowledgments

We would like to thank the anonymous reviewers and our shepherd Marc Dacier for helpful feedback on earlier versions of this paper.

References

1. Baecher, P., Koetter, M., Holz, T., Dornseif, M., Freiling, F.C.: The nepenthes platform: An efficient approach to collect malware. In: Zamboni, D., Kruegel, C. (eds.) RAID 2006. LNCS, vol. 4219, pp. 165–184. Springer, Heidelberg (2006)
2. Barham, P., Dragovic, B., Fraser, K., Hand, S., Harris, T., Ho, A., Neugebauer, R., Pratt, I., Warfield, A.: Xen and the art of virtualization. In: Proceedings of the 19th ACM Symposium on Operating Systems Principles, pp. 164–177 (2003)
3. Cymru, T.: The underground economy: Priceless. login 31(6) (2007)
4. Grizzard, J.B., Sharma, V., Nunnery, C., Kang, B.B., Dagon, D.: Peer-to-peer botnets: Overview and case study. In: Proceedings of 1st Workshop on Hot Topics in Understanding Botnets (HotBots '07) (2007)
5. Kalafut, A., Acharya, A., Gupta, M.: A study of malware in peer-to-peer networks. In: IMC '06: Proceedings of the 6th ACM SIGCOMM Internet Measurement Conference, pp. 327–332 (2006)
6. Leita, C., Dacier, M., Massicotte, F.: Automatic handling of protocol dependencies and reaction to 0-day attacks with scriptgen based honeypots. In: Zamboni, D., Kruegel, C. (eds.) RAID 2006. LNCS, vol. 4219, pp. 185–205. Springer, Heidelberg (2006)

7. Moore, D., Paxson, V., Savage, S., Shannon, C., Staniford, S., Weaver, N.: Inside the slammer worm. IEEE Security and Privacy 1(4), 33–39 (2003)
8. Moore, D., Shannon, C., claffy, k: Code-red: A case study on the spread and victims of an internet worm. In: MW '02: Proceedings of the 2nd ACM SIGCOMM Workshop on Internet Measurment, pp. 273–284. ACM Press, New York (2002)
9. Moshchuk, A., Bragin, T., Gribble, S.D., Levy, H.M.: A crawler-based study of spyware in the web. In: Proceedings of 13th Network and Distributed System Security Symposium (NDSS'06) (2006)
10. BBC News. Criminals 'may overwhelm the web'. Internet Accessed February 2007 (February 2007) http://news.bbc.co.uk/1/hi/business/6298641.stm
11. Claus, R.F.: Overbeck. Efficient Observation of Botnets. Master's thesis, RWTH Aachen University (May 2007)
12. Rajab, M.A., Zarfoss, J., Monrose, F., Terzis, A.: A multifaceted approach to understanding the botnet phenomenon. In: IMC '06: Proceedings of the 6th ACM SIGCOMM Internet Measurement Conference, pp. 41–52 (2006)
13. Rajab, M.A., Zarfoss, J., Monrose, F., Terzis, A.: My botnet is bigger than yours (maybe, better than yours): Why size estimates remain challenging. In: Proceedings of 1st Workshop on Hot Topics in Understanding Botnets (HotBots '07) (2007)
14. Saroiu, S., Gribble, S.D., Levy, H.M.: Measurement and analysis of spyware in a university environment. In: Proceedings of Networked Systems Design and Implementation (NSDI'04), San Francisco, California, United States (2004)
15. Shin, S., Jung, J., Balakrishnan, H.: Malware prevalence in the kazaa file-sharing network. In: IMC '06: Proceedings of the 6th ACM SIGCOMM Internet Measurement Conference, pp. 333–338 (2006)
16. The Honeynet Project. Know Your Enemy: Tracking Botnets (March 2005) http://www.honeynet.org/papers/bots/
17. New York Times. Attack of the zombie computers is growing threat. Internet (January 2007) http://www.nytimes.com/2007/01/07/technology/07net.html
18. Wang, Y.-M., Beck, D., Jiang, X., Roussev, R., Verbowski, C., Chen, S., King, S.T.: Automated web patrol with strider honeymonkeys: Finding web sites that exploit browser vulnerabilities. In: Proceedings of 13th Network and Distributed System Security Symposium (NDSS'06) (2006)
19. McAfee Whitepaper. Adware and spyware: Unraveling the financial web. Internet: Accessed February 2007 (August 2006) http://www.mcafee.com/us/local_content/white_papers/threat_center/wp_ad ware.pdf
20. Willems, C., Holz, T., Freiling, F.: CWSandbox: Towards automated dynamic binary analysis. IEEE Security and Privacy 5(2) (2007)
21. Yegneswaran, V., Barford, P., Ullrich, J.: Internet intrusions: Global characteristics and prevalence. In: SIGMETRICS '03: Proceedings of the 2003 ACM SIGMETRICS International Conference on Measurement and Modeling of Computer Systems, pp. 138–147. ACM Press, New York (2003)

Passive Monitoring of DNS Anomalies
(Extended Abstract)

Bojan Zdrnja[1], Nevil Brownlee[1], and Duane Wessels[2]

[1] University of Auckland, New Zealand
{b.zdrnja,nevil}@auckland.ac.nz
[2] The Measurement Factory, Inc.
wessels@packet-pushers.com

Abstract. We collected DNS responses at the University of Auckland Internet gateway in an SQL database, and analyzed them to detect unusual behaviour. Our DNS response data have included typo squatter domains, fast flux domains and domains being (ab)used by spammers. We observe that current attempts to reduce spam have greatly increased the number of A records being resolved. We also observe that the data locality of DNS requests diminishes because of domains advertised in spam.

1 Introduction

The Domain Name System (DNS) service is critical for the normal functioning of almost all Internet services. Although the Internet Protocol (IP) does not need DNS for operation, users need to distinguish machines by their names so the DNS protocol is needed to resolve names to IP addresses (and vice versa).

The main requirements on the DNS are scalability and availability. The DNS name space is divided into multiple zones, which are a "variable depth tree" [1]. This way, a particular DNS server is authoritative only for its (own) zone, and each organization is given a specific zone in the DNS hierarchy. A complete domain name for a node is called a Fully Qualified Domain Name (FQDN). An FQDN defines a complete path for a domain name starting on the leaf (the host name) all the way to the root of the tree. Each node in the tree has its label that defines the zone. An example of an FQDN is "www.auckland.ac.nz.". A domain is a subdomain when it is contained in another domain; in the previous example "auckland.ac.nz" is a subdomain of "ac.nz".

As DNS is not centrally controlled, the domain names can be abused by attackers outside any organization. Besides domain name trading, attackers can shift domain name records quickly, making access blocking difficult. Another advantage for attackers is that from the client point of view security is often relaxed around DNS traffic, even in tightly controlled organizational networks. Most organizations have strict firewall policies at least on their perimeter firewalls, but DNS traffic is usually unrestricted because it is used by many other protocols. Attackers are commonly abusing this fact, not only to covertly send data over DNS, but also to deploy rogue DNS servers that can be used to completely control victim's Internet behavior.

B. M. Hämmerli and R. Sommer (Eds.): DIMVA 2007, LNCS 4579, pp. 129–139, 2007.
© Springer-Verlag Berlin Heidelberg 2007

This paper describes a passive DNS anomaly detection project based on data captured at the University of Auckland Internet gateway. Our original motivation for deploying the passive DNS monitor was to detect and correlate domains used for botnet controls. We quickly realized that the database is also a rich source of information about spam, anti-spamming tools, typosquatting, and other anomalies.

2   Related Work

Florian Weimer presented a passive DNS replication project at the FIRST 2005 conference [17]. As a result of his project a web site was established by RUS CERT [2] that allows public access to data collected "from the public Domain Name Service (DNS) system." Weimer's software, *dnslogger* consists of sensors deployed around a network that send captured DNS responses to a central collection service. Sensors encapsulate captured DNS responses in new UDP packets which are then relayed (in real time) to the collector. The collector analyzes received UDP packets and imports them into a database. Weimer's passive DNS replication project is very similar to the one deployed at the University of Auckland, however, our setup is simpler and our database stores more information, for a longer period of time.

The University of Amsterdam [3] based their DNS capture project on Weimer's work. Schonewille et al modified Weimer's program to capture outgoing DNS queries in order to identify machines in the local network that have been compromised. Malware-infected machines tend to emit DNS queries that allow them to be easily identified.

John Kristoff's DNSwatch [4] software can be used in a similar manner, as described by Elton et al [5], but it requires an external black list of well known malicious IP addresses (servers used to spread malware or contacted by malware).

3   Data Capture Methodology

DNS traffic uses either UDP or TCP on port 53 for communication [7]. Most DNS communication happens over UDP, which is the default protocol used by resolvers, i.e. applications that communicate with DNS servers on behalf of other applications when they need to resolve a DNS query. TCP was originally used only for zone transfers, but RFC 1123 [18] expanded the use of TCP as a backup communication protocol when the answer needs to be larger than 512 octets. In cases like this, the first UDP DNS response contains only partial answers. The truncation bit is set so that the resolver can repeat the query over TCP. However, RFC 2671, "EDNS0" [19], defined a new opcode field/pseudo resource record that allows UDP DNS traffic to be bigger than 512 octets. Because almost all of today's DNS traffic uses UDP as its transport protocol, the deployment at the University of Auckland ignores TCP traffic.

DNS data is captured passively by sensors at the network edge, using an architecture designed to make implementation of sensors as simple as possible. A sensor is connected to a router SPAN port in order to get complete access to all network traffic. Sensors run *tcpdump*, configured to write captured packets to a pcap file. Since we are only interested in DNS messages, we used the following *tcpdump* filter: `udp port 53 and ( udp[10] & 0x04 != 0 )`

Note that our filter only captures UDP DNS replies from authoritative sources, since we filter on their 'Authoritative Answer' bit [7]. We ignore TCP (for now) to simplify our parsing code, and because we observe relatively little TCP DNS traffic at the router. Since DNS replies always include the query data (in the Question section), there is little need to also collect DNS queries. Alas, our filter can cause some problems on certain large responses. If the DNS reply is larger than the path MTU, the UDP message will be fragmented. If that occurs, the first fragment usually contains enough information for anomaly detection.

Since our sensor is placed at the network perimeter, we see two types of DNS responses: those destined for the University's local caching resolvers, and responses leaving the University's own authoritative nameservers. The former are most interesting for our purposes here, but we did not attempt to filter out the latter from our database.

The sensors have a cron job that runs every hour. First, a new *tcpdump* process is launched. Then, the existing *tcpdump* process is killed. The pcap file containing data from the previous hour is compressed and sent to the collector.

Our database resides on the collector. The database holds only collected DNS data relevant for our research. The relevant data includes:

- Query name (name of the original query)
- Resource Record (RR) type (query type [7], ie A for address records)
- Resource Record data (answer returned by the authoritative DNS server)
- TTL (Time To Live) – value in seconds, set by the authoritative server, that allows the client DNS server or resolver to cache the answer
- First Seen Timestamp – timestamp showing when our sensor first saw this record

Rows in the database correspond to resource records in the Answer section of the DNS reply. We do not store records from the Authority or Additional sections.

Incoming pcap files are preprocessed by a program that unpacks the DNS messages and removes any duplicate entries. Duplicates typically occur for popular names with short TTLs. Since the only timestamp in our database is the First Seen column, a duplicate answer does not update the database and can be safely discarded. The collector runs on a system with an Intel Pentium 4D 3GHz processor and 2 GB of RAM. During peak times the collector imports 270,000 DNS messages in approximately 3 minutes.

Our sensors and collector have been running at the University of Auckland since 15 May 2006. As of 15th of January 2007 we have 260 GB of raw DNS data (uncompressed pcap files) and 50 million DNS records in the database. We archive raw pcap files on the collector, but only after zeroing out the source and destination IP addresses with Minshall's tcpdpriv utility [8].

4 Results

4.1 Collected Data

Captured DNS data shows a high number of NX (non existent) DNS domains. Fig. 1 shows received authoritative DNS replies for the University of Auckland sensor, with separate traces showing nonexistant domain (NX) responses and "valid" (see Table 1) responses. The month of September 2006 exhibits a very

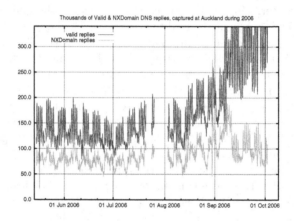

Fig. 1. Authoritative DNS replies captured at Auckland in 2006

different pattern from the previous months. During this month (and several months later), the University of Auckland network was flooded with incoming spam e-mail messages. Since the deployed anti-spam system tries to resolve all domain names and IP addresses seen in e-mail messages, this resulted in a huge increase in processed DNS replies.

4.2 Resource Record Type Prevalence

The current version of the dnsparse application running on the collector can successfully parse 15 resource record types. These types were identified as most commonly used in the first two weeks of captured data. Table 1 shows the distribution by resource record type of valid DNS response records in the collected data.

4.3 Impact of Anti-spam Tools on the DNS System

Table 1 shows that address (A) resource records are responses to the majority of queries. While Jung et al [9] attributed this type of behaviour to user activities (web site browsing) our analysis shows that the biggest contributors to a high rate of A queries are anti spam engines. Spam detection depends

Table 1. Distribution of resource record types in DNS replies (answer section only)

RR type	Number of records	Percentage
A (1)	24096932	57.00
NS (2)	757825	1.79
CNAME (5)	652126	1.54
SOA (6)	16281	0.04
PTR (12)	11261024	26.64
MX (15)	2433120	5.76
TXT (16)	3047556	7.21
AAAA (28)	2202	0.005
SRV (33)	705	0.002
Total:	42267771	100%

on DNS to retrieve data from various real time black lists (RBLs). Spam software installed at the University of Auckland includes SpamAssassin, which will query several RBLs by default. For every domain detected in a message that is scanned, SpamAssassin will attempt to resolve it by issuing an A query for the domain in question. If the domain is successfully resolved, SpamAssassin will query various RBLs in order to determine if the IP address has been blacklisted as sending spam. Queries to RBLs are also A type queries and answers. Depending on whether the tested IP address is present in the block list or not, the RBL DNS server will either return an authoritative DNS response in the 127.0.0.0/8 range (various codes are used, depending on the queried block list) or a "no such record" (NX) response. The database contains 12.2 million resource records that were responses to RBL queries. This accounts for 29% of all valid DNS responses received by the University of Auckland. We believe that this number is even higher for NX domain responses. The number of TXT resource records, while not very high, is also related to e-mail processing. The gateway at

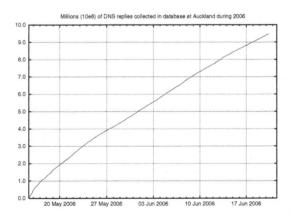

Fig. 2. Size of the database (distinct FQDNs) at Auckland during 2006

the University of Auckland uses SPF [10] to verify whether the e-mail sender's address has been spoofed, and SPF uses TXT resource records to list legitimate e-mail servers for a particular domain.

Figure 2 shows the size of our database as more FQDNs were added to it during 2006. Clearly, the database growth shows no sign of slowing; further evidence that spammers continue to fill DNS with more and more domains.

4.4 Typo Squatter Domains

Typo squatting is based on incorrect URLs entered by end users in their browsers. Mistyping of domains is very common and can be generally divided into several categories [11]:

- Spelling mistakes (www.aukcland.ac.nz or www.aukland.ac.nz)
- Typing mistakes (www.eikipedia.org)
- Top-level domain appending(www.auckland.ac.nz.com) [12]

We found, by manual inspection, several highly exposed typo squatting domains in the database. Some of these are shown in Tables 2 and 3. The IP address shown in Table 2 hosted 1377 domain names, all of which were typo squatter domains. The content on all hosted web sites was the same and consisted of a search engine with various advertisements. Microsoft recently published a list of temporarily unused (parked) typo squatting domains as a result of the Strider URL Tracer with Typo-Patrol [13].

Table 2. Typo squatting domains based on mistyped words

DNS query	Answer	RR type	Entry added	TTL
www.gmaio.com	64.20.33.131	A	16/5/2006	7200
openopffice.org	64.20.33.131	A	17/5/2006	7200
www.forcasts.org	64.20.33.131	A	18/5/2006	7200
www.hontmail.com	64.20.33.131	A	19/5/2006	7200
www.eikipedia.org	64.20.33.131	A	19/5/2006	7200
economist.com	64.20.33.131	A	23/5/2006	7200

A lot of typo squatter domains that have been identified in our database use wildcard DNS records. As wild card DNS zones allow an administrator to setup resolution of any query in the zone he is controlling (for example, a "*.auk-land.ac.nz" wildcard shown below will return the same response for any query for a host or subdomain in the aukland.ac.nz domain), all records that have been collected for such zones are directly a result of end users' activities. While the investigation of detected typo squatter domains targeting large populations (such as those targeting Wikipedia or University of Auckland) did not reveal any malicious activities, the risk associated with them is high as users who mistyped a subdomain rely on visual detection. Using cryptographic technologies for verification, such as SSL, is also of no help in this example if the attacker can install

Table 3. Typo squatter domains attacking University of Auckland users

DNS query	Answer	RR type	Entry added	TTL
aukland.ac.nz	70.85.154.28	A	16/5/2006	43200
aukland.ac.nz	64.111.218.142	A	22/12/2006	43200
www.aukland.ac.nz	aukland.ac.nz	CNAME	16/5/2006	43200
www.cs.aukland.ac.nz	aukland.ac.nz	CNAME	17/5/2006	43200
webmail.ec.aukland.ac.nz	aukland.ac.nz	CNAME	29/5/2006	43200
gateway.aukland.ac.nz	aukland.ac.nz	CNAME	18/7/2006	43200

a SSL certificate for the hosted, typo squatter domain. In such an attack, the victim would have to detect the mistyped URL in order to detect the attack.

4.5   Fast Flux Domains

Fast flux DNS domains are those that have rapidly changing resource records. They also typically have low TTLs. Fast flux DNS domains are typically used for command and control servers [14] by worms. Once a target machine has been infected, it will talk to a central command and control server for further instructions (other stages of malware download, attacks etc.). To prevent easy location and take-down of the control and command server, attackers hard code a DNS domain in malware and frequently change the IP address it points to. This makes address-based perimeter network control of infected machines difficult as an administrator can not block IP traffic towards a particular IP address. Instead, an administrator needs to block access to a certain domain name, which can be done only on the main DNS server in an organization.

We have also observed another typical use of fast flux DNS domains, on web sites running on compromised machines. Spamming operations typically use fast flux domains to change IP addresses of the target web sites per different spam runs. The domain shown in table 4 was used only for three days, for a limited

Table 4. Fast flux domain records

DNS query	Answer	RR type	Entry added	TTL
contryloansnow.com	82.155.116.90	A	22/5/2006 07:52:15	5
contryloansnow.com	80.192.79.212	A	22/5/2006 07:52:17	5
contryloansnow.com	217.209.81.86	A	22/5/2006 08:21:18	5
contryloansnow.com	62.167.58.207	A	22/5/2006 08:22:21	5
contryloansnow.com	68.85.56.47	A	22/5/2006 08:22:24	5
contryloansnow.com	193.77.253.115	A	22/5/2006 08:25:07	5

spam run and changed its IP address 80 times. By reverse resolving IP addresses and geographically locating them we see (table 5) that they are scattered around the world and mainly located on cable/DSL line connected machines. Fast flux DNS domains can be detected by deploying external agents that query the database and sort results by number of associated resource records in various time

Table 5. PTR records and geographical location of hosts used for a fast flux domain

IP address	PTR record(s)	Geographical location
82.155.116.90	bl6-116-90.dsl.telepac.pt	Portugal, Europe
80.192.79.212	80-192-79-212.cable.ubr01.edin.blueyonder.co.uk	U.K., Europe
217.209.81.86	h86n2fls33o1110.telia.com	Sweden, Europe
62.167.58.207	adsl-62-167-58-207.adslplus.ch	Switzerland, Europe
68.85.56.47	c-68-85-56-47.hsd1.ga.comcast.net	United States
193.77.253.115	BSN-77-253-115.dial-up.dsl.siol.net	Slovenia, Europe

intervals. This way it is possible to detect potentially malicious DNS domains, if a certain threshold has been reached. TTL will generally have a low value for fast flux domains as the attacker needs client machines to resolve the domain name frequently, otherwise they will try to connect to the old cached IP addresses.

4.6   Anomalous Records

Sorting the captured records by various criteria can be used to detect unusual records or activities. While searching for records with low TTL values can generally be useful in detection of fast flux domains, in order to detect anomalous records we need to perform a full database search.

A typical abuse can be detected by sorting DNS names (queries) by number of associated responses. Besides easy detection of fast flux domains, which will have hundreds, and sometimes thousands, of associated A records, this method detected some anomalous activities, as shown in Table 6, for the ntc.net.pk domain. The ntc.net.pk domain has in total 1319 A records associated. It is

Table 6. DNS records for ntc.net.pk domain

DNS query	Answer	RR type	Entry added	TTL
ntc.net.pk	202.83.160.238	A	15/5/2006 22:15:27	15
ntc.net.pk	202.83.168.98	A	16/5/2006 11:16:17	15
ntc.net.pk	202.83.168.7	A	16/5/2006 15:34:34	15
ntc.net.pk	202.83.174.29	A	16/5/2006 15:39:53	15
ntc.net.pk	202.83.175.65	A	16/5/2006 15:40:17	15
ntc.net.pk	202.83.174.174	A	16/5/2006 15:41:14	15

not clear what is the purpose of such DNS responses nor how and why were they resolved by systems or users at the University of Auckland. The WHOIS database [15] confirms that addresses 202.83.160.0–202.83.175.255 belong to the National Telecom Corporation in Pakistan so it seems that the name ntc.net.pk resolves to almost all IP addresses used by NTC. Manually querying the DNS server for ntc.net.pk returns only 8 IP addresses, which seem to randomly change every time this domain is resolved. This means that, in order to populate the DNS database, this DNS domain was resolved at least 480 times (3840 addresses in the block divided by 8 addresses per reply) by University of Auckland users.

4.7   Record Reputation

In a vast majority of cases, spammers sell their product through various web sites. The creation of SURBL (Spam URI Realtime Blocklist [16]) caused spammers to increasingly start using different domains per spam run, so called 'throw away' domains. The idea behind this is to register a new domain, run a spam campaign using that domain and then switch to a different domain. By doing this, spammers are trying to avoid their domain being blacklisted on SURBL; by the time the domain is blacklisted, the spammers have sent enough e-mails and will switch to a different domain.

By checking historical behavior of an IP address and associated DNS resource records with it, particularly NS records, it is possible to calculate the 'reputation' of a new DNS domain. The link in establishing whether the new domain is good or bad is through one of its NS records. The reputation can be calculated by checking the history of a particular record to see how many (and which) domains referred to it, or to a particular IP address. Table 7 lists domains

Table 7. Domains using ns0.quijindeshkinmas.com DNS server

DNS query	Answer	RR type	Entry added	TTL
funhderinmdasewio.com	ns0.quijindeshkinmas.com	NS	24/9/2006	300
vertionmdefunshjin.com	ns0.quijindeshkinmas.com	NS	24/9/2006	300
...	...	...	...	...
saderuijtungandsunastre.com	ns0.quijindeshkinmas.com	NS	8/12/2006	300
...	...	...	...	...
badesuijintunfeungan.com	ns0.quijindeshkinmas.com	NS	13/12/2006	300

that have been used in various spam runs, and are pointing to one DNS server. These are also the only domains associated with the ns0.quijindeshkinmas.com DNS server. Checking the 'reputation' of a DNS server in this way, we can determine whether a newly registered/seen domain has spam/malicious elements or not. For example, if the anti-spam system detects a new domain that has ns0.quijindeshkinmas.com as its NS record, the system can automatically deduce that this domain is malicious or used for spam because historically there have been no legitimate records related to this DNS server. This information can then be used similarly to all other rules in SpamAssassin.

Detected spam related domains shared the following characteristics:

– FQDNs end in a top level domain, such as .com
– Domain names are not English words
– All domains use ns0.quijindeshkinmas.com and ns0.kilonherunhasedun.com as their DNS servers.
– A records for particular domains are used only while the spam run associated with this domain is active. After it ends, the domain is left idle. A records are also spread around various providers.

5   Conclusion and Future Work

Passively collected DNS data stored in a database allows one to determine historical behavior of particular DNS records, and of the linkages between them. Since the quality of data and possibilities for analysis rise with the number of sensors (or the clients whose DNS traffic is being monitored), installing additional sensors, around the world should enable better detection of anomalies.

Automated analysis of data in the database could quickly detect anomalies and malicious attacks and thereby serve as an early alert system against spam and worm attacks.

The data should be crawled with specialized agents, such as Microsoft's Strider URL Tracer [13] to allow for near to real time detection of malicious domains. Unfortunately, our data has been already seen, i.e. a client tried to resolve it, but it should still be possible to black list the domain and alert other users which makes the viable time for an attack shorter and an attackers job more difficult.

We hope to establish a set of six to ten geographically dispersed sensors that would allow collection of DNS data from different user groups. We invite readers to contact us if they are willing to participate. We will also make the web interface for querying the database available to the public.

References

1. Mockapetris, P.V., Dunlap, K.J.: Development of the Domain Name System. In: ACM Symphosium proceedings on Communications architectures and protocols (SIGCOMM 88), vol. 18(4) (1998)
2. RUS-CERT: Passive DNS replication, http://cert.uni-stuttgart.de/stats/dns-replication.php
3. Schonewille, A., Helmond, D.v.: The Domain Name Service as an IDS. Research Project for the Master System- and Network Engineering at the University of Amsterdam (February 2006)
4. Kristoff, J.: DNSWatch, http://aharp.ittns.northwestern.edu/software/dnswatch
5. Elton, N., Keel, M.: A Discussion of Bot Networks. EDUCAUSE 2005 (April 2005) http://www.educause.edu/ir/library/pdf/SPC0568.pdf
6. TCPDUMP/libpcap public repository, http://www.tcpdump.org
7. Mockapetris, P.: Domain Names Implementation and Specification. RFC 1035 (November 1987)
8. Tcpdpriv – A program for eliminating confidential information from packets collected on a network interface (October 2005) http://ita.ee.lbl.gov/html/contrib/tcpdpriv.html
9. Jung, J., Sit, E., Balakrishnan, H., Morris, R.: DNS Performance and the Effectiveness of Caching. ACM Transactions on Networking 10(5), 589–603 (2002)
10. Wong, M.: Sender Authentication What To Do. A Messaging Anti-Abuse Working Group White Paper (November 2004) available at http://www.openspf.org/whitepaper.pdf
11. Sequitur IPS: Domain name disputes, cybersquatting and UDRP cases. http://www.sequitur-ips.com/domain-name-disputes/library.html

12. Gavron, E.: A Security Problem and Proposed Correction With Widely Deployed DNS Software. RFC 1535 (October 1993)
13. Wang, Y., Beck, D., Wang, J., Verbowski, C., Daniels, B.: Strider Typo-Patrol: Discovery and Analysis of Systematic Typo-Squatting. Microsoft Research Technical Report (to be submitted to the 2nd Usenix Workshop on Steps to Reducing Unwanted Traffic on the Internet (SRUTI 06))
    http://research.microsoft.com/URLTracer
14. Evron, G., Blog, S.: Looking behind the smoke screen of the Internet: DNS recursive attacks, spamvertised domains, phishing, botnet C&Cs, International Infrastructure and you, http://blogs.securiteam.com/index.php/archives/298
15. Daigle, L.: WHOIS: Protocol Specification. RFC 3912 (September 2004)
16. SURBL Spam URI Realtime Blocklists, http://www.surbl.org
17. Weimer, F.: Passive DNS Replication. FIRST 2005 (April 2005)
18. Internet Engineering Task Force: Requirements for Internet Hosts Application and Support. RFC 1123 (October 1989)
19. Vixie, P.: Extension Mechanisms for DNS (EDNS0). RFC 2671 (August 1999)

Characterizing Dark DNS Behavior

Jon Oberheide[1], Manish Karir[2], and Z. Morley Mao[1]

[1] Electrical Engineering and Computer Science
University of Michigan, Ann Arbor MI 48105
{jonojono,zmao}@umich.edu
[2] Networking R&D
Merit Network Inc, Ann Arbor MI 48105
mkarir@merit.edu

Abstract. Security researchers and network operators increasingly rely on information gathered from honeypots and sensors deployed on dark-nets, or unused address space, for attack detection. While the attack traffic gleaned from such deployments has been thoroughly scrutinized, little attention has been paid to DNS queries targeting these addresses. In this paper, we introduce the concept of *dark DNS*, the DNS queries associated with darknet addresses, and characterize the data collected from a large operational network by our dark DNS sensor. We discuss the implications of sensor evasion via DNS reconnaissance and empha-size the importance of reverse DNS authority when deploying darknet sensors to prevent attackers from easily evading monitored darknets. Finally, we present *honeydns*, a tool that complements existing network sensors and low-interaction honeypots by providing simple DNS services.

Keywords: DNS, reconnaissance, honeypots, sensors, darknets.

1 Introduction

The emergence of sophisticated malware has led security researchers to develop innovative tools to study and combat its malicious activities. Honeypots, intru-sion detection systems, and a multitude of other host and network based sensors have aided researchers extensively in their endeavors. These sensors provide a wide range of functionality, from simply responding to network requests, to emu-lating vulnerable services and operating systems, all the way to simulating entire virtual network and host topologies. Security researchers and network operators commonly deploy honeypots and other sensors on dark, or unused, address space to gather malware, analyze new exploit techniques, and study long-term attack trends.

To maintain their usefulness, it is vital that these sensors be resistant to re-mote identification and fingerprinting techniques that attackers may employ. As the arms race between malware authors and researchers continues, increasingly sophisticated attacks can utilize evasion techniques in order to avoid detection and identification. By performing reconnaissance to map valuable targets, an attacker can build specific target lists. Additionally, reconnaissance can identify

B. M. Hämmerli and R. Sommer (Eds.): DIMVA 2007, LNCS 4579, pp. 140–156, 2007.

monitoring systems that should be avoided. The use of DNS identifying potential targets is well known. In this paper we describe how the lack of appropriate DNS support for sensor address space can be used by malware to identify darknet monitoring systems. Such DNS reconnaissance utilizes PTR record DNS queries which attempt to resolve an IP address to a hostname. While current honeypots and darknet sensors are effective at analyzing traffic targeted *at* their addresses, they fail to consider out-of-band probes inquiring *about* their addresses, namely DNS queries. We appropriately label these queries as *dark DNS*. Dark DNS queries are not received by the darknet sensors themselves; instead, they are directed at the DNS nameserver that is authoritative for the darknet. Such dark DNS traffic is due to one of these reasons: DNS mapping efforts, backscatter, misconfiguration, or malicious reconnaissance.

In this paper, we measure and characterize dark DNS activity. We obtained DNS authority over two class B (/16) darknets and were able to direct this dark DNS traffic to our sensor for collection. We measured three distinct datasets, each collecting a week's worth of data: one from passively monitoring the incoming queries, one from actively responding with a NXDOMAIN (non-existent domain) error code, and one from actively responding with a valid hostname IP address queries. We present the behavioral patterns of dark DNS via these measurements and provide insight into the origin of such anomalous traffic.

Reverse DNS probing can be an effective technique for evading darknet monitors. Due to the recursive nature of queries and the hierarchical operation of DNS, an attacker can perform reconnaissance on a target network without sending any probe traffic directly to that network and without revealing the attacker's source. These characteristics make DNS reconnaissance a lucrative feature for sophisticated malware and a viable method for evasion. We show how this technique can be used maliciously to evade several large-scale darknet monitoring systems while still maintaining effectiveness against live hosts.

In order to mitigate the threat posed by this evasive technique, we discuss the proper methodology for delegating reverse DNS for darknet sensor deployments. We also present a defensive countermeasure, designed to complement current honeypot systems, to prevent sensor evasion based on DNS reconnaissance. Our tool, *honeydns*, implements a lightweight DNS responder which is able to reply to PTR queries for large darknets with appropriate records. Honeydns can be easily used to complement and properly configure a large-scale honeypot deployment.

To summarize, our work has the following contributions. We present the first detailed study to characterize and illustrate a significant amount of dark DNS traffic consisting of over 1.48M queries over three weeks. A significant portion of the dark DNS traffic is observed to originate from DNS mapping efforts by Akamai. Aside from dark DNS analysis, our work is the first to highlight the importance of properly configuring darknet DNS servers to prevent the use of PTR reconnaissance as an effective evasion vector. Our honeydns tool provides a lightweight and flexible way to build a more complete darknet sensor by facilitating the ability to correctly respond to DNS queries for a particular darknet and making it appear to contain valid hosts.

The rest of this paper is organized as follows: In Section 2, we provide an introduction to the operation of the Domain Name System and describe common queries types and response codes. Next, in Section 3, we discuss recent related work. In Section 4, we discuss our collection and experimentation setup. We then present a thorough analysis of our experiment results in Section 5. In Section 6, we discuss the implications of our results, and finally, in Section 7, we summarize our contributions and describe some future work.

2   Domain Name System

The Domain Name System (DNS), defined in RFCs 1034 [1] and 1035 [2], is a hierarchical, distributed database which provides essential name-resolution services to Internet applications. In order to perform a DNS query, a resolver will traverse the DNS hierarchy to locate the appropriate authoritative server that can answer its query. Given the address of a root nameserver, which resolvers are typically seeded with, the resolver can query for the address of the next level authoritative nameserver. By recursively performing this process through the hierarchical tree, the resolver will eventually reach the nameserver that is authoritative for the specified query. Once that server is identified, the answer to the query is retrieved by the resolver, completing its query. The DNS infrastructure supports many different query types, of which Address (A) and Pointer (PTR) are the most common.

Address (A) Records. Address record lookups perform the translation from a hostname to an IP address and are the most common DNS query performed. When a user connects to a service which is referred to by a domain name, a DNS query is performed to determine the endpoint IP address to connect to.

Pointer (PTR) Records. PTR records provide the reverse translation of A records by mapping an IP address to a hostname. The lookup is performed by transforming the queried IP address into a special, yet legitimate, domain name. For example, the domain name formed for a query for the IP address aa.bb.cc.dd is dd.cc.bb.aa.in-addr.arpa. The ".arpa" portion is a special top-level domain created specifically for these reverse PTR queries. A PTR query operates in the same manner as an A query by starting at the root and traversing the DNS hierarchy. Once the authoritative zone is reached, the authoritative server will return the hostname associated with the queried IP address. PTR queries are commonly used by network services such as SSH and SMTP to validate connecting clients.

Query Responses. For A record query, the DNS server responds with the appropriate IP address and for a PTR query the server responds with the hostname associated with the query IP address. Additionally, there are numerous status codes that are returned for a DNS query, three of the most common ones are SERVFAIL, NXDOMAIN, and NOERROR. If a resolver is able to determine the address of an authoritative server, but the server is not responding, the resolver will return SERVFAIL. On the other hand, if the authoritative server is responding but does not possess any records that correspond to the query, it will return NXDOMAIN. If all goes well and the authoritative server is able to answer the resolver, the NOERROR code will be sent. If a darknet sensor is configured without the accompanying DNS configuration changes, PTR queries for the darknet would result in NXDOMAIN replies being generated.

3   Related Work

Our work is related to several areas of previous studies on DNS and darknets which we briefly describe here.

DNS has long been a favorite target for attackers due to its critical role in the Internet infrastructure and the inherent lack of security in the operation of DNS. One of the earliest uses of DNS for malicious attacks was described in 1990 and demonstrated how attackers could utilize a weakness in DNS lookups to subvert system security [3]. Given that the purpose of DNS is provide information about hosts, it is not surprising that it could be used for attack reconnaissance. A common way to perform such probing was the use of a zone transfer [4] to obtain the entire set of hosts that a server is authoritative for. Many administrators subsequently started to secure their servers with proper access controls. As zone transfers are rarely effective anymore, attackers have turned to tools such as TXDNS [5] to map the namespace of a domain strictly through brute-force A record queries using a dictionary.

While network and host based intrusion detection have been studied extensively, attack detection by monitoring DNS is just starting to get the attention it deserves. Malware employing spamming services can easily be detected by their emission of a large number of MX queries [6]. Botnet activity can be inferred via DNS query patterns and maintained blacklists [7,8]. Correlation of DNS activity with regular IP traffic can even be used to detect malware scanning and zero-day worm outbreaks [9]. While these techniques have focused on detecting malicious activity by observing DNS queries, in this paper we focus on characterizing DNS activity for unused portions of the IP address space.

Given the very purpose of monitoring darknet is to detect malicious activities, it is critical to avoid revealing the location of the darknet sensors to prevent evasion. Previous work demonstrated the ease of detecting the location of general network sensors [10,11] through active probing. Recent work by Rajab et al. [12] describes how evasive techniques can be used by malware to detect honeypots by selective sampling of IP address space. Discrepancy in the behavior in responding to incoming probes can also be exploited for sensor detection, as shown by a honeyd scanner called Winnie [13]. Our proposed honeydns tool provides the darknet sensors with higher resistance to discovery and complements other tools for configuring darknets such as [14].

Our work builds on previous DNS characterization work of both DNS root servers [15,16,17] as well as local resolvers [18]. DNS can be used to estimate network distance between hosts by exploiting a large number of open-resolver DNS servers [19]. Similar to the AS112 Project, which uses separate servers to answer PTR queries for RFC1918, dynamic DNS updates and other ambiguous addresses, our work focuses on measuring DNS behavior in address spaces with no legitimate live hosts.

4   Methodology

For our experiments we obtained two class B (/16) darknet address blocks and delegated DNS authority for these subnets to our dark DNS collector. We then proceeded to gather three datasets for our experiments, collecting a week of DNS traffic for each dataset. For the first dataset we simply passively recorded all incoming queries to our delegated subnets without any active responses. The goal of this experiment was to obtain an accurate measure of DNS activity for these subnets without any external influence. The second dataset was obtained by repeating the first experiment, but, instead of passively monitoring, replying to the queries with the NXDOMAIN (non-existent domain) error code. NXDO-MAIN is the error code usually received when no resource record is found for a query. The third dataset was obtained by replying to incoming PTR queries with a valid hostname response. The format used for this hostname was *host-{a-b-c-d}.merit.edu* in response to PTR queries for any IP *a.b.c.d* within our darknet. The DNS time-to-live of the responses was set to zero to ensure resolvers would not cache our response. The goal of collecting these three distinct datasets is to examine DNS probe traffic under three common scenarios.

Table 1. The Measurement Datasets

Response Type	A/16	B/16	A/16+B/16	Duration
No Response	NR_A	NR_B	NR_TOTAL	7 days
NXDOMAIN Response	NX_A	NX_B	NX_TOTAL	7 days
Valid Response	VR_A	-	VR_TOTAL	7 days

Table 1 shows our three datasets and the terminology we will use to refer to them throughout the rest of the paper. The first dataset where the DNS server sent out no responses to any queries are called NR_A and NR_B (No Response) respectively for the two /16 darknets A and B. Similarly, the second one where the DNS server responded with NXDOMAIN replies are called NX_A and NX_B. The third dataset, where we replied with valid responses to PTR queries, is called VR_A (Valid Response). Due to an administrative issue, response dataset VR_B was not captured. Each of the three datasets represents 1 week of data collection. We refer to the combined data from both subnets if available as NR_TOTAL, NX_TOTAL, and VR_TOTAL.

During collection periods, our dark DNS sensor archived each incoming query in a SQLite database backend for subsequent analysis. An extensive schema was used to capture various aspects of each DNS query. The information collected includes IP layer details such as the source IP, identification number, and time-to-live (TTL) value, transport layer details such as the source port, and DNS details such as the type, id, and query.

For the second part of our study, we obtained one day of NetFlow data from a regional ISP to help identify the feasibility of using PTR scanning to detect live hosts on the Internet. We extracted only IP addresses from the NetFlow data where the TCP ACK flag was set. This ensures that SYN scanning or spoofing does not influence our results. For each of these addresses we performed a query to determine whether that particular live host had an associated PTR entry.

5   Data Analysis

Next we describe our analysis of the three datasets illustrating the presence of potentially malicious DNS activities of the monitored darknets, as aside from DNS mapping there should not be any legitimate DNS traffic for such address space. We expect the darknet DNS traffic to be caused by one of these reasons: (1) DNS mapping efforts such as that by Internet Systems Consortium [20], (2) Backscatter [21] due to spoofed darknet traffic triggering subsequent DNS queries by monitoring systems, (3) misconfiguration, (4) PTR reconnaissance by attackers to identify live hosts for attack targeting.

5.1   Basic Statistics

Table 2 illustrates the basic statistics of our three datasets. As described earlier, our first dataset is designed to gather the raw queries that are associated with the addresses of our delegated darknets. The second dataset shows the continued query activity despite correct NXDOMAIN responses. By comparing these two datasets we can establish the primary characteristics of dark DNS queries. We observe an order of magnitude more queries for the first dataset, which we believe is due to query timeout retries. Interestingly, the unique target probed in the first dataset is more than 88% of all the addresses covered by the two /16s monitored, indicating the behavior of PTR scanning for these two address blocks.

Table 2. Basic dark DNS query statistics. Query rates are per 5 minute interval.

Dataset	Queries	Unique Sources	Unique Targets	Avg Query Rate	Max Query Rate
NR_A	714K	11.2K	64.1K	353.70	5501
NR_B	606K	11.8K	52.2K	300.34	2725
NR_Total	1.32M	17.0K	116K	654.8	5553
NX_A	57K	8.59K	28.9K	27.56	552
NX_B	58K	9.09K	29.4K	28.79	560
NX_Total	115K	13.1K	58.4K	57.1	825
VR_A	45K	7.45K	24.2K	22.35	321
VR_B	-	-	-	-	-
VR_Total	45K	7.45K	24.2K	22.35	321

Table 3. Query Type Distribution for NX_Total

Query Code	Query Type	Count	Percentage
1	A	81	0.0704%
6	SOA	683	0.5937%
12	PTR	114214	99.2846%
15	MX	4	0.0035%
33	SRV	32	0.0278%
255	ANY	23	0.0199%

For the third dataset, in which our DNS responder replies with *host-{a-b-c-d}.merit.edu* in response to PTR queries for any IP *a.b.c.d* within our darknet, we observe slightly lower query rate compared to the second setting with NX-DOMAIN responses. We conjecture this can be due to resolvers being satisfied with replies likely to indicate legitimate hosts and therefore stop probing early rather than continuing its scanning activity.

Over the course of our three-week experiment, our darknet DNS sensor received over 1.48 million queries. They originate from more than 8000 IP prefixes and 3900 ASes. Table 3 shows the distribution of various query type codes observed in the incoming DNS queries for the second dataset. We observed similar distribution for the other two datasets. The vast majority of these as expected are PTR queries though we do observe an occasional A record request and even a few MX queries.

5.2   Query Rate

Figure 1 presents the query rate that is observed via our dark DNS monitor for the A/16 subnet. The figure shows the number of queries received in 30 minute intervals for the NR_A, NX_A, and VR_A datasets during the course of our experiments. It shows a fairly high rate of queries over the one week measurement time period for all three datasets. There are two distinct bands visible in the data. The lower band represents query rates observed in the NX_A and VR_A datasets. These are significantly lower than the query rates observed in the NR_A dataset. We believe that the higher rates observed for the NR_A dataset are caused by servers attempting to repeatedly retrying to resolve the same IP address in the absence of any reply.

The average number of queries observed in the NX_A and VR_A datasets over a 5 minute interval is 27.5 and 22.3 respectively while the query rate for the NR_A dataset is an order of magnitude greater at 353.7. The maximum rate observed is also significantly different depending on whether our server actively responds to dark DNS queries.

Figure 1 shows a couple of interesting features as well. The first is the sporadic peaks in the query rate observed in the NX_A and VR_A datasets from the lower band. These peaks are roughly a value of 256 above the lower band, or the size of a /24 subnet, caused by a deliberate scan of that subnet. The second

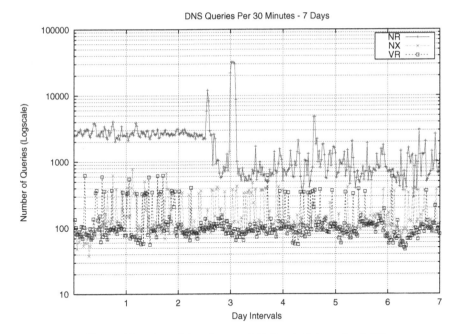

Fig. 1. Number of Queries per 30 Minute Interval - A/16

interesting feature is the significant reduction in the query rate observed in the NR_A dataset around day 4 following a short-lived spike. We will discuss this particular anomaly in greater detail in Section 5.4.

5.3 Query Targets

In order to better understand the nature of dark DNS queries, we analyzed the distribution of IP address that these queries were attempting to resolve. For this analysis we used all three datasets obtained via our collector on the A/16 subnet and for each dataset we computed the number of queries for hosts in each /24 subnet of this address space. A clustering or unusually large number of queries for a particular target address would indicate a bias in query targets. Figure 2 shows the resulting graph from our analysis. The x-axis represents each /24 subnet of our /16 and the y-axis depicts the number of queries. There are no obvious spikes or clusters visible indicating that the queries are roughly randomly distributed across the entire A/16 subnet. The NR_A query rate is clearly much higher than the query rates for the VR_A and NX_A datasets, which exhibit similar behavior.

5.4 Query Sources

One of the most intriguing characteristics of the dark DNS data is the source from which the queries originate. In this section, we discuss and illustrate several important aspects of the source of these dark DNS queries.

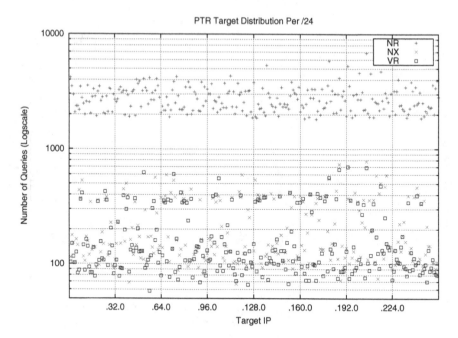

Fig. 2. Query Target IP Address Distribution - A/16

Table 4. Top 10 Sources by Percentage of Total Queries

Rank	Source IP	Percentage
1	69.15.35.X	29.0315%
2	156.45.232.X	1.2431%
3	24.93.41.X	0.5537%
4	65.24.7.X	0.4198%
5	200.169.8.X	0.4172%
6	24.92.226.X	0.4085%
7	212.27.54.X	0.3833%
8	212.27.54.X	0.3712%
9	24.25.5.X	0.3694%
10	216.219.254.X	0.3659%

Top Talkers. Table 4 lists the 10 largest contributors to our dark DNS data measurements. These measurements are based on the NX_TOTAL dataset. What is perhaps the most interesting feature of this data is that a single source IP is responsible for almost 30% of the queries. We believe that this is largely a result of large scale DNS mapping performed during our study. We discuss this characteristic further in the following sections.

Source Distribution. The left graph of Figure 3 shows the number of unique source IP addresses we observed in the NX_TOTAL dataset over time. As the figure is of linear shape, indicating that over time we are continuing to receive queries from more unique sources that have not queried us before instead of repeated queries from the same set of hosts. This indicates that it is infeasible to block such traffic from the network via simple firewall rules. However, as this figure does not show a completely straight line, given fairly constant query rate over each day, we can conclude that a very small fraction of the total sources are in fact continuing to send queries to our dark DNS collectors over time.

The right graph of Figure 3 shows the percentage of sources as a function of the percentage of total queries. The figure shows a sharp initial increase indicating that a small percentage of the sources are contributing to a large percentage of queries in our NX_TOTAL dataset. The increasing width of the boxes indicate that an increasingly greater percentage of unique sources is needed to account for each additional 5% of the total queries.

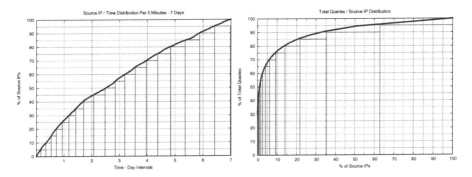

Fig. 3. Source IP distribution: growth over time, query contribution

Table 5. Top 10 Contributing Autonomous Systems by Query Volume

Rank	Query Count (% of total)	ASN	Name
1	33407 (29%)	AS17184	ATL-CBEYOND COMMUNICATIONS
2	4678 (4%)	AS7132	SBIS-AS - SBC Internet Service
3	4140 (4%)	AS12322	PROXAD AS for Proxad/Free ISP
4	2302 (2%)	AS3320	DTAG Deutsche Telekom AG
5	1438 (1%)	AS22773	CCINET-2 - Cox Communications
6	1430 (1%)	AS20170	MARITZFENTONMO - Maritz Inc.
7	1277 (1%)	AS19262	VZGNI-TRANSIT - Verizon Internt
8	903 (1%)	AS3215	AS3215 France Telecom - Orange
9	890 (1%)	AS3269	ASN-IBSNAZ TELECOM ITALIA
10	861 (1%)	AS3352	TELEFONICA-DATA-ESPANA Internet

Autonomous Systems. While there are a number of sources sending PTR queries to our dark DNS sensor, it is helpful to get a high-level view of the organizations that these IPs belong to. In Tables 5 and 6, we have ranked the top contributing organizations with their Autonomous System Number (ASN). Table 5

ranks by the total number of queries received from source IPs owned by the
AS, while Table 6 ranks by the unique number of source IPs. Most of these
networks are well known ISPs offering DSL and Cable modem services, along
with several large ISPs such as Qwest, Deutsche Telekom, and France Telecom.
It is surprising that the top query volume contributor CBEYOND accounts for
more than 29% of all queries, indicating highly nonuniform source distribution
of dark DNS traffic. The distribution for unique source IPs contributed by each
AS is less skewed with SBC accounting for more than 4.5% of all sources observed. Also note that both SBC and Deutsche Telekom appear as the top 10
contributing ASes by query rate as well as by unique sources.

Table 6. Top 10 Contributing Autonomous Systems by Number of Unique Sources

Rank	Unique Sources (% of total)	ASN	Name
1	594 (4.5%)	AS7132	SBIS-AS - SBC Internet Service
2	268 (2.0%)	AS3320	DTAG Deutsche Telekom AG
3	214 (1.6%)	AS7018	ATT-INTERNET4 - AT&T WorldNet
4	204 (1.5%)	AS6128	CABLE-NET-1 - Cablevision Systems
5	202 (1.5%)	AS4230	Embratel Brazil
6	194 (1.4%)	AS5617	TPNET Polish Telecom commerce
7	192 (1.4%)	AS209	ASN-QWEST - Qwest
8	190 (1.4%)	AS5089	NTL NTL Group Limited
9	174 (1.3%)	AS21844	THEPLANET-AS - THE PLANET
10	164 (1.2%)	AS577	BACOM - Bell Canada

Operating Systems. Figure 4 shows the distribution of IP header TTL values
from the PTR queries. The three distinct clusters signify the three classes of
initial TTL values: 64, 128, and 255. As these initial TTL values result from
network stack characteristics of different operating systems, we can estimate
the operating system distribution of the source IPs. Linux/BSD systems set the
initial TTL to 64, Windows systems set it to 128, and Solaris systems set it to
255. Table 7 summarizes the OS distribution percentages observed by our dark
DNS collector.

Table 7. Query source OS distribution based on TTL

Operating System	Initial TTL	Unique Sources	Percentage
Linux/BSD	64	10480	72.93%
Windows	128	1043	7.26%
Solaris/Other	255	2846	19.81%

The vast majority of the resolvers appear to be Linux/BSD based systems,
followed by a modest percentage that may be Solaris based, and finally a small
percentage of Windows based resolvers. This in contrast with the resolver OS
percentages reported in a previous study [17] where, of all the sources querying
the F-root server, 49% were reported to be Linux/BSD based and almost 40%

were reported to be Windows based. It is clear the queries of dark DNS are not consistent with the behavior expected of a normal DNS system. It is important to note that the origins of of such queries are not necessarily end hosts, but also local resolvers querying on behalf of the end hosts via recursive DNS queries.

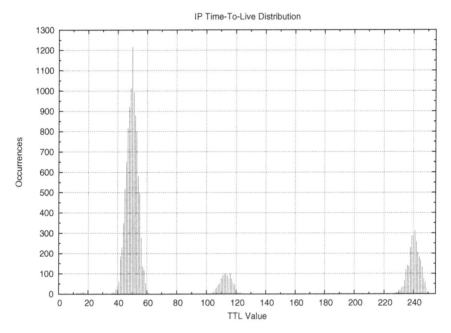

Fig. 4. TTL Distribution in PTR query packets

Akamai Mapping. Akamai is a company that provides a distributed content delivery network (CDN) to accelerate and cache web content. Their platform depends on the ability to determine network locality and distance between hosts. During our experimentation, we noticed that the majority of the top queriers were from hosts deployed by Akamai. These hosts were verified as belonging to Akamai via hostname, Internet routing registries, and SSH banner strings. Our hypothesis that Akamai is using PTR querying to supplement their network locality algorithms is partially confirmed by the DNS-based distance estimation techniques described in previous work [19].

We also determined that 11 distinct Akamai-deployed hosts are responsible for the anomalous spike in the query rate in Figure 1 of Section 5.2. Around day 3 of our NR_A dataset, an order-of-magnitude increase was observed and abruptly followed by an overall decrease in the query rate. By separating out the 11 Akamai hosts from the rest of the source hosts, we are able to more effectively highlight this anomalous behavior.

As shown in Figure 5, the query rate for the Akamai hosts is steady for the first couple days, then drops off briefly, then skyrockets up to 12000 queries per 30 minutes, then drops off again and is not observed at all for the rest of the dataset collection. Whether this sequence of events represents a potential issue with Akamai's deployments is unknown. More importantly, separating this anomaly from the rest of our dataset demonstrates the relative consistency that all other hosts exhibit in their query rate.

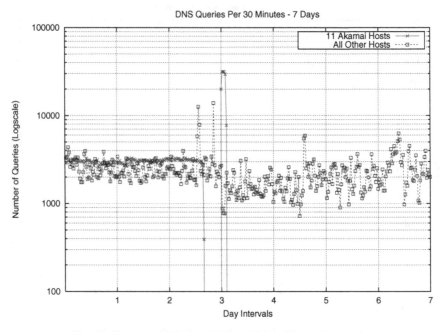

Fig. 5. Query rate distinguishing Akamai hosts from others

6   Discussion

Detailed analysis in the previous section demonstrates significant DNS activities for dark address space, originating from diverse operating systems and a large number of networks, but with a small number of hosts or networks contributing to a large percentage of queries. This data provides preliminary evidence of potentially malicious darknet DNS activities, given the presence of scanning activities and slightly lower query rate for valid response compared to the no domain response. In this section, we discuss the implications of PTR reconnaissance, verify the assumption that most live hosts have valid PTR records, and propose a solution to prevent sensor evasion using PTR reconnaissance.

6.1   PTR Reconnaissance

The PTR query type, as previously discussed, is used to perform the mapping from an IP address to a hostname. Given an address range selected for attack, an attacker can send a PTR query for each address in the range and note the result. Operating under the assumption that IP addresses with associated PTR records are usually live hosts with potentially exploitable services, an attacker can easily determine whether certain hosts or subnets are worthy of attention. Therefore, if an attacker sees a valid PTR response with an associated hostname, he can continue to attack that target with an increased level of confidence. Otherwise, he can move on to potentially more valuable targets. It is important to note that these PTR queries will not be seen by the sensors monitoring the traffic of the dark address space, but instead by the DNS server authoritative for that address space.

More importantly, an attacker can mask his identity and source IP address while performing this reconnaissance. The DNS infrastructure and its resolvers offer functionality known as recursive querying. If a client requests a recursive query from a resolver with recursive query enabled, that resolver will perform all the necessary communication on behalf of that client and simply return the final result. The other DNS servers involved in the query will have no way of knowing the attacker's true identity as they will only be communicating with the resolver the attacker has chosen. An attacker may choose resolvers located at his local ISP or, for more anonymity, one of the many open resolvers around the Internet that accept recursive queries.

6.2   Validating Usefulness of PTR Reconnaissance

To verify our assumption that most live hosts have associated PTR records and monitored unused address space does not, we performed several measurements.

First, we wanted to determine the distribution of live hosts with PTR records. We obtained 24 hours worth of NetFlow data (of size 268MB compressed) from a large regional provider, containing TCP conversations involving a total of 1,234,842 unique IP addresses. By performing a PTR query on each of these IP addresses, we received a total of 980,835 valid responses, indicating 79.43% of the hosts have associated PTR records. This high percentage confirms our assumption and affirms the effectiveness of PTR reconnaissance.

In addition, given that home users on broadband connections are more frequently targeted by malicious activity, PTR scanning techniques would even more successful against as most ISPs assign PTR records for their addresses. Table 8 shows the PTR record format template for a number of major broadband ISPs obtained from our probes.

We were also able to use PTR reconnaissance to successfully evade several large-scale, distributed systems that monitor dark address space for malicious activity. We actively probed one of these systems, which consists of sensors installed at numerous ISPs around the world monitoring over 17 million routable IP addresses. Of all the various deployments of this sensor network, only a single class C subnet (256 addresses) was configured with reverse DNS and responded to our PTR queries. Utilizing PTR reconnaissance, an attacker would successfully evade 99.9985% of that sensor's darknet monitoring.

Table 8. Common PTR record formats (anonymized)

Organization	PTR Format
AT&T	{ID.detroit-ID-ID}.mi.dial-access.att.net
Belgacom	{A.B-C-D}.adsl-dyn.isp.belgacom.be
Bellsouth	host-{A-B-C-D}.bhm.bellsouth.net
Blueyonder	adsl-{A-B-C-D}.blueyonder.co.uk
Charter	{A-B-C-D}.dhcp.bycy.mi.charter.com
Comcast	c-{A-B-C-D}.hsd1.ma.comcast.net
Earthlink	user-{ID}.cable.earthlink.net
Qwest	{A-B-C-D}.albq.qwest.net
Roadrunner	cpe-{A-B-C-D}.carolina.res.rr.com
Rogers	{ID-ID}.cpe.net.cable.rogers.com
SBC Yahoo	adsl-{A-B-C-D}.dsl.rcsntx.sbcglobal.net
Shawcable	{ID}.vs.shawcable.net
Speakeasy	dsl{A-B-C}.sea1.dsl.speakeasy.net
Telus	d{A-B-C-D}.bchsia.telus.net
Tiscali	{A-B-C-D}.dsl.ip.tiscali.nl
Verizon	pool-{A-B-C-D}.esr.east.verizon.net
XO	{A.B.C.D}.ptr.us.xo.ne

6.3   Honeydns to Combat PTR Reconnaissance

In order to subvert the effectiveness of sensor evasion via PTR reconnaissance, a countermeasure must be deployed. The underlying approach is straightforward: a valid DNS reply must be generated when an attacker performs a PTR query for a sensor address.

Sending responses for an attacker's PTR query requires DNS authority for the targeted address space. Fortunately, as many network sensors have already been delegated permission to monitor dark IP address space, the additional requirement of gaining DNS delegation is not usually a significant technical nor administrative burden. Once DNS authority has been delegated, it becomes possible to reply to an attacker's PTR query with an arbitrary hostname that appears reasonable for a live host.

While such responses can be provided by existing DNS software packages, it is desirable to deploy a solution that decreases deployment complexity and increases functionality and flexibility. DNS servers such as BIND can be cumbersome to configure and deploy as an authoritative server, especially when only a small subset of DNS functionality is required. In addition, many sensor deployments employ sampling and dynamic topologies which require a flexible framework that static configuration files cannot provide.

We kept these design goals in mind when implementing *honeydns*, a simple yet flexible daemon providing PTR response functionality. Honeydns is written in Python and contains less than 200 lines of code. By providing a flexible response framework, honeydns complements the needs of any low-interaction honeypot deployment. Honeydns also provides passive monitoring capabilities to detect and alert an operator when a malicious attacker is employing PTR reconnaissance techniques.

7 Conclusions and Future Work

Our work is the first detailed study to characterize DNS queries of darknet address space, known as dark DNS. We observe a significant amount of DNS queries to these darknets which are likely due to DNS mapping (*e.g.*, by Akamai), backscatter traffic, misconfiguration, and PTR reconnaissance by attackers. Our work is the first to describe the importance of properly configuring DNS authority for darknet address space to reduce the possibility of sensor evasion. Towards this goal, we develop a lightweight tool called honeydns to provide flexible PTR response functionality in addition to passive DNS traffic anomaly detection capability. As future work, we plan to correlate observed dark DNS traffic with data traffic to the associated darknets to further validate the presence of DNS reconnaissance.

References

1. Mockapetris, P.: RFC 1034: Domain names: concepts and facilities (November 1987), ftp://ftp.internic.net/rfc/rfc1034.txt
2. Mockapetris, P.: RFC 1035: Domain names: implementation and specification (November 1987), ftp://ftp.internic.net/rfc/rfc1035.txt
3. Bellovin, S.: Using the domain name system for system break-ins. In: Proceedings of the 5th USENIX UNIX Security Symposium (1995)
4. Samwalla, R., Sharma, R., Keshav, S.: Discovering Internet Topology. Unpublished manuscript
5. Silveira, A.: TXDNS: an aggressive multithreaded DNS digger, http://www.txdns.net/.
6. Ishibashi, K., Toyono, T., Toyama, K., Ishino, M.: Detecting mass-mailing worm infected hosts by mining DNS traffic data. In: Proceedings of the Special Interest Group on Data Communications (SIGCOMM) (2005)
7. Kristoff, J.: Botnets, detection and mitigation: DNS-based techniques. NU Security Day (2005)
8. Schonewille, A., van Helmond, D.-J.: The Domain Name Service as an IDS: How DNS can be used for detecting and monitoring badware in a network (February 2006), http://staff.science.uva.nl/delaat/snb-2005-2006/p12/report.pdf
9. Whyte, D., Kranakis, E., Van Oorschot, P.: DNS-based Detection of Scanning Worms in an Enterprise Network. In: Proceedings of the Network and Distributed Systems Symposium (NDSS) (2005)
10. Bethencourt, J., Franklin, J., Vernon, M.: Mapping Internet Sensors with Probe Response Attacks. In: Proceedings of Usenix Security Symposium (2005)
11. Shinoda, Y., Ikai, K., Itoh, M.: Vulnerabilities of Passive Internet Threat Monitors. In: Proceedings of Usenix Security Symposium (2005)
12. Rajab, M., Monrose, F., Terzis, A.: Fast and Evasive Attacks: Highlighting the Challenges Ahead. Proceedings of the 9th International Symposium on Recent Advances in Intrusion Detection (RAID) (September 2006)

13. Oberheide, J., Karir, M.: Honeyd Detection via Packet Fragmentation. Technical report, Merit Networks Inc. (2006)
14. Sinha, S., Bailey, M., Jahanian, F.: Shedding Light on the Configuration of Dark Addresses. In: Proceedings of NDSS (2007)
15. Brownlee, N.: DNS Root/gTLD Performance Measurements. IETF Meeting (2001), http://www.caida.org/publications/presentations/ietf0112/
16. Nemeth, E.: DNS Damage - Measurements at a Root Server. IETF Meeting (2001), http://www.caida.org/publications/presentations/ietf0112/
17. Wessels, D., Fomenkov, M.: Wow, That's a Lot of Packets. In: Proceedings of Passive and Active Measurement Workshop (September 2003)
18. Jung, J., Sit, E., Balakrishnan, H., Morris, R.: DNS Performance and the Effectiveness of Caching. In: Proc. ACM SIGCOMM Internet Measurement Workshop (2001)
19. Gummadi, K.P., Saroiu, S., Gribble, S.D.: King: Estimating Latency between Arbitrary Internet End Hosts. In: Proceedings of SIGCOMM IMW (2002)
20. Internet Systems Consortium. ISC Internet Domain Survey Background (2006), http://www.isc.org/index.pl
21. Moore, D., Voelker, G., Savage, S.: Inferring Internet Denial of Service Activity. In: Proceedings of the 2001 USENIX Security Symposium (2001)

Distributed Evasive Scan Techniques and Countermeasures

Min Gyung Kang, Juan Caballero, and Dawn Song

Carnegie Mellon University,
{mgkang,jcaballero,dawnsong}@cmu.edu

Abstract. Scan detection and suppression methods are an important means for preventing the disclosure of network information to attackers. However, despite the importance of limiting the information obtained by the attacker, and the wide availability of such scan detection methods, there has been very little research on evasive scan techniques, which can potentially be used by attackers to avoid detection. In this paper, we first present a novel classification of scan detection methods based on their amnesty policy, since attackers can take advantage of such policies to evade detection. Then we propose two novel metrics to measure the resources that an attacker needs to complete a scan without being detected. Next, we introduce *z-Scan*, a novel evasive scan technique that uses distributed scanning, and show that it is extremely effective against TRW, one of the state-of-the-art scan detection methods. Finally, we investigate possible countermeasures including hybrid scan detection methods and information-hiding techniques. We provide theoretical analysis, as well as simulation results, to quantitatively measure the effectiveness of the evasive scan techniques and the countermeasures.

Keywords: scan detection, evasion, distributed scanning, information-hiding.

1 Introduction

Network scans have become a common and useful means for hackers to obtain information on a specific network, such as detecting active hosts and ports in service [3] or as a tool for reconnaissance before attacking the vulnerable hosts. In an effort to detect and prevent these scan activities, various scan detection methods have been proposed [11,12,15,16,19,20,21,22,23]. These *scan detection* methods have been widely deployed, often in combination with *scan suppression* methods that try to limit the information obtained by the attacker. Typically, the output of the scan detection method becomes one input to the scan suppression method. For example, the scan detection method may output the IP address of a remote host performing a scan on the local network. Then, the suppression method takes care of blocking any further traffic from that address.

However, despite the importance of limiting the information obtained by the attacker, and the wide availability of scan detection methods, there has been very little research on the *evasive scan techniques* that can potentially be used by attackers to avoid detection. Moreover, the metaphor for security co-evolution, "security arms race", is also true for this case as attackers develop new evasive scan techniques to elude scan detection methods. Multiple techniques have been developed for this purpose such as *dumb*

B. M. Hämmerli and R. Sommer (Eds.): DIMVA 2007, LNCS 4579, pp. 157–174, 2007.

scan [1], distributed scan, and several stealthy port scan techniques [2]. In particular, distributed scans have recently become cheap to perform due to the wide availability of botnets, and current state-of-the art scan detection methods such as TRW [12] were not designed for such a threat. Thus, it is imperative to analyze evasive scan techniques and explore countermeasures against them.

In this paper, we make the following contributions:

Classify scan detection methods according to their amnesty policy: Scan detection methods assign anomaly scores to a host's activities. As this score will only ever increase, they use an amnesty policy to lessen scores in the case of normal activities. These amnesty policies usually constitute a vector for evasive scan techniques and thus need to be properly studied. We present a novel classification for scan detection methods based on their amnesty policy: *Positive-Reward*-based and *Timeout*-based methods. Such a classification allows us to abstract the essence of these scan detection methods and facilitates the analysis of evasive scan techniques against each family.

Propose two new evaluation metrics: Scan detection methods have been mostly evaluated with respect to their accuracy and detection delay. We propose using two additional metrics to incorporate the notion of how many resources the attacker needs to complete the scan, in the presence of that scan detection method, and yet remain undetected. That is, how easy it is to obtain the information while evading that scan detection method. The metrics are: 1) the time that it takes for an attacker to complete the scan of a network and 2) the number of IP addresses that the attacker needs to complete the scan. In both cases we assume the presence of the scan detection method, and that the attacker wishes to remain undetected.

Introduce z-Scan, a new evasive scan technique: We introduce *z-Scan*, a new evasive distributed scan technique against Positive-Reward-based methods. In particular, we show z-Scan to be effective against Threshold Random Walk (TRW), which has been shown to be one of the most effective scan detection methods in terms of speed and accuracy. Our z-Scan technique is extremely effective against TRW; it can scan without being detected, a given address space protected with TRW, using a small number of source addresses. The number of source addresses is bounded logarithmically with respect to the size of the address space.

Propose a hybrid solution to z-Scan: We propose using a hybrid scan detection method that combines Positive-Reward-based and Timeout-based detection to defend against evasive scan techniques. Through our analysis, we demonstrate that Positive-Reward-based detection methods and Timeout-based detection methods are synergistic and when combined, can be much more effective at defending against evasive scan techniques.

Analyze information-hiding as a solution to z-Scan: We explore information-hiding techniques as another type of countermeasure against evasive scan techniques. These information-hiding techniques, rather than trying to detect and block scans, try to hide the true information about the network, and hence reduce the utility of the scans. Through theoretical analysis and simulation results, we show that information-hiding based countermeasures are promising against evasive scan techniques; in particular, in the case of TRW, this can completely render z-Scan ineffective.

The rest of the paper is organized as follows. In Section 2, we classify scan detection methods according to their amnesty policy and introduce the metrics we use to evaluate them. In Section 3 we introduce and analyze z-Scan, our new evasive scan technique. Then, in Section 4, we propose a hybrid scan detection method to counter z-Scan, and provide theoretical analysis and evaluation results on its effectiveness. In Section 5, we analyze the effectiveness of other countermeasures against z-Scan based on information-hiding techniques. Finally, we discuss related work in Section 6 and conclude in Section 7.

2   Classification of Scan Detection Methods and Evaluation Metrics

In this section, first we introduce a novel classification of scan detection methods based on their amnesty policy, and then we propose new metrics that can be used to evaluate the effectiveness of a scan detection method when faced with evasive scan techniques.

2.1   Classification of Scan Detection Methods

There has been ample research on scan detection methods [12,16,19,20,21,23]. However, all these methods are based on one common principle: if the accumulated score for a host's activities exceeds a certain threshold value, the host is considered a scanner. As this accumulated score will only ever increase and eventually hit the threshold, detection methods usually provide policies to lessen the scores in the case of normal activities, which we call *amnesty policies*.

Such policies are important, because attackers try to scan stealthily and amnesty policies, if exploited maliciously, can provide a way for an attacker to make its behavior look normal. As such, amnesty policies are a likely vector for evasive scan techniques and we need to understand how these policies work and how they can be exploited. As a first step, we propose a novel classification of scan detection methods based on their amnesty policy, which yields three categories: *(1) Positive-Reward-based* methods; *(2) Timeout-based* methods; and *(3) No-Amnesty* methods.

Positive-Reward-based Methods. Positive-Reward-based methods lessen the accumulated anomaly score upon the occurrence of normal events such as successful connection attempts or connections to highly visited hosts. Threshold Random Walk (TRW) [12] and its variants [21,23] as well as Leckie et al.'s probabilistic approach [15] fall into this category.

TRW uses a random walk to decide whether a new connection initiated by a host is benign or malicious. We explain it in detail in Section 3 but simply put, it keeps a ratio for each host and in the case of a successful connection started by that host, multiplies its ratio by a value less than 1, making the ratio farther from a fixed threshold (and vice versa in the case of failed connection attempt). Leckie et al. assign anomaly scores to probes, based on the access probability for each target host and thus connections to highly visited hosts are considered normal.

Timeout-based Methods. Timeout-based methods assign a lifetime to each event. The lifetime is decreased periodically (i.e. events age) and events expire when their lifetime is expired. Thus, the amnesty policy is based on expiration of events. Events that have expired are no longer used to compute the anomaly score for each host. These methods can be again categorized into two groups according to their methods for assigning a lifetime to each event:

- Uniform lifetime (Block Scan Detection)
  The methods in this class count the number of events (or sum of the anomaly scores for all events) contained in a fixed time window and check if a threshold is exceeded. Snort [20] counts the total number of connection attempts, while Kato et al. [13] consider only failed connection attempts. Basu et al.'s approach [8] uses neural networks to assess the score for each event and compares the sum of scores, during a fixed time window, with the threshold.
- Lifetime proportional to how anomalous the event is considered
  The Spice engine [22] grants each packet a lifetime proportional to its anomaly score [1] to impede evasion attacks using *delayed scan* techniques.

No Amnesty Methods. There are a few traditional scan detection methods that don't provide any way to reduce the anomaly score of a host such as Bro[2] [16] However, as this accumulated score will only ever increase and eventually hit the threshold (or several thresholds in the case of Bro), these scan detection methods are prone to false positives as any host, given enough time, will eventually be flagged as a scanner.

2.2 Evaluation Metrics for Scan Detection Methods

Evaluation metrics are needed to measure the effectiveness of scan detection methods. Although previous work has used different metrics to evaluate the effectiveness of a scan detection method, these metrics have been targeted at measuring the false positive rate, false negative rate and detection delay of the scan detection method.

In this work we propose two additional metrics that allow us to measure the effectiveness of a scan detection method under a specific scan technique used by an attacker. The idea behind these metrics is that the more resources the attacker needs to complete the scan in the presence of that detection method, the more difficult it is to evade the scan detection method under that scan technique.

Time to complete the scan. The first metric we propose is the time that it takes for an attacker to complete the scan of a network in the presence of the scan detection method, using a specific scan technique. Note that this is different from measuring detection delay, since we are interested in how long it takes for *the attacker* to complete the scan of a certain address space without being detected, rather than how long it takes for the *scan detection method* to detect an attacker.

---

[1] The Spice engine uses Bayes network to build up a profile for each source address.

[2] Here we refer to the classical scan detection method in scan.bro. Bro also has an option to employ the TRW algorithm for enhanced scan detection and it has also recently introduced methods to evict state [10].

Clearly, due to the frequent changes in the address space usage of any network (e.g. dynamic IP assignments, laptops, hosts being replaced, etc), the longer it takes for an attacker to complete the scan, the less truthful the information gathered at the beginning of the scan is compared to the current state. Also, the topological information gathered by the attacker, can have a lifetime after which it becomes useless. For example after the public announcement of a vulnerability, an attacker might be interested in promptly locating all vulnerable hosts in a protected network to try to compromise them. The time window for the attacker to perform the scan and the following attack is the time needed by the system administrator to identify the vulnerability, download a patch (if available) and install it on all vulnerable hosts.

Number of addresses needed to complete the scan. The second metric is the number of IP addresses that the attacker needs to complete the scan in the presence of the scan detection method, using a specific scan technique. For example, for a Timeout-based method, given the attacker has no time constrains, the attacker will need a single IP address to complete the scan, as it just needs to use a scan rate below the lowest detected by the method. We call the evasive scan technique of probing at a rate below the minimum detected by a method, a *delayed scan*.

But when the attacker has a time constraint, it needs to increase the number of addresses performing the scan in parallel, if it wants to complete the scan satisfying the time constraint while remaining undetected. For a Positive-Reward-based method, given an attacker, which randomly probes addresses in the target network using a single source address, the detection method will eventually flag the address as a scanner. If the network employs scan suppression, blocking any further probes from that address, then the attacker needs to use another address to continue with the scan, thus requiring multiple IP addresses to send scans from.

To summarize, given an IP address space to scan, we can evaluate the effectiveness of a scan detection method against a specific scan technique, i.e. the amount of resources needed by the attacker to complete the scan while remaining undetected. For this, we use a tuple (α, T), where α denotes the number of source addresses needed to complete the scan and T is the time needed for the attacker to complete the scan.

3   z-Scan: Evasion Attacks Against TRW

Positive-Reward-based methods lessen the accumulated anomaly scores for a scanner upon the occurrence of benign events. Thus, they provide an opportunity to the intelligent attacker for evading detection if it is able to replicate or forge the existence of such benign events. In this section we propose new evasive scan techniques to evade detection by Positive-Reward-based methods that decrease the anomaly score of a scanner based on successful connections. We focus on TRW [12] as a representative of this family.

TRW is a well accepted scan detection method mainly used for detecting horizontal scans, where an attacker probes multiple protected hosts to obtain information about which hosts/services are available in the protected network. It can also be applied to detect vertical scans, as well as detecting misbehaved hosts inside the protected network.

Table 1. Notation

N: the size of address space to scan (number of active hosts + inactive IP addresses)
a: the number of active IP addresses in the address space
P_s: the fraction of active hosts. *i.e.*, $\frac{a}{N}$
α: the number of source IP addresses for the attack to scan the entire address space
H_0: the hypothesis that the source is a benign user
H_1: the hypothesis that the source is a scanner
$\Lambda(Y)$: the likelihood ratio for TRW
θ_0: the probability that a connection attempt succeeds given the hypothesis H_0
θ_1: the probability that a connection attempt succeeds given the hypothesis H_1
η_1: the upper threshold of the likelihood ratio $\Lambda(Y)$
which if crossed, flags the source as a scanner
n: the number of probes that attackers can perform before being blocked
n_i: the number of probes which the attacker can perform before
being blocked at i-th round
s_i: the estimated number of accumulated active known hosts at i-th round
t: threshold of Block Scan Detection method, *i.e.*, the number of
failed connection attempts within the time window.
β: the fraction of correct scan result
w: the size of the time window in Block Scan Detection method (in time ticks)
T: time constraint within which scan should complete
r: probing rate (the number of probes per time tick)

In this paper, for simplicity, we focus on horizontal scans. Similar techniques can be applied to other cases.

We first show *naive scan* as a straw-man case, and then describe a more sophisticated evasive scan technique which we call *z-Scan*, that is very effective against TRW. For both techniques we analytically compute the values of α, the number of IP addresses that the attacker needs to complete the scan. Table 1 shows the notation used in the analysis.

3.1   Naive Scan Against TRW

Naive scan. A determined attacker who wants to complete the scan of a network, and controls a set of IP addresses, can perform what we call *naive scan*. A naive scan is a distributed scan. In its most basic form the scan is performed sequentially. The attacker selects one of the addresses it controls and starts scanning the target network. Assuming that the target network uses scan suppression, after several probes the address will be flagged as a scanner and further probes will be blocked. At that point the attacker selects a different scanner address and commands it to scan a new set of addresses, not yet scanned, until it gets blocked again. The process continues until the complete target address space has been scanned.

Note that an attacker that wants to optimize the naive scan, rather than use its addresses sequentially, can make them scan in parallel. This allows the attacker to reduce the time employed to complete the scan. Here, the attacker divides the target address space into disjoint subsets of addresses and assigns one such subset to a different scanner address under its control. The scanner addresses probe their corresponding subset until being blocked and report back to the attacker any target addresses that it could not scan before being blocked, so they can be assigned by the attacker to a different scanner, not yet blacklisted.

Analysis. Here, we compute the number of distinct source IP addresses, α, needed to scan an address space of size N addresses, when a naive scan technique[3] is used against TRW.

Let H_0 be the hypothesis that the source of a connection attempt is a benign user; and let H_1 be the hypothesis that it is a scanner. TRW defines an indicator variable Y_i that represents the outcome of the first connection attempt from a scanner to a target host, where $Y_i = 0$ if the connection attempt was successful and $Y_i = 1$ if it failed. Each connection attempt regardless of its success is considered as an event.

Then conditional on the hypothesis H_0 and H_1, the TRW framework defines:

$$Pr[Y_i = 0|H_0] = \theta_0 \qquad Pr[Y_i = 1|H_0] = 1 - \theta_0$$
$$Pr[Y_i = 0|H_1] = \theta_1 \qquad Pr[Y_i = 1|H_1] = 1 - \theta_1$$

that is, the parameters θ_0 and θ_1 represent the conditional probabilities of an event given the hypothesis H_0 and H_1.

TRW keeps a likelihood ratio $\Lambda(Y)$ for each source address that has generated an event. For every successful connection the likelihood ratio is reduced by multiplying it by $\frac{\theta_1}{\theta_0}$, and for each unsuccessful connection the likelihood ratio is increased by multiplying it by $\frac{1-\theta_1}{1-\theta_0}$. If the likelihood ratio for a scanner address exceeds the upper threshold η_1, the address is flagged as a scanner. The reader can refer to [12] for a detailed explanation of the framework and how to set the associated parameters.

We assume that scan suppression is used in addition to TRW, so that any probes received from an address that has been determined by TRW to be a scanner are dropped.

Let n be the total number of events generated by the scanner address, that is, the total number of unique connection attempts to different target addresses, let s be the number of unique connection attempts that were successful, and let $n - s$ be the number of unique connection attempts that were unsuccessful. Then the likelihood ratio for the scanner address is:

$$\Lambda(Y) = \Pi_{i=1}^{n} \frac{Pr[Y_i|H_1]}{Pr[Y_i|H_0]} = (\frac{\theta_1}{\theta_0})^s (\frac{1 - \theta_1}{1 - \theta_0})^{n-s} \tag{1}$$

In order to be flagged as a scanner the likelihood ratio for an address needs to exceed the upper threshold η_1, thus meeting the following condition:

$$(\frac{\theta_1}{\theta_0})^s (\frac{1 - \theta_1}{1 - \theta_0})^{n-s} \geq \eta_1 \tag{2}$$

For simplicity, we assume that the active hosts are uniformly distributed across the target address space and define P_s to be the fraction of active hosts in the address space

---

[3] In this case, we assume that the attacker selects a random target and sends a probing packet without any evasion technique.

having open the port that the attacker is using for the horizontal scan. Then, $s = nP_s$ and solving $(\frac{\theta_1}{\theta_0})^s(\frac{1-\theta_1}{1-\theta_0})^{n-s} \leq \eta_1$ for n we obtain:

$$n \leq \frac{\log \eta_1}{P_s \log \frac{\theta_1}{\theta_0} + (1 - P_s) \log \frac{1-\theta_1}{1-\theta_0}} \tag{3}$$

Equation 3 shows an upper bound on the number of target addresses that a scanner address can probe before being detected.

For each scanner address used, the attacker is able to gain information about n new addresses, before the address is blocked by the scan suppression method. Thus, in a naive scan the number of source addresses needed by the attacker to complete the scan of the whole address space of size N, which we denote by α as stated in Section 2.2, is:

$$\alpha \geq \frac{N}{n} = N \frac{P_s \log \frac{\theta_1}{\theta_0} + (1 - P_s) \log \frac{1-\theta_1}{1-\theta_0}}{\log \eta_1} \tag{4}$$

This result shows that the number of addresses that an attacker, using a naive scan technique, needs to completely scan a target network is bounded by a function which grows linearly with the size of the address space being scanned.

3.2   z-Scan Against TRW

Section 3.1 introduced a basic attacker that performed a distributed scan on a target network. In this section we propose a more intelligent attacker that takes advantage of the positive rewards awarded by TRW for successful connections. This attacker performs what we call *z-Scan*.

A z-Scan is a distributed scan where the attacker uses each of its available scanner addresses to scan a subset of the target network. The main difference with the naive scan is that in a z-Scan the set of scanners controlled by the attacker collude, sharing the addresses of previously-found active hosts.

A known limitation of TRW is that if the attacker knows a set of active hosts in the target network, it can evade detection by alternating a random probe with a probe to a known active host, thus making the likelihood ratio oscillate without reaching the upper threshold η_1.

Assuming that the attacker has no information whatsoever about the target network at the beginning of the scan and that the target network once again uses scan suppression, the attacker proceeds as follows. First, the attacker selects one of its scanner addresses and performs random probing until the address becomes blocked. At that point, it commands the host owning that address to pass the set of active hosts found to another host which starts scanning alternating a known active host with a random probe till exhausting the set of known active hosts. Once that set is exhausted the new host continues with random probes until being blocked. The procedure is repeated until the complete address space of the target network has been scanned. Note that the attacker could also split the target address space into smaller spaces and perform z-Scan in parallel on them using multiple addresses.

We will refer to the sequence of scan probes from a scanner address before it gets blocked as a *round*. Intuitively, we can anticipate that the number of active hosts probed at each round will increase exponentially, thus bounding the value of α, the number of IP addresses needed to scan an address space of size N, logarithmically with respect to N. This technique is named "z-Scan" because it zigzags its targets from known active hosts to unknown hosts and vice versa.

Analysis. In round i, the attacker uses a scanner address to probe part of the target address space, using information gathered in all previous rounds. Let n_i denote the total number of probes to distinct target addresses performed by the scanner address in round i, and s_i denote the number of successful connections (or probes) to distinct target addresses performed by a scanner address in round i. Since we defined α to be the number of addresses needed by z-Scan to complete the scan of the target network, we know that $i \in [1, \alpha]$.

Note that the attacker begins probing with no known active hosts, then the number of probes the attacker can perform at the first round n_1 before being blocked, is given by Equation 3:

$$n_1 \leq \frac{\log \eta_1}{P_s \log \frac{\theta_1}{\theta_0} + (1 - P_s) \log \frac{1-\theta_1}{1-\theta_0}}$$

Thus, the number of active hosts found at the first round, $s_1 = P_s n_1$.

Since the attacker has yielded s_1 active host addresses, he can move to another source address and repeat this process until being blocked by TRW. At this second round, the attacker can employ s_1 known active hosts to alternate probing between the known active host addresses and the unknown, making TRW oscillate below the threshold, η_1. However, after consuming all the known active addresses, the attacker needs to perform naive random probing. Therefore, we can find the accumulated number of active addresses by the second round, s_2, by solving the following two equations for s_2:

$$\left(\frac{\theta_1}{\theta_0}\right)^{s_2} \left(\frac{1-\theta_1}{1-\theta_0}\right)^{n_2-s_2} \geq \eta_1 \tag{5}$$

$$s_2 = s_1 + (n_2 - s_1)P_s \tag{6}$$

Therefore,

$$s_2 = \left(1 - \frac{P_s \log \frac{\theta_1}{\theta_0}}{P_s \log \frac{\theta_1}{\theta_0} + (1 - P_s) \log \frac{1-\theta_1}{1-\theta_0}}\right)s_1 + \frac{P_s \log \eta_1}{P_s \log \frac{\theta_1}{\theta_0} + (1 - P_s) \log \frac{1-\theta_1}{1-\theta_0}}$$

Since $\left(1 - \frac{P_s \log \frac{\theta_1}{\theta_0}}{P_s \log \frac{\theta_1}{\theta_0} + (1-P_s) \log \frac{1-\theta_1}{1-\theta_0}}\right)$ and $\frac{P_s \log \eta_1}{P_s \log \frac{\theta_1}{\theta_0} + (1-P_s) \log \frac{1-\theta_1}{1-\theta_0}}$ are constants, we can simplify s_2 by replacing them with k and l respectively. Hence:

$$s_2 = ks_1 + l$$

If the attacker repeats this process, the estimated number of accumulated active known hosts in the i-th round, s_i, is:

$$s_i = ks_{i-1} + l \tag{7}$$

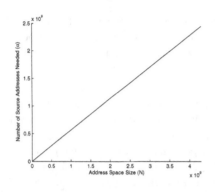

Fig. 1. Naive random scan against TRW ($P_s = 0.3$)

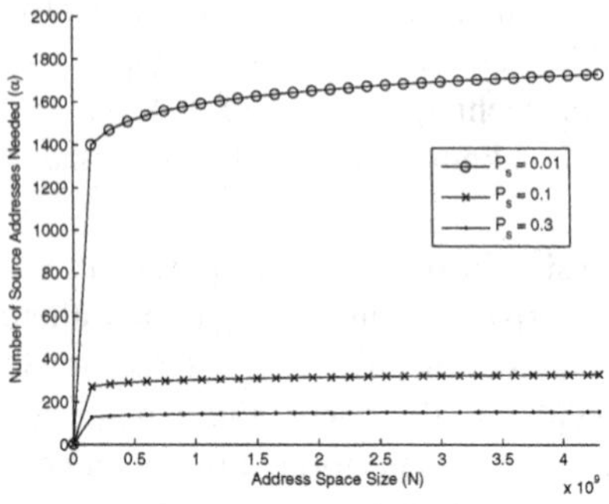

Fig. 2. z-Scan against TRW

We can derive the single general form for s_i:

$$s_i = k^{i-1}(s_1 + \frac{l}{k-1}) - \frac{l}{k-1} \tag{8}$$

Let $m_i = n_i - s_{i-1}$, where m_i denotes the number of new IP addresses probed in the i-th round. We can compute m_i as $m_i = k^{i-2}(k-1)(s_1 + \frac{l}{k-1})\frac{1}{P_s}$.

By the last round, round α, the total number of new IP addresses probed in all the rounds should be N. Thus α is the smallest value such that

$$n_1 + \sum_{2 \leq i \leq \alpha} m_i \geq N$$

and solving for α, we obtain:

$$\alpha = \left\lceil \log_k \left(1 + \frac{P_s(N - n_1)}{s_1 + \frac{l}{k-1}} \right) \right\rceil + 1 \tag{9}$$

This result shows that the number of addresses needed to completely scan a target network using z-Scan, is bounded by a function which grows logarithmically with the size of the address space being scanned.

As an example, we assume an attacker uses z-Scan with the following parameters: $P_s = \theta_1 = 0.3$, $\theta_0 = 0.99$, $\eta_1 = \frac{P_D}{P_F} = \frac{0.99}{0.01}$ where P_D and P_F are desired detection probability and false positive probability as in [12]. If this attacker wants to scan a /8 network (i.e. 2^{24} addresses), then it only needs to use 110 addresses to complete the scan versus 9.5 million when using a naive scan.

Figures 1 and 2 plot Equations 4 and 9 respectively using the above parameters. Compare the logarithmic bound of z-Scan with the linear bound of the naive scan. Clearly, an attacker that wants to avoid detection can take advantage of the positive reward method of TRW to limit the amount of resources (i.e. IP addresses) needed to complete the scan, which shows the vulnerability of TRW to z-Scan.

4   Hybrid Detection Method and Evaluation

Section 3 has shown the vulnerability of Positive-Reward-based detection methods to distributed scans, where the attackers collude to create extra rewards for each other.

The other main type of scan detection methods shown in Section 2 are Timeout-based methods. It is well known that Timeout-based methods are easily eluded by using delayed probing, i.e., sending probing packets with enough time delay between them to allow expiration of previous events, so the anomaly score does not increase.

Positive-Reward-based methods based on successful connections, such as TRW, are resilient against evasion attacks using delayed probing. For example Weaver et al. [23] show a TRW variant that can detect attackers probing at a rate larger than one probe per minute. On the other hand, Timeout-based methods will not be eluded by z-Scan. We propose then to combine both approaches to create a scan detection method which is highly resistant to known evasion techniques. We call it a hybrid detection method.

In the remainder of this section, we present a simple example of the hybrid detection methods using TRW and Block Scan Detection (BSD) and show how the detection methods can complement each other. After a brief analysis on delayed probing against BSD, we provide numerical analysis on the robustness of the hybrid detection method.

4.1   Delayed Scan Against BSD

BSD methods usually work as follows. There are two parameters: a time window of fixed length w and a threshold value t. BSD keeps a counter for the current number of events for each remote IP address. Examples of usual events are the number of destinations contacted or the number of unsuccessful connections attempted. Every time a new event occurs, the counter is incremented and compared to the threshold. If the threshold has been exceeded an alarm is thrown. Each event has an age of length equal to the value of the time window parameter. The age of an event is set to zero when the event is observed, and after the age has become larger than the time window, the event is expired and the counter is decremented.

Timeout-based methods are easily eluded by using delayed probing. In particular, BSD methods can be eluded by sending probing packets with enough time delay between them to escape a preset time window and never reach the preset threshold.

When the attacker can determine the values of the window and threshold parameters and is free of time limit, it is able to scan the whole address space using a single IP address without being detected. However, when a constraint is given on time T, the attacker should probe simultaneously using multiple source IP addresses to evade detection by BSD.

Since α source hosts should complete probing N target addresses in the protected network address space:

$$\alpha r T \geq N \tag{10}$$

where r is a probing rate (the number of probes per time tick). In addition, the number of events per time tick should not exceed $\frac{t}{w}$, where w is the size of the time window, and t is the threshold for the number of events allowed in that window. Assuming the

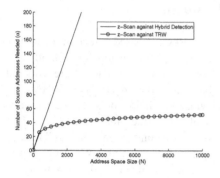

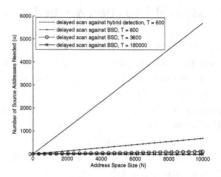

Fig. 3. z-Scan against Hybrid detection, TRW ($P_s = 0.3$)

Fig. 4. Delayed scan against Hybrid detection ($P_s = 0.3, t = 10, w = 600$time ticks)

BSD method uses failed connection attempts as events (e.g. Kato et al [13]), then the maximum probing rate r_{max} is:

$$(1 - P_s)r_{max} = \frac{t}{w}$$

If the BSD method uses any probe attempt as an event (e.g. Snort [20]) then $P_s = 0$ in the above expression.

By setting r in Equation 10 to r_{max}:

$$\alpha \geq \frac{1 - P_s}{T} \frac{w}{t} N$$

This result shows that using delayed scan, the minimum number of addresses that an attacker needs to complete the scan, when subject to a time constraint T, grows linearly with N.

Figure 4 plots α as a function of the size of the address space of the scanned network N for different values of T. The window, threshold and fraction of active hosts are set to: $P_s = 0.3$, $t = 10$ probes, $w = 600$ time ticks. As shown, delayed scan evades BSD with only one source IP address when it has sufficient time ($T = 180,000$ time ticks); but otherwise α is directly proportional to address space size N.

4.2 Hybrid Detection Method

In our hybrid detection method we adopt a combination of TRW and BSD. We show that the hybrid detection method forces the attacker to use more addresses in order to complete the scan when compared with the case where only one of the two methods is deployed. In this hybrid method, we assume that TRW and BSD are operating independently in parallel, and a detected scan source will be blocked regardless of which detection method detected it. Simply put, the attackers' scan efficiency is bounded by the more effective of the two detection methods against the attackers' strategy.

In the remainder of this section we show how the Hybrid detection method performs when faced with three different scan techniques: z-Scan, delayed scan and a combination of both.

z-Scan against Hybrid detection. When z-Scan is performed against BSD, assuming that the time needed to send probing packets is relatively small compared to the time window of BSD, we can suppose that all failed connection attempts will fall within the window. Thus, the number of times the attacker will be blocked, that is, the number of source addresses it needs, equals $\alpha = \frac{N(1-P_s)}{t}$, where t is the threshold of failed connection attempts within the time window of the BSD methods.

Delayed scan against Hybrid detection. Conversely, if a delayed scan is performed against TRW, α is equal to that of performing a naive random scan against TRW as shown in Section 3 since TRW is agnostic to the time frame where the probing events occur. Thus, from Equation 4:

$$\alpha_{trw} \geq N \frac{P_s \log \frac{\theta_1}{\theta_0} + (1 - P_s) \log \frac{1-\theta_1}{1-\theta_0}}{\log \eta_1}$$

Since the Hybrid detection method uses both TRW and BSD in parallel, then:

$$\alpha = max\left(\alpha_{trw}, \alpha_{bsd}\right) = max \left(N \frac{P_s \log \frac{\theta_1}{\theta_0} + (1 - P_s) \log \frac{1-\theta_1}{1-\theta_0}}{\log \eta_1}, \frac{1 - P_s}{T} \frac{w}{t} N \right)$$

Accordingly, the values of α in both z-Scan and delayed scan are linearly bounded by TRW and BSD. As Figures 3 and 4 show, the hybrid detection method forces both z-Scan and delayed scan to use a number of addresses that is linear with the size of the address space. However, these results are dependent on multiple parameters for configuring detection methods and network environment such as t, w, T, and P_s.

Combined scan against Hybrid detection. The attackers can also combine the evasion techniques to elude this hybrid detection method. We give a simple example of combining delayed scan and z-Scan to evade the hybrid method provided in this paper. That is, the attacker can perform z-Scan with a low scan rate set to evade the threshold value of BSD. In order to complete the scan of the address space of size N in time T, the attacker needs to divide the address space into different *subspaces* and simultaneously perform z-Scan on each subspace using multiple addresses. If the address space is divided into D subspaces of the same size, each subspace is of size $\frac{N}{D}$, and the active host ratio in that subspace is P_s. Then, the number of source addresses, σ, needed to scan one subspace using z-Scan is, from Equation 9:

$$\sigma = \log_k \left(1 + \frac{P_s(\frac{N}{D} - n_1)}{s_1 + \frac{l}{k-1}} \right) + 1 \tag{11}$$

To evade BSD with the threshold value of t and the window size of w, the maximum scan rate r_i in the i-th round of z-Scan should satisfy:

$$(1 - \frac{s_i}{n_i})r_i = \frac{t}{w}$$

In addition, since each z-Scan task on a subspace should be finished within the constraint T, the sum of time consumed in each round of z-Scan should be equal to or less than T.

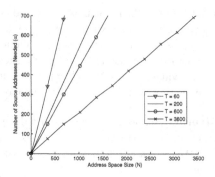

Fig. 5. Combined scan against hybrid detection ($P_s = 0.3, t = 10, w = 600$ time ticks)

$$\sum_{i=1}^{\sigma} \frac{n_i}{r_i} \leq T \tag{12}$$

Finally, the total number of source addresses, α, needed in this combined scan is $D\sigma$. Since there can be multiple possible values of D which meet constraint T, the attacker can choose the minimum of the possible $D\sigma$ values which satisfy equation 11 and 12. Therefore:

$$\alpha = min\{D\sigma \mid \sigma \text{ and } D \text{ satisfy Equation 11 and 12}\} \tag{13}$$

Through numerical iterations, we obtain the values of α with respect to N. The results indicate that the number of source addresses the attacker needs in the combined scan is proportional to the address space size N. So, as expected, when faced with a hybrid detection method, the attacker would prefer the combined scan, since it achieves better performance than the individual z-Scan or delayed scan methods.

Figure 5 shows how the combined scan performs in the face of a hybrid detection method with varying values for the time constraint T. Clearly, the more constrained the attacker is (i.e. smaller values of T) the larger the number of addresses it needs to use to complete the scan in the given time.

Limitations. Even though the hybrid approach provides higher effectiveness in detecting evasion attacks, it has some limitations. In terms of administrative efficiency, it requires supporting two different scan detection methods, or a new combined one. Regarding the detection efficiency, simply combining detection results could aggravate the total false positive rate; *i.e.*, the false positive rate of the hybrid method is additive.

5   Information-Hiding Countermeasures Against Evasion Techniques

In Section 4 we presented a hybrid detection method to thwart both z-Scan and delayed scan. The presented hybrid method tries to thwart the attacker's evasion attack. Another promising type of defense is rather than raising the bar for the scan technique, trying to hide the address space usage, thus reducing the utility of the scan itself. In this section, we explore one such countermeasure. Despite its simplicity, we show that the effectiveness is promising in augmenting the current detection methods to curb evasion attacks.

The methods we study is *All-Positive Response* (APR). APR is a technique that gives false responses when receiving packets destined to unassigned IP addresses or to closed ports on active hosts. The generated responses falsely indicate that a host exists on that address and has the probed port open. From the attacker's point of view, information obtained during the scan cannot distinguish which host is active and which port is open since all of them appear active/open. In addition, the APR method can be easily implemented by applying virtual honeypot technology [14,17].

There are other such countermeasures that could potentially help against evasion using z-Scan, such as Antonatos et al.'s Network Address Space Randomization (NASR) [7], where hosts are forced to periodically change their IP addresses. We leave the study of such other countermeasures for future work.

z-Scan against TRW with APR. Since the z-Scan technique is highly dependent on the set of known active hosts, say s_a, we can show that its performance against APR will be significantly degraded. When TRW is employed with APR, contrary to the attacker's expectation, s_a is just a set of addresses with active hosts ratio P_s. Without APR, all hosts in s_a would be active.

Therefore, in this case, the z-Scan behaves similarly to a naive scan. Initially, when an attacker begins the z-Scan, it will be blocked after n probes as shown in Equation 3. At that point the attacker believes that it knows a set of n active hosts when in fact only nP_s of those are active.

Thus in the next round when the attacker alternates one probe to an unknown address with one probe to an address it believes to be an active host, TRW will detect it and block it after n probes because the fraction of active hosts in the probes will be P_s, the same as in the case of a naive scan. So, in every round each scanner address from the attacker is allowed to probe n addresses rather than an increasing number with z-Scan. Even worse for the attacker, in this case only half of n is newly-scanned hosts since the attacker alternates probing targets between the addresses in s_a and a randomly selected probing target (from the rest of the address space). This cycle will be repeated until the whole address space is scanned. To summarize, the attacker can probe n new hosts in the first round and $\frac{n}{2}$ new hosts each in the subsequent rounds. Thus, the number of source addresses required for the attacker is:

$$\alpha = \frac{N - n}{\frac{n}{2}} + 1$$

that is:

$$\alpha = \frac{2N}{n} - 1 \tag{14}$$

which is about twice as large as that of naive scan against TRW.

Thus, z-Scan is completely inefficient against APR since a naive scan would approximately require half the number of addresses. In this case the use of APR in the protected network forces the attacker to use a more sophisticated probing technique. A nice property of information-hiding countermeasures is that they can be combined with any scan detection method such as the proposed hybrid detection method, to form a more complete defense solution that both obscures the address space usage of the network and raises the bar for the scan techniques used by the attacker.

6   Related Work

There has been a wealth of research on scan detection methods. Early proposals such as the Network Security Monitor (NSM) and the old Snort scan detection method (port scan preprocessor) [11,20] counted probes in a fixed window of time, flagging an external host as a scanner if the probe count exceeded a preset threshold.

Following work built on the observation that unsuccessful connections are a better indication of scanning than just the number of probes generated by a host [16,19]. The performance of these methods greatly varied with the values of its parameters.

More recent work also using unsuccessful connections as events, employs a random walk framework to decide between the hypothesis that a remote host is a scanner or benign [12]. Followup work using the random walk framework includes [21] where the authors focus on detecting internal, rather than remote, scanners present in the monitored network. It also includes [23] where the authors use several approximations in order to limit to a minimum the resources (e.g. memory) needed to operate it.

There is a separate group of scan detection methods that assigns anomaly scores to events, based either on the access probability for each internal host [15] or conditional probabilities extracted from the addresses and ports pairs [22].

There has been little previous research on evasion techniques. Ptacek and Newsham show different insertion and evasion techniques that affect Intrusion Detection Systems [18]. There is also previous research work on overloading detection systems [9] and several tools have been developed with the same purpose [5,6]. Some tools have been created for information-hiding at the end host, such as Morph which allows the user to emulate any operating system by forging replies to probes [4]. In general, most evasion work comes from the underground literature [1,3].

7   Conclusion

Numerous approaches have been proposed to detect network scans. However, despite the importance of limiting the information obtained by the attacker, and the wide availability of such scan detection methods, there has been very little research on the evasive scan techniques, which can potentially be used by attackers to avoid detection. In this paper, our contributions are five-fold.

First, we categorize current scan detection methods using a novel point of view, their amnesty policy. Such a classification allows us to distill the essence of each class of detection methods and facilitate us in analyzing their vulnerability to evasive scan techniques and countermeasures. Second, we propose two novel metrics to measure the resources that an attacker needs to complete a scan without being detected: the time and the number of IP addresses; needed by an attacker to complete the scan of a certain network space, while remaining undetected.

Third, as a concrete example demonstrating evasive scans against Positive-Reward based detection methods, we propose a new distributed evasive scan attack, z-Scan, which is extremely effective against TRW. With z-Scan, an attacker can complete the scan of a given IP address space using only a small number of different source IP addresses (where the number is only logarithmic to the size of the IP address space to be scanned). Fourth, as a countermeasure, we propose a hybrid approach which combines Positive-Reward and Timeout-based methods and demonstrate its effectiveness against evasive scans through analysis and simulation.

Finally, we also study information-hiding countermeasures, where we actively respond to scans with false information, and demonstrate that this type of countermeasures are extremely effective against evasive scan attacks. Moreover, the hybrid approach and the information-hiding based countermeasures are complementary, and can be combined for even greater benefits. To conclude, evasion techniques and countermeasures have not been thoroughly studied before. We hope this work will serve as a first step and encourage more study in this direction.

Acknowledgments

The authors would like to thank Xeno Kovah and the anonymous reviewers for their insightful feedback. Support for this material was provided by the National Science Foundation under Grants No. 0433540 and 0448452. Partial support was also provided by the U.S. Army Research Office under the Cyber-TA Research Grant No. W911NF-06-1-0316 and under Grant DAAD19-02-1-0389 through CyLab at Carnegie Mellon. The views and conclusions contained here are those of the authors and should not be interpreted as necessarily representing the official policies or endorsements, either expressed or implied, of ARO, CMU, the U.S. Government or any of its agencies.

References

1. antirez. IP ID reverse scan,
   http://www.kyuzz.org/antirez/papers/dumbscan.html
2. Fyodor. The Art of Port Scanning. Phrack 51, vol. 7 (September 1, 1997),
   http://www.phrack.com/phrack/51/P51-11
3. hybrid Distributed information gathering. Phrack 51, vol. 9 (September 9, 1999)
   http://www.phrack.org/phrack/55/P55-09
4. Morph, http://www.synacklabs.net/projects/morph/
5. Snot. http://www.l0t3k.org/security/tools/ids/
6. Stick. http://www.l0t3k.org/security/tools/ids/
7. Antonatos, S., Akritidis, P., Markatos, E., Anagnostakis, K.G.: Defending against Hitlist Worms using Network Address Space Randomization. In: ACM Workshop on Rapid Malcode (Fairfax, VA, USA, 11 (November 2005)
8. Basu, R., Cunningham, R.K., Lippmann, R.P.: Detecting Low-Profile Probes and Novel Denial-of-Service Attacks. In: Proceedings 2nd Annual IEEE Systems, Man, and Cybernetics Information Assurance Workshop (West Point, NY, USA) (June 5–6, 2001)

9. Crosby, S., Wallach, D.: Denial of Service via Algorithmic Complexity Attacks. In: Proceedings of the 12th USENIX Security Symposium (Washington DC, USA) (August 4–8, 2003)

10. Dreger, H., Feldmann, A., Paxson, V., Sommer, R.: Operational Experiences with HighVolume Network Intrusion Detection. In: 11th ACM Conference on Computer and Communications Security, Washington DC, USA, October 25–29, 2004, ACM Press, New York (2004)

11. Heberlein, L.T., Dias, G.V., Levitt, K.N., Mukherjee, B., Wood, J., Wolber, D.: A network security monitor. In: Proceedings of the IEEE Symposium on Research in Security and Privacy

12. Jung, J., Paxson, V., Berger, A.W., Balakrishnan, H.: Fast Portscan Detection Using Sequential Hypothesis Testing. In: IEEE Symposium on Security and Privacy, Berkeley/Oakland, CA, USA, May 9–12, 2004, IEEE Computer Society Press, Los Alamitos (2004)

13. Kato, N., Nitou, H., Ohta, K., Mansfield, G., Nemoto, Y.: A Real-Time Intrusion Detection System(IDS) for Large Scale Networks and its Evaluations. IEICE Transactions on Communication E82B(11), 1817–1825

14. Kreibich, C., Crowcroft, J.: Honeycomb –Creating Intrusion Detection Signatures Using Honeypots. In: 2nd Workshop on Hot Topics in Networks Boston, MA, USA (November 20–21, 2003)

15. Leckie, C., Kotagiri, R.: A Probabilistic Approach to Detecting Network Scans. In: Proceedings of the Eighth IEEE Network Operations and Management Symposium. Florence, Italy (April 15–19, 2002)

16. Paxson, V.: Bro: a system for detecting network intruders in real-time. Computer Networks (Amsterdam, Netherlands) 31(23–24), 2435–2463 (1999)

17. Provos, N.: A Virtual Honeypot Framework. In: Proceedings of the 13th USENIX Security Symposium San Diego, CA, USA (August 9–13, 2004)

18. Ptacek, T.H., Newsham, T.N.: Insertion, Evasion, and Denial of Service: Eluding Network Intrusion Detection. Technical report

19. Robertson, S., Siegel, E.V., Miller, M., Stolfo, S.J.: Surveillance Detection in High Bandwidth Environments. In: Proceedings of the 2003 DARPA DISCEX III Conference Washington DC, USA (April 22–24, 2003)

20. Roesch, M.: Snort-Lightweight Intrusion Detection for Networks. In: Proceedings of LISA'99: 13th Systems Administration Conference Seattle, WA, USA (November 7–12, 1999)

21. Schechter, S.E., Jung, J., Berger, A.W.: Fast Detection of Scanning Worm Infections. 7th International Symposium on Recent Advances in Intrusion Detection Sophia Antipolis, French Riviera, France (September 15–17, 2004)

22. Staniford, S., Hoagland, J.A., McAlerney, J.M.: Practical Automated Detection of Stealthy Portscans. In: Proceedings of the 7th ACM Conference on Computer and Communications Security. Athens, Greece (November 1–4, 2000)

23. Weaver, N., Staniford, S., Paxson, V.: Very Fast Containment of Scanning Worms. In: 13th USENIX Security Symposium. San Diego, CA, USA (August 9–13, 2004)

On the Adaptive Real-Time Detection of Fast-Propagating Network Worms

Jaeyeon Jung[1], Rodolfo A. Milito[2], and Vern Paxson[3]

[1] Mazu Networks
jyjung@mazunetworks.com
[2] Consentry Networks
rodolfo@consentry.com
[3] International Computer Science Institute
and Lawrence Berkeley National Laboratory
vern@icir.org

Abstract. We present two light-weight worm detection algorithms that offer significant advantages over fixed-threshold methods. The first algorithm, RBS (*rate-based sequential hypothesis testing*), aims at the large class of worms that attempts to quickly propagate, thus exhibiting abnormal levels of the rate at which hosts initiate connections to new destinations. The foundation of RBS derives from the theory of sequential hypothesis testing, the use of which for detecting randomly scanning hosts was first introduced by our previous work developing TRW [6]. The sequential hypothesis testing methodology enables us to engineer detectors to meet specific targets for false-positive and false-negative rates, rather than triggering when fixed thresholds are crossed. In this sense, the detectors that we introduce are truly adaptive.

We then introduce RBS+TRW, an algorithm that combines fan-out rate (RBS) and probability of failure (TRW) of connections to new destinations. RBS+TRW provides a unified framework that at one end acts as pure RBS and at the other end as pure TRW. Selecting an operating point that includes both mechanisms extends RBS's power in detecting worms that scan randomly selected IP addresses. Using four traces from three qualitatively different sites, we evaluate RBS and RBS+TRW in terms of false positives, false negatives, and detection speed, finding that RBS+TRW provides good detection of high-profile worms as well as internal Web crawlers that we use as proxies for targeting worms. In doing so, RBS+TRW generates fewer than 1 false alarm per hour for wide range of parameter choices.

1 Introduction

If a network worm penetrates a site's perimeter, it can quickly spread to other vulnerable hosts inside the site. The infection propagates by the compromised hosts repeatedly attempting to contact and infect new potential victims. The traffic pattern of fast worm propagation—a single host quickly contacting many different hosts—is a prominent feature across a number of types of worms, and detecting such patterns constitutes the basis for several worm detection approaches [2,8,13].

B. M. Hämmerli and R. Sommer (Eds.): DIMVA 2007, LNCS 4579, pp. 175–192, 2007.

The problem of accurately detecting such worm scanning becomes particularly acute for enterprise networks comprised of a variety of types of hosts running numerous, different applications. This diversity makes it difficult to tune existing worm detection methods [2,13] that presume preselected thresholds for connection rates and window sizes over which to compute whether a host's activity is "too quick." First, finding a single threshold rate that accommodates all (or almost all) benign hosts requires excessive tuning because of diverse application behaviors (e.g., a Web browser generating multiple concurrent connections to fetch embedded objects vs. an SSH client connecting to a server). Second, the window size chosen to compute the average rate affects the detection speed and accuracy; if too small, the detection algorithm is less resilient to small legitimate connection bursts, but if too big, the detection algorithm reacts slowly to fast propagating worms, for which brisk response is vital.

In this paper, we first develop an algorithm for detecting fast-propagating worms that use high-quality *targeting* information. We base our approach on analyzing the rate at which hosts initiate connections to new destinations. One such class of worms are those that spread in a *topological* fashion [11,16]: they gather information on the locally infected host regarding other likely victims. For example, the Morris worm examined .*rhosts* files to see what other machines were known to the local machine [4,10]. A related technique is the use of *meta-servers*, such as worms that query search engines for likely victims [5]. These targeting worms can spread extremely quickly, *even using relatively low-rate scanning*, because the vulnerability density of the addresses they probe is so much higher than if they use random scanning. Furthermore, these worms can evade many existing worm defense systems that rely on the artifacts of random scanning such as number of failed connections and the absence of preceding DNS lookups [2,8,17,18].

Our detection algorithm, *rate-based sequential hypothesis testing* (RBS), operates on a per-host and per-connection basis and does not require access to packet contents. It is built on a probabilistic model that captures benign network characteristics, which allows us to discriminate between benign traffic and worm traffic. RBS also provides an analytic framework that enables a site to tailor its operation to its network traffic pattern and security policies.

We then present RBS+TRW, a unified framework for detecting fast-propagating worms independent of their scanning strategy. RBS+TRW is a blend of RBS and our previous *threshold random walk* (TRW) algorithm, which rapidly discriminates between random scanners and legitimate traffic based on their differing rates of connection failures [6]. Wald's sequential hypothesis testing [14] forms the basis for RBS+TRW's adaptive detection.

We begin with an overview of related work in §2. §3 then presents an analysis of network traces we obtained from two *internal* routers of a medium-size enterprise. The traced traffic includes more than 650 internal hosts, about 10% of the total at the site. We examine the distribution of the time between consecutive *first-contact connection requests*, defined by [8] as a packet addressed to a host with which the sender has not previously communicated. Our analysis finds that for benign network traffic, these interarrival times are bursty, but within the bursts can be approximately modeled using exponential distributions with a few hundred millisecond average intervals.

In §4, we develop the RBS algorithm, based on the same sequential hypothesis testing framework as TRW. RBS quickly identifies hosts that initiate first-contact connection requests at a rate n times higher than that of a typical benign host. RBS updates its decision process upon each data arrival, triggering an alarm after having observed enough empirical data to make a distinction between the candidate models of (somewhat slower) benign and (somewhat faster) malicious host activity.

In §5, we evaluate RBS using trace-driven simulations. We show that computing a simple trimmed mean suffices to automatically discover an effective set of parameters for running RBS. Moreover, we show that RBS triggers few false positives when n is small (0 false positives when $n \leq 5$) when assessed against a trace that includes a variety of applications.

§6 presents RBS+TRW, which automatically adapts between the rate at which a host initiates first-contact connection requests and observations of the success of these attempts, combining two different types of worm detection. Using datasets that contain active worms caught in action, we show that RBS+TRW provides fast detection of scanners and two hosts infected by Code Red II worms, while generating less than 1 false alarm per hour.

2   Related Work

Williamson first proposed limiting the rate of outgoing packets to new destinations [19] and implemented a virus throttle that confines a host to sending packets to no more than one new host a second [13]. While this virus throttling slows traffic that could result from worm propagation below a certain rate, it remains open how to set the rate such that it permits benign traffic without impairing detection capability. For example, Web servers that employ content distribution services cause legitimate Web browsing to generate many concurrent connections to different destinations, which a limit of one new destination per second would significantly hinder. If the characteristics of benign traffic cannot be consistently recognized, a rate-based defense system will be either ignored or disabled by its users.

Numerous efforts have since aimed to improve the simple virus throttle by taking into account other metrics such as increasing numbers of ICMP host-unreachable packets or TCP RST packets [2], number of failed first-contact connections [8,17], and the absence of preceding DNS lookups [18]. However, these supplementary metrics will be not much of use if worms target only hosts that are reachable and have valid names (e.g., topological worms).

This work is inspired by our previous paper [6], which first used sequential hypothesis testing for scan detection. Our previous paper develops the threshold random walk (TRW) portscan detection algorithm based on the observation that a remote port scanner has a higher probability of attempting to contact a local host that does not exist or does not have the requested service running.

Weaver et al. [17] present an approximation to TRW suitable for implementation in high-performance network hardware for worm containment. For the same problem of detecting scanning worms, Schechter et al. [8] combine credit-based rate-limiting and reverse sequential hypothesis testing optimized to detect infection instances. In comparison, our RBS+TRW provides a unified framework built on sequential hypothesis testing with two metrics, a rate and a probability of success of a first-contact connection, that cover a broad range of worms, mostly independent of their scanning strategy or propagation speed.

There have been recent developments of worm detection using *content sifting* (finding common substrings in packets that are being sent in a many-to-many pattern) and automatic signature generation [7,9,15]. These approaches are orthogonal to our approach based on traffic behavior in that the former require payload inspection, for which computationally intensive operations are often needed. Moreover, although our approach requires a few parameter settings, it requires no training nor signature updates. However, content-based approaches are capable of detecting slowly-propagating (stealthy) worms that are indistinguishable from benign hosts by their connection-level traffic behaviors.

3   Data Analysis

We hypothesize that we can bound a benign host's network activity by a reasonably low fan-out per unit time, where we define fan-out as the number of first-contact connection requests a given host initiates. This fan-out per unit time, or *fan-out rate*, is an important traffic measure that we hope will allow us to separate benign hosts from relatively slowly scanning worms. In this section, we analyze traces of a site's internal network traffic, finding that a benign host's fan-out rate rarely exceeds a few first-contact connections per second, and time intervals between these connections can be approximately modeled as exponentially distributed.

We analyze a set of 22 anonymized network traces, each comprised of 10 minutes' of traffic recorded at Lab on Oct. 4, 2004. These were traced using tcpdump at two *internal* routers within Lab, enabling them to collect bidirectional traffic originated by internal hosts to both *external* hosts outside Lab and to other *internal* hosts inside Lab. Although we present the results from one particular site in this section, we studied 4 additional traces collected from three different sites. We used the additional traces to double-check empirical findings and later to evaluate our detection algorithm.

Table 1 summarizes the Lab dataset after some initial filtering to remove periodic NTP traffic and "triggered" connections in which a connection incoming to a host causes the host to initiate a secondary connection outbound. Such triggered connections should not be considered as first-contact connections when assessing whether a host is probing. The table shows that the traffic between internal Lab hosts consists of about 70% of the total outbound traffic recorded in the datasets. Had we traced the traffic at the site's border, we would have seen much less of the total network activity, and lower first-contact connections accordingly.

For each 10-minute trace, we observe a varying number of internal hosts initiating outbound traffic during the observation period. The last row in Table 1 shows that the largest number of active internal hosts in a 10-minute trace is 652.[1]

---

[1] Because each trace was anonymized separately, we are unable to tell how many distinct internal hosts appear across all of the traces.

Table 1. Lab dataset summary: This analysis does not include NTP traffic or triggered outgoing connections such as Ident, Finger, and FTP data-transfer

Outgoing connections	49,049 (100%)
to internal hosts	32,967 (67.21%)
to external hosts	16,082 (32.79%)
Internal hosts	≥ 652

From the traces we observe that over 99.5% of the hosts contacted fewer than 60 different hosts in 10 minutes, corresponding to an average fan-out rate below 0.1/sec. We categorize these hosts as benign. (Note that Twycross and Williamson [13] use fan-out rate of 1/sec as a maximum allowed speed for throttling virus spreads.)

Only 9 hosts exceed this threshold in this trace. Of these, 4 were aliases (introduced by the traces having separate anonymization namespaces) for an internal scanner used by the site for its own vulnerability assessment. Of the remainder, 3 hosts are main mail servers that forward large volumes of email, and the other 2 hosts are internal web crawlers that build search engine databases of the content served by internal Web servers. By manual inspection, we also later found another appearance of the internal scanner that we missed using our 0.1/sec fan-out rate threshold, as in that instance the scanner contacted only 51 different IP addresses during the 10-minute period. We exclude the scanners and the crawlers[2] from our subsequent analysis. In what follows, we develop a model that captures fan-out rate statistics of this set of "purely" benign hosts.

3.1   Time Interval to Visit New Destinations

A host engaged in scanning or worm propagation will generally probe a significant number of hosts in a short time period, yielding an elevated first-contact connection rate. In this section, we analyze our dataset to determine the distribution of first-contact interarrivals as initiated by benign hosts. We then explore the discriminating power of this metric for a worm whose first-contact connections arrive a factor of n more quickly.

Figure 1 shows the distribution of the amount of time between first-contact connections for individual hosts. Here we have separated out the scanners (identified as discussed above). While the average interarrival time is 39.2 sec, we often see benign, non-scanner hosts initiating multiple first-contact connections separated by very little (< 1 sec) time. In fact, these short time intervals account for about 40% of the total intervals generated by benign hosts, which makes it impractical to use 1/sec fan-out rate to identify possible worm propagation activity.

However, when focusing on sub-second interarrivals, we find that a benign host's short-time-scale activity fits fairly well to an exponential distribution, as illustrated in Figure 2. Here the fit to the empirical data uses $\mu = 261$ msec. We note that a scanner could craft its probing scheduling such that its fine-grained scanning behavior matches that of benign users, or at least runs slower than what we model as benign activity. However, this will significantly slow down the scanning speed, so compelling attackers

---

[2] Note that we do not include the mail servers in the set of scanners, as they are not scanners per se, but rather applications that happen in this environment to exhibit high fan-out.

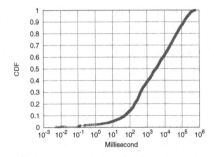
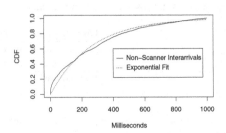

Fig. 1. Cumulative distribution of first-contact connections' interarrival time, per host

Fig. 2. First-contact interarrivals initiated by benign hosts roughly follow an exponential distribution with mean $\mu = 261$ msec

to make this modification constitutes an advance in the ongoing "arms race" between attackers and defenders.

We also note that we could extract significantly more precise interarrival models—including differing mean interarrival rates—if we partitioned the traffic based on its application protocol. While investigating this refinement remains a topic for future work, in our present effort we want to explore the efficacy of as *simple* a model as possible. If our algorithm can prove effective without having to characterize different protocols separately, we will benefit a great deal from having fewer parameters that need to be tuned operationally.

In the next section, based on these characteristics of benign activity, we develop our detection algorithm, RBS, for quickly identifying scanners or worm infectees with a high accuracy.

4   RBS: Rate-Based Sequential Hypothesis Testing

In this section, we develop a rate-based sequential hypothesis testing algorithm, RBS, which aims to quickly identify hosts issuing first-contact connections at rates higher than what we model as benign activity.

Let H_1 be the hypothesis that a given host is engaged in worm propagation, and let H_0 be the null hypothesis that the host exhibits benign network activity. A host generates an *event* when it initiates a connection to a destination with which the host has not previously communicated, i.e., when the host initiates a first-contact connection. As discussed in the previous section, we assume that the interarrival times of such events follow an exponential distribution with mean $1/\lambda_0$ (benign host) or $1/\lambda_1$ (scanner). When a host generates the ith event at time t_i, we can compute an interarrival time, $X_i = t_i - t_{i-1}$ for $i \geq 1$ and t_0 the initial starting point, and update the likelihood ratio of the host being engaged in scanning (or benign).

Define $X_1, X_2, \ldots, X_n$ as a sequence of such interarrival times. Since we model each X_i as IID non-negative exponential random variables, their sum, T_n, is the n-Erlang distribution:

$$f_n(T_n|H_1) = \frac{\lambda_1(\lambda_1 T_n)^{n-1}}{(n-1)!} \exp^{-\lambda_1 T_n} \tag{1}$$

Based on Equation (1), we can develop a sequential hypothesis test in which we define the likelihood ratio as:

$$\Lambda(n, T_n) = \frac{f_n(T_n|H_1)}{f_n(T_n|H_0)} = \left(\frac{\lambda_1}{\lambda_0}\right)^n \exp^{-(\lambda_1 - \lambda_0)T_n} \tag{2}$$

and the detection rules as:

$$\text{Output} = \begin{cases} H_1 & \text{if } \Lambda(n, T_n) \geq \eta_1 \\ H_0 & \text{if } \Lambda(n, T_n) \leq \eta_0 \\ \text{Pending} & \text{if } \eta_0 < \Lambda(n, T_n) < \eta_1 \end{cases}$$

where we can set η_1 and η_0 in terms of a target false positive rate (the proportion of benign hosts that are erroneously reported as scanners), α and a target detection rate (the proportion of scanners that are correctly reported as scanners), β [14]:

$$\eta_1 \leftarrow \frac{\beta}{\alpha} \tag{3}$$

$$\eta_0 \leftarrow \frac{1-\beta}{1-\alpha} \tag{4}$$

Wald shows that setting thresholds as above guarantees that the resulting false positive rate is bounded by $\frac{\alpha}{\beta}$ and the false negative rate is by $\frac{1-\beta}{1-\alpha}$ [14]. Given that β is usually set to a value higher than 0.99 and α to a value lower than 0.001, the margin of error becomes negligible (i.e., $\frac{1}{\beta} \approx 1$ and $\frac{1}{1-\alpha} \approx 1$).

An essential advantage of RBS over a simpler scheme using a fixed-rate threshold is that RBS is more robust to legitimate bursty connections. Figure 3 illustrates how an average arrival rate can fluctuate a great deal depending on the window size over which we compute the average. However, RBS effectively can *adapt* its window size until it finds consistency over a sufficient number of observations to reach a decision.

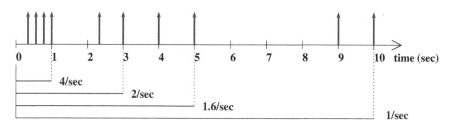

Fig. 3. 10 first-contact connection arrivals in 10 seconds: The figure illustrates that the average arrival rate can vary depending on the window size

For instance, if a host has initiated n first-contact connections and the elapsed time for the nth connection is T_n, RBS chooses H_1 (scanner) only if the likelihood ratio

$\Lambda(n, T_n)$ exceeds η_1. Using Equations (2) and (3), we can obtain a threshold on the elapsed time, T_{H_1}, below which we arrive at an H_1 (scanner) decision:

$$\frac{\beta}{\alpha} \leq \Lambda(n, T_n)$$

$$\frac{\beta}{\alpha} \leq \left(\frac{\lambda_1}{\lambda_0}\right)^n \exp^{-(\lambda_1 - \lambda_0)T_n}$$

$$\ln \frac{\beta}{\alpha} \leq n \ln \frac{\lambda_1}{\lambda_0} - (\lambda_1 - \lambda_0)T_n$$

$$T_n \leq n \frac{\ln \frac{\lambda_1}{\lambda_0}}{\lambda_1 - \lambda_0} - \frac{\ln \frac{\beta}{\alpha}}{\lambda_1 - \lambda_0} = T_{H_1} \tag{5}$$

Likewise, we can obtain a threshold elapsed time T_{H_0}, above which we conclude H_0 (benign host):

$$T_{H_0} = n \frac{\ln \frac{\lambda_1}{\lambda_0}}{\lambda_1 - \lambda_0} - \frac{\ln \frac{1-\beta}{1-\alpha}}{\lambda_1 - \lambda_0} \tag{6}$$

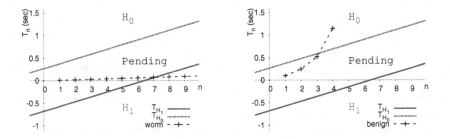

(a) Fast spreading worm with 100 first-contact connections/second will be detected by RBS at the 8th connection attempt

(b) Benign host with 4 first-contact connections/second will bypass RBS at the 4th connection attempt

Fig. 4. T_{H_1} and T_{H_0} when $\lambda_0 = 3$/sec, $\lambda_1 = 20$/sec, $\alpha = 10^{-5}$, and $\beta = 0.99$. The X axis represents the nth event and Y axis represents the elapsed time for the nth event.

Figure 4 shows how those threshold elapsed times, T_{H_1} and T_{H_0}, partition the area into three decision regions—H_1, H_0, and Pending. Figure 4(a) illustrates T_n of a host issuing first-contact connections at 100/second. At the 8th event, T_8 falls below T_{H_1}, which drives the likelihood ratio to reach the H_1 decision. Note that with the set of parameters used in Figure 4, RBS defers making a decision until it sees at least 7 events; this occurs because the elapsed time, T_n, is always greater than T_{H_1} up to $n = 6$. (T_i is a non-negative, non-decreasing random variable and T_{H_1} becomes positive when $n > 6.1$, given $\lambda_0 = 3$/sec, $\lambda_1 = 20$/sec, $\alpha = 10^{-5}$, and $\beta = 0.99$.) This initial holding period makes RBS robust against small traffic bursts. We can shorten this initial holding period, however, if we use a smaller β or larger α.

In general, Equation (5) provides important insights into the priors and the performance of RBS. T_{H_1} is a function of n, taking a form of $g(n) = a(n - c)$, where $a = (\ln \frac{\lambda_1}{\lambda_0})/(\lambda_1 - \lambda_0)$ and $c = (\ln \frac{\beta}{\alpha})/(\ln \frac{\lambda_1}{\lambda_0})$:

1. α and β affect only c, the minimum number of events required for detection (i.e., the minimum window size). For fixed values of λ_1 and λ_0, lower values of α or higher values of β (i.e., greater accuracy in our decisions) let more initial connections escape before RBS declares H_1. One can shorten this initial holding period by increasing α or decreasing β. But we can only do so to a limited degree, as c needs to be greater than the size of bursty arrivals that we often observe from Web or P2P applications, in order to avoid excessive false alarms. Another different way to prevent damage from those initially allowed connection attempts is to hold them at a switch until proven innocent [8].
2. λ_0 and λ_1 determine a, the slope of T_{H_1} over n. The inverse of the slope gives the minimum connection rate that RBS can detect. Any host generating first-contact connections at a higher rate than λ_1 intercepts $g(x)$ with probability 1. There is a built-in robustness in this, because the slope is strictly larger than $\frac{1}{\lambda_1}$ (what we model as a scanner), which follows from the inequality $\ln(x) < x - 1, 0 < x < 1$.
3. Although we use λ_1 to model a scanner's first-contact connection rate, RBS can detect any scanner with a rate λ' provided that:

$$\lambda' > \frac{1}{a} = \frac{\lambda_1 - \lambda_0}{\ln \lambda_1 - \ln \lambda_0} \tag{7}$$

because a host with a rate higher than λ' will eventually cross the line of T_{H_1} and thus trigger an alarm.

Finally, Equations (5) and (6) show that RBS bases its decision on two parameters—the number of attempts, n, and the elapsed time, $T(n)$—and not the actual realization of the arrival process.

5   Evaluation

We evaluated the performance of RBS in terms of false positives using a trace-driven simulation of the Enterprise dataset. RBS is in essence an algorithm that provides a tight bound of benign hosts' fan-out rate, enabling us to detect worms and scanners that employ higher-than-normal fan-out rates.

The Enterprise packet trace was captured at internal routers of a small enterprise network in November 2006. The trace contains 184 active hosts that initiated 238,407 TCP connections during the 1-hour collection period. To establish a ground truth, we extensively analyzed the trace using well-known application signatures and the Ethereal program [3] and found that about 76 applications were running at the time, including P2P clients such as BitTorrent and KaZaA, and VoIP programs such as Skype. Moreover, we found no infected machines nor scanners in the trace, making it suitable for testing RBS's accuracy in terms of false positives.

We need to set four parameters (α, β, λ_0, and λ_1) in order to run RBS. For high accuracy, we set $\beta = 0.99$ (99% target detection rate) and $\alpha = 10^{-6}$ (0.0001% target false alarm rate). Note that we set α very low because the detection algorithm executes for every first-contact connection initiated by a local host, which adds up to a very large number of tests.

The typical fan-out rate of benign hosts (λ_0) can change according to time (e.g., weekdays vs. weekend) and site (e.g., a small company where most network traffic is related to database transactions vs. a big ISP). To accommodate such changes, rather than asking an administrator to provide a magic number, we automatically infer the parameter λ_0 as follows:

– **Observation:** We observe interarrival times of first-contact connections generated by each host (i) and keep a list of mean interarrival times per host ($\mu_1, \mu_2, \mu_3, \ldots$) for a 10-minute period.
– **Inference:** At the end of an observation run, we compute a 10% trimmed mean [12] of the μ_i's: we first sort the data and remove the top and bottom 10% of the data before evaluating the arithmetic mean. As such, the inferred mean will not be affected by newly infected machines as long as the population of the infected machines stays below 10%. We set $1/\lambda_0$ equal to the inferred mean. Figure 5 shows the inferred values of λ_0 for the Enterprise dataset.

However, there is no obvious pick for λ_1, since a worm can choose an arbitrary propagation rate. If λ_1/λ_0 is close to 1, RBS takes longer to make a decision; but on the other hand, it can detect slower scanners than for higher λ_1/λ_0 ratios, per Equation (7).

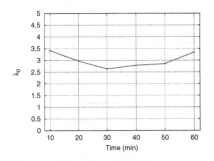 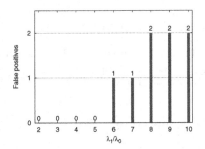

Fig. 5. 10% trimmed mean of first-contact connection arrival rate updated every 10 minutes

Fig. 6. Trace-driven simulation results of RBS varying λ_1 when $\alpha = 10^{-6}$, and $\beta = 0.99$

Figure 6 shows the simulation results of RBS for the Enterprise dataset as we vary λ_1 as a multiple of λ_0. As described above, both λ_0 and λ_1 get updated every 10 minutes. RBS generates no false positives when λ_1/λ_0 is less than 6. However, RBS erroneously triggers for 2 hosts (a BitTorrent client and a chatty Web browser) when the ratio is higher than 7. The main reason for these false positives is short bursts. As discussed in §4, when λ_1/λ_0 is high, RBS becomes sensitive to short bursts, making it prone to generating false positives. Given that bursty connections are somewhat prevalent among many applications, this result leads us to recommend a small λ_1/λ_0 ratio. A caveat of using a small ratio is that RBS may miss carefully crafted scan traffic if the scanner repeatedly generates short bursts followed by a long idle time.

Thus, while this assessment is against a fairly modest amount of data, we find the results promising. We conduct a more extensive evaluation in §6.

6 Hybrid Approach: RBS+TRW

RBS uses *fan-out rate* to differentiate benign traffic from scanners (or targeting worms), which we model as Poisson processes with rates λ_0 (benign) and λ_1 (scanner), with $\lambda_0 < \lambda_1$. Another discriminatory metric proved to work well in detecting scanners is the *failure ratio* of first-contact connections [6,17,8]. TRW [6] works by modeling Bernoulli processes with **success** probabilities, θ_0 (benign) and θ_1 (scanner), with $1 - \theta_0 < 1 - \theta_1$. In this section, we develop a combined worm detection algorithm that exploits *both* a fan-out rate model and a failure ratio model. We evaluate the hybrid using trace-driven simulation, finding that this combined algorithm, RBS+TRW, improves both overall accuracy and speed of detection.

Suppose that a given host has initiated connections to n different destinations, and that the elapsed time until the nth connection is T_n. Among those n destinations, S_n accepted the connection request (success) and $F_n = n - S_n$ rejected or did not respond (failure). Applying the models from RBS and TRW [6], we obtain a conditional probability distribution function for scanners:

$$f[(S_n, T_n)|H_1] = P[S_n|T_n, H_1] \times f[T_n|H_1]$$
$$= \binom{n}{S_n} \theta_1^{S_n} (1 - \theta_1)^{F_n}$$
$$\times \frac{\lambda_1 (\lambda_1 T_n)^{n-1}}{(n-1)!} \exp^{-\lambda_1 T_n}$$

where $P[S_n|T_n, H_1]$ is the probability of getting S_n success events when each event will succeed with an equal probability of θ_1, and $f[T_n|H_1]$ is an n-Erlang distribution in which each interarrival time is exponentially distributed with mean $1/\lambda_1$.

Analogous to $f[(S_n, T_n)|H_1]$, for benign hosts we can derive:

$$f[(S_n, T)|H_0] = \binom{n}{S_n} \theta_0^{S_n} (1 - \theta_0)^{F_n}$$
$$\times \frac{\lambda_0 (\lambda_0 T_n)^{n-1}}{(n-1)!} \exp^{-\lambda_0 T_n} .$$

We then define the likelihood ratio, $\Lambda(S_n, T_n)$, as

$$\Lambda(S_n, T_n) = \frac{f[(S_n, T_n)|H_1]}{f[(S_n, T_n)|H_0]}$$
$$= \left(\frac{\theta_1}{\theta_0}\right)^{S_n} \left(\frac{1 - \theta_1}{1 - \theta_0}\right)^{F_n}$$
$$\times \left(\frac{\lambda_1}{\lambda_0}\right)^n \exp^{-(\lambda_1 - \lambda_0)T_n} .$$

It is interesting to note that $\Lambda(S_n, T_n)$ is just the product of Λ_{TRW} and Λ_{RBS}. Moreover, $\Lambda(S_n, T_n)$ reduces to Λ_{TRW} when there is no difference in fan-out rates between benign and scanning hosts ($\lambda_1 = \lambda_0$). Likewise, $\Lambda(S_n, T_n)$ reduces to Λ_{RBS} when there is no difference in failure ratios ($\theta_1 = \theta_0$).

We evaluate this combined approach, RBS+TRW, using two new sets of traces, each of which contains different types of scanners that happen to wind up contrasting the strengths of RBS and TRW. We first categorize hosts into four classes based on their fan-out rates and failure ratios. In what follows, we discuss types of scanners falling into each region and detection algorithms capable of detecting such hosts.

- **Class LH** (low fan-out rate, high failure ratio): Slow-scanning worms or scanners that probe blindly (randomly or sequentially) will likely generate many failures, triggering TRW with a high probability.
- **Class HH** (high fan-out rate, high failure ratio): Fast-scanning worms (e.g., Code Red, Slammer) that exhibit both a high fan-out rate and a high failure ratio will very likely to drive both TRW and RBS to quickly reach their detection thresholds.
- **Class HL** (high fan-out rate, low failure ratio): Flash, metaserver, and topological worms [16] belong to this class. These worms build or acquire a list of target hosts and then propagate over only those potential victims, so their connection attempts tend to succeed. While these targeting worms can bypass TRW, their high fan-out rate should trigger RBS.
- **Class LL** (low fan-out rate, low failure ratio): Most benign hosts fall into this class, in which their network behavior is characterized by a low fan-out rate and a low failure ratio. Typically, a legitimate host's fan-out rate rarely exceeds a few first-contact connections per second. In addition, benign users do not initiate traffic to hosts unless there is reason to believe the host will accept the connection request, and thus will exhibit a high success probability. Neither TRW nor RBS will trigger hosts in this class, which in turn, allows particularly stealthy worms, or passive "contagion" worms that rely on a user's behavior for propagation [16], to evade detection. Worms of this type represent a formidable challenge that remains for future work to attempt to address.

We use an average 5 Hz fan-out rate (λ_0) and 0.5 failure ratio ($1-\theta_0$) as baselines in order to categorize hosts in our trace. Ideally, we should investigate all the hosts in the traces to obtain a ground truth, but because of the sheer amount of traffic volume (more than 2 million connections), we resort to this screening process to sift out the many hosts with quite limited activity.

We compute a fan-out rate with a sliding window of size 5 in order to capture bursty arrivals that often result from concurrent Web connections addressed to different Web sites for embedded objects. Figure 7 classifies hosts in the datasets based on the 5 Hz fan-out rate and 0.5 failure ratio thresholds.

Table 2 shows the details of the datasets we use for evaluation. The Lab-II dataset was collected at the same enterprise network as Lab. It is composed of 137 one-hour long traces from December 2004 and Janunary 2005, recorded at internal routers connecting a variety of subnets to the rest of the enterprise and the Internet. The ISP dataset was recorded using tcpdump at the border of a small ISP in April 2003. It contains

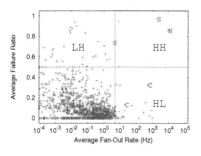 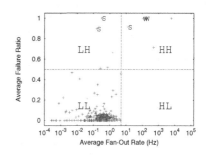

(a) Lab-II (S: scanner, N: host running nmap, (b) ISP (S: scanner, W: Code Red II infectee)
C: internal Web crawler)

Fig. 7. Classification of hosts present in the evaluation datasets: Each point represents a local host that generated more than 5 first-contact connections

traffic from 389 active hosts during the 10-hour monitoring period (The high number of connections is due to worm infections during the time of measurement.).

The table shows the division of the internal hosts into the four categories discussed above. Manual inspection of the hosts in **HH**, **HL**, and **LH**[3] reveals that there are 5 hosts each in both of Lab-II and ISP whose behavior qualifies them as scanners and worms that we aim to detect (H_1) because of their high-fan-out or high-failure behaviors: For Lab-II, the 2 **HH** hosts are one internal vulnerability scanner and one host that did a fast nmap [1] scan of 7 other hosts; 1 **LH** host is another internal vulnerability scanner; 2 **HL** hosts are internal Web crawlers that occasionally contacted tens of internal Web servers to update search engine databases. For ISP, the **HH** hosts are two Code Red II infectees plus an HTTP scanner, and the **LH** hosts are 2 slower HTTP scanners.

The one **HH** host in the Lab-II dataset that we classify as benign (H_0) turns out to be a NetBIOS client that often (benignly) made connection requests to absent hosts. The 2 benign **HH** hosts in the ISP dataset are all clients running P2P applications that attempt to contact a large number of transient peers that often do not respond. Most benign **LH** hosts are either low-profile NetBIOS clients (Lab-II) or P2P clients (ISP), and most benign **HL** hosts from Lab-II are caused by Web clients accessing Web sites with many images stored elsewhere (e.g., a popular news site using Akamai's content distribution service, and a weather site having sponsor sites' images embedded).

Table 2 also shows that while those two thresholds are useful for nailing down a set of suspicious hosts (all in either **HH**, **LH**, or **HL**), a simple detection method based on fixed thresholds would cause 66 false positives because of benign hosts scattered in the **LH** and **HL** regions, as shown in Figure 7. However, using dynamic thresholds based on the previously observed behavior, RBS+TRW accurately identifies those 10 target hosts while significantly reducing false positives.

---

[3] We looked into each host in those three classes for the ISP dataset, and the 66 of such hosts for the Lab-II dataset that generated more than 20 first-contact connections in a one-hour monitoring period.

Table 2. Evaluation datasets: scanning hosts include vulnerability scanners, worm infectees, and hosts that we use proxies for targeting worms because of their anomalous high-fan-out rate

			Lab-II	ISP
		Outgoing Connections	796,049	1,402,178
		Duration	137 hours	10.5 hours
H	**HH**	scanning	2	3
		benign	1	2
O	**LH**	scanning	1	2
		benign	34	3
S	**HL**	scanning	2	0
		benign	26	0
T	**LL**	scanning	0	0
		benign	1321	260
	≤ 5 first-contact connections		2,621	119
S	Total	scanning	5	5
		benign	4,003	384
		Total	4,008	389

We evaluate RBS+TRW by varying λ_1 from λ_0 to $10\lambda_0$, and θ_1 from $0.2\theta_0$ to θ_0. As discussed in §5, we infer λ_0 and θ_0 using 10% trimmed means.[4] We set $\beta = 0.99$, and $\alpha = 10^{-6}$. Figures 8 and 9 show the number of detections and false positives for each pair of λ_1 and θ_1. In particular, for $\lambda_1 = \lambda_0$, the combined algorithm reduces to TRW (dashed vertical lines along the θ axis), and when $\theta_1 = \theta_0$, to RBS (dashed vertical lines along the λ axis).

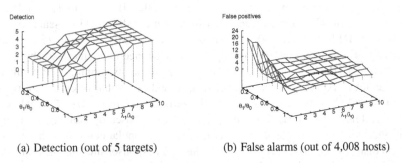

(a) Detection (out of 5 targets)   (b) False alarms (out of 4,008 hosts)

Fig. 8. Simulation results of RBS+TRW for the Lab-II dataset, varying λ_1 and θ_1

Table 3 compares the performance of the combined algorithm against that of RBS and TRW alone. First, we find the priors that make RBS (TRW) the most effective (0 false negatives) in identifying scanners in the Lab-II (ISP) dataset. The nature of our test datasets keeps either algorithm from working better across both datasets. In fact,

---

[4] We placed an upper bound (0.9) on θ_0, since a small value of θ_0 (e.g., 0.9999) causes TRW to trigger for a few spurious failures.

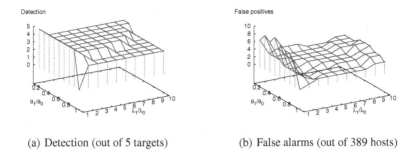

(a) Detection (out of 5 targets)   (b) False alarms (out of 389 hosts)

Fig. 9. Simulation results of RBS+TRW for the ISP dataset, varying λ_1 and θ_1

Table 3. Evaluation of RBS+TRW vs. RBS and TRW. Both Lab-II and ISP each have 5 scanners. $\overline{N}|H_1$ represents the average number of first-contact connections originated by the detected hosts upon detection.

	λ_1	θ_1	Lab-II False -	False +	$\overline{N}|H_1$	ISP False -	False +	$\overline{N}|H_1$
RBS	$10\lambda_0$	$=\theta_0$	0	2	5.6	2	3	6.4
TRW	$=\lambda_0$	$0.2\theta_0$	3	21	18.5	0	7	10.0
RBS+TRW	$5\lambda_0$	$0.6\theta_0$	0	3	6.9	1	3	5.0

when $\lambda_1 = 10\lambda_0$ and $\theta_1 = \theta_0$, RBS has 0 false negatives for Lab-II, but misses 2 **LH** scanners in ISP. In comparison, when $\lambda_1 = \lambda_0$ and $\theta_1 = 0.2\theta_0$, TRW has 0 false negatives for ISP, but misses 3 scanners in Lab-II, including the two Web crawlers.

We could address the problem of false negatives for either algorithm by running TRW and RBS in parallel, raising an alarm if either algorithm decides so. However, this approach comes at a cost of an increased number of false alarms, which usually result from **LH** hosts (e.g., Windows NetBIOS connections, often made to absent hosts) or **HL** hosts (e.g., a busy mail server or a Web proxy).

In general, improving the accuracy of a detection algorithm requires iterative adjustments of decision rules: first improving the detection rate by loosening the decision rule, and then decreasing the false positive rate by tightening the decision rule without losing too many correct detections. For this iteration, our combined algorithm, RBS+TRW provides two knobs, λ_1 and θ_1, that we can adjust to tune the detector to a site's traffic characteristics.

The trace-driven simulation shows that RBS+TRW with $\lambda_1 = 5\lambda_0$ and $\theta_1 = 0.6\theta_0$ misses only one low-profile target host (a slow HTTP scanner from ISP) while generating no more than 6 false positives, per Table 3. Had we run RBS and TRW in parallel, we could have eliminated all the false negatives, but at the cost of 33 false alarms altogether.

Overall, RBS+TRW provides the good detection of high-profile worms and scanners (no more than 2 misses across both datasets) while generating less than 1 false alarm per hour for a wide range of parameters ($\lambda_1 \in [4\lambda_0, 8\lambda_0]$ and $\theta_1 \in [0.4\theta_0, 0.7\theta_0]$), and reaching its detection decisions quickly (less than 7 first-contact connections on average).

7 Discussion

This section discusses several technical issues that may arise when employing RBS+TRW in practice. While addressing these issues is beyond the scope of this paper, we outline ideas and directions based on which we will pursue them in future work.

Operational issues: A worm detection device running RBS+TRW needs to maintain per local host information. For each host, a detector must track first-contact connections originated by the host, their failure/success status, and the elapsed time. The state thus increases proportional to the number of local hosts in the network (N) and the sum of all their currently pending first-contact connections. Given that RBS+TRW requires ≤ 10 first-contact connections on average to reach a decision (§6), we can estimate amount of state as scaling on the order of $10N$. Note that every time RBS+TRW crosses either threshold, it resets its states for the corresponding host.

When constrained by computation and storage resources, one can employ cache data structures suggested by Weaver *et al.* [17] that track first-contact connections with a high precision. However, we note that running RBS+TRW on aggregate traffic across hosts (as opposed to the per-host operation for which it is designed) can significantly affect the detection performance due to the uneven traffic distribution generated by each end-host [20].

Post-detection response: The results in Table 3 correspond to RBS+TRW generating 0.07 false alarms per hour at the Lab-II site and 0.57 per hour at the ISP site. This low rate, coupled with RBS+TRW's fast detection speed, make it potentially suitable for automated containment, crucial to defending against fast-spreading worms. Alternatively, a network operator could employ connection rate-limiting for hosts detected by RBS+TRW, automatically restricting such hosts to a low fan-out rate.

Extensions: One can complement RBS+TRW with a classification engine and run the algorithm with specific parameters per application. For instance, many peer-to-peer applications probe other neighboring hosts in order to find the best peer from which to download a file. For a peer-to-peer client having a large number of transient peers, this probing activity can generate many failed connections, leading to an alarm. In such a case, grouping peer-to-peer traffic and running a separate instance of RBS+TRW with the parameters particularly tuned for this application should significantly improve the algorithm's performance.

Limitations: As indicated in Figure 7, RBS+TRW is unable to detect targeting worms using high-quality hit lists comprised of at least 70% active hosts and spreading no faster than several first-contact connections per second. Detecting such worms might be possible by working on larger time scales. For example, a scanner that generates first-contact connections at a rate of 1 Hz will end up accessing 3,600 different hosts in an hour, far outnumbering the sustained activity of a typical benign host. Thus, a natural avenue for future work is assessing the operation of RBS on longer timescales.

Finally, attackers can game our detection algorithm by tricking end users into generating first-contact connections either at a high rate (RBS), or that will likely end up failing (TRW). For instance, similar to an attack in [8], an attacker could put content on a web site with numerous embedded links to non-existent destinations.

8 Conclusion

We have presented a worm detection algorithm, RBS (*rate-based sequential hypothesis testing*), that rapidly identifies high-fan-out behavior by hosts based on the rate at which the hosts initiate connections to new destinations. RBS uses the sequential hypothesis testing [14] framework. While built using a model that the time between connection attempts to new destinations is exponentially distributed (which we show is a reasonable approximation for bursts of activity), RBS decisions reflect the aggregate measurement of the total elapsed time over a number of attempts, not the characteristics of individual arrivals. We define RBS in terms of a single discriminating metric—the rate of connection attempts—which differs substantially between benign hosts and an important class of worms. While the choice of such a metric evokes the measurement of an average rate over a window of certain size (and the comparison of the measured rate to a fixed threshold), RBS is more elaborate. The algorithm draws from sequential hypothesis testing the ability to adapt its decision-making in response to the available measurements in order to meet specified error requirements. We can view this as an adaptation of both the window size (i.e., how many attempts to make a decision) and the threshold (i.e., what is the minimum measured rate over that window that leads to a trigger). This adaptation gives RBS a robustness unseen in fixed window/threshold schemes.

We evaluated RBS using trace-driven simulations. We find that when the factor of speed difference, n, between a scanner and a benign host is small, RBS requires more empirical data to arrive at a detection decision but stays robust against short bursts. When n is less than 6, RBS generates no false positives for a 1-hour trace that includes P2P clients and VoIP programs known to connect to a set of peers.

We then presented RBS+TRW, a hybrid of RBS and TRW [6] which combines *fan-out rate* and *probability of success* of each first-contact connection. RBS+TRW provides a unified framework for detecting fast-propagating worms independent of their scanning strategy (i.e., topological or scanning worms). Using two traces from two qualitatively different sites, containing 389 active hosts and 4,008 active hosts, we show that RBS+TRW provides fast detection of hosts infected by Code Red II, as well as the internal Web crawlers that we use as proxies for topological worms. In doing so, it generates less than 1 false alarm per hour.

Acknowledgements

Our thanks to anonymous reviewers for their helpful comments. This work was supported by NSF Awards STI-0334088, NSF-0433702 and CNS-0627320, for which we are grateful. Any opinions, findings, and conclusions or recommendations expressed in this material are those of the authors or originators and do not necessarily reflect the views of the National Science Foundation.

References

1. Nmap — free security scanner for network exploration & security audits, http://www.insecure.org/nmap/
2. Chen, S., Tang, Y.: Slowing Down Internet Worms. In: Proceedings of the 24th International Conference on Distributed Computing Systems (ICDCS'04) Tokyo, Japan (March 2004)
3. Ehtereal.com. Ethereal, http://www.ethereal.com/
4. Eichin, M.W., Rochlis, J.A.: With Microscope and Tweezers: An Analysis of the Internet Virus of November 1988. In: Proceedings of the IEEE Symposium on Research in Security and Privacy (1989)
5. F-Secure. F-Secure Virus Descriptions: Santy, http://www.f-secure.com/v-descs/santy_a.shtml
6. Jung, J., Paxson, V., Berger, A. W., and Balakrishnan, H. Fast Portscan Detection Using Sequential Hypothesis Testing. In: Proceedings of the IEEE Symposium on Security and Privacy (May 9–12, 2004)
7. Kim, H.-A., Karp, B.: Autograph: Toward Automated Distributed Worm Signature Detection. In: Proceedings of the 13th USENIX Security Symposium (August 9–13, 2004)
8. Schechter, S.E., Jung, J., Berger, A.W.: Fast Detection of Scanning Worm Infections. In: Jonsson, E., Valdes, A., Almgren, M. (eds.) RAID 2004. LNCS, vol. 3224, Springer, Heidelberg (2004)
9. Singh, S., Estan, C., Varghese, G., and Savage, S. Automated Worm Fingerprinting. In: Proceedings of the 13th Operating Systems Design and Implementation OSDI (December 2004)
10. Spafford, E. H. A Failure to Learn from the Past. In: Proceedings of the 19th Annual Computer Security Applications Conference. December 8–12, 2003 pp. 217–233 (2003)
11. Staniford, S., Paxson, V., Weaver, N.: How to Own the Internet in Your Spare Time. In: Proceedings of the 11th USENIX Security Symposium Berkeley, CA, USA, August 5–9, 2002 USENIX Association, pp. 149–170 (2002)
12. Turkey, J.W.: A survey of sampling from contaminated distributions. In: Contributions to Probability and Statistics, Stanford University Press (1960)
13. Twycross, J., Williamson, M.M.: Implementing and Testing a Virus Throttle. In: Proceedings of the 12th USENIX Security Symposium (August 4–8, 2003)
14. Wald, A.: Sequential Analysis. J. Wiley & Sons, New York (1947)
15. Wang, K., Cretu, G., Stolfo, S.J: Anomalous payload-based worm detection and signature generation. In: Valdes, A., Zamboni, D. (eds.) RAID 2005. LNCS, vol. 3858, Springer, Heidelberg (2006)
16. Weaver, N., Paxson, V., Staniford, S., Cunningham, R.: A Taxonomy of Computer Worms. In: Proceedings of the 2003 ACM Workshop on Rapid Malcode, October 27, 2003, pp. 11–18. ACM Press, New York (2003)
17. Weaver, N., Staniford, S., and Paxson, V. Very Fast Containment of Scanning Worms. In: Proceedings of the 13th USENIX Security Symposium (August 9–13, 2004)
18. Whyte, D., Kranakis, E., van Oorschot, P.: DNS-based Detection of Scanning Worms in an Enterprise Network. In: Proceedings of the Network and Distributed System Security Symposium (NDSS'05) (February 2005)
19. Williamson, M. M. Throttling Viruses: Restricting propagation to defeat malicious mobile code. In: Proceedings of The 18th Annual Computer Security Applications Conference (ACSAC 2002) (December 9–13, 2002)
20. Wong, C., Bielski, S., Studer, A., Wang, C.: Empirical analysis of rate limiting mechanisms. In: Valdes, A., Zamboni, D. (eds.) RAID 2005. LNCS, vol. 3858, Springer, Heidelberg (2006)

Targeting Physically Addressable Memory

David R. Piegdon and Lexi Pimenidis

Aachen University of Technology,
Computer Science Department Informatik IV,
Ahornstr. 55, D-52074 Aachen, Germany

Abstract. This paper introduces new advances in gaining unauthorised access to a computer by accessing its physical memory via various means. We will show a unified approach for using IEEE1394, also known as firewire, file descriptors and other methods to read from and write into a victim's memory. Thereafter we will show the power of this ability in several example attacks: stealing private SSH keys, and injecting arbitrary code in order to obtain interactive access with administrator privileges on the victim's computer.

These advances are based on data structures that are required by the CPU to provide virtual address spaces for each process running on the system. These data structures are searched and parsed in order to reassemble pages scattered in physical memory, thus being able to read and write in each processes virtual address space.

The attacks introduced in this paper are adaptable to all kinds of operating system and hardware combinations. As a sample target, we have chosen Linux on an IA-32 system with the kernel-options CONFIG_NOHIGHMEM or CONFIG_HIGHMEM4G, CONFIG_VMSPLIT_3G and CONFIG_PAGE_OFFSET= 0xC0000000.

1 Introduction

All modern operating systems do not grant processes and users access to physically addressed memory, as this addressing mode circumvents any protection methods provided by virtual addressing to separate processes from each other and the operating system. Only the operating system may use physical addressing to prepare address spaces for each running process, manage these, access special memory of extension cards and alike, or even only during bootstrapping as Linux does. Having access to a computer's memory is equal to have the same rights and possibilities as the operating system. Thus access to it should require system administrator rights or physical access to the hardware of the underlying system. Therefore it is crucial for a system's security to prevent attackers from gaining direct access to a computer's memory.

Up to recently, protecting access to a computer's memory was equal to defend against physical attacks on the hardware, given that the operating system had no vulnerabilities. Thus, reading and writing to a computer's memory was only possible by booting custom operating system, opening the case and attacking the hardware directly, stealing the whole system, installing specially crafted PCMCIA cards, or the like.

B. M. Hämmerli and R. Sommer (Eds.): DIMVA 2007, LNCS 4579, pp. 193–212, 2007.

However, IEEE1394, also known as "firewire" and so called in the rest of the paper, does not require to boot a custom operating system, to open the case, steal parts of the hardware, install new hardware (except plugging in the firewire cable) or specially crafted hardware. Access via firewire is as easy as plugging in a firewire device, like e.g. an iPod, letting it do its job and unplugging it.

In this paper we will introduce several advances in attacking computers via firewire. As a foundation for the attacks, we introduce two libraries that are used as a step stone for further work. These libraries are used to access virtual address spaces of any process on the victim's host. They also provide a simple, generic interface for all kinds of physical memory sources. As an example, we implemented backends for IEEE1394 and filedescriptors so far, but other sources can be trivially added.

Once, access to the physical memory of a system is obtained, there are two obvious ways to extract useful information from it:

- It is possible to parse the operating systems internal data structures holding all relevant information about loaded drivers, running processes et al.
- It is possible to use the information that the operating system provides to the hardware to tell it about the virtual address spaces of each process.

The first scenario will not work between different operating systems and architectures, since it is necessary to write a parser for each combination of them, possibly even for different versions of the same operating system.

The latter uses an information structure that only changes between different architectures, as the architecture relies on it. Furthermore there is a well defined algorithm for using this information (implemented in hardware in the architecture, but well defined in the reference manuals for this architecture, so system designers can provide valid data to the hardware). On the other hand, the second approach does not give as much information about the system as the first, since the first obtains all information directly from the kernel structures, while using the second approach we only can enter virtual address spaces of processes. However, in the following we will use the second approach for most attacks, as it is more robust.

In [Bur06], an approach is introduced that parses kernel-structures of Windows and Linux kernels. Since the paper is about *finding an attacker* and not *attacking a system*, it can be savely assumed that the architecture, the operating system and its version are known. An attacker, on the other hand, is usually left with guessing the architecture and operating system and needs more robust tools for his attacks.

Latest state of the art was shown in [BDK05], where Dornseif et al. demonstrated how to connect to a remote computer over an IEEE1394 connection and changed the user of all running processes to the super user "root". However, their work left the victim's machine in a fragile state, often prone to crashing, and without direct gain for the attacker.

Other advances in memory analysis have been introduced in [Bur06], where kernel-structures are searched and parsed to identify processes and meta-information about processes and the system itself.

Our contributions in to this area are twofold:

- We demonstrate how to access the memory of a remote machine in a structured and portable manner, making information retrieval as easy as reading local memory.
- With the help of our tool-set we demonstrate that it is not only possible to read or change data in the remote machine, but also to execute code and obtain interactive access, possibly with superuser privileges.

1.1 Roadmap

In **Section 2**, we will introduce `libphysical`, a library providing an attacker with a simple, generic interface to interact with physical memory via a simple interface. Thereafter, in **Section 3**, `liblinear`, an interface to access virtual address spaces, will be introduced. It incorporates a backend for IA-32[1] and functions to find virtual address spaces. We introduce several attacks basing on these results in **Section 4**, ranging from simple information gathering up to obtaining an interactive shell.

In **Section 5**, prospects will be given, what further kinds of attacks seem to be possible and are of interest. The paper ends with conclusions in **Section 6**.

2 Physically Addressable Memory Sources: `libphysical`

This section presents a simple, generic interface for all kinds of physical memory sources. The implementation is modular, so that backends for new memory sources may be plugged in with only little extra effort. This interface is called `libphysical` and currently includes backends for IEEE1394 and file descriptors.

Modern computer hardware provides many protection and memory management mechanisms in hardware. This includes mechanisms implemented in hardware to provide a virtual address space for each process, and to restrict a process to its own resources only; paging to extend memory to harddisks and fragment available memory; caching to access frequently used memory faster, and more. Obviously, all these features are architecture and operating-system dependent. An interested reader may read documentation on system programming (e.g. [Int06d, Int06e]) to obtain further information.

Consider a process with its virtual address space and its corresponding set of pages. Each page in this virtual address space may be:

- a physical memory page that is mapped into the virtual address space, possibly cached in the CPU's cache,
- a page that is swapped to other media, like a harddisk

---

[1] This backend is missing algorithms for less-used operation-modes of the IA-32 architecture, but it will work at least for most kinds of the *Linux* kernels ($\leq$ 4GB RAM). It has not yet been tested with *Windows* or *MacOS X* and is missing features (Virtual-8086 mode) to work with DOS-processes running inside Windows.

- (depending on the operating system) a mapped buffer or file
- not used, and thus not mapped

Swapped pages will and mapped pages may be loaded only on demand (i.e. when the process tries to access the page), as access to a non-mapped page by a process will generate a page fault and the operating system then may map the demanded page. Access to completely unused pages, via this mechanism, will create the well known segmentation fault.

When access to physically addressed memory is obtained, each page that an attacker can access may be either a page of memory of a random process, a buffer page of a process, a page used by the operating system (kernel code, kernel data, kernel stack, IO buffer, ...), an unused page or a page used to give the CPU information on how to handle virtual addresses, as this is done in hardware. The latter pages will be called address translation tables (for more information on these, see section 3).

2.1   Swapping, Multiple Accessors, Caching, Address Translation

Access to physical memory only gives, per definition, access to pages that are mapped from this physical memory. Thus this kind of access will be unable to read or write swapped pages and buffers that have not been mapped. There is no simple solution to circumvent this restriction; it is required to call special operating system routines to do this. However, access to physical memory does not include access to the CPU by itself, and these routines may be different from operating system to operating system.

Depending on the method used to access the memory, a parallel accessor may be using the same memory at the same time. E.g. when using firewire (see 2.2) to read a page of a currently running task, this task may access, i.e. read or write, this page at the same time. For instance, if the CPU and another accessor write at the same moment to the same address location, it depends on unpredictable timing and caching, which write access will be performed first and thus is overridden by the other one; as an external accessor we have no information, when the system's CPU accesses a page and whether it is cached, thus leaving us with no simple means to determine the success of a writing operation. Also, reading and writing at the same time may be impossible via the given method; thus many atomic commands used for process synchronization, like "test and set", do not exist.

Caching may also prevent certain actions from external accessors: if a page is cached in another, faster memory, a copy of it will typically reside in physical memory. In the general case it is difficult to know if a page is cached or not; on IA-32 however the address translation tables contain a flag for each page telling the CPU if it may be cached or not. Depending on the way used to access the memory, it may circumvent the cache or not have access to it at all. When accessing a page, changes made by a task running in parallel may not be visible immediately and changes made by us may be invisible to a parallel task or maybe even overwritten by the cache at any time. Special care needs to be taken to minimize this risk. When writing to pages, pages should be chosen that are not cached or unlikely to be cached while writing; when reading pages, it must be taken into consideration that the data may change at any time or may have changed at the time of reading.

On systems using paging, physical memory will mostly be a concatenation of "random" pages, each one either used by some process or the operating system. A minor part of these pages will be address translation tables, telling the CPU what the virtual address space of different processes looks like. Where these pages are is only known to the operating system and the CPU. For a detailed discussion, see section 3.

2.2   IEEE1394

IEEE1394, also known as ❦ firewire (Apple) or iLink (Sony), is an extension bus available on many modern computer systems and devices. In contrast to USB, which is a serial periphery bus, firewire is a high-speed serial expansion bus with features like guaranteed bandwidth (which is of interest for many real-time applications, like media crunching), DMA[2] and the ability to connect multiple nodes with a single firewire-bus. The concept of bus master and bus slaves, as known from USB, is only virtual. Typically when plugging together a firewire bus, a node is randomly selected to be the master and manages this bus. Most of these nodes have the ability to be bus master.

DMA is implemented in hardware by the OHCI chip set; it is used to release the CPU from I/O operations. OHCI filters provide a mechanism to prevent unwanted access by specific devices identified by their node ID or by all devices (which negates most of the advantages of firewire), but as the node ID can change with every bus reset, these filters are rudimental. And even though these rudimental filters exist, many drivers do not use them.

With every bus reset, these filters need to be reconfigured by the operating system, but there are no ways to securely identify or authenticate known trusted devices by means of hardware - a secure software-based authentication protocol would be required (but none are known to us).

The only thing that may be used to identify "dumb"[3] trusted devices like external storage controllers or video equipment (which are the major clients of DMA) is the globally unique *GUID* that a device has branded into its config ROM - however this GUID may be overwritten until the next hardware reset and thus faked by an attackers firewire controller. Windows XP on the other hand does use *device class descriptions* stored in the config ROM of firewire devices to allow or deny DMA by means of OHCI filters (e.g. storage devices may use DMA while other PCs may not). Adam Boileau, "TMASKY" and others have shown in [Boi06] that, by pretending to be a device like an iPod, which "deserves" DMA (in terms of marketdroid[4]-logik), it is possible to circumvent this "protection" and to trick Windows into giving an attacker DMA. This attack is

---

[2] Direct Memory Access.

[3] Read as "unable to do cryptographic operations".

[4] See jargon-files, http://catb.org/esr/jargon/html/M/marketroid.html

as simple as reading an iPod's config ROM from its CSR and using `libraw1394`'s
`raw1394_update_config_rom()` to use the copy. Adam Boileau has implemented
a simple script to do this. We have written our own tool in C using `libraw1394`,
which can be downloaded on request.

Access to memory of a node will require a 10 bit field for the bus ID, a 6 bit
field for the node ID and a 48 bit address field. On Linux, `libraw1394`[5] provides
an easy and portable interface to access the memory of a node. Using `libraw1394`
under Linux, it is possible to read different block sizes of data via firewire on
the remote computer. Our experiments showed that different hardware allows
bigger blocks to be read at different addresses: 4 byte blocks should always work;
1024 byte blocks may be read with some hardware, if the address resolves to the
physical memory. Control state registers are likely to be readable only in 4 byte
blocks.

For more information on the underlying hardware or protocols, please refer
to [Pro00, And99] or the `libraw1394`[5] documentation.

2.3   Filedescriptor: `/dev/mem`, Memory Dumps

Another source for physical memory may be given to an attacker via a filedescriptor. This filedescriptor may refer to a memory dump or the Linux `/dev/mem`
device. In case of a plain memory dump, many of the mentioned problems lapse:
no caching will be performed, no concurrent process will change the dumped
data. In the case of a filedescriptor referring to `/dev/mem`, other accessors will
exist, as `/dev/mem` is referring to the systems memory; caching on the other hand
should not be a problem as we are not circumventing any caching system (like
the CPU), but using it directly.

2.4   Other Sources

The ideas described in this paper should be easily adoptable to all memory
sources giving access to physically addressable memory, this may include e.g. remote management cards, suspend-2-disk images or virtual machines that have an
interface to access the virtual machines' memory. `qemu` is such a virtual machine,
providing a `gdb` remote stub to attach a debugger.

To use a new physical source with the methods introduced in the later sections,
it is only required to write a new backend for `libphysical`.

3   Translating Virtual to Physical Addresses

While we discussed in the last section methods to gain access to a computer's
memory and their limitations, we will discuss in this section a method for structured access to these sources.

Multitasking environments that fulfill modern requirements have to provide
virtual address spaces for each running process or thread. For performance and

---

[5] `libraw1394`: http://www.linux1394.org/

security reasons this address translation from a processes virtual address to an address valid in physical memory is normally performed in hardware. These mechanisms can include e.g. segmentation and paging.

A normal process's memory is divisible into several blocks or *segments*: the *code segment* contains all the code that may be run; the *data segment* contains the static data that is known at compile time, global structures or deliberately allocated memory (including the heap); the *stack segment* contains the stack, including local variables. On some architectures, it is possible to assign segment descriptors, referring to defined memory regions, to segment registers. This assignment will influence the further behaviour of address translation: all addresses will from there on be taken to be relative to the bound of the memory region specified by the segment descriptor. This mechanism is called *segmentation*.

Paging will divide the virtual address space of a process into several consecutive *frames* of a specific page-size (typically 4096 bytes). Virtual addresses can be split into frame number and frame offset; the frame number is translated (mapped) via a translation table into a physical page number and the frame offset is used as an offset into this physical page. If a frame does not have a corresponding physical page, it is called to be unmapped. Unmapped pages can be non-existing pages or can e.g., be swapped to slower media like harddisks.

With `liblinear`, we provide a software solution for address translation. The provided interface is similar to `libphysical`; it needs a physical memory source (in form of a `physical_handle`), and information about the target architecture. It provides some functions to find address translation tables in the raw memory and functions to use them to access the induced virtual address space.

3.1 Example Implementation: IA-32 Backend for `liblinear`

On the IA-32 architecture, the CPU can run in various modes of operation; for modern multitasking operating systems the *protected mode* is the preferred one. The protected mode can use a two-level address translation: first it will translate the *logical address*, consisting of a segment selector (which is an index into either the local or the global segment descriptor table) and an offset to the *linear address*. The linear address is then translated via paging to the *physical address*. (The paging translation is optional and needs to be enabled by setting a special flag in a control register of the CPU.)

A Linux process runs in a simple 4GiB flat virtual address space; no segmentation is required. Thus, Linux will create (among others that are not of interest for us) four special segments during boot-up: for each privilege level (i.e. kernelspace and userspace), it will create segments for both code and data. These four so called *flat* segments will span the full virtual address space of 4GiB, thus effectively eliminating segmentation. The address of the *global descriptor table*, holding the description of these segments, is then loaded into the *global descriptor table register* (GDTR) and the specific segment registers are loaded with segment selectors referring to the segments[6].

---

[6] This initialization is done in `linux/arch/i386/kernel/head.S`, GDTs are defined at symbols `boot_gdt_table` and `cpu_gdt_table`

The IA-32 architecture divides the 4GiB virtual address space into 1024 4MiB-frames. This splitting is defined by the *pagedirectory*. Each entry of a pagedirectory is 4 bytes long, thus the pagedirectory is $4 \cdot 1024 = 4096$ Bytes long. Each of these *pagedirectory entries* (PDEs), if present (its **PRESENT**-flag is set), can either refer to a 4MiB physical page or a pagetable dividing this virtual 4MiB frame further into 4KiB frames. A *pagetable* is again consisting of 1024 4-byte *pagetable entries* (PTEs), each corresponding to a 4KiB frame.

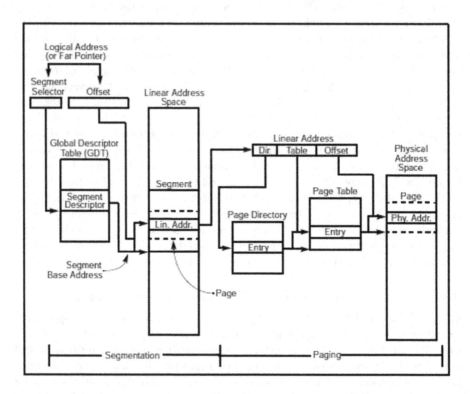

Fig. 1. IA-32 Segmentation and Paging process (image taken from [Int06d])

As newer IA-32 CPU features like *36 bit page size extension* (PSE-36) and *physical address extension* (PSE) are not used in case of the proposed circumstances[7], their reflection is omitted here. Furthermore it is not always possible to know from the physical memory only, if these features are enabled. A sample-installation of a system to be attacked should give these informations. Also, PAE and PSE-36 are not yet implemented in `liblinear`. PSE though (not PSE-36) is enabled with the given options (and implemented), as one can determine by the use of 4MiB-pages.

---

[7] `CONFIG_NOHIGHMEM` or `CONFIG_HIGHMEM4G`, `CONFIG_VMSPLIT_3G`.

For an extensive documentation of the IA-32 architecture one should refer to the *Intel 64 and IA-32 Architectures Software Developer's Manual* ([Int06a, Int06b, Int06c, Int06d, Int06e]), especially [Int06d].

3.2 Finding Address Translation Tables

When accessing a range of memory via physical addressing, it is necessary to find address translation tables to make sense out of the vast, unsorted number of pages. Typically, translation tables are not marked as such and as we can not access the processor or the operating system to ask, where these are, we have to search them. The following methods have proven themselves when being combined: for all pages we make a simple test if a page *could* be a pagedirectory (3.2) and if so, analyse this page in detail (3.3).

Obviously, address translation tables are architecture and operating system specific; but within an architecture and an operating system, they will often share data or specific patterns that are identifiable. For instance, when searching for Linux IA-32 address translation tables, one can omit searching the segment descriptor tables (see section 3.1) and concentrate on finding pagedirectories. There are several special patterns that can be found in a typical pagedirectory of a Linux process running on IA-32. Following is a layout of the typical virtual address space of a userspace process:

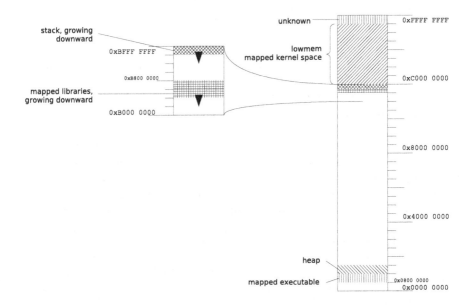

Fig. 2. Layout of the virtual address space of a typical Linux process

- *code and heap* will be starting around 0x0800 0000, consecutively following with a minor number of unused frames in between
- *libraries* and *custom mappings* will be mapped below 0xb800 0000
- the *userspace stack* will be mapped below 0xc000 0000, possibly directly starting from 0xbfff ffff
- starting from 0xc000 0000 up to approx. 0xf800 0000 the "lowmem" (approx. lower physical 900 MiB of physical RAM) will be mapped
- the *kernelspace stack* will be located in this lowmem
- several so far unidentified pages are mapped after 0xf800 0000
- all *unused frames* will have 4-byte entries consisting of zeroes (0x0000 0000)

Stack- and memory randomization techniques like *PaX* randomize the base addresses of these locations within several pages, but the general layout stays the same.

Besides searching pages that show non-zero values around these positions and zero values elsewhere, it is much easier and faster to just check, if the virtual address 0xc000 0000 maps to the physical address 0x0, because typically the PDE for 4MiB-page no. 0x300 will point to the 4MiB physical page at 0x0. This test only requires reading the 4byte PDE entry 0x300 and does sort out a vast majority of non-pagedirectory pages.

Furthermore in the combination Linux/IA-32 we only have to search the lower 1GB of RAM for pagetables.

3.3   Matching Via Statistics: NCD (Normalized Compression Distance)

For a detailed introduction to and analysis of the NCD and sample applications, the reader may refer to [LV97] and the text given below.

The *normalized information distance* (NID), a form of parameter-free similarity distance measurement, can be understood as a measurement for the minimal amount of changes required to change one information into another one. A NID of 1 means that two informations are totally unrelated; a NID of 0 means that they are the same. Due to its relation to the *Kolmogorov complexity* (a measurement for an information's shortest description in a fixed description language) it is incalculable. As an approximation, it is possible to use data compressors instead of the Kolmogorov complexity to measure the size of a minimal representation of information.

The resulting *normalized compression distance* has proven to be useful in a vast area of applications; for instance, it has shown its usefulness during analysis of DNA sequences or languages for relatedness ([CV05, LCL+04]), MIDI music files for relations in style and creator ([CV05]) and attack schemes of viruses and worms ([Weh05]).

As the NCD is only an approximation of the NID based on compressors, its resulting "normalized" value can be slightly larger that 1.0 and will never reach 0.

`liblinear` uses the NCD to measure the distance between a known true pagedirectory and a page of unknown data to determine whether this page could be a pagedirectory. The NCD has been chosen, because it is a *parameter-free* measurement, i.e. it does not depend on specific, known structures of the data in question. As different architectures will have significantly different address translation schemes, even depending on the operating systems used, this choice should be adequate. The `complearn`-toolkit [8] provides a suite of functions for generating NCD distance matrices between information, generating relational trees from these and more. As we only need to compare two pages, this set of functions is far too big and the interface far too complex for this application. Thus, we implemented a very short version of the NCD (`simple_ncd()` in `liblinear/simple_ncd.c`) using BZip2[9] as compressor.

4 Attacking

In this section we will show how the two libraries discussed in sections 2 and 3 can be used to gain unauthorized access to remote computer systems.

Subsection 4.1 will discuss passive attacks that only *read* from a physical memory source. An overview over gathering information from a virtual address space is given, including finding processes on a host, obtaining their environment, arguments and the path of the processes binary. Afterwards, an additional attack is introduced that is capable of copying public/private keypairs for SSH from a running `ssh-agent` process.

In **subsection 4.2**, we will introduce attacks that change data in the virtual address space. Further details about executables, libraries and processes will be given as an introduction. Then we will show how to find mapped libraries, binaries and the stack of a process and how to inject code into a running process. We then introduce a specially crafted code that can be used to obtain an interactive shell using firewire access only.

4.1 Information Gathering

Identifying processes. Once an address translation table has been found, it is of interest, what kind of process resides in this virtual address space. For userspace applications on IA-32-Linux there is a simple way to identify a process's *filename*, its *arguments* and even its full set of *environment variables*: This information is often required by a process and thus the kernel will provide it to the process by copying it to the bottom pages of the application's stack[10].

We wrote a tool `remote-ps`, that uses a function `proc_info()` to seek the stack-bottom, parse it and return ready-for-use environment vectors, command-line vectors and the full path of the binary for a given linear address space. For

---

[8] `complearn`-toolkit: http://complearn.org/

[9] BZip2: A high-quality data compressor, http://www.bzip.org/

[10] i.e. the stack-pages that are found first when seeking downward from virtual address `0xbfff f000`.

each found address space it will print a list of all found processes with their arguments.

Places to find secrets. Many applications keep confidential data in their memory, some of them even locking them into the main memory[11] to prevent the operating system from swapping them to slower (permanent) media. While in general this is a good idea, as an attacker may reconstruct the data from e.g. thrown-away harddisks, it increases the chance of an attacker that can obtain access to the memory of the system in question, as the confidential material will be stored in memory completely and not fragmented.

"Secrets" includes, among other information, *authentication data, cryptographic key material, random data* (e.g. to seed a cryptographic algorithm) and sometimes even *algorithms (proprietary software)*. Authentication data can be e.g. passwords or private keys for signature algorithms. Cryptographic key material are keys for usage with cryptographic algorithms (like signature algorithms). The latter two will be of main interest in the remainder of this section.

Many applications using a cryptographic infrastructure for communications will keep once loaded passwords or keys in their main memory for successive usage. The operating systems protection model ensures the safety of this information from other processes running on the same system; but by accessing the main memory we do have full access to this material. The only remaining task is to find and reconstruct the key material and passwords from the memory.

As an example, the following applications are of interest:

- GnuPG and PGP: applications to sign and encrypt arbitrary data with public/private keypairs. They are wide spread for email-encryption and -signing.
- sshd, ssh and ssh-agent: the *secure shell* application is an extended, encrypted version of telnet using strong cryptography, including passwords, skey, x509 certificates, RSA and DSA keys.
- Apache and other SSL-enabled web servers.
- OpenVPN, Cisco-VPN and other VPN-servers and clients
- Instant Messaging Applications, e.g. Psi, keeps the authentication information and possibly the GnuPG keypair in memory.
- The computer BIOS password, ATA password or PGP-Wholedisk password: the computer or its drives can be locked with a BIOS password or the harddisk can be encrypted. For a sample attack, see [Boi06].

Example attack: ssh-agent snarfer. To show how easy it is to obtain secret keys from a process we have written a sample attack to obtain (snarf[12]) *ssh public/private keypairs* from ssh-agents via *firewire*.

When using ssh for accessing remote computers it is possible to authenticate via passwords, public/private keypairs and various other methods. The

---

[11] e.g. via the *mlock* function.

[12] To snarf: To grab, esp. to grab a large document or file for the purpose of using it with or without the author's permission. // To acquire, with little concern for legal forms or politesse (but not quite by stealing). (source: Jargon Files)

usage of public/private keypairs is wide-spread among people using ssh on a regular basis. These keypairs can either be a DSA or a RSA keypair, they are typically created with ssh-keygen and stored somewhere in $HOME/.ssh/, e.g. /root/.ssh/id_dsa and /root/.ssh/id_dsa.pub. Keypairs can and should be encrypted with a passphrase to prevent attackers from using them, if they were able to obtain them by some means. Thus to use a keypair it is required to enter this passphrase each time. This can be disturbing during frequent usage, e.g. when using ssh+svn or scp with remote-tab-completion (zsh is capable of this).

For these and other reasons, the ssh-agent has been developed. This agent will run in the background; the user can store a keypair into it (once entering the passphrase to unlock the keypair) and successively use the keypair without the requirement to enter the passphrase each time. The keypair can be wiped from memory on demand and also be loaded only for a specified period of time.

During our tests we found that the key is *not* wiped from memory when the time limit is hit. It will be wiped the next time the ssh-agent is queried (via its socket), but the agent is stalled in a *read* system call until this query and thus can not wipe the key[13]. That makes it possible to obtain long overdue keys from ssh-agents, although their owners believed them to be safe. A simple timer could have prevented this. But even with such a timer enabled it would be possible to acquire the key during its lifetime.

To obtain a keypair from an agent via firewire, a staged attack is required:

1. Seek the first GiB of physical memory for pagetables.

2. For each pagetable: check with the introduced proc_info(), if the found userspace belongs to a ssh-agent process. If not, seek next pagetable.

3. Use the obtained environment to resolve the users home directory ($HOME) and create a path where keypairs most likely reside in the file system (e.g. "$HOME/.ssh/") and seek this string in the heap. This approach will only find keypairs that have been loaded with this key-location.[14] Keypairs loaded from different locations or via a relative path can thus not be found by this search.

4. All loaded keypairs have a corresponding *identity-struct* in an agent. Among other fields, this identity-struct contains a link to a key struct, the above mentioned path/comment-field and the lifetime of the key. Thus to find the identity struct corresponding to a found comment-field, one has to search the address of the comment-field in the heap of the agent.

5. Once the *key-struct* that is linked to by the identity-struct, has been found, one can determine whether the found key is a RSA or a DSA key. The key-struct

---

[13] This bug has been fixed upon request in openssh-4.5p1 or earlier.

[14] Actually this field is the key's comment-field that is mostly unused and overwritten with the filename of the key. Keypairs that are used with SSH protocol version 2 (virtually all) do not have a comment-field; during loading, the comment-field is always initialized with the keys pathname.

contains a type-field and two pointers to either the RSA or the DSA key. These referenced structures are the *OpenSSL*[15]-structures RSA and DSA.

6. For both RSA and DSA structures , all important fields need to be recovered to obtain valid keypairs. [Sch96, MvOV01] give an overview of both cryptographic algorithms, [VMC02] introduces OpenSSL concepts and implementation details. OpenSSL's arbitrary precision integer implementation is the BIGNUM-struct (often abbreviated "BN"). It consists of a variable-length array of bit-vectors forming the value and a length-field defining the length of this array. As RSA and DSA both operate on finite fields, both are implemented with BIGNUMs. Therefore, the RSA and DSA structures contain several BIGNUMs that need to be recovered to obtain a valid copy of the keypair.

7. Some validity tests may be done to verify that the acquired BIGNUMs fulfill algorithm-specific properties and thus form a valid keypair.

8. Attach the obtained BIGNUMs back into valid RSA or DSA structures and save these keys to a file using openssl-functions.

Once *one identity*-struct is found, *all* structs of the same key-type (RSA or DSA) could be found by walking the list this key is linked into.

As stated above, the keypairs reside decrypted in the memory of the agent (even if overtime) and thus, when snarfed and stored to a file, can be immediately used by the command `ssh -i keyfile user@host`[16]. Such an attack will not take much longer than searching the first 1 GiB of physical RAM for pagedirectories, that is *typically no more than 15 seconds*. If an attack fails but an agent was found, it would be possible to just dump the heap of the agent to a permanent storage and stage a more thorough attack at a later time. Once the heap is dumped, all required data is obtained. A similar attack via *ptrace* should be possible as well.

[SvS99] introduces some schemes to find secret keys in random data and some countermeasures. It takes a special look at finding private RSA keys if their corresponding public keys are known and finding keys by searching high-entropy regions. Though we encourage the reader to read this interesting paper, the circumstances are most likely very different: cheap and small storage media like flash-memory and small harddisks have increased portable storage to a huge size, equal or larger than the memory a computer system typically has. Thus, an attacker can just dump the full memory or a subset of it (like the virtual address space of a single process) that is promising to contain a secret. A thorough attack can then be staged later. Still, searching private keys with the introduced methods can be very helpful, if reconstruction of the used data-structures is impossible or more expensive. Furthermore, when trying to obtain a private key, often enough the corresponding public key is unknown. This invalidates the approaches introduced to find RSA secret keys that require the public key.

---

[15] OpenSSL (http://openssl.org) is a free open-source implementation of the secure socket layer protocol also providing a general purpose cryptography library ().

[16] Only by stealing a key, an attacker will not know, which hosts can be accessed with a retrieved key.

4.2   Userspace Modifications

Each executable object, including libraries and executables, is usually separated
into code and data sections, where the code is marked as read-only during execution. The data can further be separated into read-only data, read-write data
and uninitialized global variables (local variables will be allocated from the stack,
runtime-allocated memory is allocated from the heap). Thus an executable object may be split into four regions: *code*, *rodata* (constants), *rwdata* and *dynamic
data* (rwdata may also be implemented by copying the initial data from rodata
to dynamic data); stack and heap are process-specific.

As many different processes may use the same executable objects, it would be
a waste of memory if the operating system created a copy of the object for each
reference to it.

Code and rodata may not be written to by a process, thus the operating
system can share these two regions among processes that are using the same
objects (binaries or libraries). Thus, once an operating system *ensures* that a
process can not write to code-regions and read-only data-regions or introduces
a copy-on-write mechanism, it can map these once loaded regions into multiple
virtual address spaces. This enforcement is done in hardware, on IA-32 by setting
a flag in the page directory or a page table referencing the specific physical
memory pages containing the region.

Newer CPUs provide *page-level no-execute enforcements* (AMD's NX *No eXecute bit*, Intel's EXB *EXecute disable Bit*); equal segment-level enforcements exist for years but never have been used in mainstream as Linux and many other
operating-systems using a flat memory-model (with only one big segment span-
ning the full virtual address space). Once these page-level enforcements are used
in systems, attacks that inject code into data-regions or the stack are rendered
completely useless. However with access to the data-structures (page directory
and page tables) containing the information, which pages are executable and
which not, it is trivial to remove the protection before injecting code e.g. into
an applications stack.

On Linux, programs and libraries are in *Executable and Linker Format* (ELF).
This format is described in the manpage elf(5). When a binary is mapped into
a process's memory, it is mapped including the full ELF header containing all
information that is required to link all references between different objects; ELFs
are always mapped at page-bounds. Due to this, all mapped ELFs (that includes
executables and libraries) can be found by scanning all pages for the ELF Magic
(0x7f E L F) at offset 0 in the page. Libraries, executables and other ELF objects
can be distinguished by evaluating the e_type field of the ELF header.

Overwriting executable or library code. When code of executables or libraries is changed, all programs using these ELF objects are influenced at the
same time. An attacker thus has the ability, but also the burden, to possibly
infect several processes at the same time. Such an attack has to be carefully
prepared and conducted, as each system may have a different version of a binary
and overwriting the wrong parts of an ELF or writing the wrong code may result

in an almost immediate crash of all processes using the ELF. Though this is an interesting approach, there are easier ways to inject code into a *single* process (see 4.2).

Such an attack could be conducted by searching a single virtual address space for the glibc and then parsing the ELF-headers and searching for the entry-point of the `printf`-function (or some other function). Then a piece of code could be injected into the unused fragment of the last page of the libc-mapping. It is important to inject the shellcode into the mapping, as all processes that will be affected have to be able to reach the shellcode. The intention is to overwrite the `printf` functions code with a *relative*[17] jump to this injected code. But as we need to overwrite some instructions inside the function, we need to parse the functions code to separate each instruction[18], so that after our code is executed, it executes a copy of the overwritten instructions and jumps to a fully intact instruction right after the injected jump. After this has been done, the jump can be injected into the functions code. This last write has to be as atomic as possible, as a process may just be executing these bytes and thus get astray. On IA-32, entry-points of functions are most likely aligned to 32-bit addresses[19]. Firewire also provides an interface to write 32-bit aligned 32-bit values ("quads") atomically. Unfortunately, a *relative short* jump (2 bytes) can only jump within ± 256 bytes from the jump itself and *relative long* and *absolute* jumps are 5 bytes wide (1 byte command + 4 bytes address). A short jump is most likely incapable of reaching the last page of the ELF and writing a long relative jump is not atomic.

A lot of interesting methods to inject code into a running process have been developed; e.g. [Ano02] gives an introduction into using *ptrace*, including injecting whole shared objects using the runtime linker *libdl*. The usability of this approach has not yet been analysed.

Overwriting the stack and return addresses. Besides stealing SSH-keys, we have put most of our efforts into injecting code into the stack and overwriting return-addresses on the stack to point to the injected code. This modification of the classic *stack overflow* method has some advantages over the previous approach:

- Each process, even each thread, has its own stack. Thus only a single thread will be affected by the attack.
- If the attack fails and the thread dies, only a *single* thread will fail on the target system, not e.g. *all* processes using the glibc or *all* instances of */bin/sh.*

---

[17] An ELF may be mapped at different locations in different processes, if it is "PIC" or "PIE" (Position Independent Code/Executable) and the kernel supports this. Thus, unless the ELF is only mapped in one process or the overwritten function is only used in one process, the jumps target has to be addressed relative to the current position.

[18] On IA-32, different machine instructions can have different length.

[19] Due to optimizations by the compiler.

- The process can read and write to the stack as well, thus we can communicate with the injected shell-code in a rather easy way (see 4.2).
- During the attack we do not need to modify parts of the code of the target-process, reducing the risk of an astray process. The final part consists of overwriting 4 byte wide return-addresses on the stack and this can almost always be done automatically.

The attack consists of the following steps:

1. Search a free location in the stack-pages. If the shellcode is small, we can use the zero-padded area of the pages containing the environment and argument vectors (see section 4.1). If the shellcode does not fit into this area, we could try to just overwrite these vectors. Most programs will parse environment and arguments only once during startup of the program, thus overwriting them at a later time usually has no effects. But note that these vectors are also evaluated whenever someone accesses a processes *procfs* entries /proc/$PID/environ and /proc/$PID/cmdline. Thus if these are over-written with new data, it is possible to see the difference by querying these procfs-entries or using ps[20].

2. Scan the stack for stack-frames and for each found: overwrite the return address. This can be simplified into: overwrite all 32-bit aligned 32-bit values that contain a value that might be a pointer into the main code area (0x08** ****, see figure 2) with a pointer to the injected code. A more aggressive approach might also overwrite return-values pointing into the library section (0xB7** ****).

Once the attacked process leaves a stack frame with an overwritten return value, it will jump to the injected code and execute it.

An implementation of this attack, including some sample shellcodes like a bindshell and a simple printf has been implemented.

Direct communication with shellcode via DMA. The royal league of attacking remote hosts is to inject code that is executed and spawns an interactive shell (thus it is also called "shellcode") and additionally is as invisible on the target system as possible. An interactive shell has to communicate with its user, so typically a network-based shell is used for attacking purposes. The downside of this technique is the visibility of the communication on the network-layer: an administrator can easily spot the network connection by either sniffing on the network or by asking the system what kind of sockets and files a process is using[21]. A network intrusion system (NIS) can easily spot shell connections in an automated way or firewalls could be configured in a way that a network connection is impossible. But when using e.g. firewire to attack a host there is usually no network connection between the attacker and the victim at all.

In our example attack, we will use a similar attack vector to inject a "beach-head" with our methods of physical memory access.

---

[20] Ps relies on these procfs entries.

[21] e.g. by using lsof -i (LiSt Open Files).

The overall mechanism is introduced in figure 3. The injected shellcode will fork a shell and communicate with stdin/stdout of the shell via two pipes. The shellcode then creates a second thread, thus having one thread for each direction of *master to shell* and *shell to master*. If the master (attacker) wishes to send a command to the shell, it writes the command string into the *FromMaster* ring-buffer via DMA. Once the ReaderThread sees that the ring-buffer is not empty, it reads the data inside the buffer and writes it into the pipe to the shell. The WriterThread will read data coming from the shell from the pipe and then write it into the *ToMaster* ring-buffer, so the master can read it via DMA.

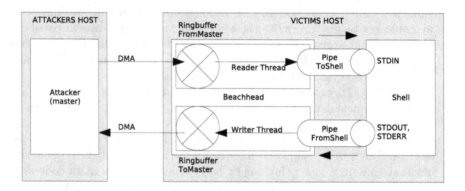

Fig. 3. Functionality of the beachhead

We thus have shown that it is possible to gain interactive, unauthorized, administrative access to a remote computer system by simply plugging a cable into the device's firewire port.

5   Future Prospects

In this section we will show future work that can be done in this area.

5.1   Kernelspace Modifications

The Linux character device /dev/kmem gives a process read and write access to its virtual address space, including the kernel-space area. /dev/kmem has not only been used for its legitimate purpose (i.e. debugging the kernel) but also to inject code into the running kernel and install kernel-based rootkits. [sd01] describes an attack using /dev/kmem to inject a new syscall-handler (a regularly used rootkit technique).

With our provided toolkit, we plan to do extend our work to include root-kit injection in the future.

5.2   Bootstrapping Custom Operating Systems

As an attacker has complete access to a systems memory, it is possible to take over the system completely, reset it to a known state and boot a custom operating system on it (and e.g. use firewire storage as the root-device for the new system). A special bootloader would be required to do this and it might also be necessary to reset the system and attached hardware in a special way, depending on the operating system running on it before the approach.

6   Conclusion

It has been shown that firewire and other DMA technology are a mature attack vector having a serious impact on a systems security. DMA interfaces should always be sealed or disabled if untrusted persons can access them; this particularly includes laptops, as more and more of them are equipped with a tiny firewire port. Security "solutions" that deny DMA for some devices and allow DMA for others should be tested very carefully, as these schemes may be tricked by pretending to be a different, "trusted" device (see [Boi06]).

Though most of the tools introduced are designed to attack a system, `libphysical` and `liblinear` can also be used for forensic purposes to analyse memory dumps (with the filedescriptor backend). The statement "There is little experience in reconstructing logical/virtual memory from physical memory dumps" from [BDK05] is no longer true: `liblinear` can be used to access virtual address spaces of each process (independent of the operating system), e.g. IDETECT (by Mariusz Burdach, [Bur06]) can be used to analyse kernel data structures to obtain other information.

References

[And99]   Anderson, D.: FireWire System Architecture - IEEE 1394. Addison Wesley, Reading (1999)

[Ano02]   Anonymous. Runtime Process Infection. Phrack, vol. 0x0b(0x3b) Phile 0x08 (2002) http://www.phrack.org/archives/59/p59-0x08.txt

[BDK05]   Becher, M., Dornseif, M., Klein, C.N.: FireWire - all your memory are belong to us (2005), http://md.hudora.de/presentations/firewire/2005-firewire-cansecwest.pdf

[Boi06]   Boileau, A.: Ruxcon 2006: Hit by a Bus: Physical Access Attacks with Firewire (2006), http://security-assessment.com/

[Bur06]   Burdach, M.: Finding Digital Evidence In Physical Memory pdf (2006), http://forensic.seccure.net/pdf/mburdach_physical_memory_forensics_bh06.pdf

[CV05]   Cilibrasi, R., Vitányi, P.M.B.: Clustering by Compression. IEEE transactions on information theory, vol. 51 (2005) http://www.cwi.nl/paulv/papers/cluster.pdf

[Int06a]   Intel Corp. Intel 64 and IA-32 Architectures Software Developer's Manual, vol. 1 Basic Architecture (2006), http://developer.intel.com/

[Int06b]   Intel Corp. Intel 64 and IA-32 Architectures Software Developer's Manual, vol. 2A: Instruction Set Reference, A-M (2006), http://developer.intel.com/

[Int06c]   Intel Corp. Intel 64 and IA-32 Architectures Software Developer's Manual, vol. 2B: Instruction Set Reference, N-Z (2006), http://developer.intel.com/

[Int06d]   Intel Corp. Intel 64 and IA-32 Architectures Software Developer's Manual, vol. 3A: System Programming Guide, Part 1 (2006), http://developer.intel.com/

[Int06e]   Intel Corp. Intel 64 and IA-32 Architectures Software Developer's Manual, vol. 3B: System Programming Guide, Part 2 (2006), http://developer.intel.com/

[LCL+04]   Li, M., Chen, X., Li, X., Ma, B.: Vitányi, P.M.P.: The Similarity Metric. IEEE transactions on information theory (August 2004), http://arxiv.org/pdf/cs.CR/0111054

[LV97]   Li, M., Vitányi, P.M.B.: An Introduction to Kolmogorov Complexity and Its Applications, 2nd edn. Springer, Heidelberg (1997)

[MvOV01]   Alfred, J., Menezes, P.C.: Handbook of Applied Cryptography. CRC Press, Boca Raton, USA (2001), http://www.cacr.math.uwaterloo.ca/hac/

[Pro00]   Promoters of the 1394 Open HCI. 1394 Open Host Controller Interface Specification (January 2000)

[Sch96]   Schneier, B.: Applied Cryptography, 2nd edn. John Wiley & Sons, Inc, Chichester (1996)

[sd01]   sd, devik,: Linux on-the-fly kernel patching without LKM. Phrack, Vol. 0x0b, Issue 0x3a, Phile 0x07 (December 2001), http://www.phrack.org/archives/58/p58-0x07.txt

[SvS99]   Shamir, A., van Someren, N.: Playing Hide and Seek with Stored Keys. In: Franklin, M.K. (ed.) FC 1999. LNCS, vol. 1648, pp. 118–124. Springer, Heidelberg (1999)

[VMC02]   Viega, J., Messier, M., Chandra, P.: Network Security with OpenSSL. O'Reilly (2002)

[Weh05]   Wehner, S.: Analyzing Worms and Network Traffic using Compression (April 2005), http://arxiv.org/pdf/cs.CR/0504045

Static Analysis on x86 Executables for Preventing Automatic Mimicry Attacks

Danilo Bruschi, Lorenzo Cavallaro, and Andrea Lanzi

Dipartimento di Informatica e Comunicazione
Università degli Studi di Milano
Milano, Italy
Via Comelico 39/41, I-20135, Milano MI, Italy
{bruschi,sullivan,andrew}@security.dico.unimi.it

Abstract. In 2005, Kruegel *et al.* proposed a variation of the traditional mimicry attack, to which we will refer to as *automatic mimicry*, which can defeat existing system call based HIDS models. We show how such an attack can be defeated by using information provided by the Interprocedural Control Flow Graph (ICFG). Roughly speaking, by exploiting the ICFG of a protected binary, we propose a strategy based on the use of static analysis techniques which is able to localize critical regions inside a program, which are segments of code that could be used for exploiting an automatic mimicry attack. Once the critical regions have been recognized, their code is instrumented in such a way that, during the executions of such regions, the integrity of the dangerous code pointers is monitored, and any unauthorized modification will be restored at once with the legal values. Moreover, our experiments shows that such a defensive mechanism presents a low run-time overhead.

1 Introduction

In their seminal work [13,12] about anomaly-based Host Intrusion Detection System (HIDS), Forrest *et al.*, introduced the idea that anomalous behavior of a process p can be detected by learning the sequences of system calls executed by p in a sterile environment, comparing them against those executed in a production environment, and detecting any significant deviation among them. Such an approach has been investigated by many researchers, who proposed several improvements over the original model, thus obtaining more efficient and more precise (i.e., which recognize broader classes of intrusions) anomaly detection HIDS. In [31,30] Wagner *et al.* observed that all the system call-based HIDS suffer a particular form of attack called mimicry. In its simplest form, to which we will refer to as *traditional mimicry*, it basically consists of forcing a process to execute an attack vector by *mimicking* the system calls sequences and learnt by the HIDS. Subsequently, several strategies (see [23,11,5]) have been proposed for inhibiting traditional mimicry attacks.

In a recent paper, Kruegel *et al.* [17] observed that even if the introduction of such techniques in anomaly-based HIDS [5,11,23] has significantly reduced the possibility to perform successful traditional mimicry attacks [26,25,31], they do not impose any kind of restriction on the execution of arbitrary code which does not directly invoke system

B. M. Hämmerli and R. Sommer (Eds.): DIMVA 2007, LNCS 4579, pp. 213–230, 2007.
© Springer-Verlag Berlin Heidelberg 2007

calls (i.e., system call-free code). For example, a piece of code that is able to modify writable memory segments represents a threat by itself. This observation, brought Kruegel *et al.* to devise a variation of the traditional mimicry attack which is able to hijack a program execution flow, execute malicious system call-free code, relinquish the execution flow to the diverted program to regain it later on.

This malicious code is usually executed as a preamble of in-trace syscalls. Its main objective is either to change the value of the system call parameters in order to eventually execute arbitrary code, or to modify the value of some control-dependent data variable in order eventually influence the process execution flow. In [17] a proof of concept tool is provided which is able to automatically identify, inside a program, the instructions which can be used for such a scope. For this reason we refer to such an attack as automatic mimicry. More precisely, the main goal of the automatic mimicry is to elude HIDS checks by continuously diverting the process execution flow in order to execute arbitrary code with the purpose of changing system calls parameters without directly invoking any system call. However, most of the time these steps cannot be completed at once. Thus, any piece of malicious code has to take care of continuously regaining the control of the execution flow. Such a task is usually performed by modifying appropriate code pointers.

On the basis of the previous observation we devised a strategy for containing automatic mimicry attacks. Such a strategy consists of localizing, inside a IA32 binary p, all the *dangerous regions* $a_i, \cdots, a_n$, where by dangerous region, known also as *liveness area*, we mean the code area between the definition d and use u of the values v of the system calls parameters. After the liveness areas have been determined we collect, at run-time, for any area a_i $1 \leq i \leq n$, the "trusted values" $t_1, \cdots, t_k$ of the code pointers defined in a_i. Subsequently, we instrument the process p image so that at run-time code pointers in a_i will always be restored to their corresponding trusted values, before their use. Consequently the attacker will not be able to regain the control of p's execution flow and the attack will not be feasible.

A static analysis tool and a kernel-level module on a Linux system have been developed in order to assess the viability of our approach. Several experiments has been performed both for verifying the correctness of the approach and its overheads. The results obtained showed that our strategy defeats the automatic mimicry attack guaranteeing a low overhead impact in term of process execution time.

The paper is organized as follows. Related works are described in § 2 while § 3 introduces some preliminary notions about static analysis and automatic mimicry attacks that will be useful throughout the paper. The core of our code pointers integrity verification is faced in § 4, and § 5 shows the effectiveness of this defensive mechanism. Technical details and experimental results are given in § 6 and § 7, while conclusion, future works and final remarks are given in § 8.

2   Related Works

Generally speaking, memory error exploits which corrupt code pointers aim at pursuing two main goals (or a combination of them), that is, (i) to perform IPE attacks [30] (to bypass security critical checks), and (ii) to execute arbitrary malicious code.

Several strategies have been proposed to deal with this problem. Some of them, such as StackGuard [7] (SG) and Pro Police Stack Detector (also known as Stack Smashing Protector, i.e., SSP) [10], aim at protecting the integrity of particular code pointers (e.g., return address for SG and mainly return address and saved frame pointer for SSP). However, beside stack smashing attacks [18], they do not address other kind of memory error exploits based on the corruption of others code pointers (GOT, .dtors, heap management information, and so on).

In [1], Abadi *et al.* propose Control-Flow Integrity (CFI), an approach to guarantee the integrity of the execution control flow of a protected application p. By forcing p's execution to dynamically follow only paths defined by its Control Flow Graph (CFG), their approach defeats attacks which, as a final goal, attempt to hijack a program execution flow to alter its behavior. CFI leverages on fewer assumptions to achieve its goals. In particular, it relies on non-writable code, and non-executable data segments. While, generally, these are common sense requirements, as noted by the authors, the assumptions can be somewhat problematic in the presence of self-modifying code, run-time code generation, and the unanticipated dynamic loading of code.

Program shepherding, proposed by Kiriansky *et al.*, monitors control flow transfers to enforce a security policy [16]. While CFI could be enforced by program shepherding, the approach proposed by Kiriansky *et al.* is more general. In fact, it prevents execution of data or modified code and ensures that libraries are entered only through exported entry points, without making any assumption a priori. Moreover, program shepherding provides sandboxing that cannot be circumvented, allowing construction of customized security policies. On the other hand, this monitoring technique may impose a quite moderate overhead for certain types of programs. Moreover, existing code attacks can be stopped only in some cases.

In [29], a technique based on process address space layout randomization (ASLR) has been proposed and realized by developing a kernel level patch which is in charge of loading the process' memory segments (code, data, heap, stack and mmap'd region) at different, randomized memory locations. Since no knowledge on the process behavior or structure is required, the approach can only guarantee the randomization of the segments base addresses but it lacks a more fine-grained randomization. Unfortunately, the approach is vulnerable to information leakage attacks or it has been proved to be not so effective on 32-bit Intel Architecture platforms [14].

Other address obfuscation techniques have been proposed in [21,20] by Bhatkar *et al.* as a particular form of program transformations to combat memory error exploits. Such approaches differ from the one proposed in [29] since they aim at providing a more fine-grained address space obfuscation. The objectives of these transformations are to randomize the absolute locations of all code and data in order to achieve protection from a broad class of memory corruption attacks, and to randomize the relative distance between different data objects in order to defeat relative addressing attacks, which are a subclass of non-control data ones [6]. To this end, various obfuscating transformations have been proposed; they range from the randomization of the base addresses of common memory regions (stack, heap, mmap'd area, text and static data), the permutation of the order of variables and routines, and the introduction of random gaps between objects. A further improvement over such an idea has been proposed in [21], where a source-to-source transformation on C programs has been developed to produce self-randomizing programs.

All the aforementioned randomization approaches share a common concept: they provide a *probabilistic* defensive mechanism that, in general, cannot provide *certainty* in protecting from memory errors exploits. In this sense, quite recently, newer approaches have been devised [9,4] that make use of diversified process replicæto provide protection from a broad class of memory error attacks which mainly corrupt application's code and data pointers. Even if the approach seems sound, promising, and an on-going research topic, it currently presents a quite high overhead, and fewer practical not fully solved limitations involving the management of shared memory, signals, and threads.

In this paper, we address the problem of memory error attacks which corrupt code pointers in order to perform an automatic mimicry attack. We believe that our technique can defeat most of the memory error attacks, while experiencing a low overhead and a transparent deployment[1] in all the HIDS architectures. It is worth noting that our technique is symbiotic with the HIDS and, consequently, several checks about stack integrity, some form of traditional mimicry and some IPE attacks, are performed by the HIDS itself.

3   Preliminaries

In this section we recall some basic notions about program static analysis that will be useful to understand our approach, as well as further remarks on the automatic mimicry attack.

Liveness Analysis. Given a program p, we use data-flow analysis techniques in order to gather information about the data used by p. In particular, we use the *liveness analysis* to define the liveness region of the program. From our point of view, a liveness region is a sequence of instructions where a particular system call parameter is alive; a parameter is alive if it holds a value that will/might be used in the future. Figure 1 shows the liveness area of the variable a, which is defined at line 6 and used at line 10. All application paths defined between the *definition* and *use* of the variable belong to the liveness area of the variable itself. More precisely:

- **Definition:** the *definition* of a variable occurs when it is defined either by input-related system call-aware functions, that is, functions that eventually invoke system calls (e.g., `read`, `recv`, `fgets`), or, in according to the classic definition, with an assignment of that variable. More precisely, we can classify the assignments in two main categories:
  - *dynamic assignment.* Such a kind of assignment is associated to the data coming directly from the input. In such an assignment are involved all the input-related system-call aware functions;
  - *static assignment.* Such a kind of assignment is associated to the data whose values do not come from input but are statically defined into the application by constant values.

---

[1] That is, without modifying neither the HIDS nor the binary code.

- **Use:** the *use* of a variable occurs when it is used by some security sensitive system call (e.g., `write`, `execve`, `read`) or by some function which eventually invokes security sensitive system calls (e.g., `fprintf`). Any modification of the variable achieved through arithmetic transformation, is not considered like an use. Roughly speaking, we consider the use of a variable when it is only used by some security sensitive routine.

```
1    int main(int argc, char **argv)
2
3        int a, b, c;
4        c = 40;
5        b = 30;
6        a = 25;
7        b = 2 * c;
8        c = c * 2;
9        c = c + 1;
10       b = a + 1;
11       c = c + 10;
```

Fig. 1. The Liveness Area of the Variable a

For the sake of clarity, we have reported in Figure 2 an example of the liveness region of the parameter `cmd` of the `execl` system call-aware function, which is defined between line 26 and line 30. At line 26 the parameter `cmd` is defined through the `fgets` system call-aware function, whilst at line 30 `cmd` is used by `execl`. All the statements between these lines represent the zone where the `cmd` parameter is alive. In order to compute the liveness regions, we will apply the classic data-flow algorithms [19] according to the aforementioned description of *use* and *definition*.

Automating Mimicry Attack. The main purpose of the automatic mimicry is to compromise an application overcoming any protection mechanism provided by an anomaly-based system call-based HIDS. The applications which can be compromised using an automatic mimicry attack have to satisfy some particular characteristics. More precisely, an application a has to contain a vulnerability that allows the injection of malicious code, and a sequence of system calls $s_1, \ldots, s_n$ which can be triggered for performing some unauthorized action. The main task which the injected code j has to perform is (i) to modify the code pointers inside a so that j can be executed before the legal in-trace syscall s_i is invoked, (ii) to relinquish the execution flow to a, and (iii) to eventually regain the execution flow to modify others code pointers used in a to change the behavior of a system call s_j.

For the sake of clarity and to better understand this evasion technique, we describe two successful automatic mimicry attacks[2] performed against the code snippet shown in Figure 3 and 4 proposed in [17]. In the former attack, the attacker exploits the stack-based buffer overflow [18] vulnerability related to the `strcpy` (line 8) in order to overwrite the return address of check_pw, and point it to the attacker code. In writing such a code he may follow two options, that is, to either (i) directly invoke an in-trace

---

[2] Assuming no particular OS protection mechanisms, such as Address Space Layout Randomization (ASLR) [29,20,27] and non-executable data area [28,15,29] are deployed.

```
1    #define CMD_FILE "commands.txt"
2
3    int enable_logging = 0;
4
5    int check_pw(int uid, char *pass)
6    {
7        char buf[128];
8        strcpy(buf, pass);
9        return !strcmp(buf, "secret");
10   }
11
12   int main(int argc, char **argv)
13   {
14       FILE *f;
15       int uid;
16       char passwd[256], cmd[128];
17
18       if ((f = fopen(CMD_FILE, "r")) == NULL) {
19           perror("error: fopen"); exit(1);
20       }
21
22       uid = getuid();
23       fgets(passwd, sizeof(passwd), stdin);
24
25       if (check_pw(uid, passwd)) {
26           fgets(cmd, sizeof(cmd), f);
27           if(enable_logging)
28               printf("uid[%d]: %s", uid, cmd);
29           setuid(0);
30           if (execl(cmd, cmd, 0) < 0) {
31               perror("error: execl"); exit(1);
32           }
33       }
34   }
```

Fig. 2. The Liveness Area of the Parameter *cmd*

system call, but, due to the system call coordinates checks [11], he cannot neither invoke a system call from an illegal call site nor returning into different location after the system call-aware function termination, or (ii) set enable_logging, overwrite the printf GOT entry with the address of the injected malicious code, fix the stack layout in order to restore the original check_pw return address (the one at line 26, supposing the function does not return 0) and saved frame pointer and, finally, voluntarily relinquish the execution flow to the application code. Since no system call has been executed so far, no HIDS checks are performed and everything runs smoothly until the execution flow reaches the printf at line 28. At this point, before executing the real syscall-aware library function that, however, has to be executed in order to keep the write syscall performed by the printf in-trace, the malicious code is executed in order to change the content of the cmd "string" so that arbitrary command will eventually be executed (line 30) with full privileges (thanks to the setuid at line 29). After this simple little black magic, the attack ends by relinquishing the execution flow to the application code so that the legal in-trace printf can be executed from the permitted call site with a correct return address.

Obviously, things can be much harder from the attacker perspective than the one just described. In fact, if the attacker is not able to find suitable GOT entries to overwrite, he has to find out different code pointers to play with (e.g., application function pointers), as depicted in Figure 4. In this scenario, the attacker can exploit the same vulnerability as in the previous example, but this time no suitable GOT entries are available in order to regain the control of the execution flow later on. However, by carefully looking at the code, check_pw return address can be forced to point to a malicious code that will set enable_logging and uid (a signed 32-bit integer). The former variable will be

```
1    #define CMD_FILE "commands.txt"
2
3    int enable_logging = 0;
4
5    int check_pw(int uid, char *pass)
6    {
7        char buf[128];
8        strcpy(buf, pass);
9        return !strcmp(buf, "secret");
10   }
11
12   int main(int argc, char **argv)
13   {
14       FILE *f;
15       int uid;
16       char passwd[256], cmd[128];
17
18       if ((f = fopen(CMD_FILE, "r")) == NULL) {
19           perror("error: fopen"); exit(1);
20       }
21
22       uid = getuid();
23       fgets(passwd, sizeof(passwd), stdin);}
24
25       if (check_pw(uid, passwd)) {
26           fgets(cmd, sizeof(cmd), f);
27           if(enable_logging)
28               printf("uid[%d]: \%s", uid, cmd);
29           setuid(0);
30           if (execl(cmd, cmd, 0) < 0) {
31               perror("error: execl"); exit(1);
32           }
33       }
34   }
```

Fig. 3. First Vulnerable Program

used to reach the do_log function that will allow the attacker to regain the control of the code, while the latter will be used to exploit the vulnerability present in do_log function (line 14) that will enable the attacker to overflow the buffer and overwrite the return address with the malicious code address. In fact after the pointer arithmetic is performed on line 14, do_log return address is overwritten with the cmd_id value (controlled by the attacker as well), so that it can make it point into the malicious code. Once the execution flow is regained, the attacker can change the value of cmd parameter performing any privileged command.

4 Defeating Automatic Mimicry Attacks

In this section we will explain the strategy we devised in order to prevent automatic mimicry attacks. Our approach is based on the use of the information contained in the Inter-procedural Control Flow Graph (ICFG) of the binary which has to be protected.

4.1 Defensive Strategy

A fundamental requirement of any *automatic mimicry* attack is the possibility to modify a process code pointers in order to execute the injected malicious code. Thus, automatic mimicry can be defeated if the integrity of such data is guaranteed. This is exactly the strategy we adopt. It is based on a three phases process: *code analysis*, *data collection*, and *code pointers restoring*. During the *code analysis* phase, the ICFG of the program p we want to protect is computed, and it is used to recognize the *dangerous regions*.

```
 1      int enable_logging = 0;
 2      int cmd_id = 0;
 3      int uid_table[8192];
 4
 5      int check_pw(int uid, char *pass)
 6      {
 7          char buf[128];
 8          strcpy(buf, pass);
 9          return !strcmp(buf, "secret");
10      }
11
12      void do_log(int uid)
13      {
14          uid_table[uid] = cmd_id++;
15      }
16
17      int main(int argc, char **argv)
18
19          if (check_pw(uid, passwd)) {
20              fgets(cmd, sizeof(cmd), f);
21              if (enable_logging)
22                  do_log(uid);
23              setuid(0);
24              if (execl(cmd, cmd, 0) < 0) {
25                  perror("error: execl"); exit(1);
26              }
27          }
28      }
```

Fig. 4. Second Vulnerable Program

Afterwards, the *data collection* phase collects the "trusted" values of the code pointers contained in p's dangerous regions. Such a phase is performed by executing p in a sterile environment. Finally, at run-time, the *code pointers restoring* phase restores the code pointers values collected during the data collection phase.

Code Analysis. The purpose of this phase is to determine the dangerous regions of p, using p's ICFG. In particular, we consider only nodes (basic blocks) that contain dangerous system calls, as defined by Xu. *et al.* [32]. Our method works as follows. Initially, we build p's ICFG, then:

- each node of the ICFG which contains a dangerous system call, is marked with u (i.e., we determine parameters' *use*);
- Let $p_1, \cdots, p_m$ be parameters used by a dangerous system call. For any p_j, $1 \leq j \leq k$ we collect the program locations where the parameter is defined[3], according to the definition given in § 3. To achieve this goal we use the standard equations defined by the data-flow analysis [19]. Such equations provide us the list of the defined variables on a per-basic block granularity. We mark all these nodes with d (i.e., we determine parameters' *definition*);
- subsequently, we visit the entire ICFG, and every time we meet a basic block marked by u, we perform the following steps. We apply the depth first search algorithm backward, starting from a node t marked with u and visiting the ICFG until we reach nodes marked by d, which contain the definition of the parameters used in node t. The sub-graph constituted by all visited nodes represents one of the dangerous regions we are interested in, and it is stored inside a database.

Figure 5, reports a fragment of a partial ICFG of the code depicted in Figure 3. In particular, we want to build a dangerous regions that is able to protect the parameter

---

[3] p is an ET_EXEC ELF executable so, code and data hold fixed absolute references.

cmd used inside the exec1 dangerous function. Gray nodes represent the dangerous regions built around the exec1 dangerous function and the leaf of the dangerous region is represented by the node marked with 4 (fgets function) in which the variable cmd is defined.

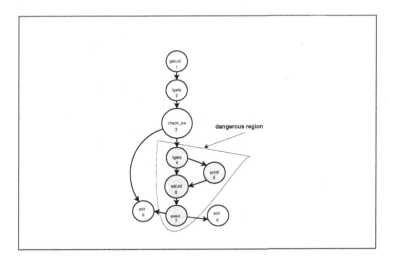

Fig. 5. Dangerous Region

Data Collection. After the code analysis phase, we collect the "trusted" addresses of the potential "dangerous" code pointers defined inside the dangerous regions. In particular, we collect the following information:

– *GOT Function Addresses*: For performance reasons we are interested only in the GOT addresses of the functions which are defined in dangerous regions[4]. GOT addresses are collected in two steps. Initially we execute the program p and we force the corresponding process to resolve all dynamic symbols collecting the address values; subsequently, we associate the GOT code pointers inside the dangerous regions with the discovered address values, and we store such relationships inside the database;

– *Function Pointers*: Another technique proposed by Kruegel *et al.* in order to perform the automatic mimicry attack is to exploit code pointers such as *application function pointers*. In order to collect such code pointers values, first we look for the program locations where the code pointers are defined, only inside dangerous regions; afterwards, through data-flow techniques we compute all code pointers destinations values and we save the correlation between program locations and such values into a database. Such operands represent the "trusted" values of the code pointers which will be used to check if an anomaly occurs during the program execution.

---

[4] We allow the attacker to regain control of the execution flow only in those locations of the application that are not dangerous to perform a successful automatic mimicry attack.

Code Pointers Restoring. The code pointers restoring is the last phase and it guarantees the integrity of the code pointers defined inside the dangerous regions. This phase is composed by two main steps. The first one, which takes place at loading time, performs a run-time *code instrumentation* of the process p, and loads the code pointers program locations and their trusted values inside a custom kernel data structures used by our kernel module component. The second step acts at run-time and performs the code pointers *integrity verification* step which is in charge of executing various checks on the "dangerous" code pointers and to restore the appropriate process execution flow.

run-time process instrumentation. The main goal of this step is to allow the execution of the *integrity verification* step in a transparent way without modifying neither the program source nor the binary code. It is performed as following. Initially it loads the kernel data structures containing the trusted values of the code pointers collected during the data collection phase. Subsequently, the code pointers instructions (i.e. call, ret) found inside the dangerous region (code analysis phase) are substituted by the int3[5] assembly instruction. The original instructions are saved inside the *saving instruction table* (see Figure 6) and will be restored after the integrity verification phase takes place.

Such a table will contain the op-codes of the substituted instructions and it is used to restore the execution flow of the process after the code pointers *integrity verification* step. Since the table is stored in p's address space, to guarantee that every tampering attempt is detected by the kernel before using the data provided by the table, its integrity is verified by using common cryptographic hash algorithms (SHA-1 and MD5). If the integrity cannot be satisfied, the kernel kills the process being protected, otherwise it is safe to use the data provided by the table to perform the next steps.

integrity verification. Due to the instrumentation process every time a potential dangerous function terminates its execution, or a (function) code pointer is invoked, the int3 instruction brings the execution in kernel land to a custom module which performs the appropriate checks. Such checks are strongly dependent on the type of code pointers we are trying to protect, and they can be classified in three main sets:

- *GOT entries*: the trusted values of GOT entries are retrieved from the entry in the kernel memory structures associated to the substituted instructions, and replaced into the appropriate GOT entries locations of p;
- *Return addresses*: in order to get the appropriate return address we instrument the call statement associated to the called function f; consequently, whenever f is invoked the integrity verification module v will be able to retrieve and store inside its own memory structures the "active" f's return address (i.e., the address of the instruction next to the considered call statement). When f has to return (ret instruction) v will check if the return address is equal to the "active" return address retrieved during the call invocation; if so, the module

---

[5] Such an instruction issues a software interrupt and it is usually used by programs debugger.

will not perform any actions[6] and the process will continue its execution. Otherwise, v will restore the appropriate return address retrieved during call invocation, raising an alarm and allowing the process to continue its execution.

- *Function Pointers*: whenever a function pointer is invoked, the integrity verification module v will check if the function pointer belongs to the set learnt during the static analysis phase; if so, v will not perform any actions and the process will continue its execution. Otherwise, the module raises an alarm and stops the process execution.

restoring process control flow. After the integrity verification phase, the module checker must restores the normal process flow. Such a process is executed by a kernel module that will perform two actions according on the type of the substituted instructions:

- call: for each substituted call, the module copies inside the saving instruction table the call instruction followed by a jmp statement. Once the kernel restores the process flow after the integrity verification phase, it brings the execution flow to the appropriate call inside the table; at this point the call is executed and the address of the next instruction, that is jmp, is saved onto p's stack; afterwards, whenever the function invoked by the call returns, the program counter (%eip register) points to the jmp instruction which will jump to inside the executable process memory after the int3 statement, restoring the normal execution process flow.
- ret: the module copies inside the saving instructions table the ret statement, which will bring the control flow to the appropriate process location, after the checks are performed.

Figure 6, reports the steps of the restoring process flow. In step 1 the process raises an exception and the control flow is transferred to kernel land then, after the check on the trusted code pointers is performed, the module checker restores the program counter value to the entry associated to the substituted instructions (step 2). At the end, after the execution of the call *%edx, the flow returns to the jmp instruction inside the saved table, which brings the process execution flow to the appropriate program location (step 3).

5 Effectiveness

In this section we will describe some properties of our defensive mechanism and in particular we will show its effectiveness on two practical examples. It is worth noting that in order to evaluate the effectiveness of our strategy we must consider the goals of our defensive mechanism and some properties of the application execution context. More in details:

- our defensive mechanism is symbiotic with the HIDS. Consequently, for performing a successful attack an attacker must elude both the HIDS and the code pointers integrity verification checks;

---

[6] The attacker should pick and change the address inside the set learnt in the static analysis phase. Such an attack, however, fall into the IPE category and the HIDS will be able to detect it.

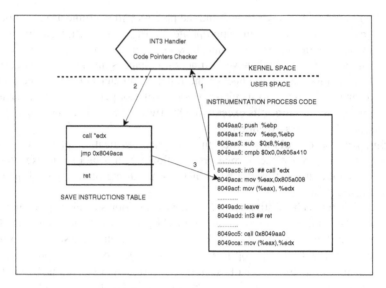

Fig. 6. Process Execution Flow Restoring Step

- the main goal of our defensive strategy is to defeat the attacks that use code pointers as a way to divert a process execution flow. It is worth noting that a vulnerability could occur inside the dangerous regions in some positions where the attacker must not use any code pointers to change the value of the syscall parameters; such an attack is generally known as non-control data [6] and it is not currently addressed by our approach[7];

In the following we will show how our technique works on the two examples of automatic mimicry attack described in [17].

5.1 GOT Protection

We apply the mechanism described in § 4 to the automating mimicry attack presented in Figure 3 . Our goal is to protect the *cmd* parameter used by the execl syscall. After the code analysis phase, we have defined the dangerous region of the program line 26-30, the Kernel module checker *c* has loaded inside its memory structures the trusted values of the code pointers (i.e execl's GOT line 30, fgets (line 26), printf (line 28), setuid (line 29) etc.) and the process has been instrumented. At this point, during the program execution, whenever the attacker exploits the vulnerability inside the check_pw function, he probably will rewrite the GOT of a function defined inside the dangerous regions which will be executed before execl function (line 30). The next attacker's action is to relinquish the control of the code to the application after the check_pw function, and regaining it when that particular function will be invoked. But after the attacker relinquished the control code to the "original" application, when

---

[7] However, some forms of such attacks can be defeated by protecting the use and definition area of the sensitive variables.

the execution flow reaches one of the checks previously set, the program flow will pass to c that will rewrite the appropriate code pointers, blocking so the attack.

5.2   Code Pointers Protection

In the example shown in Figure 4 the attacker uses a return stack as code pointer to regain code. During the learning phase the Kernel module checker retrieves the return addresses of the dangerous functions, do_log function, and during the loading it substitutes the ret instruction of such a function, with the breakpoint instruction ret.

Whenever the attacker exploits the vulnerability in the function check_pw, he changes the value of the variable uid writing a value that, once used by do_log function, will overwrite the function return address of that function bringing the execution inside the malicious code. Once the attacker has modified the uid value, it relinquishes the process execution flow back to p which will follow the normal flow. Whenever the program is about to return from do_log function, the execution flow will pass, by means of int3, to the code pointers integrity verification module which will overwrite the function return address with the "trusted" one, preventing to malicious code to regain control on the p's execution flow later on.

6   Technical Details

In this section we provide technical details of the prototype we developed for a GNU/ Linux system (kernel 2.4.28 version). We will describe the static analysis tool used to perform the static analysis phase, the process instrumentation performed at load time after the dynamic linker process takes place, and the modifications of the int3 kernel handler performed in order to manage the code pointers integrity verification process.

6.1   Static Analysis Tools

Static analysis of p has been performed using a static analysis tool for ELF IA32 binaries, developed by our group. The core of the tool is written using the Python language and some parts using the C language. Such a tool is able to obtain the Inter-procedural Control Flow Graph (ICFG) and to perform the basic data-flow analysis of the program being analyzed. In particular, the tool works following these steps:

- initially the pre-processing phase is performed in order to recognize some important ELF information such as symbol table location, code section location, dynamic section information, and so on;
- after gathering the preliminaries information, the tool disassembles the instructions contained inside the code section and converts them to an intermediate form. We used the well-known recursive traversal algorithm defined in [22] to disassemble the binary;
- the tool computes the ICFG (§ 3), afterwards the program is converted into the SSA form using the standard Ferrant's algorithm [8];
- finally, the tool uses the classic equations of the liveness analysis defined in [2] to perform this analysis.

Moreover, the tool is able to compute both the control dependencies and the classic data-flow analysis equations defined in [2].

6.2   Process Instrumentation

The process instrumentation phase is performed by the *instrumentator*, a program we have developed which trace the program p to be protected and, by using the ptrace system call, substitutes the appropriate instructions with the int3 statement. Moreover, the instrumentator has to build the saving instructions table. Such a table will be mapped at a fixed address known by the kernel code pointers integrity verification module as well; this can be easily achieved by using the mmap system call with a MAP_FIXED flag.

6.3   int3 Exception Handling

In order to perform the code pointers integrity verification checks, we have modi-fied the int3 kernel exception handler implemented in the do_trap kernel func-tion (traps.c). In particular, when the int3 exception is raised the control flow is transferred from user space application to the kernel code which calls the do_int3 kernel function (see entry.S) which eventually invokes do_trap. Figure 7, reports a snippet of the do_trap function we modified to add our code pointers integrity verification.

More in detail, when the exception int3 is executed, the do_trap function checks the exception number and the process name (line 7 and 8) which raises the exception. Consequently, if the process name[8] and the exception number are appropriate, we per-form the code pointer checks and restore the flow as already explained in § 4 (line 10 and 11); otherwise the handler will work in the usual way and the code inside the *if* statement (line 7) will not be executed.

```
1    trap_signal(...)
2    {
3        struct task_struct *tsk = current;
4        tsk->thread.error_code = error_code;
5        tsk->thread.trap_no = trapnr;
6
7        if ((trapnr == 3) && !(strcmp(tsk->comm, "process_name")))
8        {
9            check_code_pointers();
10           restore_flow() ;
11           return;
12       }
13       else
14       {
15           if (info)
16               force_sig_info(signr, info, tsk);
17           else
18               force_sig(signr, tsk);
19           return;
20       }
21   }
22   }
```

Fig. 7. Modified do_trap Function

---

[8] Indeed, a check on the program's i-node number would be better. Otherwise, the check can be easily bypassed by a local attacker by using symbolic links, for example.

7   Experimental Results

In this section we will describe the system used in order to make our experimental test and then present the set of experiments we ran to collect the measurements about the overhead introduced by our code pointers integrity verification module. All the experiments have been executed on an Intel Pentium IV processor with 3 GHz clock, running a GNU/Linux Debian operating system, 2.4.28 Linux kernel and 128 MB of RAM.

Our module acts on the code used by the kernel in order to manage the checking performed at runtime, so we focus our attention on those routines, defined into the file `traps.c`. In order to measure time lapses we used the time-stamp counter processor register (`tsc`, using the `rdtsc` assembly instruction). The counter, available on all kinds of Pentium processors is a 64-bit register that gets incremented at each clock tick. Using this measure we are able to provide the most accurate measurement of the system.

In the first phase of our experiments we have measured two main pieces of code of our obfuscation model, providing three measurements for each of them: the best time, the average time and the standard deviation of execution; in particular we have:

- *Context Switch*: this measure represents the amount of time used to perform the context switch from kernel to user mode context and vice versa, executed during the code pointers integrity verification process. The overhead in this case is $144\mu s \pm 493\mu s$ (8.5% overhead) on average (reporting $63\mu s$, i.e., 5%, on the best-case).
- *Hash Table access time*: this measure represents the amount of time needed to access the hash table (saving instruction table) used in order to replace the trusted code pointers values and for bringing the execution flow back to the process. The hash table size depends on the number of different instrumentation locations defined by the application. For the test we conducted, our hash table contained 50 locations on an average. Thus, the obfuscator overhead in this case is $114\mu s \pm 437\mu s$ (6.5% overhead) on average (reporting $61\mu s$, i.e., 1.6%, on the best-case).

As a second phase of our test we have considered three different kind of applications: server web `dhttpd` version $1.02a$, the `tftpd` server version $0.17 - 15$, and `sudo` application version $1.6.8p12$. Table 1 reportes the results of the static analysis phase; for each service we can see the number of the dangerous regions found and the total number of the code pointers that must be protected defined inside those regions.

After the static analysis phase we have performed the run-time analysis. For the HTTP server we have used a small web site with the following features: total size 500 KB, 12 static HTML pages, and 6 pdf documents (document's size 200 KB); for the `tftpd` server we have considered download and upload operations of a file which size

Table 1. Dangerous Regions

Services	# Dangerous Regions	# Code Pointers found in the Dangerous Regions
dhttpd	6	30
tftpd	7	39
sudo	14	75

Table 2. Runtime Analysis

Services	#Checks	Execution Time μs	Checking Time μs	Overhead
dhttpd	724	1407000	72400	5.1%
tftpd	467	1200000	37600	3.1%
sudo	110	99150	8800	8.8%

is 500 KB, and for the sudo utility we have considered the execution on the cat command on a small file. In Table 2 we have reported the run-time analysis overhead for each service, the number of the checks performed during the execution time, the total amount of the time spent by the process (we do not considered the I/O idle time), the time spent by the integrity verification process and, in the last column, the overhead inserted by our integrity verification module for those particular services.

8   Conclusion and Future Works

This paper presents a novel defensive technique based on the Inter-procedural Control Flow Graph; such a mechanism is represented by the code pointers checker module at the kernel-level, which is able to protect the HIDS against automatic mimicry attack with a low overhead.

One of the main problem of our defensive mechanism is represented by the accuracy of the static analysis phase performed on x86 binaries. In fact, the imprecision of such an analysis could increase both the false positive and negative in our system. In particular, there are two main problems which must be addressed when working on an executable binary: (1) the CFG's completeness and (2) the aliasing problem. In order to improve the CFG's completeness we can adopt the technique described in [24]. In this approach, the authors use the data-flow analysis in order to determine the values of the indirect calls so to improve the completeness of CFG. Instead, for the aliasing problem we can use the algorithm describe in [3]. This technique works on the x86 executable and has obtained good results. However, in future we think to work on the source code of the program in order to solve the problems that binary static analysis techniques arise.

Another problem of our approach is the size of the dangerous regions. In fact, sometimes there exists a great distance between the definition and use of a particular variable; consequently, if the region's size is very large, the attacker could have more chances to perform the attack successfully. In fact, if the vulnerability is positioned inside the dangerous regions the attacker can change the value of the system call parameters successfully without using any code pointers. We are investigating for improving our technique in order to solve these issues and to mitigate other attacks such as the non-control data.

Acknowledgements

We thank the anonymous reviewers for their helpful comments that improved the quality of the paper. We thank Monirul Sharif for help in reviewing the paper and we thank Christopher Kruegel and Lorenzo Martignoni for their extensive comments and suggestions.

References

1. Abadi, M., Budiu, M., Erlingsson, U., Ligatti, J.: Control-flow integrity. In: CCS '05: Proceedings of the 12th ACM conference on Computer and communications security, pp. 340–353. ACM Press, New York (2005)
2. appel, a.w.: Modern compiler implementation in c. Cambridge University Press, Cambridge (2004)
3. Balakrishnan, G., Reps, T.: Analyzing memory accesses in x86 executables. In: Duesterwald, E. (ed.) CC 2004. LNCS, vol. 2985, pp. 5–23. Springer, Heidelberg (2004)
4. Cox, B., Evans, D., Filipi, A., Rowanhill, J., Hu, W., Davidson, J., Knight, J., Nguyen-Tuong, A., Hiser, J.: N-Variant Systems: A Secretless Framework for Security through Diversity. In: 15th USENIX Security Symposium (2006)
5. Bruschi, D., Cavallaro, L., Lanzi, A.: An Efficient Technique for Preventing Mimicry and Impossible Paths Execution Attacks. In: 3rd International Workshop on Information Assurance (WIA 2007) (April 2007)
6. Chen, S., Xu, J., Sezer, E., Gauriar, P., Iye, R.K.: Non-Control-Data Attacks Are Realistic Threats. In: 14th USENIX Security Symposium (2005)
7. Cowan, C., Pu, C., Maier, D., Walpole, J., Bakke, P., Beattie, S., Grier, A., Wagle, P., Zhang, Q., Hinton, H.: StackGuard: Automatic adaptive detection and prevention of buffer-overflow attacks. In: Proc. of the 7th Usenix Security Symposium, pp. 63–78 (January 1998)
8. Cytron, R., Ferrante, J., Rosen, B.K., Wegman, M.N., Zadeck, F.K.: Efficiently computing static single assignment form and the control dependence graph. ACM Trans. Program. Lang. Syst. 13(4), 451–490 (1991)
9. Bruschi, D., Cavallaro, L., Lanzi, A.: Diversified Process Replicæ for Defeating Memory Error Exploits. In: 3rd International Workshop on Information Assurance (WIA 2007) (April 2007)
10. Etoh, H.: GCC extension for protecting applications from stack-smashing attacks (ProPolice) (2003), http://www.trl.ibm.com/projects/security/ssp/
11. Feng, H., Kolesnikov, O., Fogla, P., Lee, W., Gong, W.: Anomaly Detection using Call Stack Information. IEEE Symposium on Security and Privacy, Oakland, California (2003)
12. Forrest, S., Hofmeyr, S.A., Somayaji, A., Longstaff, T.A.: A Sense of Self for Unix Processes. In: SP '96: Proceedings of the 1996 IEEE Symposium on Security and Privacy, p. 120. IEEE Computer Society Press, Los Alamitos (1996)
13. Hofmeyr, S.A., Forrest, S., Somayaji, A.: Intrusion Detection Using Sequences of System Calls. Journal of Computer Security 6(3), 151–180 (1998)
14. Shacham, H., Page, M., Pfaff, B., Goh, E.-J.: On the Effectiveness of Address-Space Randomization. In: CCS '04: Proceedings of the 11th ACM Conference on Computer and Communications Security, pp. 298–307. ACM Press, New York (2004)
15. iSec.pl Development Team. kNoX - Implementation of non-executable Page Protection Mechanism (February 2005)
   http://www.isec.pl/projects/knox/knox.html
16. Kiriansky, V., Bruening, D., Amarasinghe, S.P.: Secure execution via program shepherding. In: Proceedings of the 11th USENIX Security Symposium, pp. 191–206, Berkeley, CA, USA, USENIX Association (2002)
17. Kruegel, C., Kirda, E., Mutz, D., Robertson, W., Vigna, G.: Automating Mimicry Attacks Using Static Binary Analysis. In: Proceedings of the USENIX Security Symposium, Baltimore, MD (August 2005)

18. Elias Aleph One Levy. Smashing the Stack for Fun and Profit. Phrack Magazine, vol. 0x07(#49), Phile 14–16 (December 1998)
19. Nielson, F., Nielson, H., Hankin, C.: Principles of Program Analysis (1999)
20. Bhatkar, S., DuVarney, D.C., Sekar, R.: Address Obfuscation: An Efficient Approach to Combat a Broad Range of Memory Error Exploits. In: 12th USENIX Security Symposium (2003)
21. Bhatkar, S., Sekar, R., DuVarney, D.C.: Efficient Techniques for Comprehensive Protection from Memory Error Exploits. In: 14th USENIX Security Symposium (2005)
22. Schwarz, B., Debray, S., Andrews, G.: Disassembly of Executable Code Revisited. In: Proceedings of the Ninth Working Conference on Reverse Engineering (2002)
23. Sekar, R., Bendre, M., Dhurjati, D., Bollineni, P.: A Fast Automaton-Based Method for Detecting Anomalous Program Behaviors. In: IEEE Symposium on Security and Privacy, Oakland, California (2001)
24. De Sutter, B., De Bus, B., De Bosschere, K., Keyngnaert, P., Demoen, B.: the static analysis of indirect control transfers in binaries. In: Proceedings of the International Conference on Parallel and Distributed Processing Techniques and Applications, Las Vegas, Nevada, USA, pp. 1013–1019 (June 2000)
25. Tan, K.M.C., Killourhy, K.S., Maxion, R.A.: Undermining an anomaly-based intrusion detection system using common exploits. In: Proceedings of the 5th International Symposium on Recent Advances in Intrusion Detection (2002)
26. Tan, K.M.C., McHugh, J., Killourhy, K.S.: Hiding intrusions: From the abnormal to the normal and beyond. In: Information Hiding, pp. 1–17 (2002)
27. The Linux Kernel 2.6 Development Team. The Linux Kernel 2.6 (February 2005), http://lwn.net/Articles/121845/
28. The OpenWall Development Team. The OpenWall Project (February 2005), http://www.openwall.com
29. The PaX Team. PaX: Address Space Layout Randomization (ASLR) http://pax.grsecurity.net
30. Wagner, D., Dean, D.: Intrusion Detection via Static Analysis. In: IEEE Symposium on Security and Privacy, Oakland, California (2001)
31. Wagner, D., Soto, P.: Mimicry Attacks on Host Based Intrusion Detection Systems. In: Proc. Ninth ACM Conference on Computer and Communications Security (2002)
32. Xu, H., Du, W., Chapin, S.J.: Context Sensitive Anomaly Monitoring of Process Control Flow to Detect Mimicry Attacks and Impossible Paths. In: Jonsson, E., Valdes, A., Almgren, M. (eds.) RAID 2004. LNCS, vol. 3224, pp. 21–38. Springer, Heidelberg (2004)

A Study of Malcode-Bearing Documents

Wei-Jen Li, Salvatore Stolfo, Angelos Stavrou, Elli Androulaki,
and Angelos D. Keromytis

Computer Science Department, Columbia University
{weijen,sal,angel,elli,angelos}@cs.columbia.edu

Abstract. By exploiting the object-oriented dynamic composability of modern document applications and formats, malcode hidden in otherwise inconspicuous documents can reach third-party applications that may harbor exploitable vulnerabilities otherwise unreachable by network-level service attacks. Such attacks can be very selective and difficult to detect compared to the typical network worm threat, owing to the complexity of these applications and data formats, as well as the multitude of document-exchange vectors. As a case study, this paper focuses on Microsoft Word documents as malcode carriers. We investigate the possibility of detecting embedded malcode in Word documents using two techniques: static content analysis using statistical models of typical document content, and run-time dynamic tests on diverse platforms. The experiments demonstrate these approaches can not only detect known malware, but also most zero-day attacks. We identify several problems with both approaches, representing both challenges in addressing the problem and opportunities for future research.

Keywords: Intrusion Detection, N-gram, Sandbox Diversity.

1 Introduction

In this paper, we focus on *stealthy and targeted* attacks where malcode is delivered to a host in an otherwise normal-appearing document. Modern documents and the corresponding applications make use of embedded code fragments. This embedded code is capable of indirectly invoking other applications or libraries on the host as part of document rendering or editing. For example, a pie chart displaying the contents of a spreadsheet embedded in a Word document will cause Excel components to be invoked when the Word document is opened. As a result, documents offer a convenient means for attackers to penetrate systems and reach third-party host-based applications that may harbor vulnerabilities which are not reachable, and thus not directly exploitable, remotely over the network. Disturbingly, attackers are simply exploiting deliberate features that are critical to the way modern document-handling applications operate, instead of some temporary vulnerabilities or bugs.

Several cases have been reported where malcode has been embedded in documents (e.g., PDF, Word, Excel, and PowerPoint [1,2,3]) transforming them into a vehicle for host intrusions. These trojan-infected documents can be served up

B. M. Hämmerli and R. Sommer (Eds.): DIMVA 2007, LNCS 4579, pp. 231–250, 2007.

by any arbitrary web site or search engine in a passive "drive by" fashion, transmitted over email or instant messaging (IM), or even introduced to a system by other media such as CD-ROMs and USB drives, bypassing all the network firewalls and intrusion-detection systems. Furthermore, the attacker can use such documents as a stepping stone to reach other systems, unreachable via the regular network. Hence, any machine inside an organization with the ability to open a document can become the spreading point for the malcode to reach any host within that organization. Indeed, a recent attack of this nature was reported in [4] using Wikipedia. There is nothing new about the presence of viruses in streams, embedded as attached documents, nor is the use of malicious macros a new threat [5,6], e.g., in Word documents. However, simply disabling macros does not solve the problem; other forms of code may be embedded in Word documents, for which no easy solution is available other than not using Word altogether.

The underlying problem is that modern document formats are essentially object-containers (e.g., Object Linking and Embedding (OLE) format for Word) of any executable object. Hence, one should expect to see any kind of code embedded in a document. Since malcode is code, one cannot be entirely certain that a piece of code detected in a document is legitimate or not, unless it is discovered and embedded in an object that typically does not contain code. Simply stated, **modern document formats provide a convenient object-container format and constitute thus a convenient and easy to use "code-injection platform."**

To better illustrate the complexity of the task of identifying malcode in documents through a concrete study, we limit our investigation to Microsoft Word document files; Word documents serve as a "container" for complex object embeddings that need to be parsed and executed to render the document for display. In addition to the well known macro viruses, two further possible scenarios are introduced bellow:

Execution strategies of embedded malcode: From the attackers perspective, the optimal attack strategy is to architect the injected code as an embedded object that would be executed automatically upon rendering the document. In addition to automated techniques such as the *WMF, PNG and JPEG vulnerabilities*, an attacker can also use social engineering whereby an embedded object in a document, appearing as an icon, is opened manually by the user, launching an attack including attacks against third-party vulnerable applications. The left-side screen shot of Fig. 1 is an example of a Word document with embedded malcode, in this case a copy of the Slammer worm, with a message enticing a user to click on the icon and launch the malcode.

Dormant malcode in multi-partite attacks: Another stealth tactic is to embed malcode in documents that does not execute automatically nor by user intervention when the document is opened, but rather lies dormant in the file store of the target environment awaiting a future attack that would extract the hidden malcode. This multi-partite attack strategy could be used to successfully embed an arbitrarily large and sophisticated collection of malcode components across multiple documents. The right screen shot in Fig. 1 demonstrates another simple example of embedding a known malicious code sample, in this case also Slammer, into an otherwise normal Word document. The document opens entirely normally, with Slammer sitting idly in memory. Both infected files can open normally in a Windows environment. However, the right one appears with no discernible differences from a normal document while a different document could incorporate this Slammer-laden document when it is opened, and invoke the malcode contained therein. Although real-world attacks identical to our example have not appeared, similar scenarios that combine multiple attacks have been studied. Bontchev [5] discussed a new macro attack that can be created by combining two known malicious macros. (e.g., a macro virus resides on a machine, another macro virus reaches it, and "mutates" into a third virus.) Filiol *et al.* [7] analyzed the complexity of another type of viruses named k-ary viruses, which combine actions of multiple attacks.

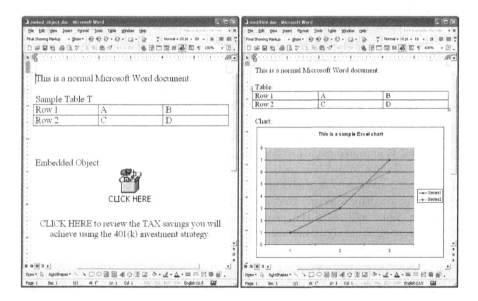

Fig. 1. Left: A screen shot of an embedded executable object to entice the user to click and launch malcode. Right: Example of malicious code (Slammer) embedded in a normal document.

Our aim is to study the effectiveness of two techniques that have been applied in the context of "traditional" network worms: statistical analysis of content to identify portions of input that deviate from expected normal content as estimated from a training corpora, and detection of malicious behavior by dynamic execution on multiple, diverse platforms. The challenge is to find a method to inspect the binary content of any document file before it is opened to determine whether it is suspicious and may indeed be infected with malicious code without *a priori* knowledge of the specific code in question or where it may be embedded in the document.

Initially, we explore the detection capabilities of statical analysis techniques. More specifically, we investigate the application of statistical modeling techniques to characterize the typical content of documents. Our goal is to determine whether we can detect embedded malcode using statistical methods on the binary file content. Furthermore, we introduce novel dynamic run-time tests that attempt to expose the attackers' actions through application diversity: we open the files using a set of different implementations of document processing application in a sandboxed environment. To quantify the detection capabilities of statistical analysis, we perform a series of experiments where statistical analysis is applied to labeled training documents to characterize both normal and malicious document content. Our experiments show that statistical analysis techniques outperform generic COTS Anti-Virus (AV) scanners. To further improve our detection capability, we designed novel tests that harness the application diversity to expose malicious byte-code. In these tests, documents are opened in a diverse set of sandboxed and emulated environments exposing malicious code execution. We show that in most cases, malicious code depend on operating system or program characteristics for successful completion of its execution. In the process of our experimentation, we discovered that attackers use existing benign documents as vehicles for their attack. Thus, we can further improve our classification if we use benign documents from the Web to train our detectors since even small deviations from normality can expose an attack.

Our results indicate that both static statistical and dynamic detection techniques can be employed to detect malicious documents. However, there are some weaknesses that make each method incomplete if used in isolation. For statistical analysis, we would like to be able to determine the "intent" and "effect" of the malicious code. On the other hand, dynamic tests may fail to detect the presence of stealthy malcode that is designed to hide its actions. Hence, neither technique alone will solve the problem in its entirety. We posit that a hybrid approach integrating dynamic and static analysis techniques will likely provide a suitable solution.

Paper Organization: The next section discusses related work and research reported in the literature. Section 3 describes the static statistical approach including an overview of the byte-value n-gram algorithm, the SPARSEGui program and the experimental results. We introduce the dynamic run-time tests and the use of application diversity in Section 4. Section 5 concludes the paper with suggestions that perhaps collaborative detection methods may provide a fruitful path forward.

2   Background and Related Work

2.1   Binary Content File Analysis

Probabilistic modeling in the area of content analysis mainly involves n-gram approaches [8,9,10]; the file binary contents are measured and the distribution of the frequency of 1-gram, as well as each fixed size n-gram, is computed. An early research effort in this area is the Malicious Email Filter [11], using a naive Bayes classifier algorithm applied to the binary content of email attachments known to be viral. The classifier was trained on both "normal" executables and known viruses to determine whether emails likely included malicious attachments that should be filtered.

Others have applied similar techniques including, for example, Abou-Assaleh et al. [12,13] to detect worms and viruses. Furthermore, Karim et al. suggest that malicious programs are frequently related to previous ones [14]. They define a variation on n-grams called "n-perms" An n-perm represents every possible permutation of an n-gram sequence, and n-perms can be used to match possibly permuted malicious code. McDaniel and Heydari [15] introduce algorithms for generating "fingerprints" of file types using byte-value distributions of file content. However, instead of computing a set of centroid models, they compute a single representative fingerprint for the entire class. This strategy may be unwise. Mixing the statistics of different subtypes and averaging of the statistics of an aggregation of examples may tend to loose information. A report from AFRL proposes the Detector and Extractor of Fileprints (DEF) process for data protection and automatic file identification [16]. By applying the DEF process, they generate visual hashes, called fileprints, to measure the integrity of a data sequence, compare the similarity between data sequences, and to identify the data type of an unknown file. Goel [17] introduces a signature-matching technique based on Kolmogorov Complexity metrics, for file type identification.

2.2   Steganalysis

There exists a substantial literature on the subject of steganography, the means of hiding secret messages embedded in otherwise normal appearing objects or communication channels. We do not provide an analysis of this area since it is not exactly germane to the topic of identifying embedded malcode in documents. However, many of the steganalysis techniques that have been under investigation to detect steganographic communication over covert channels may bear resemblance to the techniques we applied during the course of this research study. For example, Provos' work on defeating steganalysis [18] highlights the difficulty of identifying "foreign" material embedded cleverly within media objects that defeats statistical analysis while maintaining what otherwise appears to be a completely normal-appearing objects, e.g., a sensible image.

The general class of steganographic embedding of secret messages may be viewed as a "mimicry" attack, whereby the messages are embedded in such a fashion as to mimic the statistical characteristics of the objects in which the messages are embedded. Our task in this project was a more limited view of the problem, to identify embedded "zero day malcode" inside documents. The conjecture that drives our analysis is that code segments may be limited to a specific set of statistical characterizations so that one may be able to differentiate code from other material in which it is embedded; i.e., code embedded in an image may appear to have a significantly different statistical distribution to that of the class of images used to transport it. Unfortunately, this tends not to be true especially with a crafty adversary capable of generating obfuscation techniques that shape the appearance of the code's binary content to have a user-chosen statistical distribution. One presumes that the attacker knows the particular statistical modeling and testing technique applied while shaping their embedded code to pass the test. Such techniques are being honed by adversaries fashioning polymorphic attack engines that change a code segment and re-shape it to fit an arbitrary statistical distribution, to avoid inspection and detection.

2.3   Polymorphic Code Generation Tools

Polymorphic viruses are nothing new; "1260" and the "Dark Avenger Mutation Engine" were considered the first two polymorphic virus engines, written in the early 90s. Early work focused on making detection by COTS signature scanners less likely. Polymorphic worms with vulnerability-exploiting shellcode, e.g., ADMutate [19] and CLET [20], are primarily designed to fool signature-based IDSes. CLET features a form of padding, called cramming, to defeat simple anomaly detectors. However, cram bytes are derived from a static source, i.e., instructions in a file included with the CLET distribution; while this may be customized to approach a general mimicry attack, it must be done by hand. An engine crafted by Lee's team at Georgia Tech [21] had this purpose in mind; an attack vector was morphed by padding bytes guided by a statistical distribution learned by sniffing the environment in which the code would be injected, hence allowing the code to have a "normal" appearing statistical characterization. This engine targeted the 1-gram distributions computed by the PAYL anomaly detector; the obfuscation and evasion technique was subsequently countered by the Anagram sensor that implements higher-order n-gram analysis. The core algorithm in the Anagram sensor is the basis of the zero-day malcode detection algorithm employed in SPARSEGui as described briefly later, and which we consider to be related to the Shaner algorithm [22] devised to classify files into their respective types. During the course of our tests using thousands of Word documents provided, we found that performance was hard to improve without carefully redistributing training data. In addition, Song et al. [23] also suggest it is futile to compute a statistical model of malicious code, and hence identifying malcode embedded in a document may not be the wisest strategy. Hence, we also applied a dynamic test approach to compare against the static analysis approaches, implemented as the VM-based test facility described in Section 4.

2.4   Dynamic Sandbox Tests

Sandboxing is a common technique for creating virtual environments where it is safe to execute possibly unsafe code. For example, Norman Sandbox [24] simulates an entire machine as if it were connected to a network. By monitoring the Windows DLLs activated by programs, it stops and quarantines programs that exhibit abnormal behavior. Since this is a proprietary commercial system, it is unknown exactly how abnormal behavior is determined. Willems et al. present an automated system call analysis in a simulated environment, the CWSandbox [25]. They use API hooking: system calls to the Win32 API are re-routed to monitoring software that gathers all the information available to the operating system. Instead of using a virtual environment, TTAnalyze [26] runs a CPU emulator, QEMU, which runs on many host operating systems. Recently, Microsoft Research developed BrowserShield [27], a system that performs dynamic instrumentation of embedded scripts. Similar in spirit to our approach, BrowserShield is designed to detect embedded malcode implemented as HTML scripts which would otherwise be undetectable using static analysis alone.

In this paper, we employ virtual machines running Word-processing applications on diverse platforms; in one case, the native implementation on Windows, in another, a Windows emulation environment running under Linux hosted by a virtual machine. This architecture is easy to implement, and provides a safe means of learning expected behavior of Word document processing under different implementations, using the multiple platform diversity as an additional source of information to identify malcode.

3   Statistical Analysis

As a first effort to identify malcode-infected documents, we used *static inspection of the statistical byte sequences of binary content*. Our intuition is that the binary content of malicious Word documents contains substantial portions of contiguous byte sequences that are significantly different (abnormal) from typical/benign Word documents. Our approach is reminiscent of corpus-based machine learning in natural language processing of human-generated content. The goal is to explore the detection capabilities and limitations of statistical characterization given the available training data. We will start by introducing the tools we used to perform the static analysis and experiments.

3.1   The POI Parser and SPARSEGui

A document may contain many types of embedded objects. To achieve any reasonable level of detection performance, we found it necessary to "parse" the binary file format into its constituent embedded object structure and extract the individual data objects, in order to model instances of the same types together, without mixing data from multiple types of objects.

We used the open-source Apache POI [28] application, a Java implementation of the OLE 2 Compound Document, to decompose Word files into their exact, correct constituent structures. The parsed object structures in the binary content of the files will be referred "sections." We further modified the POI software so that the location of each object within a Word file is revealed. These sections include header information, summary information, word document, CompObj, 1Table, data, pictures, PowerPoint document, macros, *etc.* Fig, 2 displays the histograms of byte content of four common sections whose differences are easy to observe.

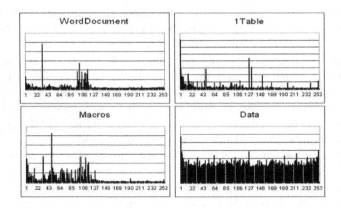

Fig. 2. Byte occurrence frequency of WordDocument, 1Table, Macros, and Data. The byte values were parsed from 120 benign Word documents containing macros. In these plots, the byte value 0 and FF were removed because they occurred relatively much more frequent than the others and will mess up the display.

SPARSEGui includes a number of the modeling techniques described and calls upon the POI parser to provide the means of displaying detailed information about the binary content of Word files as well as presenting experimental results to the user. The experimental results in the remainder of this paper were produced using this toolkit. This program was designed not only to implement the methods described herein but also to provide a user-friendly interface which can extend to analyst information for deeper inspection of a suspect Word file. A screen shot is shown in Fig. 3 in Section 3.4.

3.2   Statistical Content-Based Detection

To evaluate whether statistical binary content detectors can effectively detect malcode embedded in documents, we used the Anagram [8] algorithm. Although Anagram was originally designed to identify anomalous network packet payloads, it is essentially an *efficient approximation* of Shaner's algorithm [22] enabling us to detect malicious binary content. Anagram extracts and models high-order n-grams (an n-gram is a sequence of contiguous n byte values) exposing significant anomalous bytes sequences. All necessary n-gram information is stored to highly compact and efficient Bloom filters [29] reducing significantly the space complexity of the detection algorithm. Contrary to the original 1-class modeling technique applied to the PAYL algorithm [30], we introduce the same mutual-information strategy as suggested by Shaner. Hence, we utilize both "good" and "bad" models that are generated using labeled benign and malicious datasets, respectively. In this way, we train one benign and one malicious model and classify the files by comparing the score computed against both models.

As a next step, we had to determine the optimal n-gram size that best captures the corpus of our documents. To that end, we evaluated the detection performance and storage requirements of all Anagram models with gram size from 4 to 8 bytes. Although larger sized grams can capture more fine-grained information, they can significantly increase the space requirements of Anagram both in terms of runtime memory and in terms of storage. Therefore, for higher ordered grams, a larger Bloom filter is required to avoid having collision that can lead to false positives. The detailed discussion of the size of grams and the use of Bloom filters is beyond the scope of this paper since it depends on the memory usage, the type of data analyzed, and the implementation of Bloom filters [31]. Based on the results of our experiments, we selected the 5-gram model, which consumed reasonable memory and accurately detects attacks.

However, the performance of our statistical methodology was also dependent upon the amount and quality of our training set: without a sufficient training corpus, the detector may produce too many false positives. On the other hand, using a very broad set of documents can produce an augmented and under-trained normality model increasing our false negative rate. To minimize these issues, we generated a model of what we considered as "normal" behavior using Anagram on benign documents. Our aim is to then use Anagram in testing mode on unknown documents to ferret out documents with abnormal content, indicative of zero-day malcode embedded within the document in question. We posit that by generating organization or group specific benign and malicious behavior models, we can further facilitate the detection. The assumption is that documents being created, opened and exchanged within a specific group should be similar, and malicious documents' byte content should be significantly different from them. For the benign data corpus, we collected 4825 samples from two anonymous organizations using *wget* over their public facing web sites (1775 and 3050 documents for each group). In addition, we downloaded 2918 real-world malicious documents from VX Heavens [1] [32].

We used two different approaches to build the normality models. The first method is more coarse-grained and involves scanning and storing all the n-grams from the collected documents creating two separate training sets: one for the benign and one for the malicious model. In the testing/detection phase we compare the n-grams obtained from the documents under test with both the benign and malicious models generating a "similarity score." This score is the ratio of the number of testing n-grams that exist in the training models to the total number of testing n-grams. Testing documents are classified according to the similarity scores they receive from the two models. Documents that receive the same score for both models are deemed malicious. The other approach involves generating multiple normality models corresponding to different document sections instead of using just a single model. Thus, the training documents are parsed and the models are created using the parsed sections, one model for each section. Different sections are text, tables, macros, and other more rare data objects. For each of the section, a weight is assigned. During testing phase, we compare the grams of each of the section from the unclassified document to the ones generated during training. The final similarity scores for each testing document are computed

---

[1] These experimental datasets can be reached from our web site for interested readers: http://www1.cs.columbia.edu/ids/SPARSE/Spring07TestFiles/

by summing up all of the scores for the individual sections. Thus, we categorize the document under question based on how similar it is to the benign and the malicious section models. The advantage of this method is that different types of embedded objects are not mixed together, so the classification will be more accurate.

For this second method, it is essential to discover the appropriate weights for each section. Although we can easily parse the documents into different sections, we cannot identify which of the sections are malicious even when we know that the whole document is malicious since a document can have section interdependencies. As a result, an appropriate weight for each section cannot be "learnt" by repetitive training/testing. To address this problem, we use the normalized byte size of each testing section as weight.

3.3   Performance Evaluation

We evaluated our statistical content-based techniques using the data we collected on Web. Furthermore, we compared our approach to a COTS AV scanner to both verify and measure our detection performance. In our experiments, we used a standard 5-fold cross-validation scenario, in which data were equally split into five groups, and when each group was tested, the other four were used as training data. All of the pre-mentioned 4825 benign and 2918 malicious documents were tested. In all of our experiments we used an Intel(R) Xeon(TM) CPU 2.40GHz, with 3.6GB memory, running Fedora 3. Depending on the file size, the overhead varied when training/testing a document. The average time to parse or test a file was 0.226 seconds, and the standard deviation was 0.563 seconds. Table 1 presents the experimental results of both methods. The overall performance of Method 2, taking advantage of the parser, was highly accurate and superior to the performance of Method 1. However, the false positive rate of Method 2 was slightly higher than that of Method 1 because Method 2 provided a more detailed comparison. Unfortunately, Method 2 created a more sensitive classifier leading to a slight increase in false positives.

Table 1. Detection results of 5-fold cross-validation. Method 1: Train one single model without parsing. Method 2: Train multiple models for the parsed sections.

	Method 1	Method 2
TP/FN	92.32% / 7.68%	98.69% / 1.31%
FP/TN	0.02% / 99.98%	0.15% / 99.85%
Total Accuracy	95.79%	99.22%

The most recently patched AV scanners have the signatures of all of the malware collected from VX Heavens rendering our dataset inappropriate for further comparing our approach to general COTS AV scanners. Hence, we prepared a second malicious dataset consisting of 35 (10 benign and 25 malicious) carefully crafted files where ground truth was unknown to us before the test. A third-party evaluator created this set of test files for a complete "blind test" of our analysis results. For this test, we trained one model over the 2918 malicious documents and another model using one group of the benign documents we collected (both groups of data had the same final result). After verifying the testing results of these 35 files when ground truth was disclosed, 28 were correctly classified, shown in the first column of Table 2. Note that the numbers in the table are the actual numbers instead of percentages. We achieved zero false positive, but a significant number of false negatives appeared.

Table 2. Detection results of the 35 files. Stat.1: Statistical test, Stat.2: Statistical test with improved strategy, AV: COTS AV scanner

	Stat. 1	Stat. 2	AV
TP/FN	18/7	23/2	17/8
FP/TN	0/10	0/10	0/10
Total Correct	28	33	27

Our statistical analysis technique performed slightly better than a COTS AV scanner, whose result is shown in the third column of Table 2. Our success can be attributed to the fact that we were able to model enough information from the malicious document training set to at least "emulate" the AV scanners with up-to-date signatures. Additionally, the strategy of computing normal models over an organization's specific set of normal documents produced a model that could detect anomalous events, i.e., the zero-day attacks. However, in this 35-file test, some small, well crafted malcode cleverly embedded in malicious documents were very hard to detect mainly because of their relatively small size in comparison to the whole documents. Statistics based detection mechanism performs poorly in this case. Therefore, we introduce a further strategy.

3.4 File Content Differences Identify Embedded Malcode

It is possible that an adversary may carefully craft malcode and embed it within a document chosen from a public source. In their effort to blend, attackers would rather use existing public documents since crafting their own documents could contain private or proprietary information that might identify them. Furthermore, an attacker may devise an attack without paying particular attention to the viewable readable document text portion. Malicious documents may contain what might be regarded as "gibberish" material. To generate a benign-looking document, an attacker can mine random benign documents from the Web and embed malcode in them. In that case, comparing the test document to the original or even similar benign document found on the Web can narrow down the detection region and increase the detection accuracy.

Fig. 3 presents a screen shot of SPARSEGui comparing an original benign host document and the infected version of the same document. (The host document was a document accessible on the Internet.) The left two charts represent the byte values, ranging from -128 to 127, of these two documents, the original and infected one respectively. In addition to the byte values, the n-gram entropy values, defined as the number of distinct byte values over an n-gram, are shown in the right two charts. To clearly exhibit the anomalous portion, n is assigned to 50 (i.e., 50-gram) in this figure. In this case, the infected document has a clearly discriminable high entropy portion. Having observed several similar cases, we also discovered that such portions bearing malcode usually contain foreign grams, i.e., never-seen-before grams, which is displayed by using bold characters in the bottom panel of Fig. 3. To evaluate if foreign grams or entropy of foreign grams can provide information to locate suspicious code remains an item for future work.

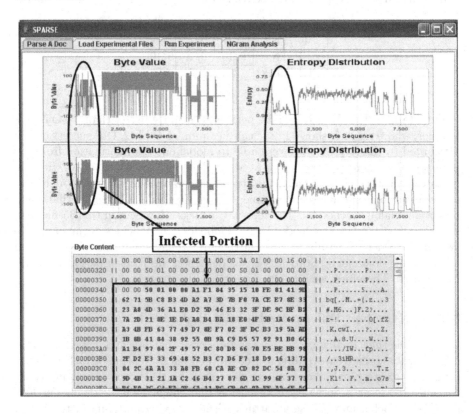

Fig. 3. SPARSEGui screen-shot: parse a benign document and compare its infected version

In the prior experiments, the detector produced 7 false negatives. It appears that some of them were crafted based on random benign documents found on the Web. Such "mimic attacks" could evade our statistical content-based detector. Therefore, we developed the following detection strategy: we first parse the inspected document (D1) by using SPARSEGui and take a portion of the text as tokens in a Google search. In case where a document (D2) is found on the Web to have at least 90% of its content in common with D1 (but less than

100%), we extract the n-grams from D1 that *do not appear* in D2. Then, they are computed against the trained Bloom filters and classified to which class it is close, i.e., benign or malicious. Without increasing false positives, this strategy detected 5 malicious documents that were misclassified in the previous 35-file test. Shown in the second column of Table 2, the result was superior to the tested COTS AV scanner.

The 35 test files were purposefully chosen and crafted to avoid detection by statistical means. Even so, we were able to detect almost all of the malicious documents without false positives. However, we did misclassify two malicious documents. Given our performance under such an adverse testing set, we believe that our results demonstrate that our approach has merit and warrants further investigation to improve upon detection performance.

Additionally, our experiments reveal another principle: to validate whether some portion of a document has embedded malcode, mutual collaboration across sites could help identify hidden malcode. Sites that cooperate to detect malcode-laden documents and that share suspect documents could validate that indeed malcode hidden in documents has been discovered. The privacy-preserving sharing of suspect documents among sites is posited as a useful next step in reducing the threat posed by malicious documents appearing openly on the Internet.

A general observation for all the static statistical approaches is that they exhibit inherent limitiations in detecting malicious documents. First, any machine learning or statistical method for that matter, is entirely dependent upon the amount and quality of the training corpus. In general, it is not known a priori if the sample of data available to train and test models is truly representative of a particular empirical distribution from which test cases will be drawn. Without sufficient and representative training data, it is both practically and theoretically infeasible to compute a meaningfull statistical model. In addition, malicious content can be crafted with extremely small portions of malcode spreading throughout a section of a document. Compared to the entire file, which is usually substantially larger, the embedded malcode is very hard to detect. The shorter the sequence of code, the higher the likelihood that a static-analysis detector will miss it. On the other hand, far too many false alarms may be generated if the sensitivity of the detector is raised too high. Lastly, statistical tests may indeed find portions of a document that contain code, but the binary content of the detected foreign code may not identify the "intent" of embedded code. Hence, we investigated an alternative dynamic run-time technique that can improve upon the statistical content-based analysis.

4   Dynamic Run-Time Tests Using Environment Diversity

In this section, we introduce a series of dynamic tests that exploit the diversity of emulation environments to expose malicious documents. Our goal is to determine whether opening a malicious document under an emulated environment can force the malicious code to exhibit easily discernible behavior which deviates from normal and hence identify malicious documents. We show that this behavioral deviation clearly indicates the existence of malicious code inside the file under inspection.

In this case, we did not implement complex instrumentation nor did we apply API hooking to monitor the execution of Word; the implementation of the experimental test bed we built is straightforward: we open documents using the same Microsoft Word executable on different environments both emulated and non-emulated. To avoid damaging our system and to be consistent in applying the same test environment to each file, we ran experiments in a virtual machine (i.e., sandbox) with an identical setup for each test. After each file is tested, we reload the VM image and test the next document. For our prototype, we used VMware WorkStation software installed on the same host machine. For the VM hosted operating system, we installed Linux (Fedora). In that hosted Linux we installed CrossOver Office Standard 5.0.1, a Windows binary translator and emulator. In addition, we had another VM hosting Windows XP and the same version of Microsoft Office (Word 2003) that was used for CrossOver. Based on the observables, we introduce a series of three tests which are referred to as Test 1 (OS crash), Test 2 (Unexpected changes), and Test 3 (Application failure).

4.1   Test 1 – OS Crashes

Applications need to interact with the operating system via libraries and system calls in order to perform even the simplest tasks such as reading or writing a file. In Windows, this happens through the loading of Dynamic Linked Libraries (DLLs), which are loaded both at the beginning of the application's execution and on demand. In large programs, such as Microsoft Word or other applications in the MS Office suite, the number of required DLLs is very large (two to three dozen, depending on the application and the features used by the file loaded). Some of these DLLs are necessary for the program to startup. Most of the rest of the DLLs that the application loads at runtime are required to execute and render the embedded objects and macros after the document is opened. We use the emulated Windows environment on Linux as a concept of changing the loading order of DLLs from the original Windows. Then, the code exceptions depending on this exact order can be revealed. We conjecture that such exceptions, which lead to program and system crashes, are indicative of malcode: normal, non-attacking objects and macros should not depend on the loading order of the DLLs but only on whether the needed DLLs are actually loaded. Based on this hypothesis, a document is opened under the emulated environment to determine if it crashes the application or the underlying operating system. If it does, we declare the document as malicious.

4.2   Test 2 – Unexpected Changes to the Underlying Environment

Test 1 limits our ability to identify malicious documents because most malicious documents may succeed in executing the embedded malcode yet may not crash the test environment.

In the second test, we expand the set of what we deem as abnormal behavior to include all easily observable malicious changes to the hosted operating system.

We run the second test after applying the first test and only to documents that fail to be labeled malicious in the first test. Thus, if the document can be opened without any fault or catastrophic error, we examine all the platform files generated or modified by the Word process, i.e., we compare the system right before and after opening a testing document. Our goal is to determine if there are unexpected differences recorded when the malcode embedded in some malicious documents are executed but do not terminate the Word process with a failure or crash.

However, executing the application on multiple environments by opening benign documents may also produce differences in runtime behavior. Hence, there is a small probability that a benign Word document might exhibit different execution behavior (but not failure) under an emulated platform. To minimize such false positive errors, we first train 1000 benign and 1000 malicious documents and gather all of the changes observed to the underlying systems after opening the files. We then generate a list of expected (benign) and unexpected (malicious) changes based on the nature of the document examined. These changes include temporary file creation, data file change such as index.dat, and registry modification. All changes, or the lack of changes, can be used to identify malcode execution. Currently, 27 registry keys are checked in our model, some of them are shown in Table 3, and a Java program is used to automatically verify the changes.

Table 3. The list of registry keys that may be modified after opening a Word document

[HARDWARE//DESCRIPTION//System//CentralProcessor//0]
[Software//Classes//Interface//A4C46780-499F-101B-BB78-00AA00383CBB //TypeLib]
[Software//Classes//TypeLib//00020430-0000-0000-C000-000000000046//2.0//0 //win32]
[Software//Microsoft//Windows NT//CurrentVersion//Fonts]
[System//CurrentControlSet//Control//Print//Environments//Windows NT x86 //Drivers//PS Driver]
[Software//Microsoft//Office//11.0//Word]
[Software//Microsoft//Office//11.0//Common//LanguageResources]
[Software//Microsoft//Office//Common//Assistant]
[Software//Wine//Fonts]
[Software//Microsoft//Office//11.0//Word//Text Converters//Import//MSWord8]
[Software//Microsoft//VBA//6.0//Common]

When we applied Test 2 to classify the same documents in Test 1, we observed a substantial increase in the true positive rate. This was something we expected since we increased the set of what we deemed as abnormal behavior. However, some malcode may be considerably more "quiet" and "stealthy" and not produce any observable malicious changes to the underlying system. Hence, we apply a third and final test to determine if any easily discernible application behavior indicates the execution of malcode.

4.3   Test 3 – Non-fatal Application Errors

When we first tested to the set of the malicious documents available, we discovered some types of pop-up messages generated by Microsoft Word. These messages do not cause the OS or emulation environment to fail, but they are clear indicators of malcode execution causing the application to gracefully terminate only some part of the application execution. Users are presented with pop-up windows requesting their input or intervention before they can proceed viewing the document. We use these pop-up messages as the last useful information we can extract from the execution of Word and utilize it for dynamic detection of malicious documents. If both Test 1 and Test 2 fail to label a document as malicious, we apply this final test to the document: we open the document and observe the application output. If one of the known pop-up messages appears on the screen, we mark the document as malicious. However, some benign documents, without embedded malcode, can spawn the same pop-up messages because of improper macro design, rare embedded objects using different versions of applications, or any incorrect use of embedded objects in a Word document.

4.4   Experiments and Analysis

We performed the first experiment by randomly choosing 400 benign and 400 malicious documents which were not in the set of the 1000 benign and 1000 malicious training documents mentioned in Section 4.2. We used the "successive" strategy as the following: Test 1 is first performed, Test 2 is performed only if the testing document is labelled benign in Test 1, and Test 3 is performed only if the testing document is labelled benign in Test 2. The terms "Test 1," "Test 1+2," and "Test 1+2+3" represent the three steps of this successive strategy, respectively. In addition to the successive strategy, we also evaluated indivisual Test 2 and Test 3 as shown in the last two columns of Table 4. Only a few malicious documents were detected by Test 1, but Test 1+2 dramatically increased the true positive rate. The best result we obtained - 97.12% accuracy - was when we employed Test 1+2+3, in which 777 documents out of 800 were correctly classified. However, when performing Test 1+2+3 after Test 1+2, the number of false positives increased by one. This false positive was actually a benign document that requires a border-control feature which is not a default feature in Word. Though Test 1+2+3 doesn't improve the performance much after Test 1+2, it provides further coarse-grained analysis given that it determines if a document contains macros that run automatically when the document is opened.

Table 4. Detection results of 400 benign and 400 malicious documents

	Test1	Test1+2	Test1+2+3	Only Test2	Only Test3
TP/FN	4/397	380/20	381/19	376/24	239/161
%	1%/99%	95%/5%	95.25%/4.75%	94%/6%	59.75%/40.25%
TN/FP	400/0	397/3	396/4	397/3	399/1
%	100%/0%	99.25%/0.75%	99%/1%	99.25%/0.75%	99.75%/0.25%
Total Accuracy	50.5%	97.12%	97.12%	96.62%	79.75%

The overhead to test a document is approximately 170 seconds, including cleaning up the image of previous test (1 sec.), duplicating the system image for next comparison (30 sec.), delaying for the observation of Test 1 and 3 (40 seconds), and comparing the image for Test 2 (130 sec. because the size of the compared image is 416MB). Although tests can be performed in parallel, the current overhead is only acceptable to offline analysis.

The next experiment is the blind test using the 35 files. In this test, shown in Table 5, we achieved 100% accuracy; all of the 35 files were correctly classified. However, we do not believe that these tests constitute a complete set of dynamic execution tests that are able to cover all possible malicious documents. First, we have some false negatives when testing the dataset we collected. Second, a stealthy successful attack may be crafted such that it produces no discernible and easily viewable change to the execution environment, i.e., a logic bomb or a multi-partite attack. In cases where malcode may attempt to install a rootkit without any discernible external failures or message pop-ups, an additional test would be necessary to compare the "dormant" virtual machine to its original image and to compare each for possible rootkit installs. Alternatively, running a fully instrumented "shadow" version of the binary of the Word application might identify anomalous program execution at the very point the malcode attempts to exploit a vulnerability or otherwise exhibits anomalous program behavior.

Table 5. Detection results of the 35 files. AV: COTS AV scanner.

	AV	Test1	Test1+2	Test1+2+3	Only Test2	Only Test3
TP/FN	8/17	8/17	25/0	25/0	17/8	12/22
TN/FP	0/10	0/10	0/10	0/10	0/10	0/10
Total Correct	27	18	35	35	27	22

Overall, neither static statistical content-based analysis nor dynamic runtime testing provides a 100% detection accuracy. A combination of both approaches will likely provide more accurate performance. For example, as a preliminary stage, objects embedded in a document can be extracted by the static parser and then subjected to the dynamic tests so the specific malicious objects can be detected. Moreover, these detected malicious objects or malcode can be sent back to patch the static content-based detection models to improve accuracy.

5 Conclusion

Our intention was to provide a better understanding of the issues involved in detecting zero-day malcode embedded in modern document formats. Although the analysis we present is applicable to several other popular file formats, we focused on Word files. Word documents constitute a large percentage of the files exchanged globally both in private and in public organizations. Furthermore, their rich semantics and the large variety of embedded objects make them an ideal attack vehicles against a wealth of applications. Unfortunately, modern proprietary document formats, exemplified by Microsoft Word, are highly complex and fundamentally provide a convenient and easy to use "code injection platform".

In an effort to explore our detection capabilities, we designed sensors using two complementary detection strategies: static content-based statistical-learning analysis and coarse-grained dynamic tests designed to exploit run-time environment diversity. For the static analysis, we employed Anagram an algorithm that generates byte-code n-gram normality models of the training set. Anagram can effectively generate a similarity score between the tested document and the normality model. We compare each document to both benign and malicious normality models and classify the documents based on their similarity scores to those models. We found it necessary to "parse" the binary file format into its constituent embedded object structure in order to extract the individual data objects. Otherwise, the statistical characterizations of different kinds of objects would be blended together, producing poor characterizations of what may be "normal" content. Having a separate weighted model for each of the section of a document increased our total accuracy to 99.22% from 95.79%. Unfortunately, statistical anomaly detection techniques have some inherent limitations: they are dependent on the training set, they require the malicious content to be significantly large and they cannot reveal the "intent" of the malicious documents.

To address these issues, we performed several experiments where we imposed a dynamic run-time environment using multiple COTS implementations of the Word application encased in virtual machines. In some cases, it was immediately obvious and trivial to observe that the document was poisoned; In other cases, validation that the document harbored malcode was dependent upon the actions of the application changing local files or registries. With well specified policies that define unwanted, malicious, dynamic events have a high chance of detecting malicious "intent" (or, at least, behavior) of the code embedded in documents. However, detecting malicious documents by observing runtime behavior also has weaknesses. On the one hand, improperly designed benign macros may cause false alarms in Test 3; on the other hand, logic bombs or stealthily multi-partite attacks may exhibit no abnormal runtime behavior either and thus would be a false negative under dynamic tests. Hence, a deep file inspection using static analysis is still warranted for such stealthy attack cases.

The experimental results indicate that no single static model, nor a single approach, will likely reach the gold standard of 100% detection accuracy, and 0% false positive rate by static analysis alone and do so with a minimum of computational expense (e.g., a small overhead while simply opening the document). However, a combination of techniques, combining statistical analysis and dynamic testing will likely provide reasonable operational value. For example, to amortize the costs of testing documents, perhaps a preliminary stage (static parsing) that extracts suspect embeddings in a document that are then subjected to dynamic tests, which can be performed in parallel among instrumented application instances, may achieve high accuracy and reasonable computational performance objectives. Furthermore, malcode detected by runtime dynamic tests can and should be integrated in a feedback loop. Malcode that is extracted should be used as training data to update static detection models to improve accuracy.

Finally, we conjecture that malcode crafted for a particular version of Word may be reused in a number of publicly available documents. Hence, a collaborative detection process may provide greater benefit. It may be harder for an adversary to craft an attack that is undetectable by all such detectors. Thus, collaboration among a large number of sites that each attempts by a variety of different means to detect malcode embedded in documents would benefit each other by exchanging suspicious content to correlate for common instances of attack data. An alternative strategy might be to create a server farm running many different versions of document applications and that are coordinated to identify documents that harbor malcode, similar in spirit and scope to the Strider Honeymonkey [35] project for collaborative malicious web site detection.

References

1. Leyden, J.: Trojan exploits unpatched Word vulnerability. The Register (May 2006)
2. Evers, J.: Zero-day attacks continue to hit Microsoft. News.com (September 2006)
3. Kierznowski, D.: Backdooring PDF Files (September 2006)
4. Broersma, M.: Wikipedia hijacked by malware. Techworld (November 2006) http://www.techworld.com/news/index.cfm?RSS&NewsID=7254
5. Bontchev, V.: Possible Virus Attacks Against Integrity Programs and How to Prevent Them. In: Proc. 2nd Int. Virus Bull. Conf. pp. 131–141 (1992)
6. Bontchev, V.: Macro Virus Identification Problems. In: Proc. 7th Int. Virus Bull. Conf. pp. 175–196 (1997)
7. Filiol, E., Helenius, M., Zanero, S.: Open Problems in Computer Virology. Journal in Computer Virology, pp. 55–66 (2006)
8. Wang, K., Parekh, J., Stolfo, S.J.: Anagram: A Content Anomaly Detector Resistant to Mimicry Attack. In: Zamboni, D., Kruegel, C. (eds.) RAID 2006. LNCS, vol. 4219, Springer, Heidelberg (2006)
9. Li, W.-J., Wang, K., Stolfo, S.J., Herzog, B.: Fileprints: Identifying File Types by n-gram Analysis. In: 2005 IEEE Information Assurance Workshop (2005)
10. Stolfo, S.J., Wang, K., Li, W.-J.: Towards Stealthy Malware Detection. In: Jha, Christodorescu, Wang (eds.) Malware Detection Book, Springer, Heidelberg (2006)
11. Schultz, M.G., Eskin, E., Zadok, E., Stolfo, S.J.: Data Mining Methods for Detection of New Malicious Executables. In: IEEE Symposium on Security and Privacy, Oakland, CA (May 2001)
12. Abou-Assaleh, T., Cercone, N., Keselj, V., Sweidan, R.: Detection of New Malicious Code Using N-grams Signatures. In: Proceedings of Second Annual Conference on Privacy, Security and Trust, October 13-15, 2004 (2004)
13. Abou-Assaleh, T., Cercone, N., Keselj, V., Sweidan, R.: N-gram-based Detection of New Malicious Code. In: Proceedings of the 28th IEEE Annual International Computer Software and Applications Conference, COMPSAC 2004. Hong Kong. September 28–30,2004 (2004)
14. Karim, M.E., Walenstein, A., Lakhotia, A.: Malware Phylogeny Generation using Permutations of Code. Journal in Computer Virology (2005)

15. McDaniel, M., Heydari, M.H.: Content Based File Type Detection Algorithms. In: 6th Annual Hawaii International Conference on System Sciences (HICSS'03) (2003)
16. Noga, A.J.: A Visual Data Hash Method. Air Force Research report (October 2004)
17. Goel, S.: Kolmogorov Complexity Estimates for Detection of Viruses. Complexity Journal 9(2) (2003)
18. Steganalysis http://niels.xtdnet.nl/stego/
19. K2. ADMmutate (2001) Available from http://www.ktwo.ca/security.html
20. Detristan, T., Ulenspiegel, T., Malcom, Y., Underduk, M.: Polymorphic Shellcode Engine Using Spectrum Analysis. Phrack (2003)
21. Kolesnikov, O., Lee, W.: Advanced Polymorphic Worms: Evading IDS by Blending in with Normal Traffic. USENIX Security Symposium, Georgia Tech: Vancouver, BC, Canada (2006)
22. Shaner: US Patent No. 5,991,714 (November 1999)
23. Song, Y., Locasto, M.E., Stavrou, A., Keromytis, A.D., Stolfo, S.J.: On the Infeasibility of Modeling Polymorphic Shellcode for Signature Detection Tech. report cucs-00707, Columbia University (February 2007)
24. Natvig, K.: SandboxII: Internet Norman SandBox Whitepaper (2002)
25. Willems, C., Freiling, F., Holz, T.: Toward Automated Dynamic Malware Analysis Using CWSandbox. IEEE Security and Privacy Magazine 5(2), 32–39 (2007)
26. Bellard, F.: QEMU, a Fast and Portable Dynamic Translator. In: proceedings of the USENIX 2005 Annual Technical Conference, pp. 41–46 (2005)
27. Reis, C., Dunagan, J., Wang, H.J., Dubrovsky, O., Esmeir, S.: BrowserShield: Vulnerability-Driven Filtering of Dynamic HTML. OSDI, Seattle, WA (2006)
28. POIFS: http://jakarta.apache.org/
29. Bloom, B.H.: Space/time trade-offs in hash coding with allowable errors. Communications of the ACM 13(7), 422–426 (1970)
30. Wang, K., Cretu, G., Stolfo, S.J.: Anomalous Payload-based Worm Detection and Signature Generation. In: Valdes, A., Zamboni, D. (eds.) RAID 2005. LNCS, vol. 3858, Springer, Heidelberg (2006)
31. Broder, A., Mitzenmacher, M.: Network Applications of Bloom Filters: A Survey. In: Allerton Conference (2002)
32. http://vx.netlux.org/
33. Totel, E., Majorczyk, F., Me, L.: COTS: Diversity Intrusion Detection and Application to Web Servers. RAID 2005 (2005)
34. Reynolds, J.C., Just, J., Clough, L., Maglich, R.: On-line intrusion detection and attack prevention using diversity, generate-and-test, and generalization. In: Proceedings of the 36th Hawaii International Conference on System Sciences (2003)
35. Wang, Y.-M., Beck, D., Jiang, X., Roussev, R.: Automated Web Patrol with Strider HoneyMonkeys: Finding Web Sites That Exploit Browser Vulnerabilities. In: NDSS 2006

Author Index

Lecture Notes in Computer Science

For information about Vols. 1–4511

please contact your bookseller or Springer

Vol. 4563: R. Shumaker (Ed.), Virtual Reality. XXII, 762 pages. 2007.

Vol. 4562: D. Harris (Ed.), Engineering Psychology and Cognitive Ergonomics. XXIII, 879 pages. 2007. (Sublibrary LNAI).

Vol. 4561: V.G. Duffy (Ed.), Digital Human Modeling. XXIII, 1068 pages. 2007.

Vol. 4560: N. Aykin (Ed.), Usability and Internationalization, Part II. XVIII, 576 pages. 2007.

Vol. 4559: N. Aykin (Ed.), Usability and Internationalization, Part I. XVIII, 661 pages. 2007.

Vol. 4558: M.J. Smith, G. Salvendy (Eds.), Human Interface and the Management of Information, Part II. XXIII, 1162 pages. 2007.

Vol. 4557: M.J. Smith, G. Salvendy (Eds.), Human Interface and the Management of Information, Part I. XXII, 1030 pages. 2007.

Vol. 4554: C. Stephanidis (Ed.), Universal Acess in Human Computer Interaction, Part I. XXII, 1054 pages. 2007.

Vol. 4553: J.A. Jacko (Ed.), Human-Computer Interaction, Part IV. XXIV, 1225 pages. 2007.

Vol. 4552: J.A. Jacko (Ed.), Human-Computer Interaction, Part III. XXI, 1038 pages. 2007.

Vol. 4551: J.A. Jacko (Ed.), Human-Computer Interaction, Part II. XXIII, 1253 pages. 2007.

Vol. 4550: J.A. Jacko (Ed.), Human-Computer Interaction, Part I. XXIII, 1240 pages. 2007.

Vol. 4549: J. Aspnes, C. Scheideler, A. Arora, S. Madden (Eds.), Distributed Computing in Sensor Systems. XIII, 417 pages. 2007.

Vol. 4548: N. Olivetti (Ed.), Automated Reasoning with Analytic Tableaux and Related Methods. X, 245 pages. 2007. (Sublibrary LNAI).

Vol. 4547: C. Carlet, B. Sunar (Eds.), Arithmetic of Finite Fields. XI, 355 pages. 2007.

Vol. 4546: J. Kleijn, A. Yakovlev (Eds.), Petri Nets and Other Models of Concurrency – ICATPN 2007. XI, 515 pages. 2007.

Vol. 4545: H. Anai, K. Horimoto, T. Kutsia (Eds.), Algebraic Biology. XIII, 379 pages. 2007.

Vol. 4544: S. Cohen-Boulakia, V. Tannen (Eds.), Data Integration in the Life Sciences. XI, 282 pages. 2007. (Sublibrary LNBI).

Vol. 4543: A.K. Bandara, M. Burgess (Eds.), Inter-Domain Management. XII, 237 pages. 2007.

Vol. 4542: P. Sawyer, B. Paech, P. Heymans (Eds.), Requirements Engineering: Foundation for Software Quality. IX, 384 pages. 2007.

Vol. 4541: T. Okadome, T. Yamazaki, M. Makhtari (Eds.), Pervasive Computing for Quality of Life Enhancement. IX, 248 pages. 2007.

Vol. 4539: N.H. Bshouty, C. Gentile (Eds.), Learning Theory. XII, 634 pages. 2007. (Sublibrary LNAI).

Vol. 4538: F. Escolano, M. Vento (Eds.), Graph-Based Representations in Pattern Recognition. XII, 416 pages. 2007.

Vol. 4537: K.C.-C. Chang, W. Wang, L. Chen, C.A. Ellis, C.-H. Hsu, A.C. Tsoi, H. Wang (Eds.), Advances in Web and Network Technologies, and Information Management. XXIII, 707 pages. 2007.

Vol. 4536: G. Concas, E. Damiani, M. Scotto, G. Succi (Eds.), Agile Processes in Software Engineering and Extreme Programming. XV, 276 pages. 2007.

Vol. 4534: I. Tomkos, F. Neri, J. Solé Pareta, X. Masip Bruin, S. Sánchez Lopez (Eds.), Optical Network Design and Modeling. XI, 460 pages. 2007.

Vol. 4533: F. Baader (Ed.), Term Rewriting and Applications. XII, 419 pages. 2007.

Vol. 4531: J. Indulska, K. Raymond (Eds.), Distributed Applications and Interoperable Systems. XI, 337 pages. 2007.

Vol. 4530: D.H. Akehurst, R. Vogel, R.F. Paige (Eds.), Model Driven Architecture- Foundations and Applications. X, 219 pages. 2007.

Vol. 4529: P. Melin, O. Castillo, L.T. Aguilar, J. Kacprzyk, W. Pedrycz (Eds.), Foundations of Fuzzy Logic and Soft Computing. XIX, 830 pages. 2007. (Sublibrary LNAI).

Vol. 4528: J. Mira, J.R. Álvarez (Eds.), Nature Inspired Problem-Solving Methods in Knowledge Engineering, Part II. XXII, 650 pages. 2007.

Vol. 4527: J. Mira, J.R. Álvarez (Eds.), Bio-inspired Modeling of Cognitive Tasks, Part I. XXII, 630 pages. 2007.

Vol. 4526: M. Malek, M. Reitenspieß, A. van Moorsel (Eds.), Service Availability. X, 155 pages. 2007.

Vol. 4525: C. Demetrescu (Ed.), Experimental Algorithms. XIII, 448 pages. 2007.

Vol. 4524: M. Marchiori, J.Z. Pan, C.d.S. Marie (Eds.), Web Reasoning and Rule Systems. XI, 382 pages. 2007.

Vol. 4523: Y.-H. Lee, H.-N. Kim, J. Kim, Y. Park, L.T. Yang, S.W. Kim (Eds.), Embedded Software and Systems. XIX, 829 pages. 2007.

Vol. 4522: B.K. Ersbøll, K.S. Pedersen (Eds.), Image Analysis. XVIII, 989 pages. 2007.

Vol. 4521: J. Katz, M. Yung (Eds.), Applied Cryptography and Network Security. XIII, 498 pages. 2007.

Vol. 4519: E. Franconi, M. Kifer, W. May (Eds.), The Semantic Web: Research and Applications. XVIII, 830 pages. 2007.

Vol. 4517: F. Boavida, E. Monteiro, S. Mascolo, Y. Koucheryavy (Eds.), Wired/Wireless Internet Communications. XIV, 382 pages. 2007.

Vol. 4516: L. Mason, T. Drwiega, J. Yan (Eds.), Managing Traffic Performance in Converged Networks. XXIII, 1191 pages. 2007.

Vol. 4515: M. Naor (Ed.), Advances in Cryptology - EUROCRYPT 2007. XIII, 591 pages. 2007.

Vol. 4514: S.N. Artemov, A. Nerode (Eds.), Logical Foundations of Computer Science. XI, 513 pages. 2007.

Vol. 4513: M. Fischetti, D.P. Williamson (Eds.), Integer Programming and Combinatorial Optimization. IX, 500 pages. 2007.